Reading Assessment

Principles and Practices for Elementary Teachers

Second Edition

Shelby J. Barrentine
University of North Dakota
Grand Forks, North Dakota, USA

Sandra M. Stokes
University of Wisconsin–Green Bay
Green Bay, Wisconsin, USA

EDITORS

INTERNATIONAL
Reading Association
800 Barksdale Road, PO Box 8139
Newark, DE 19714-8139, USA
www.reading.org

Director of Publications Dan Mangan
Editorial Director, Books and Special Projects Teresa Curto
Managing Editor, Books Shannon T. Fortner
Acquisitions and Developmental Editor Corinne M. Mooney
Associate Editor Charlene M. Nichols
Production Editor Amy Messick
Assistant Editor Elizabeth C. Hunt
Books and Inventory Assistant Rebecca A. Zell
Permissions Editor Janet S. Parrack
Assistant Permissions Editor Tyanna L. Collins
Production Department Manager Iona Muscella
Supervisor, Electronic Publishing Anette Schütz
Senior Electronic Publishing Specialist R. Lynn Harrison
Electronic Publishing Specialist Lisa M. Kochel
Proofreader Stacey Lynn Sharp

Project Editors Shannon T. Fortner and Corinne M. Mooney

Cover Design, Linda Steere; Photo, PhotoDisc

Web addresses in this book were correct as of the publication date but may have become inactive or otherwise modified since that time. If you notice a deactivated or changed Web address, please e-mail books@reading.org with the words "Website Update" in the subject line. In your message, specify the Web link, the book title, and the page number on which the link appears.

Library of Congress Cataloging-in-Publication Data

Reading assessment : principles and practices for elementary teachers / Shelby J. Barrentine, Sandra M. Stokes, eds.-- 2nd ed.
p. cm.
Includes bibliographical references and index.
ISBN 0-87207-572-9
1. Reading (Elementary) 2. Reading--Ability testing. I. Barrentine, Shelby J. II. Stokes, Sandra M.
LB1573.R2793 2005
372.48'4--dc22
Second Printing, June 2006.

2005006226

Contents

Acknowledgments

We are grateful to the authors of the articles that are included in this compilation. Their work is important to the profession of teaching and to the well-being of readers in elementary school classrooms across the United States and international arena. We offer a special note of thanks to Matt Baker, who supported the work in the early stages of development, and to the publications staff at IRA, especially Shannon Fortner and Corinne Mooney. Finally, we thank our families for their support throughout this endeavor:

Lucretius—thanks for your unique support.
SJB

Mom—thank you for listening as I read you "bits and pieces."
Andrew—thanks for your support.
Dad—thank you for your love.
SMS

Introduction

To assess or not to assess is no longer the question. In fact, assessment is a 21st-century reality—and there are many questions being asked by teachers, parents, the public, and students themselves about the subject of assessment. It is indeed no wonder that teachers today plan their assessments wisely, seek to know more, and even experience trepidation and confusion about this topic.

The Real World of Teachers

The best teachers we know have learned to use assessment to understand the readers and writers in their classrooms, to plan for instruction, to confer with students and parents, and to set achievement goals. For expert teachers, assessment is a continual cycle of inquiry: What does the reader know and need to learn? What should I teach based on my assessment information? Now that I've taught, what else does the reader need to know to become a more competent reader?

Becoming an expert is not easy. It takes time to learn to make assessment a part of the daily routine, to gather and even analyze data while "sitting right next to a student, observing him read, probing her thinking" (Routman, 2003, p. 100). But learning to do so allows teachers to take a problem-solving stance toward teaching: What's working for this reader, what isn't, and what changes need to be made in this learning opportunity? This assessment cycle and problem-solving stance allows teachers to make immediate adjustments to the lesson—to choose an easier book, build more background knowledge, encourage rereading to build fluency and confidence, and expand the time allotted for talking about comprehension or word decoding.

For all teachers, assessment is part of the daily literacy routine and goes beyond the moment-to-moment cycle of assess–instruct–assess. Inquiry-oriented assessment practices and problem-solving–type assessments are evident in the rich documentation of literacy learning that is expected in many U.S. school districts (Hill, Ruptic, & Norwick, 1998). Monthly running records on each student, retelling protocols, and portfolios are commonly required assessment tools in many districts and schools. Teachers also use many other practices—such as anecdotal records or notes, checklists, continua of developmental benchmark reading behaviors, and rubrics—to assess and describe students' reading progress. Moreover, today it is common for teachers to involve students in assessment through the portfolio process and for students to take the lead in sharing descriptions and reflections of their literacy progress during parent–teacher conferences.

How are these assessment data used? In large part, these are the data that allow teachers to make those moment-to-moment, situational teaching decisions, resulting in supportive and informed teaching for readers. These assessments and resulting information help teachers come to know the learning patterns and needs of their students and reveal what and how to teach.

The power of assessment as inquiry (refer to Serafini, this volume), as well as a problem-solving stance toward teaching, is that it motivates students. Students are intrinsically motivated because they continually engage with teachers to understand what successful readers do. Growing toward reading proficiency takes on a natural—but not necessarily easy—cycle of learning. The teacher (who is simultaneously assessing and problem solving) and the reader (who is taking learning risks and using teacher feedback) are engaged in a caring teacher–student relationship and take joint responsibility for the student's learning (Cambourne, 1995). Even when learning is a challenge, students are motivated to learn because they know what to engage with, and the task is worthy of engagement: becoming a competent reader.

Teaching and High-Stakes Testing

By contrast, students are not motivated to learn because of a high-stakes test (Stiggins, 2004). As teachers are well aware, annual high-stakes testing now reaches into the lives of every public school student in the United States. Students feel the pressure of these tests (e.g., see Hoffman, Assaf, & Paris, this volume; Phillips, this volume), but they do not try harder to become better readers because of annual high-stakes tests. Indeed, as Stiggins points out, struggling students, in particular, can be discouraged and defeated by high-pressure, high-stakes tests, which can destroy their motivation to learn and negatively affect their achievement.

High-stakes testing stands in stark contrast to classroom assessment. Classroom assessment involves a routine of caring relationships (Graves, 2002), well-chosen assessment practices aimed to understand the whole child, record-keeping, analysis, communication, and daily accountability (Routman, 2003). The information is used daily, even momentarily to adjust a lesson in progress. The data from portfolios are used to make student achievement concrete for parents, to involve the student, and to document the school curricula. High-stakes testing, however, is usually disjointed from the school curricula. To young learners it is alienating in format and implementation, and the results are supplied in untimely ways—too late to be helpful to the current teacher and too early to help the next teacher. The results are generally not meaningful to students' learning, though they can be linked to consequential events in their lives (e.g., grade retention, high school graduation, even obtaining a driver's license).

If high-stakes testing is counterproductive for students, why is it so pervasive? Policymakers use high-stakes testing as a tool for accountability—for school systems and, more personally, for teachers. Educators recognize this intent. Stiggins (2004), for example, announces that "the primary intent of these accountability-oriented assessments is to pressure educators to teach more effectively" (p. 24). Graves (2002) recognizes this as well, stating, "In reality, most of the tests the children take are really assessing their teachers" (p. 19).

When the public is polled on whether testing should be used to judge teacher performance, they lean slightly toward the attitude that testing *should* be used to judge teacher performance. The most recent Phi Delta Kappa/Gallup Poll of the public's attitudes toward public schools reports that 49% of the public believe that high-stakes testing should be used to judge the quality of teachers, and 47% believe that high-stakes testing should not be used to judge teacher quality (Rose & Gallup, 2004, pp. 48–49, Table 22). This attitude is worrisome as it implies high-stakes tests can be used as a "stick" to force teachers to improve—to teach more effectively.

What has happened as teachers have responded to the tests, in other words, as they have tried to teach more "effectively" and to raise the test scores for their students? Graves (2002) asserts that, as a result, testing has become a subject in schools. Teachers devote an enormous amount of time preparing students to take the high-stakes tests mandated by the federal, state, or district levels. Graves claims that another result is teachers and entire school systems are abandoning reading instruction that is more likely to produce lifelong readers. They are turning toward instructional approaches that are test centered and prescribed and away from approaches that are student centered and provide students and teachers with curricular choices.

As a consequence of these changes, in some schools *test scores* may be increasing, but according to a study conducted by Hoffman et al. (this volume), *student learning* is not. When teachers were asked about their perceptions of the relationship between rising scores on the Texas Assessment of Academic Skills (TAAS) and achievement, they responded that rising scores do not reflect real increases in student learning. Rather, they lament, students are better at taking the tests and teachers are better at teaching to the test.

A situation local to one of the editors, and common across the United States, illustrates that educators are dealing with *perceptions* of changes in achievement in schools due to high stakes testing. Several school districts that failed to meet the federal No Child Left Behind expectations for two years in a row were placed on school improvement plans. Some of the schools in these districts were actually high performing schools, but because especially vulnerable groups of children (e.g., children with disabilities) were not proficient in one subject area, entire schools were reported as failing—in need of improvement. Television news stories and newspaper articles expressed that educators needed to develop a plan to improve test scores. The emphasis in these stories and articles was repeatedly placed on improving test scores rather than on student learning. Administrators found themselves stating they were seeking ways to get off the list of failing schools rather than explaining their plans for improvement.

To create plans for *real* achievement is, of course, the goal in school districts. Perhaps the press and the public need to be educated about real learning, as well as the consequences of failing to make annual yearly progress, in human terms, as illustrated in the story of one elementary school that received a "needs improvement" designation. This school's parents received a letter from the district telling them that the school was failing and that parents could send their children elsewhere if they so desired. Many inservice sessions were scheduled over the summer and during the next school year, but funding was not increased to pay for these inservice sessions, which necessitated cuts in other portions of the school's budget. Nearly half of the teachers transferred to other schools in the district. The harshness of this result is not what the public wants, according to the Phi Delta Kappa/Gallup Poll: 67% of the people questioned replied that the results from one test should not be used to determine whether or not a school is in need of improvement (Rose & Gallup, 2004).

Complicating the picture further is a possible scenario described by Popham (2004/2005): Students in schools ranked as "effective" could actually be receiving poor instruction even though test scores are high. It is highly unlikely that instruction in such schools will be improved or changed in any way as long as test scores remain high.

There is an obvious tension between the need for school accountability, high-stakes testing, classroom assessment, and teaching. The tension is not all unhealthy though. For example, the push for accountability reminds teachers that information can be helpful to the public. Because schools absorb a high percentage of state taxes, citizens benefit from obtaining balanced, meaningful information about the schools. In addition, some districts, schools, and teachers are finding ways to use high-stakes testing to inform and even strengthen the curriculum. Routman (2003), for example, tells about working with teachers in a Florida school to examine the content of their high-stakes reading test. In consultation with Routman, the teachers determined that the strategic comprehension content on the test was not thoroughly taught, though they valued that content for their readers. Consequently, teachers incorporated strategic comprehension into their daily instruction and shared the strategies with parents, as well. Thus, the content of the high-stakes test was incorporated as a meaningful part of the curriculum.

But, questions remain: What is a classroom teacher to do? There are so many issues pressing teachers to assess wisely—which assessments should be used? How can teachers systematically plan for assessment? When selecting assessments, what should influence the selection process? Can information from high-stakes tests help inform teaching decisions? How can teacher-selected assessment practices be implemented more advantageously?

Assessment Planning: A Scenario

In this section, we present a scenario we created to address some of the challenges around developing an assessment plan and to model how teachers can respond to some of the challenges. We introduce a mentor teacher who is working with novice teachers. The mentor, whom we call Wanda, is a composite of several excellent mentor teachers we have worked with in recent years. The novice teachers represent the numerous new teachers we have mentored in our roles as university mentors. The assessment planning process and the plans that are modeled in the scenario not only begin to introduce you to the content of this book, but reflect the actual assessment practices of teachers we work with on a routine basis.

Wanda, a highly experienced mentor teacher, meets with her novice teachers to launch their literacy assessment plans for the year. They begin the planning by considering the tools that are district-mandated and others they want to use. Some tools are specific to developmental levels (e.g., concepts of print test for younger readers and comprehension strategies inventory for older readers), but their list (see Figure 1) includes tools that evoke discussion. Why use portfolios when they are not required? Why have students lead conferences? Why use anecdotal notes?

Wanda seizes the teachable moment and has the novices reflect on what they believe about assessment. Before proceeding with more elaborate planning, they construct a list of beliefs or principles about assessment (see Figure 2). The new teachers conclude they want to go beyond implementing assessments that uncover reading behaviors and include assessments that are empowering for students. They determine to support one another as they involve students in portfolio assessment beginning the first week of school (see Courtney & Abodeeb, this volume; Cleland, this volume). They also determine to help students develop literacy behaviors that would support student success on the state-mandated reading test. Wanda encourages the new teachers to keep track of their beliefs and use them to help make decisions about what assessment practices to use and to justify those choices.

As the novice teachers begin to collect data on their students, Wanda continually assists them with organizing and interpreting the information so they can make decisions about instruction. To organize their information, they maintain a folder of aggregated class data on skills such as phonemic awareness or sight word recognition. This folder supports making observations on differences and similarities within the class of students and reporting collective descriptive information such as class averages. The teachers also build individualized assessment files. These files are designed to paint a literacy portrait of each student using anecdotal notes, various checklists, running

Figure 1
Literacy assessment tools used by elementary teachers

Required assessment tools	Choice assessment tools
Continuum of literacy behaviors	Interviews
Concepts of print test	Interest inventories
Phonemic awareness evaluation	Family surveys and inventories
Sound-letter association assessment	Anecdotal observations
Running records with retelling guides	Diagnostic narratives
Sight words list for reading and writing	Self-concept surveys
Words you know (write them)	Portfolios
Decoding strategies inventory	Student-led conferences
Comprehension strategies inventory	
Parent-teacher conferences	
State-mandated test	

records, writing samples, letters from families, interest inventories, and lists of books read. Finally, the teachers also have students build collections of work such as literature response projects, journals, and other daily assignments.

"But, what do we *do* with all of the information?" the novices ask. Wanda has learned to expect this question and is prepared to teach them to use interpretive tools: grids of documented literacy behaviors (see West, Figure 1, this volume), standards information to interpret anecdotal notes (e.g., see Boyd-Badstone, Table 5, this volume), and continua offering lists of developmentally appropriate literacy behaviors. A reading continuum lists benchmark behaviors of successfully developing readers. A continuum helps the teachers see patterns in students' literacy development and helps them recognize achievement of expectations—i.e., achievement of benchmark literacy behaviors. A teacher, for example, can look for patterns of reading achievement that reveal a reader is meeting benchmarks of an "expanding" reader (see Figure 3): An expanding reader (Hill et al.,

Figure 2
List of assessment beliefs or principles

Assessment should
- inform teaching—be useful
- be routine (systematic)
- provide insight into individual student
- be doable for the teacher
- involve students
- provide feedback to students
- be helpful to parents
- be fair and not show favoritism
- be an integral part of the classroom instructional cycle

Figure 3
Benchmark behaviors of successful expanding readers

Expanding reader (ages 7–9)
☐ Reads beginning chapter books.
☐ Chooses, reads, and finishes a variety of materials at appropriate level with guidance.
☐ Begins to read aloud with fluency.
☐ Reads silently for increasingly longer periods (15–30 minutes).
☐ Uses reading strategies appropriately, depending on the text and purpose.
☐ Uses word structure cues (e.g., prefixes, contractions, abbreviations).
☐ Begins to use meaning cues (context) to increase vocabulary.
☐ Self-corrects for meaning.
☐ Follows written directions.
☐ Identifies chapter titles and table of contents (text organizers).
☐ Summarizes and retells story events in sequential order.
☐ Responds to and makes personal connections with facts, characters, and situations in literature.
☐ Compares and contrasts characters and story events.
☐ Makes predictions and "reads beyond the text" with guidance.
☐ Identifies own reading strategies and sets goals with guidance.

Adapted from Form 11.2: Reading Continuum in Hill, B.C., Ruptic, C., & Norwick, L. (1998). *Classroom based assessment*. Norwood, MA: Christopher-Gordon.

1998), often ages 7–9, demonstrates growing competence with behaviors such as reading beginning chapter books, reading silently for 15–30 minutes, using structural cues such as prefixes and suffixes to decode words, and summarizing text sequentially.

Wanda helps her teachers understand that these interpretive tools (e.g., grids, standards charts, continua) reveal what to teach. For example, as data from anecdotal records mount up a teacher may see that a number of students do not exhibit stamina for reading silently for more than 10 minutes at a time—an important academic skill and an important skill for success on high-stakes tests (Calkins, Montgomery, & Santman, 1998). Assessment information converges on this benchmark behavior, revealing something essential that readers need to learn. Thus, teaching students to read silently for sustained amounts of time becomes a data-based teaching decision.

Since the novice teachers want to involve students in the assessment process, they seek ways to engage students in monitoring the development of this reading ability. Students are taught to notice what disrupts their sustained reading: Choosing books that are too challenging or too easy? Forgetting to practice attentively? Needing to set goals? Being distracted by peers? Feeling tired? Once reasons for disruption are considered, the teacher and students devise plans for reading with increased stamina. They make a checklist of ideas to try out (see Figure 4). When it is time to confer with parents, the teacher, student, and parents can talk together and look at the checklist and other assessment records to evaluate the student's progress on building stamina for silent reading.

Figure 4
Checklist for increasing time spent reading silently

Directions: Mark all of the strategies you have tried this week to help you spend more time reading silently.

- ☐ I chose "just right" books to read.
- ☐ I kept my eyes on my book even when I heard my friends talking.
- ☐ I placed my bookmark five pages past the number of pages I read yesterday.
- ☐ I looked at the clock and kept reading for 10 more minutes.
- ☐ I brought several books to my desk so I didn't have to get up to find more books.
- ☐ I went to bed earlier.
- ☐ What else did you try? ______________

Teachers, as represented in this scenario, are growing more and more determined to use assessment information to support high levels of reading achievement, build caring relationships, and empower students to be responsible learners. They are also seeking ways to fit high-stakes testing into the assessment puzzle and not compromise their assessment principles. Professional development is a key aspect of learning to balance all of the demands of assessment. Identifying assessment principles and sound assessment practices is a lifelong journey—one that can be less bewildering when informed by the thoughtful scholarship of other educators, such as in this collection of articles.

Creating This Collection

This book presents articles from the last 10 years of the International Reading Association (IRA) journal *The Reading Teacher* and aims to position teachers as central to forming principled assessment policy, choosing meaningful assessment practices, and promoting literacy achievement in our schools. These aims align with the views expressed in the IRA position statement *High-Stakes Assessments in Reading*, which is the first article presented in this collection. The position statement affirms the notion that teachers must be knowledgeable to plan, implement, interpret, and act on assessment. It also aims to "guide educators who must use tests as a key element in the information base used to make decisions about the progress of individual children and the quality of instructional programs." The position statement clearly recommends that teachers involve themselves with assessment policy and construct "more systematic and rigorous assessment for classrooms." The statement also asserts that "actions to improve test scores" result in "teaching students to read better."

The 34 articles in this collection combine to form a very different edition from the first collection (Barrentine, 1999). For this edition, all of the articles were selected on the premise that they had potential to help teachers define their beliefs about assessment and to support planning systematic assessment practice to meet the needs of diverse readers in the environment of increased high-stakes testing. Several articles guide teachers to think critically about the purpose of assessment, the role of the teacher, and issues of equity. Also, many of the articles address responsiveness to high-stakes testing and were included because of the growing need for thoughtful analysis of this type of assessment. In the first edition of *Reading Assessment: Principles and Practices for Elementary Teachers*, no articles were available on the topic of responsiveness to high-stakes testing. In this edition, we include six articles addressing this topic in Section Four.

Other articles, as in the previous edition, were included for their practicality. They describe assessment practices that teachers can adapt to their own classrooms. To be included, these articles had to fundamentally serve the interests of children. It should be noted, however, that though the ideas presented in this collection are useful with all children, most of the selections focus on classroom teaching. Fully meeting the professional needs of teachers who are working with readers who require highly specialized diagnosis and assistance is beyond the scope of this book.

Due to space constraints and in the interest of avoiding overlap, many excellent articles from *The Reading Teacher* on the topic of assessment within the 10-year time frame were not included. Related to this, eight articles that were in the first edition of this book are again included here. These articles fill important niches (e.g., an instrument for assessing phonemic awareness) or are exceptionally relevant and thought provoking and provide philosophical continuity with the first edition (e.g., Tierney's article on assessment reform).

Overview of the Book

The articles in the collection are organized into seven sections, each with its own introduction that invites ongoing reader engagement. Through prereading questions, article summaries, lists of additional readings, and assessment planning tasks, teachers are challenged to discover, rethink, and plan their assessment principles and practices. We urge readers to begin the discovery process by keeping a journal or notebook to respond to questions posed at the beginning of each section and record thoughts during reading. To develop better assessment practices, or to articulate them for the first time, we invite readers to complete the tasks posed in each section introduction titled "Create a Statement of Reading Assessment Principles and Practices." Each of these tasks aims to assist readers in adding another layer to their reading assessment plans. Readers who faithfully engage with these tasks will, like the novice teachers described in this introduction, possess a principled assessment plan that is responsive to readers and promotes reading achievement.

The first three sections of the book work together, helping to lay a foundation of assessment beliefs or principles: Foundations of Reading Assessment, Equity and Diversity in Reading Assessment, and Gaining Perspective. Readers should turn to the articles in these sections to explore "principles for assessment that emanate from a mix of child-centered views of teaching, developmental views of children, constructivist views of knowing, critical theoretical views of empowerment, and pluralistic views of society" (Tierney, this volume).

Section Four, Negotiating the Influence of High-Stakes Testing, collects examples of how educators are dealing with high-stakes tests as their amount and influence have increased. Authors of these articles seek ways to help students succeed on tests but challenge practices that "raise test scores without actually changing students' underlying knowledge or achievement" (Hoffman et al., this volume). Referring to the IRA position statement may be helpful when reading the articles in this section.

Section Five, The Assessment–Instruction–Assessment Cycle, and Section Six, Involving Students in Assessment, reflect the heart and soul of assessment as inquiry and teaching as problem solving, as described earlier in this introduction. These authors describe assessment practices that "build a descriptive story of each student's learning" (West, this volume) and draw students into the assessment process to "help learners see how they think, feel, work, and change over a period of time" (Courtney & Abodeeb, this volume).

Five articles are collected in Section Seven, Formal Assessment Tools. All the articles offer an assessment protocol to use with individuals or whole groups. They help uncover what students know and need and can be a useful "starting point for productive conversations with colleagues and parents" (Dickinson, McCabe, & Sprague, this volume).

Readers who have engaged with the interactive writing task "Create a Statement of Reading Assessment Principles and Practices" throughout the text can turn to the Appendix, where we have included a culminating activity that helps build reflection and brings some closure to the writing experience. To be consistent with the notion of valuing self-assessment, we also provide a rubric to assist readers to describe their professional growth that results from engaging with this active learning opportunity.

Concluding Thoughts

We hope that all teachers benefit from the rich reading from *The Reading Teacher* collected in this book. We believe the collection has unique potential to renew experienced teachers and support novice teachers as they read to deepen their foundational, theoretical, and practical knowledge of the assessment–instruction–assessment cycle. We also believe that this collection can serve the role of mentor as described in the scenario about Wanda, the mentor teacher. Articles by premier thinkers in the field of reading education provide the depth of knowledge and a variety of formal tools required to be in charge of classroom achievement—banishing the notion that teachers require the threat of high-stakes testing to "improve" their teaching. We also anticipate that the articles on high-stakes testing can help move teachers beyond the rhetoric that focuses on the frustration of high-stakes testing and can help equip them to negotiate the role of high-stakes testing in their assessment plans.

References

Barrentine, S.J. (1999). (Ed.). *Reading assessment: Principles and practices for elementary teachers.* Newark, DE: International Reading Association.

Calkins, L., Montgomery, K., & Santman, D. (1998). *A teacher's guide to standardized reading tests: Knowledge is power.* Portsmouth, NH: Heinemann.

Cambourne, B. (1995). Toward an educationally relevant theory of literacy learning: Twenty years of inquiry. *The Reading Teacher, 49*(3), 182–190.

Graves, D.H. (2002). *Testing is not teaching: What **should** count in education.* Portsmouth, NH: Heinemann.

Hill, B.C., Ruptic, C., & Norwick, L. (1998). *Classroom based assessment.* Norwood, MA: Christopher-Gordon.

Popham, W.J. (2004/2005). Swords with blunt edges. *Educational Leadership, 62*(4), 86–87.

Rose, L.C., & Gallup, A.M. (2004). The 36th annual Phi Delta Kappa/Gallup poll of the public's attitudes toward the public schools. *Phi Delta Kappan, 86*(1), 41–52.

Routman, R. (2003). *Reading essentials: The specifics you need to teach reading well.* Portsmouth, NH: Heinemann.

Stiggins, R. (2004). New assessment beliefs for a new school mission. *Phi Delta Kappan, 86*(1), 22–27.

High-Stakes Assessments in Reading: A Position Statement of the International Reading Association

The Board of Directors of the International Reading Association is opposed to high-stakes testing. High-stakes testing means that one test is used to make important decisions about students, teachers, and schools. In a high-stakes testing situation, if students score high on a single test they could be placed in honors classes or a gifted program. On the other hand, if students score low on a high-stakes test, it could mean that they will be rejected by a particular college, and it could affect their teacher's salary and the rating of the school district as compared with others where the same test was given.

In the United States in recent years there has been an increase in policy makers' and educators' reliance on high-stakes testing in which single test scores are used to make important educational decisions. The International Reading Association is deeply concerned about this trend. The Board of Directors offers this position statement as a call for the evaluation of the impact of current types and levels of testing on teaching quality, student motivation, educational policy making, and the public's perception of the quality of schooling. Our central concern is that testing has become a means of controlling instruction as opposed to a way of gathering information to help students become better readers. To guide educators who must use tests as a key element in the information base used to make decisions about the progress of individual children and the quality of instructional programs, we offer this position in the form of a question and answer dialogue. This format is intended to ensure that important conceptual, practical, and ethical issues are considered by those responsible for designing and implementing testing programs.

What Does the Term *High-Stakes Testing* Mean?

High-stakes testing means that the consequences for good (high) or poor (low) performance on a test are substantial. In other words, some very important decisions, such as promotion or retention, entrance into an educational institution, teacher salary, or a school district's autonomy depend on a single test score.

High-stakes tests have been a part of education for some time. Perhaps the most conspicuous form of high-stakes testing, historically speaking, was in the British educational system. National exams in England and in other countries that adopted the British system separated students into different educational tracks. In the United States, tests such as the Medical College Admission Test and Law School Admission Test, as well as professional certification examinations (for example, state bar examinations, medical board examinations, state teacher examinations) all represent high-stakes tests.

The meaning of high stakes can be confusing at times. Tests that have no specific decision tied to them can become high stakes to teachers and school administrators when they must face public pressure after scores are made public. In other

From *The Reading Teacher*, 53(3), 257-264. © 1999 by the International Reading Association. Position statement adopted by the Board of Directors in May 1999. Board of Directors at time of adoption: Kathryn A. Ransom, *President*; Carol Minnick Santa, *President Elect*; Carmelita K. Williams, *Vice President*; Alan E. Farstrup, *Executive Director*; Kathryn H. Au; Betsy M. Baker; Patricia A. Edwards; James V. Hoffman; Adria F. Klein; Diane L. Larson; John W. Logan; Lesley Mandel Morrow; and Timothy Shanahan.

cases, a low-stakes state test can be transformed into a high-stakes test at a school district level if a local school board decides to make educational or personnel decisions based on the test results.

Why Are We Concerned With High-Stakes Testing?

Although high-stakes testing has been and probably will continue to be part of the educational landscape, there has been an increase in such testing in recent years, particularly at the state level. More children are being tested at younger ages, and states and local school districts are using these tests to make a greater variety of important decisions than ever before. Increased frustration with lack of achievement has led to a greater reliance on testing. In response to these frustrations, many states have adopted educational standards and assessments of those standards. The logic is that tests of standards accompanied by a reward and penalty structure will improve children's achievement. In too many cases the assessment is a single multiple-choice test, which would be considered high stakes and would not yield enough information to make an important instructional decision.

Is Testing an Important Part of Good Educational Design?

Yes, testing students' skills and knowledge is certainly an important part of education, but it is only one type of educational assessment. Assessment involves the systematic and purposeful collection of data to inform actions. From the viewpoint of educators, the primary purpose of assessment is to help students by providing information about how instruction can be improved.

Assessment has an important role to play in decision making beyond the classroom level, however. Administrators, school board members, policy makers, and parents make significant decisions that impact students. The needs of many audiences must be considered in building a quality assessment plan.

Testing is a form of assessment that involves the systematic sampling of behavior under controlled conditions. Testing can provide quick, reliable data on student performance. Single tests might be used to make decisions that do not have major long-term consequences, or used to supplement other forms of assessment such as focused interviews, classroom observations and anecdotal records, analysis of work samples, and work inventories.

Different kinds of assessment produce different kinds of information. If a teacher needs to know whether a student can read a particular textbook, there are many sources of information available to her. She can consult districtwide achievement tests in reading, estimate the level of the textbook, determine what score a student would need to read the textbook effectively, and then make a decision. However, it might be simpler for the teacher to ask the student to read a section of the text and then talk with the student about the text. This would probably be faster and more accurate than looking up test scores and conducting studies to see what kind of a test score is needed to comprehend the textbook. In general, teachers need information specific to the content and strategies they are teaching, and they can best get that information through assessments built around their daily educational tasks.

The public and policy makers have different needs from teachers. In general they need to know whether the school, school district, and state are effectively educating the students in their charge. For this purpose they need to collect information about many students and they need to know how those students stand in relation to other students across the United States or in relation to some specific standards set by the state. For these purposes, standardized norm-referenced or criterion-referenced tests are efficient and can give a broad picture of achievement on certain kinds of tasks. These kinds of tests are used most commonly for high-stakes decisions regarding schools and school districts.

Why Does Using Tests for High-Stakes Decisions Cause Problems?

There are several possible problematic outcomes of high-stakes testing. These include making bad decisions, narrowing the curriculum, focusing exclusively on certain segments of students, losing instructional time, and moving decision making to central authorities and away from local personnel.

Tests are imperfect. Basing important decisions on limited and imperfect information can lead to bad decisions—decisions that can do harm to students and teachers and that sometimes have unfortunate legal and economic consequences for the schools. Decision makers reduce the chance of making a bad decision by seeking information from multiple sources. However, the information from norm-referenced and criterion-referenced tests is inexpensive to collect, easy to aggregate, and usually is highly reliable; for those reasons it is tempting to try to use this information alone to make major decisions.

Another problem is that high-stakes tests have a tendency to narrow the curriculum and inflate the importance of the test. Schools should address a broad range of student learning needs, not just the subjects or parts of subject areas covered on a particular test. As the consequences for low performance are raised, teachers feel pressured to raise scores at all costs. This means they will focus their efforts on activities that they think will improve the single important score. Time spent focusing on those activities will come from other activities in the curriculum and will consequently narrow the curriculum. Most state assessments tend to focus on reading, writing, and mathematics. Too much attention to these basic subjects will marginalize the fine arts, physical education, social studies, and the sciences.

Narrowing of the curriculum is most likely to occur in high-poverty schools that tend to have the lowest test scores. Compared to students in schools in affluent communities, students in high-poverty schools receive teaching with a greater emphasis in lower level skills, and they have limited access to instruction focusing on higher level thinking. A recent survey in one state that uses high-stakes assessments found that 75% of classroom teachers surveyed thought the state assessment had a negative impact on their teaching (Hoffman, Paris, Patterson, Salas, & Assaf, 2003).

Another way that educators sometimes respond to test pressure is to focus their attention on particular students. Sometimes this means that only low-performing readers get the instructional resources they need, and those doing only slightly better are ignored. Sometimes there is an attempt to raise test scores by focusing instructional initiatives on those students scoring just below cut-off points, and ignoring those both above or far below cutoff points. And sometimes schools place children in expensive special education programs they do not need, discourage particular children from attending school on testing days, or encourage low-achieving students to drop out of school altogether, all in the name of getting higher test scores.

The loss of instructional time also is a negative result of high-stakes tests. The time for preparing for and taking tests is time taken away from basic instruction. The consequences of lost instructional time, particularly for low-performing students, are too great for information that can be gathered more efficiently.

Finally, we are concerned that instructional decision making in high-stakes testing situations is diverted from local teachers and is concentrated in a central authority far away from the school. The further decision making is removed from the local level of implementation, the less adaptive the system becomes to individual needs. High-stakes assessment shifts decisions from teachers and principals to bureaucrats and politicians and consequently may diminish the quality of educational services provided to students.

Do Test Scores Improve When High-Stakes Assessment Is Mandated?

Test scores in the states with high-stakes assessment plans have often shown improvement. This could be because high-stakes pressure and competition lead teachers to teach reading more effectively. An alternative interpretation is that gains in test scores are the result of "teaching to the test" even when reading does not improve. Analyses of national reading scores do not show the substantial gains claimed by state reading assessments. Studies of norm-referenced tests in states with sustained patterns of growth in state skill assessments (for example, Texas and Kentucky) show no comparable patterns of gain. Although Texas showed steady improvement on state tests, its National Assessment of Educational Progress (NAEP) reading scores are not among the highest, and the scores did not show significant improvement between 1992 and 1998 (U.S. Department of Education, 1999). This may be the result of high-stakes assessments that tend to narrow the curriculum and emphasize only parts of what students need to learn to become successful readers.

Why Don't We Just End High-Stakes Assessment?

It is unlikely that states using these assessments will abandon them. Indeed, the most likely scenario is for an increasing number of states to develop and adopt similar assessment plans. Tests can be useful for making state-level educational decisions, and they provide the public with at least a partial understanding of how well schools are doing. Less positively, politicians, bureaucrats, and test publishers have discovered that they can influence classroom instruction through the use of high-stakes tests. Tests allow these outside parties to take control away from local educational authorities without assuming the responsibilities of educating the students.

Is There a Way to Help States Monitor Student Success in the Curriculum?

If the intent of state assessments is to measure how well students are learning the outcomes identified in the state curriculum framework, then one way students' success can be monitored is by following the NAEP model with selective sampling across student populations and across content areas on a systematic basis. This model monitors achievement without encouraging high-stakes testing. The tests are directed toward particular grade levels and are not given every year. A sampling procedure is used so very few students actually participate in testing. NAEP is designed to give a report card on general achievement levels in the basic subject areas over time.

Many aspects of the NAEP assessment in reading are commendable. The NAEP sampling strategy has been useful in keeping efficiency high and maintaining a focus on the questions that the national assessment is designed to address. Sampling also has provided NAEP with an opportunity to experiment with a wide variety of testing formats and conditions. Such a strategy would avoid most of the problems associated with teaching to the test. This type of plan would reflect sound principles of instructional design and assessment.

In the book *High Stakes: Testing for Tracking, Promotion, and Graduation* (Heubert & Hauser, 1999), the following basic principles for test use are presented:

- The important thing about a test is not its validity in general, but its validity when used for a specific purpose. Thus, tests that are valid for influencing classroom practice, "leading" the curriculum, or holding schools accountable are not appropriate for making high-stakes decisions about individual student mastery unless the curriculum, the teaching, and the tests are aligned.
- Tests are not perfect. Test questions are a sample of possible questions that could be asked in a given area. Moreover, a test score is not an exact measure of a student's knowledge or skills. A student's score can be expected to vary across different versions of a test—within a margin of error determined by the reliability of the test—as a function of the particular sample of questions asked and/or transitory factors, such as the student's health on the day of the test. Thus, no single test score can be considered a definitive measure of a student's knowledge.

- An educational decision that will have a major impact on a test taker should not be made solely or automatically on the basis of a single test score. Other relevant information about the student's knowledge and skills should also be taken into account.
- Neither a test score nor any other kind of information can justify a bad decision. Research shows that students are typically hurt by a simple retention and repetition of a grade in school without remedial and other instructional support services. In the absence of effective services better tests will not lead to better educational outcomes. (p. 3)

State testing programs should respect these basic principles.

What Are the Recommendations of the International Reading Association Regarding High-Stakes Reading Assessments?

In framing our recommendations the Association would like to stress two points. First, we recognize accountability is a necessary part of education. Concerns over high-stakes tests should not be interpreted as fear of or disregard for professional accountability. Second, the intent in this position statement is not to blame policy makers for the current dilemma with high-stakes testing.

Our recommendations begin with a consideration of teachers and their responsibility to create rich assessment environments in their classrooms and schools. Next, we suggest that researchers must continue to investigate how assessment can better serve our educational goals. Third, we stress the importance of parents and community members in bringing balance to the assessment design. Finally, we offer recommendations to policy makers for developing a plan of action.

Recommendations to Teachers

- Construct more systematic and rigorous assessments for classrooms, so that external audiences will gain confidence in the measures that are being used and their inherent value to inform decisions.

Suggested readings

1. What does the term *high-stakes testing* mean?

Downing, S., & Haladyna, T. (1996). A model for evaluation of high-stakes testing programs: Why the fox should not guard the chicken coop. *Educational Measurement: Issues and Practice*, *5*(1), 5–12.

Popham, W. (1987). Can high-stakes tests be developed at the local level? *NASSP Bulletin*, *71*(496), 77–84.

2. Why are we concerned with high-stakes testing?

Pipho, C., & Hadley, C. (1985). *State activity: Minimum competence testing as of January 1985* (Clearinghouse notes). Denver, CO: Education Commission of the States.

3. Is testing an important part of good educational design?

International Reading Association. (1995). *Reading assessment in practice*. Newark, DE: Author.

4. Why does using tests for high-stakes decisions cause problems?

Allington, R.L., & McGill-Franzen, A. (1992). Unintended effects of educational reform in New York State. *Educational Policy*, *6*(4), 396–413.

Madaus, G.F. (1985). Test scores as administrative mechanisms in educational policy. *Phi Delta Kappan*, *66*(9), 611–617.

Mathison, S. (1989). *The perceived effects of standardized testing on teaching and curriculum.* Paper presented at the annual meeting of the American Educational Research Association, San Francisco, CA.

McGill-Franzen, A., & Allington, R.L. (1993). Flunk 'em or get them classified: The contamination of primary grade accountability data. *Educational Researcher*, *22*(1), 19–22, 34.

Paris, S.G. (1998). Why learner-centered assessment is better than high-stakes testing. In N.M. Lambert & B.L. McCombs (Eds.), *How students learn: Reforming schools through learner-centered education* (pp. 189–209). Washington, DC: American Psychological Association.

(continued)

Suggested readings (cont'd.)

5. Do test scores improve when high-stakes assessment is mandated?

Cornet, H.D., & Wilson, B.L. (1991). *Testing reform and rebellion.* Norwood, NJ: Ablex.

Resnick, D.P., & Resnick, L.B. (1985). Standards, curriculum, and performance: A historical and comparative perspective. *Educational Researcher, 14*(4), 5–20.

Wise, A.E. (1990, January 10). A look ahead: Education and the new decade. *Education Week*, p. 30.

6. Why don't we just end high-stakes assessment?

Madaus, G.F. (1985). Test scores as administrative mechanisms in educational policy. *Phi Delta Kappan, 66*(9), 611–617.

7. Is there a way to help states monitor student success in the curriculum?

Linn, R.L. (1993). Educational assessment: Expanded expectations and challenges. *Educational, Evaluation and Policy Analysis, 15*(1), 1–16.

Messick, S. (1993). Validity. In R.L. Linn (Ed.), *Educational measurement* (3rd ed., pp. 13–103). Washington, DC: American Council on Education.

Moss, P. (1998). The role of consequences in validity theory. *Educational Measurement: Issues and Practice, 17*(2), 6–12.

- Take responsibility to educate parents, community members, and policy makers about the forms of classroom-based assessment, used in addition to standardized tests, that can improve instruction and benefit students learning to read.
- Understand the difference between ethical and unethical practices when teaching to the test. It is ethical to familiarize students with the format of the test so they are familiar with the types of questions and responses required. Spending time on this type of instruction is helpful to all and can be supportive of the regular curriculum. It is not ethical to devote substantial instructional time teaching to the test, and it is not ethical to focus instructional time on particular students who are most likely to raise test scores while ignoring groups unlikely to improve.
- Inform parents and the public about tests and their results.
- Resist the temptation to take actions to improve test scores that are not based on the idea of teaching students to read better.

Recommendations to Researchers

- Conduct ongoing evaluations of high-stakes tests. These studies should include but not be limited to teacher use of results, impact on the curriculum focus, time in testing and test preparation, the costs of the test (both direct and hidden), parent and community communication, and effects on teacher and student motivations.

  There are few data on the impact of tests on instruction. Good baseline data and follow-up studies will help in monitoring the situation. These studies should not be left to those who design, develop, and implement tests; they should be conducted by independent researchers.
- Find ways to link performance assessment alternatives to questions that external audiences must address on a regular basis. Researchers must continue to offer demonstrations of ways that data from performance assessments can be aggregated meaningfully. This strategy will allow them to build trustworthy informal assessments.

Recommendations to Parents, Parent Groups, and Child Advocacy Groups

- Be vigilant regarding the costs of high-stakes tests on students. Parents must ask questions about what tests are doing to their children and their schools. They cannot simply accept the "we're just holding the school accountable" response as satisfactory. They must consider cost, time, alternative methods, and emotional impact on students as a result of these tests.

- Lobby for the development of classroom-based forms of assessment that provide useful, understandable information, improve instruction, and help children become better readers.

Recommendations to Policy Makers

- Design an assessment plan that is considerate of the complexity of reading, learning to read, and the teaching of reading. A strong assessment plan is the best ally of teachers and administrators because it supports good instructional decision making and good instructional design. Consider the features of good assessment as outlined in *Standards for the Assessment of Reading and Writing* (International Reading Association & National Council of Teachers of English, 1994) in designing an assessment plan. Be aware of the pressures to use tests to make high-stakes decisions.
- When decisions about students must be made that involve high-stakes outcomes (e.g., graduation, matriculation, awards), rely on multiple measures rather than just performance on a single test. The experiences in England with high-stakes assessment have been instructive. England has moved to an assessment system that values teacher informal assessments, ongoing performance assessments, portfolios, teacher recommendations, and standardized testing. The triangulation of data sources leads to more valid decision making.
- Use sampling strategies when assessments do not involve decisions related to the performance of individual students (e.g., program evaluation). Sampling is less intrusive, less costly, and just as reliable as full-scale assessment plans. Sampling strategies also provide an opportunity to design alternate forms and types of assessments. Such a variety of assessments encourages careful inspection of issues of validity and reliability.
- Do not use incentives, resources, money, or recognition of test scores to reward or punish schools or teachers. Neither the awards (e.g., blue ribbon schools) nor the punishing labels (e.g., low-performing schools) are in the interest of students or teachers. The consequences of achieving or not achieving in schools are real enough. Well-intentioned efforts to recognize achievement often become disincentives to those who need the most help.
- Do not attempt to manipulate instruction through assessments. In other words, do not initiate, design, or implement high-stakes tests when the primary goal is to affect instructional practices. Ask the question, "Is the primary goal of the assessment to collect data that will be used to make better decisions that impact the individual students taking the test?" If the answer is "no," high-stakes tests are inappropriate.

The pattern of testing as the preferred tool to manipulate teaching continues to expand. We call on educators, policy makers, community leaders, and parents to take a common-sense look at the testing in schools today. Visit classrooms. Talk to teachers. Listen to teachers talk about the curriculum and the decisions they are making. Talk to the teachers about the kinds of assessments they use in the classroom and how they use collected data. To be opposed to large-scale, high-stakes testing is not to be opposed to assessment or accountability. It is to affirm the necessity of aligning our purposes and goals with our methods.

References

Heubert, J.P., & Hauser, R.M. (1999). *High stakes: Testing for tracking, promotion, and graduation.* Washington, DC: National Academy Press.

Hoffman, J.V., Paris, S.G., Patterson, E., Salas, R., & Assaf, L. (2003). High-stakes assessment in the language arts: The piper plays, the players dance, but who pays the price? In J. Flood, D. Lapp, J.R. Squire, & J.M. Jensen (Eds.), *Handbook of research on teaching the English language arts* (2nd ed., pp. 619–630). Mahwah, NJ: Erlbaum.

International Reading Association & National Council of Teachers of English. (1994). *Standards for the assessment of reading and writing.* Newark, DE: International Reading Association; Urbana, IL: National Council of Teachers of English.

U.S. Department of Education. (1999). *The NAEP 1998 reading report card for the nation and the states* (NCES 1999-459). Washington, DC: Author.

Foundations of Reading Assessment

- What exactly is assessment?
- Does assessment differ from evaluation? If so, how?
- Is there a connection between assessment and instruction? If so, what is the connection? If not, does that mean that assessment is irrelevant to teaching?
- What principles guide assessment programs that are relevant to teaching and learning? How do you form assessment principles?
- What "vexing issues" surround the newly emerged formalized assessment of young children?
- What should an overall assessment plan for a classroom look like? For a school? For a district?
- What is your role in assessment?

More and more, teachers grapple with these questions on a routine basis—directly in conversation with colleagues or perhaps, more obliquely, when conferring with parents. The three articles in Section One address the building blocks of assessment. They create opportunity for inservice and preservice teachers to lay a foundation to understand the myriad issues that fit under the umbrella term "assessment" in preparation for developing a principled assessment program.

The first article, by Charlene Cobb, makes a distinction between assessment and evaluation. Once these terms are defined, she advocates for developing assessment programs that guide teachers' instructional decisions. She promotes the notion that teachers need to work together to plan assessment and discuss the results. School principals, she maintains, play an essential role in arranging for those discussions to occur and supporting assessment reform.

Assessment reform can occur on macro and micro levels of schooling. In his article, Robert J. Tierney lays out principles for effective assessment that can be applied to a single classroom or entire districts. He has mined the depths of educators' thinking and has surfaced with 12 principles to consider when planning learner-centered, culturally sensitive assessment. His recommendations for change aim to bring teachers "in partnership with their students" and bring students close to their own learning through self-assessment.

Monitoring literacy development and identifying young children at risk of reading failure is the somewhat delicate subject of Kathleen Roskos's article. She points out that vigorous, even high-stakes assessment of young children's literacy progress has replaced the casual and general literacy assessment inventories of the 1980s. In this climate of accountability, Roskos explains how new knowledge about literacy development as well as increased program accountability makes effective early literacy assessment an absolute essential. The article provides perspectives on the complexity of the assessment issues at hand for teachers of young children but also offers foundational thoughts to consider when designing early literacy assessment systems.

Additional Reading

- Au, K.H., Scheu, J.A., Kawakami, A.J., & Herman, P.A. (1990). Assessment and accountability in a whole literacy curriculum. *The Reading Teacher, 43*(8), 574–578.
- Falk, B. (2000). *The heart of the matter: Using standards and assessment to learn.* Portsmouth, NH: Heinemann.
- Flippo, R.F. (2003). *Assessing readers: Qualitative diagnosis and instruction.* Portsmouth, NH: Heinemann.
- Harp, B. (2000). *The handbook of literacy assessment and evaluation* (2nd ed.). Norwood, MA: Christopher-Gordon.
- Hiebert, E.H., & Calfee, R.C. (1992). Assessing literacy: From standardized tests to portfolio and performances. In A.E. Farstrup & S.J. Samuels (Eds.), *What research has to say about reading instruction* (2nd ed., pp. 70–100). Newark, DE: International Reading Association.
- Laza, A., & Mayor, S. (2004). Capturing 360 degrees of a child: Helping preservice teachers develop case studies of struggling readers. *Journal of Reading Education, 30*(1), 17–26.
- Popham, W.J. (2004). "Teaching to the test": An expression to eliminate. *Educational Leadership, 62*(3), 82–83.
- Shepard, L.A. (2000). The role of assessment in a learning culture. *Educational Researcher, 29*(7), 4–14.
- Strickland, K., & Strickland, J. (1998). *Reflections on assessment: Its purposes, methods and effects on learning*. Portsmouth, NH: Boynton/Cook.
- Sulzby, E. (1991). Assessment of emergent literacy: Storybook reading. *The Reading Teacher, 44*(7), 498–500.

Create a Statement of Reading Assessment Principles and Practices

The theme of this section of the book, foundations, invites you to identify which assessment vocabulary, principles, and issues *unite* your view of literacy assessment. What are the foundations of your literacy assessment program? Do you agree with Cobb that assessment serves as a checkpoint and reflects what instruction point is next? That teachers must work together for effective assessment in schools? Like Tierney, do you espouse the view that assessment practices must bring learners close to their own achievement—that self-monitoring is essential to building the habit of achievement and growth? That respect for diversity and parents must be embraced when planning for assessment? If you teach very young children, are there particular principles that must be considered? What is the teacher's role in all of this?

Phrase your views, beliefs, and perspectives on assessment in your own terms. Use your professional knowledge to shape your perspective. Then, in writing, define assessment. Next, list and explain your set of interrelated principles of reading assessment. You might benefit from referring back to Figure 2 in the introduction to the book (see p. 5) to review the list of beliefs generated by the novice teachers. Also, in your statement, include an explanation about the teacher's role in assessment. Plan to refer back to this list later when adding other layers to your assessment plan.

Effective Instruction Begins With Purposeful Assessments

Charlene Cobb

As levels of accountability increase, teachers and administrators frequently lament the amount of time devoted to testing. They wonder why so much time is spent assessing student knowledge. I would like to propose what I consider to be a thoughtful suggestion to administrators and reading specialists for dealing with this dilemma: We need to spend *more* time assessing students' knowledge.

Wait—before you stop reading or throw your journal across the room, let me explain. Building administrators and reading specialists can take a leadership role by helping teachers differentiate between assessment and evaluation.

Assessment and Evaluation

Here's an analogy that might help to distinguish and differentiate the two concepts. A visit to the doctor's office is to assessment what an autopsy is to evaluation. Let's say you go to see a doctor, for either a perceived need or a regular checkup. The doctor examines you, makes a diagnosis, and provides a treatment based on his or her discovery and your needs. This is a form of ongoing assessment. Suppose you come home from the doctor and find out that your neighbor has suddenly died. You're told that nobody knows what happened, but an autopsy is planned. An autopsy is an evaluation. Evaluations are done to determine what happened and result in a specific outcome.

In education, an evaluation occurs when a single score or grade is used to publicly report student learning. In it, you're looking at what has already occurred, with no possibility of intervening, reassessing, and changing eventual outcomes.

I propose more purposeful, ongoing assessment that guides and directs subsequent instruction. Further, I propose that administrators and reading specialists collaborate with teachers on assessments and use them to provide valuable information for developing alternative instruction or interventions.

Assessment is a critical component of effective teaching and learning. The relationship of curriculum, assessment, and instruction must be integrated and reciprocal. The same questions and answers can be used within any subject area to guide this process (see Figure).

The reciprocal relationship between curriculum, assessment, and instruction

Curriculum ⟷	Assessment ⟷	Instruction
Where am I going?	*How will I know that?*	*How will I get there?*
Guiding all students to achieve high levels of content standards, local benchmarks, and daily learning.	By providing students with multiple opportunities to demonstrate learning.	Through purposefully planned teaching and learning experiences.

From *The Reading Teacher*, 57(4), 386-388. © 2003 by the International Reading Association.

Assessment is frequently confused with evaluation. In its fundamental form, assessment provides teachers with information they need to help students. In effective classrooms, it is sometimes difficult to determine where instruction ends and assessment begins (Checkley, 1997). Assessment is diagnostic *and* formative. Evaluation, on the other hand, is a summation and is used upon completion of instruction. It is the final analysis of instruction and assessments and is used to assign grades or determine grade placement.

Guskey (2003) has made three recommendations that can change the approach to assessment. First, make assessments useful for students and teachers. Assessment cannot be a guessing game played between them. Teachers must inform students of (a) the concepts and skills necessary for achievement and, more important, (b) the criteria that will be used to judge successful achievement. In addition, assessment must be followed with corrective instruction. Assessment should not mark the end of learning but rather a checkpoint for the level of learning, as well as a reflection on what needs to happen next. Finally, there must be more than one opportunity to demonstrate success. After assessment, feedback, and corrective instruction, students must have an opportunity to show their new level of understanding and competence.

Assessment is more than the weekly spelling test or end-of-the-unit science test—it requires frequent opportunities to examine student performance in a variety of formats. As Black and William (1998) pointed out, assessments that are frequent and short are more effective than assessments that are infrequent and lengthy. If we are going to make a difference, then we need to start doing things differently (International Reading Association, 2000).

Making a Difference

If assessment is to be meaningful and guide instruction then teachers *and* administrators must take the time to meet and talk about student work. There is great power for teachers and administrators who share dialogue about student work, instruction methods, and specific uses of curriculum. Administrators and reading specialists are in an ideal situation to facilitate conversations about ongoing assessment. The following suggestions may help as you start to examine methods of assessment in your school.

Look for ways to capture time. Plan special schedules (music, physical education, art) so teachers can meet in horizontal (grade-level) teams for 30 to 45 minutes each week. Make these meetings a time for teachers to share and examine student work samples in reading and writing. Administrators and reading specialists can validate the importance of these meetings by attending, listening, and offering help when needed.

Establish vertical teams. Plan a minimum of three meetings throughout the year so teachers in vertical teams (across grade levels) can meet to share results and expectations for reading and writing instruction.

Talk about assessments. Examine how teachers in your school currently gather information to determine student performance in reading and writing. Talk about how to assess fluency, comprehension, and writing. Look beyond national and other tests to classroom measures including formal assessments connected to curriculum and informal assessments such as observations, running records, and homework. All of these are meaningful sources of information and should be considered and evaluated as evidence of effective instruction and student learning. Examine what you already do, then determine what you need to do.

Gather baseline data. Look at the profile of your school with other teachers and administrators and select one area of reading or writing as a focus. Use a simple, common assessment with all students to provide baseline data. Graded passages from informal reading inventories or benchmark texts can be used to assess fluency or comprehension. First-draft writing samples from common prompts can be used to assess writing. It is important that there be consistency in the selection and administration of these assessments. If they want teachers to use assessment to guide instruction, then administrators and reading specialists must be willing to jump in and give a hand—not only with the development of these assessments but also with the administration.

Work with the data. Once data are collected, meet as teams to analyze the results. Look for evidence of learning and areas in need of improvement. Think about what instruction should look like for students along the performance continuum. An effective assessment provides enough information to guide and direct instruction.

Plan the next steps. Now that you have assessed the students, what will your instruction look like? Work with teachers to develop a common set of goals for instruction. How will instruction look for students who need something more or something different? Determine when would be the best time to gather additional data—not all students need all assessments all the time. Thinking about giving a retelling to every student in a class several times a year can be overwhelming, but planning comprehension checks for select groups of students who need them can be manageable. Some students may need weekly assessment "checkups"; other students may need monthly or only quarterly checks.

A Sample Scenario

An elementary school selects writing improvement as a goal. A team of teachers, the reading specialist, and a building administrator develop a set of grade-level prompts. Students in each class use the prompt to write a first draft. Teachers randomly select three papers from their class, remove the names, make copies, and bring them to a grade-level team meeting. The principal, reading specialist, and teachers meet and score the papers, using an agreed upon rubric. They work until they establish consistency in scoring, or interrater reliability. Teachers use the rubric to score the remaining papers individually. The reading specialist and principal are available to discuss any papers that teachers have difficulty scoring.

The team meets again in two weeks to talk about how their students did as a class and what instruction will look like for students who scored in the upper, middle, and lower ranges of the rubric. Teachers share ideas and instruction strategies for supporting that range of writing levels in their classrooms. The reading specialist and principal share resources they've found on best practice, such as professional books, journal articles, and websites. They also discuss expectations for students and create a consistent instructional framework within their grade level.

Two weeks later, vertical teams of teachers meet to share the data from their grade-level writing samples and bring other samples of student work. This meeting provides teachers in all grade levels with an opportunity to discuss how students can meet the criteria they've established for good writing. It also develops consistency across grade levels through common language and expectations. The teachers and administrators decide together when they will administer the next schoolwide writing prompt.

In most schools, it takes time and patience to change perspectives on assessment. The role of principals has moved from manager to instructional leader, while the role of the reading specialist has changed to reflect a leadership position. Professionals in both roles can help teachers and students use assessment for effective instruction.

References

Black, P., & William, D. (1998). *Inside the black box: Raising standards through classroom assessment.* Retrieved April 1, 2003, from http://www.pdkintl.org/kappan/ kbla9810.htm

Checkley, K. (1997). Assessment that serves instruction. *Education Update, 39*(4), 1, 4–6.

Guskey, T.R. (2003). How classroom assessments improve learning. *Educational Leadership, 60*(5), 6–11.

International Reading Association. (2000). *Making a difference means making it different: Honoring children's rights to excellent reading instruction.* Newark, DE: Author.

Literacy Assessment Reform: Shifting Beliefs, Principled Possibilities, and Emerging Practices

Robert J. Tierney

Developing better assessment practices requires more than simply choosing a new test or adopting a packaged informal assessment procedure. Indeed, it is difficult to imagine "plastic wrapped" versions of what these new assessment systems intend. Unfortunately, some assessment practices may be repackaged versions of old tests rather than new ways of doing assessment. And some assessment practices, regardless of the label (authentic assessment, alternative assessment, student-centered assessment, responsive evaluation, classroom-based assessment, or constructive assessment), may be compromised as they are made to fit tenets or principles out of character or inconsistent with the aspirations of these possibilities. Contributing to the confusion may be reverence for certain technical attributes espoused by some psychometricians and a predilection or political climate that tends to perpetuate top-down assessment and curriculum reform. Not surprising, professionals may differ in whether or not new forms of assessment live up to their promise.

In hopes of helping to sort out some of these dilemmas—the oxymorons, compromises or, at the very least, different views of assessment, learners, and learning—I have tried to make the ramifications of my definition of assessment more explicit with the articulation of a number of principles, which I describe in this article.

These principles for assessment emanate from personal ideals and practice as much as theory and research—a mix of child-centered views of teaching, pluralistic and developmental views of children, constructivist views of knowing, and critical theoretical views of empowerment. The view that I espouse strives to be in harmony with Bruner's (1990) notion that a democratic society "demands that we be conscious of how we come to our knowledge and be as conscious as we can be about the values that lead us to our perspectives. It asks us to be accountable for how and what we know" (p. 31). Likewise, my goal is aligned with constructivists' ways of knowing and the notion of responsive evaluation that Guba and Lincoln (1989) as well as others (e.g., Lather, 1986; Stake, 1983) have espoused:

> Responsive evaluation is not only responsive for the reason that it seeks out different stakeholder views but also since it responds to those items in the subsequent collection of information. It is quite likely that different stakeholders will hold very different constructions with respect to any particular claim, concern, or issue. As we shall see, one of the major tasks of the evaluator is to conduct the evaluation in such a way that each group must confront and deal with the constructions of all the others, a process we shall refer to as a hermeneutic dialectic. (Guba & Lincoln, 1989, p. 41)

I also find my views aligning with critical theorists (e.g., Baker & Luke, 1991; Freire & Macedo, 1987; Gee, 1990; hooks, 1989, 1994) who suggest that the point of literacy is to reflect

From *The Reading Teacher*, *51*(5), 374-390. © 1998 by the International Reading Association.

upon, and be empowered by, text rather than to be subjugated by it—that literacy contributes to social transformation as we connect with what we read and write, not in acquiescence, but in reaction, reflection, and response.

In accordance with these notions, I contend that to be both accountable and empowered, readers and writers need to be both reflective and pragmatic. To do so, readers and writers need to be inquirers—researching their own selves, considering the consequences of their efforts, and evaluating the implications, worth, and ongoing usefulness of what they are doing or have done. Teachers can facilitate such reflection by encouraging students to keep traces of what they do, by suggesting they pursue ways to depict their journey (e.g., webs or a narrative or listing of steps) and by setting aside time to contemplate their progress and efforts. These reflections can serve as conversation starters—conversations about what they are doing and planning to do and what they did and have learned. I suggest moving toward conversations and notes rather than checklists, rubrics, and more formal evaluations, which seem to distance the student from what she/he is doing, has done, or might do.

These principles stem from a concern that new assessment efforts need to be principled and thoughtful rather than faddish. They reflect a need for a major paradigm shift as regards how we assess, why we assess, and the ways these assessments are manifest in the classroom. Some ramifications include a new type of professionalism on the part of teachers, a shift in the relationship between testing and teaching and between teacher, students, and parents. In general, these principles call for a willingness to recognize complexity and diversity and an approach to assessment that begins from inside rather than outside the classroom. Are we succeeding in terms of shifting such values? Currently, there are several efforts occurring that are simultaneously studying and supporting such shifts (see, for instance, Tierney et al., 1998). I am optimistic enough to think we have the makings of a movement that is beginning to establish its own identity—one that is aligned with contemporary views of learning, and more consistent with pluralistic and constructivist ethics (see especially Moss, 1996).

The Principles

Principle 1: Assessments should emerge from the classroom rather than be imposed upon it. Classrooms are places where wonderful ideas are encountered every day; where children engage with one another in a myriad of social interactions; where learning can occur as the culmination of a unit of work, in conjunction with an experiment, or as students work with others or watch others work. Learnings may be fleeting, emerging, reinforced, and challenged. Oftentimes teachers expect certain learnings; at other times, teachers are surprised at what is learned.

The learnings that occur in classrooms are difficult to predict. Children are different not only in their interests and backgrounds, but also in terms of their literacies. While most teachers may begin the year with a sense of what they want to cover, generally they do not consider their plans to be cast in stone. Indeed, they are quick to adjust to their assessment of their students' needs and even to discard and begin afresh. They are more apt to begin with a menu of possibilities and an open-ended agenda, which allows for learning that is opportunistic and individualized.

With the movement to more child-centered approaches, teaching and learning have become less prescriptive and predetermined and have given way to notions of emergent literacy and negotiated curriculums. Most teachers espouse following the lead of the child. Unfortunately, testing practices tend to abide by a different orientation. Many forms of traditional tests do not measure what is valued and what is occurring in classrooms. Changes in testing have not kept pace with shifts in our understanding of learning and literacy development. Moreover, they often perpetuate an approach to assessment that is from the outside in rather than from the inside out. Indeed, I often argue that one of the reasons for emergent assessment is to ensure that assessment practices keep up with teaching and learning rather than stagnate them by perpetuating the status quo or outdated views of literacy learning.

Compare, if you will, these two scenarios:

Students in one classroom are engaged in a wide array of reading and writing experiences, projects, book talks, conferences, and workshops. In conjunction with these activities the students keep journals in which they discuss their reflections, including their goals and self-assessment of their achievements. In addition, each student maintains a log of his or her reading and writing activities, as well as a folder that contains almost everything. Portfolios, in turn, are used to keep track of the key aspects of their work over time. During teacher conferences with the students, the teacher encourages the students to note what they have achieved and want to pursue further. The teacher keeps her/his own informal notes on what is occurring—focusing on a menu of different aspects drawn from a menu of possibilities that the teacher and some colleagues developed. The menu supports but does not constrain the notes that the teacher keeps on the students. As part of the process, these notes are shared with the students, who are encouraged to add their own comments to them. At parent–teacher conferences and student-led parent conferences both the teacher and the student refer back to these notes, portfolios, etc. to remind themselves of and share what has occurred.

The students in another classroom are engaged in a wide array of activities but are not encouraged to monitor themselves. Periodically the teacher distributes a checklist to each student with a preset listing of skills that the child has to check. Likewise the teacher may interrupt the flow of activities and check the students in terms of these preset listing of skills. The skills on the list bear some relationship to some things that are done, but there are a host of things that are not included and some other things that are included that do not seem to apply. The listing of skills was not developed by the teacher nor is it open ended. Instead, the list was developed by a curriculum committee for the district. In some ways the list reflects a philosophy and approach that do not match the current situation. Nonetheless, the teacher is expected to keep the checklist and file it. After the checklist is completed and filed it is not reexamined or revised.

The first example is representative of an inside-out approach—that is, what is assessed and the manner in which the assessment of various learnings is carried out and originates from within the classroom. An inside-out approach does not involve overly rigid a priori determinations of what should be looked for nor does it restrict the types of learning to be examined. In addition, assessment is negotiated among the parties that are involved.

Our second example may give the illusion of being inside out, but it actually perpetuates the outside-in approach. In this classroom the teacher uses informal assessment procedures, but they do not fit with or emerge from the classroom, and there is no negotiation between teacher and student. While the second type of classroom may represent an improvement over classrooms that depend upon standardized assessments and periodic checks, it has some major shortcomings in terms of what is being done and how these things are negotiated. Such a classroom does not invest in or trust the professionalism and problem-solving abilities of teachers, as well as the need for student involvement.

Principle 2: Effective testing requires teacher professionalism with teachers as learners. Many of the assessment practices in schools (especially standardized tests) have a dysfunctional relationship with teachers and learners. Whereas in most relationships you expect a give and take, actual testing practices in schools seem more estranged than reciprocal, more detached than intimate. This should come as no surprise for oftentimes testing personnel have separated themselves and their instruments from teachers and students. Testing divisions in school districts generally have detached themselves from teachers and students or have forced teachers and students to work on their terms. In some districts, the testing division may use tenets tied to notions of objectivity and reliability to leverage control of what is tested as well as how, when, and why testing occurs.

If teachers become involved in making assessment decisions, the complexity of dealing with individual differences and differences across classes and schools is apt to surface. It may become problematic to assume that different students can be assessed with the same test, that comparisons across students are straightforward, or that students' performance and progress can be adequately represented with scores derived by periodical administrations of tests.

Quite often teachers will make reference to the tests that they are required to use, principals will allude to the district and state policy, and the district and state lay the responsibility on the public. Some systems seem to be either resistant to change or entrenched in their commitments.

But, teachers relinquishing control of assessment leads to a loss of self-determinacy and professionalism, which is problematic for a number of reasons. It seems to accept and reinforce the view that teachers cannot be trusted. It removes responsibility for instructional decisions from the hands of those who need to be making them. As a result, it decreases the likelihood that assessment will be aligned with teaching and learning and increases the separation between how learning is occurring in classrooms and how it is tested and reported. It depersonalizes the experience and serves as an excuse for relinquishing responsibility. Essentially, the external control of testing and standardization of testing procedures tend to perpetuate teacher and student disenfranchisement.

Teachers are in a better position to know and learn about an individual's development than outsiders. They are with the student over time across a variety of learning situations. As a result they become aware of the subtle changes and nuances of learning within and across individuals. They are sensitive to student engagement, student interests, student personalities, and the idiosyncrasies of students across learning activities. They are less likely to overstate or ascribe too much significance to results on a single test that may have an alienating impact upon a student. They are in a better position to track and assess learning in the context of teaching and child watching, and therefore to help students assess themselves. Effective teachers are effective learners themselves; they are members of a community of learners in a classroom.

So how might assessment be changed? Teachers, in partnership with their students, need to devise their own classroom assessment systems. These systems should have goals for assessment tied to teaching and learning. These goals should be tied to the types of learning and experiences deemed desirable and, therefore, should be established by those most directly invested in the student's education—the teachers and the students themselves. These standards/features should be open ended and flexible enough to adjust to the nuances of classroom life. Tied to these goals might be an array of assessment activities from formalized procedures to very informal, from student self-assessment activities to teacher observations to periodical assessments via portfolios or other ways of checking progress.

Teachers and students need to be willing to change and recognize that there exists no quick fix or prepackaged way to do assessment. Indeed, prepackaged assessments are apt to be the antithesis of what should be developed. Unfortunately, teachers, students, and caregivers may have been enculturated to view assessment as predetermined rather than emergent and as having a look and feel quite different from more direct and classroom-derived assessments.

More direct forms of assessment might involve ongoing monitoring of students by sampling reading and writing behaviors, maintaining portfolios and journals, holding periodic conferences, and keeping anecdotal records. Several teachers and state efforts suggest that the community will support, if not embrace, such changes. We have numerous affidavits from teachers to that effect, which are corroborated by published reports of others such as Shepard and Bliem (1995), who found community support for performance assessments or more direct methods of assessment over traditional assessments was forthcoming and considerable when caregivers were presented with examples of the options.

Principle 3: Assessment practices should be client centered and reciprocal. The notion that assessment should empower students and caregivers suggests an approach consistent with a more client-centered approach to learning. A client-centered approach to assessment is not novel. In areas such as psychotherapy and medicine, client-centered orientations are more the rule than the exception. In a court of law the judicial process hinges upon the notion of advocacy for a client. In attempts at being client centered, teachers are apt to consider what students take away from tests or teacher-student conferences. A shift to client-centered approaches addresses how assessment practices are helping students assess themselves—i.e., the extent to which students might know how they can check their own progress. Indeed, the development of assessment practices with such provisions may have far-reaching consequences. It suggests that we should shift the whole orientation of assessment from developing better methods of assessing students toward better methods of helping students assess themselves.

So how might client-centered assessment look? It would look like child-centered learning. Teachers would strive to help students assess themselves. Their orientation would shift from subjecting students to assessment practices to respecting students for their self-assessment initiatives. This entails a shift from something you *do to* students to something you *do with* them or help them *do for themselves*—a form of leading from behind.

A number of classrooms have in place the beginnings of student self-assessment vehicles via the use of journals, logs, and portfolios. But this is just a beginning; self-assessment should extend to every aspect of the classroom, from helping students formulate their own learning goals, to helping students make decisions on what they can handle and need, to having them collaborate in the development of report cards and parent–teacher conferences. Too, the involvement of students in their own assessment helps with the management of such activities. This might entail having students set their own goals at the beginning of a unit (not unlike what is proposed with K-W-L); hold conferences with teachers, parents, or peers as they progress or wrestle with issues; look at their efforts and study their progress; and set future goals at the end of a unit in conjunction with parent conferences, or as alternatives to report cards.

There are numerous ways to start these conversations. I ground my conversations about assessment for and with students in the actual portfolio without the intrusion of a grade or score. Scores and grades only give the illusion of accuracy and authority; conversations connected to portfolios or other forms of more direct assessment unmask the bases for decision making and spur the conversation toward a consideration of the evidence, an appreciation of assumptions and the negotiations of goals. "Let's look," "I can show you," "It's like this," "I see what you mean," and "Do you think" displace more general and removed conversations, which tend to be categorical rather than contributory.

Various forms of self-analysis can complement portfolios and be wonderful springboards for such conversations. For example, sometimes I will have students represent their progress and goals with bar graphs or other visual representations (e.g., Venn diagrams, landscapes) in a fashion akin to "then," "now," and "future" and use these graphs as conversation starters. In turn, the visuals serve as the basis for having students delve into their portfolios and examine evidence about what they have achieved and what they might focus upon or set their sights on.

Principle 4: Assessment should be done judiciously, with teachers as advocates for students and ensuring their due process. A useful metaphor, if not rule, for rethinking assessment can be derived from aligning assessment with judicial processes. In a court of law, an individual on trial is given an advocate who presents evidence, including testimony, to present a case on behalf of the client. The client and the lawyer work in tandem. The trial is judged upon whether or not the client was given a just hearing and whether or nor her or his representation was adequate. The client has the right to see the evidence presented for and against her or him, the right to reports developed, the right to present his or her own evidence and arguments, and the right to appeal. Also, in the event the client is not satisfied with his or her representation, the client has the right to request someone else to support his or her making a case or, if concerned about procedure, to request a retrial.

Now consider how students are put on trial in our school systems. They may or may not have an advocate, they may or may not be given adequate representation, and the evidence that is presented may or may not best represent their cases. They may not see the reports that are developed. Indirect indicators such as standardized tests, of questionable (if not circumstantial) quality, serve as the basis for decisions that restrict opportunities. In a host of ways assessment activities appear less judicious than they should be. Indeed, students are rarely given the right to appeal or to provide their own evidence—it is as if the students' right to due process is violated.

An examination of the law governing public schools raises some interesting concerns regarding schooling. Over the last 30 years, some key U.S. Supreme Court decisions have been offered that should direct our thinking. In *Tinker v. Des Moines Independent School District*, 393 U.S. 503 (1969), a case involving freedom of speech, the Court established some key principles undergirding students' rights. The Court wrote: "In our system, state operated schools may not be enclaves for totalitarianism.... Students in schools, as well as out of school are possessed of fundamental rights which the State must respect." This position was reaffirmed in the case of *Goss v. Lopez*, 419 U.S. 565 (1975). As Justice White stated, "young people do not 'shed their constitutional rights' at the schoolhouse door"—the right to due process is of particular importance when the impact of an event "may interfere with later opportunities."

I would hope that legislators pursue practices that place students' rights at a premium rather than displace such a goal with practices that serve first to protect themselves against legal challenges. At a minimum, I would hope that any assessments afford students better due process, including the right of disclosure and presentation of evidence on behalf of the student, as well as the right to appeal the use of indirect or circumstantial evidence. Moreover, I would hope my appeal for judicious assessment shifts the pursuit of such to being both a goal and a right.

Unfortunately, some U.S. state legislators may be more intent on protecting themselves against possible litigation than ensuring that students' rights have been fully supported. For example, they might consider that the spirit of due process has been satisfied when students have been given advance notice of tests and what these tests will entail—that is, in lieu of opportunities to appeal or students providing their own "alternative" evidence of progress or proficiencies. Also, an insipid development occurs when teaching to the test is used to maximize the legal defensibility of tests. In particular, states will often try to finesse the possibility of legal challenges of test bias by ensuring that students have had the opportunity to learn the content covered on tests. To avoid litigation and appear to address local needs, they will establish programs to prepare students for the tests and therefore "make" their tests unbiased by definition. The attitude of most institutions and states is to emphasize legal defensibility ahead of protection for and advocacy on behalf of students.

Principle 5: Assessment extends beyond improving our tests to the purposes of assessment and how results from assessment are used, reported, contextualized, and perceived. Any consideration of assessment needs to be broadly defined to encompass an exploration of the relationship between assessment and teaching, as well as facets such as report cards, parent–teacher–student conferences, and the student's ongoing record. These facets should not be viewed as exempt from scrutiny in terms of the principles described herein. They should be subjected to the same guidelines.

Just as the goals for developing better classroom-based assessment procedures are tied to the principles discussed herein, so report cards, records, and other elements must be examined in terms of whether they adequately serve the ends for which they are intended. Take, if you will, report cards. Do report cards serve the needs of the student, teacher, and parent? Do they represent a vehicle for ongoing communication and goal setting? Are they done judiciously? If not, how might the method of reporting be changed to afford such possibilities? Or, take, if you will, the student's records. For what purposes are the records used? Are the records adequate for these purposes?

Changes in assessment should be viewed systemically. When teachers contemplate a shift in classroom assessment, it is rarely a matter of simply making selected adjustments or additions. What a teacher does with one facet should and will affect another. For example, a teacher who incorporates a portfolio approach is likely to become dissatisfied with traditional forms of reporting progress. The solution is not to shy away from such changes, but to realize that they will need to occur and, if they do not, to realize that the failure to make such changes may undermine the changes already made. Teachers start to feel as if their new assessment initiatives are being compromised. Students may begin to sense mixed messages if teachers advocate student decision-making and then reassert their singular authority via the determination of a grade without any student input or negotiation. That is, teachers move in and out of assessment practices tied to very different underlying principles. I feel as if the worth of assessment efforts such as portfolios may be diminished if the portfolios are graded or graded inappropriately either without any student input or without consideration for diversity and richness—especially, what the portfolio might mean to the student. We need to keep an eye on achieving students' engagement in their own learning as we negotiate future goals and possibilities against the type of judgments that are made and reported by whom and how.

We should not underestimate the importance of parent or caregiver involvement in such efforts. Rather than keep the parent or caregiver at arm's length in the negotiations over reform, we need to embrace the concerns that parents have and the contributions that they can make. In those situations where teachers pursue alternatives to report cards, parent contributions may be crucial. Parents need to be informed of the goals and engaged in contributing to the efforts. Because not all parents might see the advantages, they may need choices. And, there are ways to avoid holding all parents hostage to what one parent or a small number express as concerns. For example, in pursuit of student-led conferences as an alternative to report cards, Steve Bober (1995) presented parents in Massachusetts with a description of two alternatives and offered them a choice—student-led conferences or more traditional report cards. Parents choosing student-led conferences were also expected to write letters to their children after each conference. Apart from the distinctiveness of the practice, what is notable is how Bober engaged parents as informed partners in the practice.

Principle 6: Diversity should be embraced, not slighted. Oftentimes those assessing students want to remove any cultural biases rather than recognize diversity and support individual empowerment. They often pursue culture-free items and analysis procedures as a way of neatening and comparing. In pursuit of straightforward comparisons they assume that to be fair more items are needed, and therefore, the use of authentic assessment procedures will create problems, especially since the "time-consuming nature of the problems limits the number" (Linn, Baker, & Dunbar, 1991, p. 18). In addition, they seem to support as a given the use of the same analysis systems for the responses of all students. They expect a respondent to interpret a task in a certain way and respond in a set manner and may not tolerate variation in response, even if such variation might be justified. Whereas they might allude to the context-specific nature of any assessment, they tend to retreat from considering individuals on their own merits or in their own ways.

The term *culture-free tests* seems an oxymoron. I suspect that it is well nigh impossible, and certainly questionable, to extract cultural influences from any test or measure of someone's literacy. Literacy, your own and my own, is inextricably connected to cultural background and life experiences. Culture-free assessments afford, at best, a partial and perhaps distorted understanding of the student. In other words, assessments that do not build upon the nature and nuances of each individual's experiences should be viewed as limited and perhaps flawed. Just as teachers attempt to engage students by building from their background of experiences, so assessment should pursue a goal of culture sensitivity. Classroom teaching does not occur by ignoring or removing diversities. Nor should such a view of assessment be dismissed because of its ideological or sociopolitical considerations: Recognition or validation of one's own experience would seem a basic human right.

We need to aspire to culturally based assessment practices. In some ways I see this pursuit consistent with John Ogbu's (1988, 1991) notions about beginning to meet the needs of African American students—namely, an approach to educational reform that has a cultural ecological orientation. I envision cultural ecological assessments that build upon, recognize, and value rather than displace what students have experienced in their worlds.

For a number of years literacy educators have been willing to sidestep complex issues of culturally sensitive assessments by appealing to the need to make straightforward comparisons. For years standardized test developers and the National Assessment of Educational Progress have retreated from dealing with issues of nonuniformity and diversity as they have pursued the development of scales for straightforward comparisons across individuals. In conjunction with doing this, they have often revised their assessment instruments to ensure that results fit their models or views of literacy. For example, they are apt to exclude items on topics tied to specific cultural interests and to remove items that show an advantage for one group over another. Even recent attempts espousing guidelines for new approaches to performance assessment (e.g., Linn et al., 1991) or exploring bias in testing minorities (Haney, 1993) may have fallen prey to the same view of the world.

Principle 7: Assessment procedures may need to be nonstandardized to be fair to the individual. As teachers try to avail students of every opportunity within their control, they are constantly making adjustments as they "read" the students—their dispositions, verbal abilities, familiarities, needs, and so on. We look for ways to maximize the learning for different students, and we know that different students may need different amounts of encouragement and very different kinds of support. If we standardized our teaching, we know what would apt to be the end result—some students with wonderful potential would reveal only certain sides of themselves and might not achieve their potential or even reveal who they are and what they might contribute and learn.

Allowing for individual or even group differences creates havoc with the desire to standardize assessment. Standardization approaches each individual and group in the same way—that is, students perform the same tasks at the same time, and then their responses are assessed using the same criteria. But if different students' learning repertoires are different and different students enlist different strategies and have different values, etc., and different approaches to testing, then what may be standard for one student may be unique for another.

Studies across cultures, across classrooms, and within classrooms suggest that different students respond in different ways to different forms of assessment depending upon their histories—cultural, classroom, or personal. As my previous principle suggested, how students respond should be looked at as different across situations and against a "comparative canvas, one that takes into account the nature of the community that students inhabit, both the community of the classroom and the community of society with all of its past and present conditions and hopes for the future" (Purves, 1982, p. 345). Green and Dixon (1994) have emphasized that students construct "situated repertoires associated with particular models for being a student...not generic ones" (p. 237). We have ample demonstrations as to how the responsiveness of various groups and individuals in testing situations depends on their view of the social dynamics of the situation (Basso, 1970; Crumpler, 1996; Ogbu, 1988; Philips, 1983).

Indeed, there is always a tension between a need for uniformity across individuals and groups and the use of procedures that are sensitive to the different literacy developments of students, as well as the students' own predispositions to respond differently to different people in different ways at different times. On numerous occasions my assessment of some students has been revised as a result of pursuing more than one mode of response, as well as establishing different kinds of partnership with them or watching them interact over time in different situations with different individuals or groups. In turn, what may serve as a vehicle for uncovering the literacies of one student may not be a satisfactory method for uncovering those of another student or those of the same student at another time. Teachers need to be willing to use different means with different students whether they are assessing or teaching.

The decision-making process may also be complicated by certain of our own predilections. In conjunction with my work on portfolios, I am always surprised at the analyses that learners have done of their progress and the types of goals that they choose to pursue. They ascribe to elements in their portfolios significance that I may have overlooked or not have been able to see. And, their decisions to proceed are often at variance with what I would have suggested.

Principle 8: Simple-minded summaries, scores, and comparisons should be displaced with approaches that acknowledge the complex and idiosyncratic nature of literacy development. Straightforward comparisons across individuals are usually arbitrary, biased, and narrow. Assuming an approach to assessment with a new openness to complexity, respect for diversity, and interest in acquiring a rich picture of each student, then how might decisions be made about students? Those decisions that require reflection upon the individual's progress and prospects will likely be bountiful. Teachers who pursue an open-ended and diverse view of students will find little difficulty negotiating new areas of pursuit with and for individual students. Decisions that demand comparisons from one individual to the next will be problematic, but these difficulties are not insurmountable. They require a willingness to deal with uncertainties, to entertain possibilities, and to negotiate decisions, including the possibility that there will be lack of agreement. The problems with comparisons are confounded when people assume that straightforward continuums or single scores can adequately describe students.

Comparisons based upon scores are so problematic for a host of reasons: (a) Each student's development is unique; (b) the literacies of one student will be different from another, and even the same literacies will involve differing arrays of facets; and (c) some of these facets will be unique to a certain situation. Literacy development is sufficiently different from one student to the next that the types of comparisons that might be made are quite complex and multifaceted. The term *literacy abilities* rather than *literacy ability* seems in order. If you were trying to portray the character of these developments, you might find yourself gravitating to describing individuals on their own terms. Unfortunately, the terms of comparison in place with standardized tests and NAEP assessments and implicit in many of the attempts to score portfolios and other classroom-based data are often insensitive to such complexity. Looking at different individuals in terms of a single score masks variability and individuality. Again, test makers err on the side of a level of simplification not unlike a massive "conspiracy of convenience" (Spiro, Vispoel, Schmitz, Samarapungavan, & Boerger, 1987, p. 180).

The drive for uniformity is quite pervasive. Our assessment and instructional programs oftentimes include long lists of skills as outcomes to be assessed, taught, and mastered. It is assumed that skills are neatly packaged and discrete and that each makes a uniform contribution to literacy development. It is assumed that students acquire these skills to mastery and that their ability to use them is uniform across literacy situations. In authentic reading and writing situations within which genuine purposes are being pursued, this is unlikely. Across literacy situations certain attributes may be more likely to be enlisted than others, and they are apt to be enlisted as clusters rather than one by one or discretely.

Too often literacy educators have ignored the complexities of the issues and have fallen back on convenience rather than exploring possibilities. Take, if you will, the attempts to wed some of the data emerging from performance assessment (e.g., portfolios) with rubrics. The data generated from a portfolio might involve a rich array of samples or observations of the students' work across situations and time. These samples are apt to represent the students' pursuit of different goals, utilizing different resources, including content, under varying conditions. In some ways student classroom samples may vary as much as the works of art from an artist's portfolio. Each sample may represent very different achievements and processes. When you hold them, examine them, and discuss their significance you are in touch with the actual artifact and not some distant derivative.

It is at this point, some would argue, that we can use a rubric to affix a score or scores or a sum total score to the student's work. But we need to examine a question that is the reverse of what is often asked. Instead of asking how we rate the portfolio, we should be asking whether the rubric measures up to the portfolio or to the assessment of complex performance. Moreover, in classrooms do we need a measure that is a distant derivative when we have the primary sources—the actual samples—to examine and reexamine using an array of lenses or perspectives? Whereas I argue for the context-specific nature of any assessment, advocates of rubrics seem to want to dismiss idiosyncrasies and variation—that is, they would retreat from being willing to consider individuals on their own merits or in their own ways. Unless rubrics are used to prompt a consideration of possible ways to analyze work or as conversation starters in conjunction with revisiting the students' work samples, I see few advantages to their use in classrooms.

Sometimes assessment of reading and writing becomes more far-fetched by adding together a set of subscores. A key assumption often undergirding the use of such scores—especially the suggestion that they can be added and used as the basis of comparative decision making—is that the full and detailed portrait of an individual's literacies has been afforded. Unfortunately, these dimensions are not exhaustive, these determinations of degree are not accurate, and they should not be added. To be able to do so, we would have to do the following:

1. include all of the attributes or be assured that the partial listing that was developed is representative;
2. determine how these attributes are configured across situations;
3. assume that ample evidence will be provided for assessing these attributes;
4. develop scales for assessing attributes; and
5. generate an algorithm that works across individuals by which we might combine the elements and their dimensions.

I would posit that we do not have such samples, sampling procedures, ways of procuring evidence, adequate scales, or algorithm. And it is problematic to assume that an algorithm that simply represents sums would ever be adequate. The complexity of literacy is such that we cannot assume a basis for generating or combining scores.

Literacy assessments cannot and should not be so rigid. Perhaps there are some benchmarks that are appropriate across all students. Perhaps there are benchmarks appropriate to some readers and not others. But such benchmarks are likely to represent a partial view of any student's literacies. The use of scores and continua as ways of affording simplification and comparability has a tendency to camouflage the subjectivity of assessment and give test developers the allusion of objectivity. The use of scores and continua is not more objective; it is arbitrary. Guba and Lincoln

(1989) have suggested the shift toward accepting the inevitability of relativism and the complexities across different settings may require the ongoing, ecumenical, and recursive pursuit of shared possibilities rather than a single set of absolute truths.

Principle 9: Some things that can be assessed reliably across raters are not worth assessing; some things that are worth assessing may be difficult to assess reliably except by the same rater. Oftentimes, test makers and researchers will perseverate on whether or not they can consistently measure certain abilities. They tout reliability as the major criteria for whether or not a test is valid. The end result is that some things that are worth measuring are discarded and some things that are not worth measuring or valuing achieve an elevated level of importance. Typically, complex and individualistic learning tends to be shortchanged whereas the currency of learnings that are easier to define may be inflated. For example, in writing assessment, constructs such as style or voice may be shortchanged, while spelling and punctuation may be inflated. In reading, constructs such as self-questioning, engagement, and interpretation may be shortchanged, while speed, factual recall, and vocabulary may be elevated.

Unfortunately, reliability is translated to mean that two different scorers or raters will be able to assess the same thing in the same way. Unless a high degree of agreement across raters is achieved, test makers will deem a measure unreliable and therefore question its worth. In so doing, they may be making the mistake of assuming that reliability equates to agreement when verifiability may be a better approach.

We should be willing to accept differences of opinion in terms of how certain abilities are rated or discerned. Some abilities and strategies are difficult to pin down in terms of clear operational definitions. Different raters or even the same raters at different times are apt to develop different constructions of the same phenomena. Sometimes these shifts arise as a result of the different predispositions of the raters. Sometimes they arise as different facets of the phenomena are taken into account either by different raters or the same rater. Sometimes they arise as a result of differences in how students enlisted certain abilities. Such differences should not be viewed as surprising, for they coincide with two key tenets of most current views of learning: the notion of an ongoing constructive nature of knowing; and the situation-specific nature of learning. Differences are apt to exist across and within an individual's literacies (e.g., reading a newspaper for purposes of locating an advertisement versus reading a romance novel for pleasure) and from one individual to the next. In other words, some features may or may not apply to some students' literacy, and some facets may apply uniquely to individuals.

One should not be seduced into thinking that variables that are easy to define should be looked at to the exclusion of those that are difficult to assess. It may be foolish to exclude some facets because they are difficult to assess or because they look different either across students or situations or by the raters. Likewise, one should not be seduced into thinking that every reading and writing act is the same and involves the same variables. If the only literacy facets scored are those common across students and those that can be scored with high reliability across different students' responses, then certain facets will be given more weight than they deserve, and some important facets may be excluded.

Principle 10: Assessment should be more developmental and sustained than piecemeal and shortsighted. To assess how well a student is doing, our vision or vistas need to change. If assessment goals are tied to development, then we need to look at patterns and long-term goals. What we see or look for in a single selection or case may not be helpful in looking for patterns across cases, selections, or circumstances. For example, as a reader or writer reads and writes a single selection, we might look for engagement and active involvement. Across situations we might want to consider the extent to which the interest and engagement are maintained across a range of material for different purposes. We also might be interested in the extent to which the student has developed a value for reading and writing that is reflected in how he or she uses reading and writing inside and outside the class. This may be apparent in her or his self-selection of books or self-initiated writing to serve different purposes.

Within areas such as the students' abilities to read with understanding, our goal for a single selection might be the extent to which a reader understands the main idea or theme or can draw conclusions using selected details, etc. Across selections or in the long term, we might be interested in how the students use different books to contribute overall understandings tied to units or projects or their own developing understandings of the world. Or, we might be interested in self-assessment. With a single selection we could focus on the reader's or writer's ability to monitor reading and writing, to set goals for a specific selection, and to problem-solve and wrestle with meaning-making. Across selections we might be interested in the reader's or writer's ability to set goals and assess progress across several selections. In looking across selections, you should not expect that students will always appear to reveal the same level of sophistication with skills and strategies or necessarily use the same skills and strategies. See the Table for other short-term, long-term contrasts.

A shift toward assessment that examines students over time aligns assessment with classroom practices that pursue sustained engagement and aim to help students derive an understanding of patterns. It shifts our teaching and learning to long-term possibilities rather than the specific and short-term objectives of a lesson.

Principle 11: Most interpretations of results are not straightforward. Assessment should be viewed as ongoing and suggestive, rather than fixed or definitive. In many ways teaching involves constant redevelopment or continuous experimentation and adjustments to plans, directions, and future goals. To appreciate the complexities and sophistication of teaching, consider the image one conjures up for a sportsperson. In certain sports (e.g., baseball, tennis) involving eye-hand coordination with racquets or bats, players will begin their swing and constantly be making subtle adjustments as balls with different velocities, rotations, and angles are thrown at them. But sporting events pale in comparison with the dynamics of teacher-student interactions—the adjustments, just in time decision making, and ebb and flow of activities that occur. Teachers deal with students whom they may be trying to respond to, motivate, mobilize, develop, and coach while understanding their needs, beliefs, strategies, and possible ways of responding as they are interacting with one another and dealing with the rest of their lives. Not surprising, teachers have to be a mix of ecologist, developer, advocate, coach, player, actor-director, stage manager, mayor, and sometimes counselor. Teachers are always planning and recognizing the need to make constant adjustments to what they are doing and what they might do next.

For these purposes, the typical assessment data (e.g., scouting reports of students provided by school records, premeasures of abilities, standardized or even informal assessments) may provide limited guidance to teachers in terms of the moment-by-moment decision making and even planning for the next day or week or even month. Too often typical student records seem as limited as a mug shot taken of the learner; you may be able to identify the learner (depending upon your ability to see likenesses) but may not. Certainly, the mug shot will not afford you an appreciation of the character of the student, nor will it help you understand the range of things that the student can do, nor will it support your ability to negotiate either long-term or short-term learning goals.

Most classroom-based assessments offer more promise but are still limited. Classroom-based assessment procedures may give teachers a better sense of how students will proceed in like circumstances and may also afford a fuller picture of the student across time. Portfolios, for example, are equivalent to scrapbooks involving multiple snapshots of the learner in a variety of

Short- and long-term contrasts in assessment

Short-term/single instance	Long-term/multiple situations
Affect	
Engaged	Value
Active	Self-seeking ongoing
Thoughtful	Habit
Strategies	
Planning	Flexible, reflective, coordinated, selective, customized
Fixing up and troubleshooting	
Making connections	
Looking back, forward, and beyond	
Collaborating	Community building
Outcomes	
Main idea	Overall understandings, intertextual connections
Details	Projects
Conclusions	Applications
Implications	Range of problems and activities
	Overall understandings and themes
Self-assessment	
Self-monitoring	Self-scrutiny, goal setting, self-determinations
Online problem solving	Overall goals, progress, patterns

contexts. Such assessments might afford a fuller and richer depiction of the learner and his or her pattern of development, but judgments—especially prescriptions—are never as straightforward as they might appear. The possibility of obtaining a complete vision of a learner is complicated by our inability to constantly monitor a learner, delve into and interpret his or her innermost thoughts, and achieve more than one perspective on the learner. It is also tied to the ever-changing nature of learning. Apart from the fact that our snapshots of classroom learning tend to be still shots of the learner, these images are tied to a place and time that has become more historical than current. Such limitations might be viewed as a problem if we were to perseverate on wanting to pin down what to do next with a student and be sure to stick to a set course. Instead, they should be anticipated and viewed as tentative bases for where and when one might begin. While we can develop short- and long-term goals and plans, we should not approach our teaching as if our prescriptions should not be altered, assessment fixed, nor directions more than suggestive.

Likewise, we should not approach assessment as if our results need be final or base our subsequent actions as if we have derived a decision that is any better than a hunch. We should avoid assuming that our assessments do anything more than afford us information that we might consider. No assessment should be used as restrictively or rigidly as decisions made in courts of law, yet I fear that many are. Instead we should reinforce what needs to occur in classrooms—constant adjustments, shifts, and ongoing decision making by teachers who are constantly watching, learning, coaching, and responding to students, peers, and others.

Principle 12: Learning possibilities should be negotiated with the students and stakeholders rather than imposed via standards and assessment that are preset, prescribed, or mandated. The state within which

I reside (along with many other states) has been seduced into thinking that standard setting may be the answer to improving education by ensuring that teachers teach and students learn certain basic skills. I find myself quite discouraged that our professional associations have aligned with similar efforts. Historically, standard setting (and the proficiency testing that it spurs) has tended to restrict access and experimentation at the same time as it has tended to support agendas tied to gatekeeping and exclusion.

The standard-setting enterprise and the proficiency-testing industry have the potential to perpetuate the view that we can set targets that we can easily reach. Unfortunately, it is problematic to assume that development is simply setting a course for the student from A to B—especially when A is not taken into account and B is tied to views of outcomes looking for expertise rather than individual assessment of development. Without ample consideration being given for where students are and how and why they develop and their aspirations, we are apt to have our targets misplaced and our learning routes poorly aligned. I was in attendance at one of the many sessions on standards sponsored by the International Reading Association and the National Council of Teachers of English, when a speaker talked about standards using the analogy of a basketball player of the caliber of Michael Jordan as the "standard." As the speaker discussed the worth of setting standards based upon what we view as aspirations, I mulled over my height and my skill and what I might do to improve. Then I reminded myself of my reasons for playing basketball and where I am insofar as my background in basketball. I play basketball for fun, to be with my sons, and for exercise. We need to realize that we should be asking, who is deciding? Whose standards are being represented? In some ways the quest for educational improvement via standards and in turn proficiency testing places a premium on uniformity rather than diversity and favors prepackaged learning over emerging possibilities.

In a similar vein, advocates of standards emphasize the importance of the role of making judgments by comparisons to Olympic skating and other activities where success is measured by the trophies one achieves or the graded measures that are applied. I think we need to challenge this metaphor and question the emphasis on judgment rather than support. I prefer to think of a teacher as a coach rather than a judge—a supporter and counselor versus a judge and award- or grade-giver. I would like to see teachers view their role as providing guidance, handholding, and comments rather than As, Bs, and Cs or some score. In my view of a more ideal world, I see teachers, students, and caregivers operating in a kind of public sphere where they are part of the team negotiating for a better self. In this regard, I find myself fascinated with several classroom projects: with the kind of self-reflection and analysis occurring amidst the community-based preschool efforts of Reggio Emilia (Forman, 1993, 1994) where teachers, students, and community work together developing and implementing curriculum plans, ponder the right questions to ask to spur students' reflections, develop insights, and learn; with the work of Short, Harste, and Burke (1996) on developing inquiry in Indianapolis schools (as they engage students and teachers in considering the anomalies, patterns, and ways of looking at themselves); with the work of the Santa Barbara Classroom Discourse Group (1992a, 1992b), a community of teachers, researchers, and students interested in understanding how life in classrooms is constructed and how expectations and practices influence opportunities to access, accomplish, and learn in school; and with the work of Fenner (1995) who uses a general form of Toulmin's (1958) analysis of argumentation to examine classroom conversations and student self-assessments with portfolios and looks for ways to help students look at themselves in terms of evidence, assumptions, claims, and goals. Fenner's approach to self-assessment moves us away from the typical checklist that asks students to detail in rather vague and unsubstantiated fashion their strengths and goals in a kind of "hit and miss" fashion.

Unfortunately, rather than language that suggests a view of classrooms as developmental and nurturing, oftentimes the metaphors adopted by those involved in the testing, proficiency, and standards enterprises seem more appropriate to developing consumer products connected to prescribed guidelines and uniform inspection procedures. That is, they seem to fit with our views of industry rather than nurturing human potential (Wile & Tierney, 1996). With this in mind, I would suggest that we should assess assessment based on whether it is parsimonious with a society's bill of rights and our views of individual rights, opportunities, and freedoms.

I fear that standards will perpetuate the effects uncovered when Ellwein, Glass, and Smith (1988) surveyed the history of the effects of various statewide proficiency testing—gatekeeping and the removal rather than enhancement of opportunities. Indeed, in Ohio and I would suspect other states, Ellwein et al.'s (1988) findings are being replicated. With the introduction of proficiency testing more students are dropping out. Ironically, the tests were intended to improve instruction, but fewer students are taking them, which in turn suggests that more students are passing them. So by keeping these dropouts invisible, advocates of proficiency testing and legislators claim the reform is having positive effects—that is, as more students leave or drop out, abhorring or deterred by the situation, legislators and advocates (including the media) erroneously suggest or advertise falsely that more students are passing.

Closing Remarks

My principles for assessment emanate from a mix of child-centered views of teaching, developmental views of children, constructivist views of knowing, critical theoretical views of empowerment, and pluralistic views of society. I view them as suggesting directions and guidelines for thinking about the why, how, where and when, who, and what of assessment.

Why?

To develop culturally sensitive versus culturally free assessments

To connect assessment to teaching and learning

To connect assessment to students' ongoing goal setting, decision making, and development

To become better informed and make better decisions

To develop assessment that keeps up with teaching and learning

How?

Collaborative, participatory, client centered

Coach-like, supportive and ongoing rather than judgmental, hard-nosed, and final

Supplemental and complementary versus grade-like and summative

Individually, diversely, not prepackaged

Judiciously

Developmentally

Reasoned

Where and when?

Amidst students' lives

Across everyday events and programs

In and out of school

Opportunistically, periodically, continuously

Who?

Students, teachers, and stakeholders

What?

Ongoing learning: development, resources, and needs

Complexities

Individuals and groups

Evidence of progress and decision making

Programs, groups, individuals

In describing the essence of my proposition, I would like to return to where I began. I believe an overriding principle, which is perhaps my 13th or more of a penumbra, is **assessment should be assessed in terms of its relationship with teaching and learning, including the opportunities learners are offered and the rights and respect they are accorded**.

Shifts in my own thinking about assessment began occurring when I asked myself this question: If I were to assess assessment, what criteria might I use? My answer to this question was that assessment practices should empower teachers, students, and their caregivers. In other words, assessment practices should enrich teaching and learning. As I explored how tests might be used as tools of empowerment for teachers and learners, I became interested in whether this type of assessment actually helped teachers and students (as well as the student's caregiver, resource teachers, principal, and others) achieve a more expanded view of the student's learning. I also wanted to know whether testing contributed to developing goals and formulating plans of action, which would suggest that assessment practices were empowering. My view of empowerment includes:

- Teachers having a fuller sense (expanded, refined, different) of the students' abilities, needs, and instructional possibilities;
- Students having a fuller sense of their own abilities, needs, and instructional possibilities;
- Teachers integrating assessment with teaching and learning (this would entail the dynamic/ongoing use of assessment practices, as well as assessment tailored to classroom life); accommodating, adapting, adjusting, customizing—shifting assessment practices to fit with students and their learning and adjusting teaching in accordance with feedback from assessments;
- Students engaging in their own self-assessments as they set, pursue, and monitor their own goals for learning in collaboration with others, including peers, teachers, and caregivers.
- Communities of teachers, students, and parents forming and supporting one another around this assessment process.

The use of standardized tests, tests accompanying the published reading programs, and even teacher-made tests do not expand teachers' views of their students' learning over time, nor suggest ways the teacher might help them. Nor are such tests integrated into classroom life. They tend to displace teaching and learning activities rather than enhance them.

Likewise, students rarely seem to be engaged in learning how to assess themselves. When my colleagues and I interviewed teachers with whom we began working in assessment 10 years ago, most teachers did not conceptualize the goal of testing to be helping students reflect or obtain feedback on their progress, nor did they envision tests as helping students establish, refine, or achieve learning goals. When we interviewed students, we found that students in these classes tended to have a limited and rather negative view of themselves, and they had set few learning goals. Attempts to examine the impact of more learner-based assessments yielded quite contrasting results. In classrooms in which portfolios were becoming an integral part of classroom life, teachers and students had developed a fuller sense of their own abilities (Carter, 1992; Carter & Tierney, 1988; Fenner, 1995; Stowell & Tierney, 1995; Tierney, Carter, & Desai, 1991).

A study by Shavelson, Baxter, and Pine (1992) provides other confirmation of the worth of aligning assessment to the teaching and learning in classrooms. In their attempts to examine variations in instructional programs, they concluded that direct observations and more emergent procedures captured the shifts in learning while traditional methods (multiple choice, short answer) did not. Such findings should come as no surprise to those of us who have been involved in research on the effects of teaching upon learning; that is, very few literacy researchers would rely upon a standardized test to measure the effectiveness of particular teaching strategies with different students. Instead, we are apt to pursue a range of measures, and some of us would not develop our measures a priori. In fact, several efforts have demonstrated the power of new assessment approaches to evaluate and guide program development and teacher change effectively (see Tierney et al., 1993).

Designing these new assessment approaches has to do with a way of teaching, testing, and knowing that is aligned with a set of values different than what has been and still is espoused by most educational reformers. Unfortunately, the power of some of the psychometricians and their entrenched values related to testing make the emergence of alternative assessment procedures difficult. Indeed, I see the shift as involving a cultural transformation—a shift away from what I view as a somewhat totalitarian practice tied to "old science" and metaphors that equate student learning to quality control.

Mike Rose (1995) suggests in *Possible Lives* that classrooms are created spaces, and the successful ones create spaces where students feel safe and secure; they are the classrooms in which students are willing to stretch, take risks, and pursue their interpretive authority for themselves and with others. In a similar vein, Kris Gutierrez and her colleagues (Gutierrez, Rymes, & Larson, 1995), in discussing teacher-student discourse, assert the need for spaces where students and teachers can connect or transact with each other, rather than pass by one another. The key is finding ways to effect involvement and transaction rather than detachment and monolithic responses.

Assessment must address making futures possible and pursuable rather than impossible or improbable. We must create spaces where students, teachers, and others can achieve futures and spaces wherein the dynamics and practices are such that they challenge but do not undermine the ecology of who students are and might become.

References

Baker, A., & Luke, A. (1991). *Toward a critical sociology of reading pedagogy*. Philadelphia: John Benjamin's.

Basso, K. (1970). "To give up on words": Silence in Western Apache culture. *Southwest Journal of Anthropology, 26*, 213–230.

Bober, S. (1995, July). *Portfolio conferences*. Presentation at Lesley College Literacy Institute, Cambridge, MA.

Bruner, J. (1990). *Acts of meaning*. Cambridge, MA: Harvard University Press.

Carter, M. (1992). *Self-assessment using writing portfolios*. Unpublished doctoral dissertation, The Ohio State University, Columbus.

Carter, M., & Tierney, R.J. (1988, December). *Writing growth: Using portfolios in assessment*. Paper presented at the National Reading Conference, Tucson, AZ.

Ellwein, M.C., Glass, G.V., & Smith, M.L. (1988) Standards of competence: Propositions on the nature of testing reforms. *Educational Researcher*, 17(8), 4–9.

Fenner, L. (1995). *Student portfolios: A view from inside the classroom*. Unpublished doctoral dissertation, The Ohio State University, Columbus.

Forman, G. (1993). Multiple symbolizations in the long jump project. In C. Edward, L. Gandini, & G. Forman (Eds.), *The hundred languages of children* (pp. 171–188). Norwood, NJ: Ablex.

Forman, G. (1994). Different media, different languages. In L. Katz & B. Cesarone (Eds.), *Reflections on the Reggio Emilia approach* (pp. 41–54). Urbana, IL: ERIC/EECE.

Freire, P., & Macedo, D. (1987). *Literacy: Reading the word and the world*. South Hadley, MA: Bergin & Garvey.

Gee, J. (1990). *Social linguistics and literacies: Ideologies in discourse*. New York: Falmer Press.

Green, J., & Dixon, C. (1994). Talking knowledge into being: Discursive and social practices in classrooms. *Linguistics and Education, 5*, 231–239.

Guba, E.G., & Lincoln, Y.S. (1989). *Fourth generation evaluation*. Newbury Park, CA: Sage.

Gutierrez, K., Rymes, B., & Larson, J. (1995). Script, counterscript, and underlife in the classroom: James Brown versus Brown v. Board of Education. *Harvard Educational Review, 65*, 445–471.

Haney, W. (1993). Testing and minorities. In L. Weis & M. Fine (Eds.), *Beyond silenced voices* (pp. 45–74). Albany: State University of New York Press.

hooks, b. (1989). *Talking back*. Boston: South End Press.

hooks, b. (1994). *Teaching to transgress: Education as the practice of freedom*. New York: Routledge.

Lather, P. (1986). Research as praxis. *Harvard Educational Review, 56*, 257–277.

Linn, R.L., Baker, E.L., & Dunbar, S.B. (1991). Complex performance assessment: Expectations and validation criteria. *Educational Researcher, 20*(8), 15–21.

Moss, P. (1996). Enlarging the dialogue in educational measurement: Voices from interpretive research traditions. *Educational Researcher, 25*(1), 20–28.

Ogbu, J. (1988). Literacy and schooling in subordinate cultures: The case of Black Americans. In E. Kintgen, B. Kroll, & M. Rose (Eds.), *Perspectives on literacy* (pp. 227–242). Carbondale, IL: Southern Illinois University Press.

Ogbu, J. (1991). Cultural perspective and school experience. In C. Walsh (Ed.), *Literacy as praxis: Culture, language and pedagogy* (pp. 25–50). Norwood, NJ: Ablex.

Phillips, S. (1983). *The invisible culture: Communication and community on the Warm Springs Indian reservation.* New York: Longman.

Purves, A. (1982). Conclusion to an international perspective to the evaluation of written composition. In B.H. Choppin & T.N. Postlethwaite (Eds.), *Evaluation in education: An international review series* (Vol. 5, pp. 343–345.). Oxford, England: Pergamon Press.

Rose, M. (1995). *Possible lives.* Boston: Houghton Mifflin.

Santa Barbara Classroom Discourse Group. (1992a). Constructing literacy in classrooms; literate action as social accomplishment. In H. Marshall (Ed.), *Redefining student learning: Roots of educational change* (pp. 119–150). Norwood, NJ: Ablex.

Santa Barbara Classroom Discourse Group. (1992b). The referential and intertextual nature of classroom life. *Journal of Classroom Interaction,* 27(2), 29–36.

Shavelson, R., Baxter, G.P., & Pine, J. (1992). Performance assessment: Political rhetoric and measurement reality. *Educational Researcher, 21*(4), 22–27.

Short, K.G., Harste, J.C., & Burke, C. (1996). *Creating classrooms for authors and inquirers.* Portsmouth, NH: Heinemann.

Spiro, R.J., Vispoel, W.L., Schmitz, J., Samarapungavan, A., & Boerger, A. (1987). Knowledge acquisition for application: Cognitive flexibility and transfer in complex content domains. In B.C. Britton & S. Glynn (Eds.), *Executive control processes* (pp. 177–200). Hillsdale, NJ: Erlbaum.

Stake, R. (1983). The case study method in social inquiry. In G. Madaus, M. Scriven, & D. Stufflebeam (Eds.), *Evaluation models* (pp. 279–286). Boston: Kluwer-Nijhoff.

Tierney, R.J., Carter, M., & Desai, L. (1991). *Portfolio assessment in the reading-writing classroom.* Norwood, MA: Christopher Gordon.

Tierney, R.J., Clark, C., Fenner, L., Herter, R.J., Simpson, C., & Wiser, B. (1998). Portfolios: Assumptions, tensions, and possibilities. *Reading Research Quarterly, 33,* 474–486.

Tierney, R.J., Wile, J., Moss, A.G., Reed, E.W., Ribar, J.P., & Zilversmit, A. (1993). Portfolio evaluation as history: Evaluation of the history academy for Ohio teachers (occasional paper). National Council of History Education, Inc.

Toulmin, S. (1958). *The uses of argument.* Cambridge, England: Cambridge University Press.

Wile, J., & Tierney, R.J. (1996). Tensions in assessment: The battle over portfolios, curriculum and control. In R. Calfee & P. Perfumo (Eds.), *Writing portfolios in the classrooms: Policy and practice, process and peril* (pp. 203–218). Hillsdale, NJ: Erlbaum.

Early Literacy Assessment—Thoughtful, Sensible, and Good

Kathleen Roskos

My first encounter with early literacy assessment occurred in the early 1980s when our Title I (a federally funded program for at-risk students) team organized a screening for all incoming kindergartners in a small, rural U.S. school district. We set up "centers" in the school gym to assess what we thought were basic readiness skills of our young entrants. In a game-like fashion, we probed them: Can you write your name? What letter is this? Tell me about this [a toy car]. Count the tiny plastic bears. Hop on one foot, now the other. Walk the balance beam.

In total, it took about 20 minutes to gather information about each child's oral language, alphabet knowledge, one-to-one correspondence, and motor skills, not to mention a general willingness to participate at all. We conducted these screenings for several years in a row, but they were not without dilemmas and controversies as to their purpose, appropriateness, and usefulness.

That was a long time ago, and our knowledge of early literacy and assessment has grown considerably in the intervening years, although it has certainly not been free of dilemmas and controversies.

Why Is Early Literacy Assessment Important?

The building blocks of high-quality early literacy education include strong standards, appropriate and fair assessments, well-built curricula, and research-based instruction. There are two reasons, one leading the other, why assessment in the United States is becoming more important with every passing day.

The primary reason is the tremendous progress in understanding the developmental foundations of early literacy (National Research Council, 2001; Neuman & Dickinson, 2001; Snow, Burns, & Griffin, 1998; Stanovich, 2000; Yaden, Rowe, & MacGillivray, 2000). Research syntheses indicate four developmental "drivers" of early literacy linked to later reading achievement: oral language comprehension (including vocabulary), phonological awareness, print knowledge, and print motivation (Lonigan, 2004). Children's growth in these areas is critical not only to their learning to read but also to their general cognitive capacity to learn more, and more complex, content (National Research Council, 2000, 2001; National Research Council & Institute of Medicine, 2000). Assessment is the necessary means for systematically collecting and analyzing information on children's literacy development in these areas. Engaging in this practice (as an integral part of our professional work) contributes directly to improvements in the educational services provided to children and their families.

The other key reason is the accountability that comes with an enlightened emphasis on early literacy in early childhood. Solid evidence of the effect of high-quality early education on children's later academic achievement has created a strong push for early learning standards and assessments that interface with K–12 education (National Association for the Education of Young Children & National Association of Early Childhood Specialists in State Departments of

From *The Reading Teacher*, 58(1), 91–94, 99–100. © 2004 by the International Reading Association.

Education, 2002, 2003; National Institute for Early Education Research, 2003; Scott-Little, Kagan, & Frelow, 2003). Pressure is especially intense in the early literacy-learning domain where U.S. federal and state funding is tied to evidence of the scientific research base in curricula and evaluations of program effectiveness (e.g., Early Reading First; Good Start, Grow Smart; Head Start Child Outcomes Framework). Documenting results and demonstrating improvements in children's literacy achievement in the early grades rest on quality assessment information from preschool through grade 3. Thus, the need for "good" assessment data is rapidly growing. Policymakers want data to determine what works and to identify gaps in children's early learning experiences. Parents and teachers want information to monitor children's progress and to make instructional decisions. Early childhood programs and elementary schools want accurate data to establish a baseline of children's strengths and weaknesses, to manage instructional goals, and to evaluate their overall effectiveness. Satisfying these many "wants" responsibly elevates the importance of early literacy assessment during the early years of preschool and primary education.

What Are the Vexing Issues?

The issues surrounding early literacy assessment are not new to the field of assessment, although they are accentuated in the early childhood context because the children are so young and because the link between assessment and accountability is a new and scary notion. Purpose is one of the more problematic issues.

Assessments can serve varied purposes from instructional decision making and identifying children with special needs to program monitoring and accountability evaluations. Dangers lurk, however, in the mismatch of purpose and tool and the misuse of assessment results. Consider, for example, readiness screening for kindergarten. Its intended purpose is to "flag" children who may need more assistance and further diagnosis upon entry to school (Kame'enui, 2002). Yet it happens, unfortunately, that screening information can be misused to judge children "unready" for kindergarten or to place them in programs without follow-through assessment (National Association of Early Childhood Specialists in State Departments of Education, 2000). This screening does not help children learn to read and write; it does not help them obtain the instruction they need to make progress; and, sadly, it puts them in harm's way.

Let me be clear, though, that this issue of purpose does not hinge on whether we should or should not conduct early literacy assessments. We should (and must) conduct them because we possess scientific knowledge about literacy development that can help children. The problem instead is how to ensure clarity of purpose and appropriate, ethical use of assessment information for children's benefit. Addressing this issue in early literacy assessment requires a "strong hand" on our part to decide what structures and strategies must be in place in early childhood programs and schools so as to first do no harm (Jones, 2004). In this situation professional development is pivotal. Administrators and teachers need opportunities to acquire the knowledge and skills to design and implement sound early literacy assessment systems that meet the needs of the families and children they serve. They need real, tangible, everyday support from knowledgeable reading professionals.

Another issue involves the complexities of assessing young children. Granted, the literacy assessment of any age learner is a complicated business. But it is more so, many argue, when it targets preschoolers and kindergartners (National Education Goals Panel Early Childhood Assessment Group, 1998). This is because their nascent literacy concepts and skills are deeply involved with other developing systems (e.g., physical, cognitive, emotional, language), exceedingly unstable, and thus more difficult to locate by means of traditional standardized measures. To assess young children's literacy requires evidence gathered from multiple methods over time in order to "see" emerging skills and forming concepts. Moreover, it's much easier for young children to show what they know (e.g., in play) than to talk, much less write, about what they know and can do. Consequently, assessments should be embedded in activities young children do or, at the very least, closely resemble them. Furthermore, unlike school-age children with built-up classroom experience, young children come to assessment activities with widely divergent learning experiences—some having been in family or home care, others at day care, and still others in public preschools. Their participation in assessment activity, therefore, is colored by their prior experience with school-like settings. Some children have far more familiarity with such settings than others.

The issue is made more complex by the design and selection of early literacy assessment instruments. Not only should such tools be psychometrically sound (e.g., reliable, valid), but they should also be of clear purpose, age appropriate, culturally and linguistically sensitive, and fair. Growing concern about the assessment of young children has led to several published position statements and guidelines that include early literacy assessment (e.g., National Education Goals Panel Early Childhood Assessment Group, 1998) In our professional work we need to be alert to these concerns and positions so as to inform and influence local early childhood programs and schools increasingly faced with the challenge of selecting early literacy assessment instruments.

A third and no less complicated issue involves assessment procedures and how they are carried out in classrooms. This issue is all about logistics: Who? When? For how long? Where? At what cost? Early literacy assessments have a variety of requirements for data collection. Some require a specialist trained to use the measure and interpret results (e.g., the 1981 Peabody Picture Vocabulary Test—Revised), while others can be administered by teachers with appropriate training (e.g., *Get Ready to Read!*, Whitehurst & Lonigan, 2001). Some need quiet conditions where adult and child work alone (e.g., rapid picture naming), while others can be handled in daily activities (e.g., concepts of print). Some are short; others are long and require extended time to collect information. Some are more expensive than others. Considerable thought is needed to ensure a realistic match between the requirements for collecting early literacy assessment information and the setting's capability to meet them.

For early literacy assessment to be "good" (i.e., to benefit children, their families, and their teachers), reading educators need to come to grips with procedural issues at a practical level. They need to ask detail-oriented questions like these: How will this assessment measure work in the school or classroom setting? Is it affordable in terms of cost, time, and professional development? How well does it contribute to a comprehensive picture of a child's early literacy development and growth? What are the accommodations for children with disabilities? The answers to such questions then need to be carefully considered to implement effective and efficient assessment procedures that produce high-quality information.

What Is an Early Literacy Assessment System?

The growing need for norm-referenced screening and progress monitoring measures to identify children at risk for reading failure and to track growth in relation to instructional approaches argues for the design and implementation of an early literacy assessment system. The outcome measures of such a system must indicate whether an early literacy program is helping children learn essential literacy concepts and skills. The fundamental complexity of a multipurpose assessment system is that no one purpose can function in isolation from the others. Rather, the different purposes of early literacy assessment must forge a linked system that is comprehensive, integrated, and trustworthy (McConnell, 2000). This goal calls for the thoughtful consideration of several factors.

- The extent to which assessment measures and procedures complement one another across the entire system is important. Screenings need to mesh with diagnostics that inform instruction and intervention.

These, in turn, must include formal and informal tools for monitoring children's growth, and the salient goals of these assessments must be adequately captured in outcome measures to judge child achievement and program results.

- Measures and procedures that can be used to directly and repeatedly monitor progress toward desired long-term reading outcomes are important (Fuchs & Deno, 1990). Instruction needs to rest on more than the monitoring of curriculum-based literacy concepts and skills of a specific literacy program. It also needs to be grounded in normative information about children's progress in essential areas of the early literacy learning domain (i.e., oral language; phonological processing; orthographic processing; fluency; vocabulary; and reading comprehension, including early print awareness). Teachers need to know, in short, where children stand relative to their peers and in relation to general outcomes in order to plan effectively and to judge responsibly. Valid, reliable, multiple measures are therefore critical in a linked assessment system. Yet, the system must be efficient and parsimonious in its use of resources (e.g., time). Not all of the children need to be assessed all of the time. Rather, a sampling system can be used (i.e., some of the children some of the time) to obtain assessment information for different purposes.
- An overarching theory of action for decision making across the system is very important to pull together assessment information gathered from multiple sources, settings, and occasions. Without it, an assessment system can easily slip into a fragmented set of activities—assessment bits and pieces that are difficult to manage and use. A theory of action includes principles that "balance the need for information with concern for children"; adheres to the "best practices" of early literacy assessment (e.g., information collected from more than one source); and ensures assessment safeguards related to informed consent, confidentiality, sampling, and information management (Scott-Little & Niemeyer, 2003, pp. 10, 26). Reading educators need to take a leadership role in helping to map a theory of action for early literacy assessment on the basis of strong principles, best assessment practices, and safeguards. They need to help their colleagues determine what early literacy assessment information is needed and why, to weigh the options in a given situation, and to plan for measures and practices grounded in literacy development research and the professional knowledge of early childhood.

References

Fuchs, L.S., & Deno, S.L. (1990). Paradigmatic distinctions between instructionally relevant measurement models. *Exceptional Children, 57*, 488–499.

Jones, J. (2004). *Early literacy assessment systems: Essential elements*. Retrieved from http://www.ets.org/research/pic/earlylit.pdf

Kame'enui, E. (2002). *An analysis of reading assessment instruments for K–3*. Retrieved from http://novel.nifl.gov/nifl/partnershipforreading/publications/pdf/assessment/assessmentDocument.pdf

Lonigan, C. (2004). Getting ready to read: Emergent literacy and family literacy. In B. Wasik (Ed.), *Family literacy programs: Current status and future directions* (pp. 55–83). Mahwah, NJ: Erlbaum.

McConnell, S. (2000). Assessment in early intervention and early childhood special education: Building on the past to project into our future. *Topics in Early Childhood Special Education, 20*(1), 43–48.

National Association for the Education of Young Children & National Association of Early Childhood Specialists in State Departments of Education. (2002). *Early learning standards: Creating the conditions for success*. Retrieved from http://www.naeyc.org/resources/position_statements/creating_conditions.asp

National Association for the Education of Young Children & National Association of Early Childhood Specialists in State Departments of Education. (2003). *Early childhood curriculum, child assessment and program evaluation:*

Building an accountable and effective system for children birth through age eight. Retrieved from http://www.naeyc.org/resources/position_statements/CAPEexpand.pdf

National Association of Early Childhood Specialists in State Departments of Education. (2000). *Still unacceptable trends in kindergarten entry and placement*. Retrieved from http://ericps.crc.uiuc.edu/naecs/position/trends2000.html

National Education Goals Panel Early Childhood Assessment Group. (1998). *Principles and recommendations for early childhood assessments*. Retrieved from http://www.negp.gov/reports/prinrec.pdf

National Institute for Early Education Research. (2003). *Child outcome standards in preschool programs: What are standards; what is needed to make them work?* Retrieved from http://www.nieer.org/resources/policybriefs/5.pdf

National Research Council. (2000). *How people learn: Brain, mind, experience and school*. Washington, DC: National Academy Press.

National Research Council. (2001). *Eager to learn: Educating our preschoolers*. Washington, DC: National Academy Press.

National Research Council & Institute of Medicine. (2000). *From neurons to neighborhoods: The science of early childhood development*. Washington, DC: National Academy Press.

Neuman, S.B., & Dickinson, D. (Eds.). (2001). *Handbook of early literacy research*. New York: Guilford.

Scott-Little, C., Kagan, S.L., & Frelow, V.S. (2003). *Standards for preschool children's learning and development: Who has standards, how were they developed, and how are they used?* Retrieved from http://www.serve.org/_downloads/full2print.doc

Scott-Little, C., & Niemeyer, J. (2003). *Assessing kindergarten children: What school systems need to know*. Retrieved from http://www.ecs.org/html/offsite.asp?document=http%3A%2F%2Fwww%2Eserve%2Eorg%2Fpublications%2Frdakcg%2Epdf

Snow, C.E., Burns, M.S., & Griffin, P. (1998). *Preventing reading difficulties in young children*. Washington, DC: National Academy Press.

Stanovich, K.E. (2000). *Progress in understanding reading: Scientific foundations and new frontiers*. New York: Guilford.

Whitehurst, G.J., & Lonigan, C. (2001). *Get ready to read! An early literacy manual: Screening tool, activities and resources*. Columbus, OH: Pearson.

Yaden, D., Rowe, D.W., & MacGillivray, L. (2000). Emergent literacy: A matter (polyphony) of perspectives. In M.L. Kamil, P.B. Mosenthal, P.D. Pearson, & R. Barr (Eds.), *Handbook of reading research* (Vol. 3, pp. 425–454). Mahwah, NJ: Erlbaum.

Equity and Diversity in Reading Assessment

- What type of assessment is fair to all students?
- Are all standardized tests fair to all students?
- Are there some types of assessment that either favor or work against certain groups of students?
- How are students in other countries assessed?
- Should you include students with special needs in all types of assessment?

The four articles in this section instruct literacy educators to develop assessment programs that are equitable and effective for all learners. Robert T. Jiménez presents practical information on how to more fairly assess the achievement of Latino students. A problem with traditional and standardized reading tests is that they rank students by ethnicity and socioeconomic backgrounds and also "confound knowledge of English with literacy." Jiménez asks teachers to augment traditional literacy assessments with those that value Latino students' nonschool literacies, such as translating for parents and other "language brokering" tasks. Further, he reminds teachers that honoring native identity is fundamental to student achievement and equitable assessment.

Obviously, not all learners demonstrate their highest levels of achievement when presented with traditional modes of assessment, such as paper-and-pencil tasks. Rather, performance-based assessment, explains Marshá Taylor DeLain, provides *all* students opportunity to learn to read by reading and to be assessed simultaneously. She points to the mutualism in performance-based assessment: The experience of performance enables learners to be successful in assessment activities. An article in Section Six by John T. Guthrie, Peggy Van Meter, and Ann Mitchell elaborates on DeLain's view and presents a classroom example of performance assessment in action.

Research on international assessments of literacy reminds us that literacy achievement is used by the international community to measure the human condition. What is measured by such assessments, why countries assess reading achievement, and how the results can be used are instructive. Gerry Shiel and Judith Cosgrove's article demonstrates how international test results can prompt nations to achieve greater equity in education, for example, for girls or for children of low socioeconomic backgrounds.

Lee Gunderson and Linda S. Siegel reveal in their article that when a student whose second language is English scores low on an IQ test due to cultural differences, that student is labeled inappropriately and does not get the reading help needed. They urge teachers to play a role in preventing this misuse of testing—this inequitable treatment of diverse students—and, instead, administer assessments that uncover student needs, leading to appropriate instruction for the learner.

Additional Reading

- Bracey, G.W. (2004). Value-added assessment findings: Poor kids get poor teachers. *Phi Delta Kappan*, *86*(4), 331–333.
- D'Angiulli, A., Siegel, L.S., & Maggi, S. (2004). Literacy instruction, SES, and word-reading achievement in English language learners and children with English as a first language: A longitudinal study. *Learning Disabilities Research & Practice*, *19*(4), 202–213.
- Herrell, A., & Jordan, M. (2003). *Fifty strategies for teaching English language learners* (2nd ed.). Alexandria, VA: Association for Supervision and Curriculum Development.
- Krashen, S. (2004/2005). Skyrocketing scores: An urban legend. *Educational Leadership*, *62*(4), 37–39.
- Ladson-Billings, G. (1999). Toward a theory of culturally relevant pedagogy. *American Educational Research Journal*, *32*(3), 465–491.
- Perez, B. (1994). Spanish literacy development: A descriptive study of four bilingual whole-language classrooms. *Journal of Reading Behavior*, *26*(1), 75–93.
- Shannon, P. (1998). *Reading poverty*. Portsmouth, NH: Heinemann.
- Shaywitz, S.E., & Shaywitz, B.A. (2004). Reading disability and the brain. *Educational Leadership*, *61*(6), 6–11.
- Stanovich, K.E. (1986). Matthew effects in reading: Some consequences of individual differences in the acquisition of literacy. *Reading Research Quarterly*, *21*(4), 360–407.

Create a Statement of Reading Assessment Principles and Practices

You are laying the foundation to ensure that students from diverse backgrounds have an equitable opportunity to do well on the assessments you would include in your assessment system. Referring to the principles you identified in Section One, obtain feedback from peers on how well your principles address issues of equity. Ask, whose interests are being served by these principles? Do your principles include children whose needs are diverse? Do they help you weed out assessment practices that might lead to inequities? Refine your stated principles accordingly.

More Equitable Literacy Assessments for Latino Students

Robert T. Jiménez

A teacher recently came to me with the end-of-year reading test scores for her Latino students. Her principal wanted to know what she was going to do to improve their scores. The teacher was not provided with any other information useful for interpreting the scores—information that would give her a sense of how well or poorly her students were performing in comparison with other students like hers or mainstream students. One of the problems with assessments like these is that they serve to hierarchically rank children according to their ethnic and social-class backgrounds. Such inequitable assessments often confound students' knowledge of English with literacy. Consider for a moment how literate you might appear if you were given a reading test in the foreign language you studied in high school. Such a test might indicate something about your knowledge of the foreign language but probably not much else. While more in-depth information for assessing the literacy of Latino students is available, my goal is to help you assess your linguistically diverse students more equitably (García, 1994; Pérez & Torres-Guzmán, 1996).

As teachers, we need to assess students within three domains. The first domain involves traditional assessments that indicate how well students are learning the literacy valued in schools. These abilities and forms of knowledge constitute a type of capital necessary for success in the mainstream. Failure to provide students with these forms of literacy constitutes a kind of inequity. The second dimension involves assessing students' knowledge of other literacies. Schools often treat these abilities as a kind of foreign currency, but including them could radically improve perceptions of these students as literate persons. Such a change has the potential to provide Latino students with a more equitable learning experience. In the third domain of assessment, information is needed on how students perceive and respond to the process of learning a new language, a new culture, and its associated forms of literacy. Understanding these feelings and beliefs can help us understand how larger inequitable forces adversely affect students' performance and that language and literacy are more than simply what we know and can do—they are a part of who we are.

Traditional Literacy Assessments

The information derived from traditional assessments can be greatly enhanced with a language profile and an educational history. The profile should include information concerning languages with which the child has had contact and where they were encountered (such as home, school, neighborhood, or church). Some children in countries like Mexico have had the most contact with an indigenous language and encounter Spanish only outside the home. Equitable instruction for these children would include the language necessary to succeed on school literacy tasks. Students might need more contact with native speakers of English, overt instruction on specific linguistic forms, or opportunities to use their native language to clarify misunderstandings. For example, in some schools in Mexico children are not asked to author texts but only to

From *The Reading Teacher*, 57(6), 576–578. © 2004 by the International Reading Association.

faithfully reproduce them (Smith, Jiménez, & Martínez-León, 2003). Students coming from this background will need extra support to understand different uses of writing.

An educational history also is important for understanding students' learning needs. It is most important to determine whether a student has had gaps in schooling. Students from rural backgrounds are especially vulnerable because schooling may have been unavailable due to a lack of teachers or classroom space, or family poverty may have precluded school attendance because of costs involving school supplies, uniforms, or books. Other students miss portions of their schooling because of frequent mobility.

In addition, students from diverse backgrounds can experience highly fragmented schooling. For example, a child may begin his or her schooling in a mainstream all-English preschool or kindergarten. When the child fails to make adequate or expected progress, he or she might be moved into an English as a Second Language (ESL) or special education classroom. Some children have experienced all of these placements within three to four years of schooling. The changes in placement are seldom planned within a cohesive program but instead reflect educators' confusion. In short, some instruction is repeated and some is omitted. By considering the child's history of schooling, those concerned with equity should identify what components of literacy instruction have been provided and which are still necessary.

Students' test scores should be compared with those of other English-language learners and considered in light of what is expected from native English-speaking children. Factors to consider include the child's age when first exposed to English, the amount of exposure to English, the quality of previous instruction, the child's language learning aptitude, and the quality of current instructional offerings. Research demonstrates that the amount of time necessary to achieve grade-level expectations can vary between two to seven years (Thomas & Collier, 1997). Without making excuses, ask yourself how much time you would need to be as literate as an educated native speaker of another language. As teachers, we can accelerate students' progress by providing excellent instruction (Reyes & Halcón, 2001) and by exposing students to meaningful forms of English. Equity demands that these last two items be considered carefully when assessing English-language learners.

Assessing Students' Nonschool Literacies

It is absolutely essential to assess students' native-language literacy. Students who are literate in their non-English language, particularly Spanish, have an immense advantage in becoming literate in English if we recognize this "treasure trove" and help students link it to English literacy (August & Hakuta, 1997). Too often this knowledge is rejected as "foreign currency." Teachers can get a rough understanding of their students' non-English literacy abilities by conferring with ESL teachers, bilingual teachers, students' parents, and the students themselves. Specific ways to assess students' native-language literacy, like dictations, cloze tests, retellings, and think-alouds, can be found in the work of Pérez and Torres-Guzmán (1996).

Nonschool-based literacies may be more motivating and purposeful to some Latino students, and understanding what students do with these literacies can be informative (Jiménez, 2001). For example, some students have parents who struggle with English. These students often translate for their parents in a process known as language brokering. Research shows that the more young people broker language, the better they perform in school (Orellana, Reynolds, Dorner, & Meza, 2003). A simple and direct way to find out if students serve as language brokers is to ask them about it. Educators can learn more by asking students to keep a journal of their language-brokering activities. Many students see income-tax forms, credit applications, and rental agreements outside of the classroom but seldom see such texts as part of their literacy curriculum. Other alternative literacies include letter writing to distant relatives, the study of popular music lyrics, and the use of handmade texts to communicate commercial interests found in students' communities. By recognizing and valuing these other literacies, we can help students understand the ways that school literacy can support their efforts to be good family and community members.

Assessing Students' Literate Identities

In the United States, it is not unusual for students from linguistically diverse backgrounds to voice feelings of shame, dislike, and alienation toward their non-English language. They may refuse to speak it, or they may make statements to the effect that their language is "stupid," confusing, or not as good as English. While it is almost an irresistible force of nature that children immersed within any given speech community will desire to learn that language, such desire need not be associated with efforts to abandon their native language. Negative feelings toward the non-English language are fueled by messages produced within school. Students who experience debits or bankruptcy in their literate identity accounts will often exhibit related problems with academic learning and may drop out or be attracted by gangs (Flores-Gonzalez, 2002). Although alienation is more prevalent at the secondary school level, researchers recommend that educators establish meaningful relationships with students through extracurricular activities to ameliorate this problem.

Children who do not understand the relationship between their first and second languages often experience more difficulties with English literacy than those students who view their native tongue as a source of strength. For example, Jiménez, García, and Pearson (1996) noted that higher performing bilingual/biliterate Latino students are more likely to see their knowledge of Spanish as a source of information useful for comprehending English text. The students in the 1996 study drew from their prior knowledge of topics learned in Spanish, noted similarities between the meanings of cognate vocabulary items across the two languages, and strategically translated information when they did not understand text in their weaker language. Students who were struggling with English-language literacy reported that Spanish and English were different, that they should not be confused with one another, and that the process of reading was essentially a matter of pronunciation. Equitable instruction needs to include spaces where students can discuss these language relationships. Students are willing to share this information with individuals who want to hear it and with those committed to advocating students' interest, even in the face of inequitable assessment practices.

References

August, D., & Hakuta, K. (1997). *Improving schooling for language-minority children*. Washington DC: National Academy Press.

Flores-Gonzalez, N. (2002). *School kids/street kids: Identity development in Latino students*. New York: Teachers College Press.

García, G.E. (1994). The literacy assessment of second-language learners: A focus on authentic assessment. In K. Spangenberg-Urbschat & R. Pritchard (Eds.), *Kids come in all languages: Reading instruction for second-language learners* (pp. 183–208). Newark, DE: International Reading Association.

Jiménez, R.T. (2001). "It's a difference that changes us": An alternative view of the language and literacy learning needs of Latina/o students. *The Reading Teacher, 54*, 736–742.

Jiménez, R.T., García, G.E., & Pearson, P.D. (1996). The reading strategies of Latina/o students who are successful English readers: Opportunities and obstacles. *Reading Research Quarterly, 31*, 90–112.

Orellana, M.F., Reynolds, J., Dorner, L., & Meza, M. (2003). In other words: Translating or "para-phrasing" as a family literacy practice in immigrant households. *Reading Research Quarterly, 38*, 12–34.

Pérez, B., & Torres-Guzmán, M.E. (1996). *Learning in two worlds*. White Plains, NY: Longman.

Reyes, M., & Halcón, J. (2001). *The best for our children: Critical perspectives on literacy for Latino students*. New York: Teachers College Press.

Smith, P.H., Jiménez, R.T., & Martínez-León, N. (2003). Other countries' literacies: What U.S. educators can learn from Mexican schools. *The Reading Teacher, 56*, 772–781.

Thomas, W., & Collier, V. (1997). *School effectiveness for language minority students*. Washington DC: National Clearinghouse for Bilingual Education.

Equity and Performance-Based Assessment: An Insider's View

Marshá Taylor DeLain

Equity. Opportunity to learn. Appreciation for diversity. Recently these terms have been tossed about in academia, district offices, schools, and classrooms. What does it all mean? How will our interpretation of these terms, particularly in assessment, impact our children?

I am an African American, but my interests in these issues extend far beyond my personal perspective. It is important to me that all children learn to their highest potential. This simply is not possible if we think of these terms (equity, opportunity to learn, appreciation for diversity) as only having relevance for minorities. Besides, who is the minority? Today we consider minorities to be Hispanics, African Americans, Native Americans, Asians; the list goes on. However, demographic projections tell us that by the year 2000 people of color will be the majority in the United States. But that really shouldn't matter. If our focus is on what's best for children, the definition of "best" shouldn't change when the demographic characteristics of the classroom change.

So what is best for all children? Children should be expected to achieve levels of excellence and afforded the opportunities and environment to do so. This is a critical part of my definition of equity. Expectations for success should not vary dependent upon race, gender, ethnicity, where you live, how many parents you have, or whether your mom went to college. We teach the mix of students who walk through the door—black, white, yellow, tall, short, rich, or poor. Our responsibility does not change. The paths we take to actualizing and evaluating success for our students may vary, but the bottom line stays the same. All children need to be given the tools they need to "be all that they can be." However, for years the definition of what children are and what they can be has been influenced by the results of assessments.

Until recently, assessment has been based upon the validity of breaking reading processes into discrete pieces; the assumption has been that if you know the pieces, you know the whole. Therefore, assessment of the pieces was presumed to provide evaluative information on a student's achievement of the processes. In reading, this meant testing vocabulary knowledge using lists of words or testing comprehension using short, artificially created paragraphs. These assessment methods provided a relatively quick and inexpensive way of testing large numbers of students. However, performance on these assessments was most often reported in terms of how well students measured up against each other, not against clear standards of what the student was supposed to know and be able to do. Ironically, the assessments provided very little information on how well a student could actually read and comprehend real literature.

But what does this have to do with equity, and what does equity mean? For me, equity includes the following:

- equitable access to resources,
- equitable opportunities to learn new and challenging information,
- equitable expectations for outcomes of excellence, and

From *The Reading Teacher*, *48*(5), 440–442. © 1995 by the International Reading Association.

- sensitivity to and appreciation for diversity and how that diversity can enhance learning for all students.

Performance-based assessment has brought a new slant on these issues, particularly as they relate to evaluating student achievement of the "outcomes of excellence" previously mentioned. Performance-based assessment involves actual demonstrations, which involve integration of several processes, skills, and concepts. Student achievement is assessed by evaluating some type of student product that is planned, constructed, or developed.

Performance assessment in reading and other language arts is not new. For years students have read books and plays, written reports, given oral presentations, and dramatized scenes. Research has been conducted on topics of interest through trips to the library, interviews with experts, and collaboration with peers. All of these "performance" activities take place under the watchful eye of teachers who firmly believe that students must be actively involved in the process of learning. Simply put, students had to *do* in order to learn. What is different in this era of reform is the importance of attaching the activities to clearly stated instructional outcomes and evaluating student success on these activities against clearly stated criteria. Also, this type of assessment has gained acceptance because it is more aligned with how students actually learn and more useful for instructional improvement and accountability.

Aspects of performance assessment are provided in the following example, which is adapted from a project generated by an Interstate Teacher Team at the 1991 New Standards Project Workshop in Snowmass, Colorado, USA.

***

West End Elementary is planning a Visitors' Night. Students will give presentations on their favorite authors, the school choir will sing, artwork will be displayed, a science experiment will be done, and a storyteller will be present. The students in Mrs. Edwards's class are asked to (a) prepare presentations based on their favorite authors, (b) create an invitation for Visitors' Night, and (c) write directions or draw a map from their homes to the school.

Performance-based assessment can:

- **be aligned with instructional practice.** For example, we expect that students will apply what they have learned in school to real-life activities. In the example, reading and using texts in a decision-making process is a real-life activity. The map drawing activity is not only authentic, but it also draws on communication skills, spatial understanding, and reasoning abilities.

- **provide students opportunities to express or represent their knowledge in different ways.** In the example, students have the opportunity to express what they have learned by writing compositions, oral presentations, drawing, and cutting and pasting. In the activities planned for Visitors' Night, opportunities are broadened even more to include singing, constructing experiments, and retellings.

- **provide better indicators of the depth of a student's knowledge.** When students supply information or explain their understandings, we develop much richer insight into what they really know. In the example, students are asked to select and give a presentation on their favorite author. In the presentation they are expected to articulate reasons for their choices. This requires the students to have a deep understanding of the materials and identify and translate key elements of that understanding for an audience.

- **stretch students' minds by requiring them to construct, design, compose, model, or build their response rather than select it from an array of choices.** In the sample above, students are asked to develop a presentation that convinces, invitations that entice and excite, maps and directions that clearly point the way, and an activity schedule that gives the presenters adequate time while keeping things flowing at a nice pace. All of these activities stretch students' minds by requiring them to draw on, integrate, and apply skills from several areas in ways that are creative yet useful to a real audience.

• **be aligned with ongoing classroom instruction so that it ceases to become an end in and of itself.** Assessment can and should be an ongoing and integral part of classroom activity. The closer assessment is aligned with instruction and curriculum, the better it can inform the teacher and the student, and the less likely it is to become a separate, unrelated activity.

While performance assessment can provide useful information, like all other assessments it has limitations. Performance-based assessment cannot:

• **answer all questions about what a child knows and is able to do.** As noted above, assessment should be an ongoing, integral part of classroom activity, and performance-based assessment is simply one way to attain evaluative information. There may also be a need for more traditional types of assessments. Once the purpose of the assessment and the type of student behavior to be evaluated are decided, the methods or formats that best accomplish those purposes are chosen.

• **be a panacea to all the assessment and instructional ills of the current educational system.** If assessment is the only change in the classroom, it simply becomes a fad. Instruction and curriculum within the context of the total school climate must all be evaluated and systematically aligned if change is going to make a difference.

As the stakes attached to all forms of assessment become higher and higher, those who typically have been disenfranchised by normed assessments may ask "Is performance assessment another obstacle that blocks the success of our children?" This question speaks directly to the issue of equity. My response is "yes and no."

I believe that performance-based assessment provides more opportunity for teachers to get a clearer understanding of what their students actually know and more opportunity for students to demonstrate what they know. Some students do not perform well on multiple choice, timed assessments. With performance-based assessment, these same students have the opportunity to show what they know in different formats. Instead of darkening in the bubbles of a machine-scored test, they can write a play, give an oral presentation, build a model, or conduct an experiment.

On the other hand, no assessment or series of assessments, regardless of their validity or usefulness, can compensate for students not being exposed to information; not having the opportunity to participate in hands-on learning; or not being engaged in discussions that force them to expand, reflect upon, critically evaluate, justify, and defend their thinking. Without the appropriate support, performance-based assessment will only emphasize what's not happening in the classroom and the school—what opportunities the student has not had.

So what are the options? How should equity be integrated into a reconceptualization of assessment? We must first have a clear vision of where we are going. Most of our conversations as educators have been based on an oft-repeated premise that "All children can learn." I have to add, "All children can learn at high standards." If this is truly believed, then the following must be considered to achieve the goal.

• **Everything must reflect the commitment to high standards.** "Everything" includes not only a careful conceptualization and use of assessment, but issues pertaining to school climate (e.g., how the classes are organized, how discipline is administered, how instruction is delivered, and how curriculum is determined).

• **Change or reform must first be structured and systematic.** Changing one part of the system without considering the context of that system often results in failed reform.

• **The demands created by equity must be considered when assessments are redesigned.** The design of the assessments (e.g., format, content, language), the development and application of scoring criteria (e.g., who participates in setting standards, or how the criteria may be differentially interpreted based on cultural knowledge), the integration of assessment within curriculum, and the interpretation and use of the assessment results should all reflect the commitment to equity. If these issues are not addressed, performance-based measures have the potential of being one more "No, you can't do it" message to those who can least afford to hear it.

In conclusion, we cannot afford to have differing expectations for success. All children must be provided the opportunity to achieve excellence. This premise should be the cornerstone of our commitment to students. Clearly stated instructional outcomes tied to standards of excellence and performance assessments can provide students with new and engaging ways to demonstrate their knowledge. They can also provide useful information on a student's achievement. Equitable opportunities and equitable success. That's what education should be about.

International Assessments of Reading Literacy

Gerry Shiel and Judith Cosgrove

Many countries implement national assessments of reading literacy in order to monitor progress in reading over time and to gain insights on the factors associated with achievement. Such assessments, which use nationally representative samples of schools and students, have been conducted in England since 1948 (Brooks, 1998) and in the United States, as part of the National Assessment of Educational Achievement (NAEP), since 1971 (Campbell, Hombo, & Mazzeo, 2000). In recent years, many countries have also participated in international assessments of reading literacy, which, like national assessments, draw on representative samples of schools and students. In this month's column, we look at why countries participate in international assessments, how reading literacy is measured, what such assessments have told us to date, and what the future might hold.

Why Do Countries Take Part in International Assessments?

International comparative assessments of reading literacy are not new. As part of the six-subject study conducted by the International Association for the Evaluation of Educational Achievement (IEA) in the early 1970s, 10- and 14-year-olds in 15 countries were assessed on their reading comprehension skills, while 14-year-olds were also assessed on their ability to interpret literary texts (literature) (Thorndike, 1973; Walker, 1976). In noting the challenge that such studies present, Thorndike wrote,

> There would be general agreement that children should be able to get meaning efficiently from written material of various styles and content areas. On the other hand, the preparation of genuinely equivalent tests in reading, where the essence of the task very intimately involves the language of a particular country, would seem to present very serious difficulties. (p. 14)

Despite such difficulties, the impetus for comparative international studies has increased in recent years as countries seek to improve their competitiveness or stock of "human capital" through evaluating and improving their educational systems and learning programs.

International studies have been likened to a horse race in which countries strive to attain the highest ranking (Owen, Stephens, Moskowitz, & Guillermo, 2000). The reality, however, is that differences between countries are generally small in comparison with differences within countries. On the positive side, international studies provide countries with the opportunity with examine factors associated with reading literacy across a range of levels, including the system level (e.g., national policy on curriculum content or teacher education), school level (e.g., the provision of programs for lower achieving students, use of resources for the teaching of reading), class level (e.g., use of particular strategies in teaching reading), and student level (e.g., gender, attitude toward reading, reading habits). A particular advantage of international studies is that associations between variables such as gender or socioeconomic status and reading literacy can vary across countries, prompting individual countries to examine their own situations more critically and to implement change if necessary.

From *The Reading Teacher*, 55(7), 690–692. © 2002 by the International Reading Association.

What Do International Assessments Measure?

International assessments of reading literacy have evolved over time in three related areas: (a) definitions of reading literacy, (b) assessment frameworks, and (c) the types of texts and questions used to measure reading literacy.

The IEA Reading Literacy Study (IEA/RLS) was administered to intact classes in representative school samples in 32 countries in 1990–1991. Within participating countries, the survey was administered at the grade levels in which the majority of 9- and 14-year-olds were enrolled. IEA/RLS defined reading literacy as the "ability to understand and use those written language forms that are required by society and/or valued by the individual" (Elley, 1992, p. 3). Hence, the requirements of society (which increase all the time), as well as those of individual students, were acknowledged. Reading literacy was evaluated using three text types—*narrative prose* (continuous text in which the writer's main aim is to tell a story, whether fact or fiction), *expository prose* (continuous text designed to describe or explain factual information), and *documents* (structured information displays presented in the form of charts, tables, maps, and notices). The majority of questions (90% for 9-year-olds and 75% for 14-year-olds) followed a multiple-choice format, while the remainder were items students answered with a short response.

The Program for International Student Assessment (PISA), which included the assessment of reading literacy, was administered to representative samples of 15-year-olds in 32 countries in 2000 under the auspices of the Organisation for Economic Cooperation and Development (OECD; 2001). (For more information, see the International Reading Association's website, http://www.reading.org/resources/issues/reports/pisa.html.) PISA focused on the skills needed for adult life rather than mastery of school curricula. It defined reading literacy as "understanding, using and reflecting on written texts, in order to achieve one's goals, to develop one's knowledge and potential, and to participate in society" (OECD, 1999, p. 20). This definition underpins an assessment framework that referred to three aspects of comprehension: *retrieve* (retrieving information in texts and forming a general understanding), *interpret* (interpreting information in texts), and *reflect/evaluate* (reflecting on and evaluating the content and form of texts). Two types of texts were used: *continuous* (e.g., descriptions, narrations, and arguments) and *noncontinuous* (e.g., advertisements, charts, graphs, forms, maps, and tables). PISA 2000 included a combination of multiple-choice (55%) and constructed-response (45%) items. The latter included closed-constructed response items (where the range of acceptable answers is limited), and open-constructed response items (where divergent responses and opposite viewpoints were acceptable, and partial credit was possible).

IEA's Progress in International Reading Literacy Study (PIRLS) was administered to students in fourth-grade classes in representative samples of schools in 37 countries in 2001. PIRLS defined reading literacy as follows:

> the ability to understand and use those written language forms required by society and valued by the individual. Young readers construct meaning from a variety of texts. They read to learn, to participate in communities of readers, and for enjoyment. (Campbell, Kelly, Mullis, Martin, & Sainsbury, 2001, p. 3)

This definition extends the one used in IEA/RLS by focusing on the interactive nature of reading, including its social aspects. The assessment framework underpinning PIRLS focused on three aspects of reading—the purposes for reading, the processes of comprehension, and reading behavior and attitudes. Two broad purposes, each encompassing 50% of test items, were identified: *acquiring and using information* (focusing mainly on expository texts), and *literacy experience* (focusing mainly on narratives). Four reading comprehension processes were identified: *focus on and retrieve explicitly stated information*; *make straightforward inferences*; *interpret and integrate ideas and information*; and *examine and evaluate content, language, and textual elements*. These processes are broadly similar to those assessed in

PISA and again reflect a constructivist, interactive view of the reading process.

All three studies involved the administration of questionnaires to obtain background information that could be used to interpret scores. In all three studies, questionnaires were completed by school principals and students, while the IEA/RLS and PIRLS questionnaires were also completed by students' teachers. The absence of a teacher questionnaire in PISA reflects its use of an age cohort (where students may be drawn from several different classes in a school) and its concerns with system and school-level policy issues rather than with the content or methodologies of classroom instruction. PIRLS, on the other hand, was designed to provide information on instructional factors associated with achievement in reading literacy.

What Have We Learned From International Assessments?

The results of two assessments, the IEA/RLS (Elley, 1992, 1994) and PISA (OECD, 2001), are available and focus both on achievement outcomes and on factors underlying those outcomes.

In IEA/RLS, the highest scoring country on overall reading literacy at ages 9 and 14 was Finland, which also had the highest scores on the three assessment domains (narrative, expository, and documents) at both levels. Other countries with high overall scores included the United States and Sweden at age 9 and France, Sweden, and New Zealand at age 14. Elley (1992) noted that the performance of Finland was higher than would be expected, given social and economic circumstances, and might be attributed to a number of factors such as the regularity of the Finnish orthography, the relative wealth of the country (reflected in a low student–teacher ratio), the linguistic homogeneity of Finnish schools, the importance attributed to literacy in Finland, and the implementation by teachers of student-centered approaches to assessment. Statistically significant differences in achievement between boys and girls were observed in 19 of 27 countries at age 9 and in 13 of 31 at age 14, suggesting a bridging of the gender gap between 9 and 14. Countries with the largest gender differences were Denmark, Iceland, and New Zealand at age 9 and Thailand, Trinidad and Tobago, Ireland, and Canada (British Columbia) at age 14. Among the variables that were most strongly associated with country-level achievement were easy access to books in students' homes, access to well-stocked school libraries, and moderate amounts of television viewing. More detailed analyses of the IEA/RLS data may be found in Elley (1994), Postlethwaite and Ross (1992), and Lundberg and Linnakyla (1993).

In PISA, Finland was again the highest-scoring country on overall (combined) reading literacy and on two of the three reading subscales (retrieve and interpret) (OECD, 2001). Other high-achieving countries included Canada (which had the highest score on the reflect/evaluate scale), New Zealand, Australia, and Ireland. Countries with levels of achievement close to the OECD average included Belgium, Norway, France, and the United States. PISA also reported on the performance of countries in terms of the proportions of students at each of five reading proficiency levels. For example, in Germany, a country with an overall mean score near the OECD country average, 9% of students scored at Level 5 (the highest level), while 23% scored at or below Level 1 (the lowest level). Girls achieved significantly higher mean scores than boys on combined reading literacy in all participating countries and were more strongly represented at the highest reading proficiency levels, while boys were more strongly represented at the lowest levels. Hence, the gender differences observed among 15-year-olds in PISA are greater than those observed among 14-year-olds in the earlier IEA/RLS study and may relate to the inclusion of a greater proportion of items dealing with reflection on and evaluation of texts in PISA.

PISA also reported associations between student factors and reading literacy. Across all participating countries, variables such as student-level socioeconomic status, average school-level socioeconomic status, student gender (favoring females), students' use of school resources, whether or not a student was born in a different country (favoring those who weren't), and the quality of student–teacher relations were found to be the strongest predictors of achievement in reading literacy (OECD, 2001). In Ireland, variables associated with performance in reading literacy included diversity of reading (the average frequency with which students read different types of text), frequency of borrowing library books, frequency of leisure reading (reading for enjoyment), and attitude toward reading (Shiel, Cosgrove, Sofroniou, & Kelly, 2001). Higher achieving students were those who held a positive attitude toward reading, who borrowed library books at least once a month, who engaged in moderate amounts of leisure reading, and who read a broad range of text types. More detailed analyses of the data showed that variables such as attitude to reading and frequency of leisure reading explained performance in reading literacy, even after school and student socioeconomic status had been accounted for.

What Does the Future Hold?

Many educators look forward to the publication of the PIRLS results, which are due for release in 2003 and will include comparisons with performance in the 1991 IEA/RLS. PISA also plans to issue a thematic report on reading literacy in 2002/03, when performance on continuous and noncontinuous texts will be compared across countries. Already, it is planned to repeat the PIRLS assessment in fourth grade in 2005 and 2009, while PISA is scheduled to assess reading literacy among 15-year-olds again in 2003 and 2006. Hence, the emphasis in the future will be on looking at trends over time, though whether countries can implement changes that will have a substantial impact on achievement levels in just 3 or 4 years remains to be seen. A challenge likely to face some countries is how best to integrate international and national assessments without overburdening schools and students while at the same time containing costs.

Studies such as PIRLS and PISA have gone to great lengths to ensure their assessment frameworks are grounded in current research, that texts and questions are comparable across countries and cultures, that translation procedures meet the highest standards, that samples of students are comparable across countries, that response rates are uniformly high, and that rigorous procedures are implemented in scoring student responses (an important issue in light of the gradual shift away from multiple-choice type items). Future developments are likely to focus on issues raised by Thorndike (1973), including the effects on students' comprehension of translating texts from one language to another and their being asked to read a series of texts that are grounded in cultures other than their own. According to Lafontaine (2000), such concerns still persist, despite the stringent translation procedures implemented in studies like PIRLS and PISA and their attempts to include a broad range of texts reflecting a range of diverse cultures. Finally, future international assessments of reading literacy will need to address students' use and understanding of electronic texts.

References

Brooks, G. (1998). Trends in standards in the United Kingdom, 1948–1996. *TOPIC, 19*, 1–8.

Campbell, J.R., Hombo, C.M., & Mazzeo, J. (2000). *NAEP 1999: Trends in academic progress: Three decades of student performance—Reading, 1971–1999, Science, 1969–1999, and Mathematics, 1973–1999*. Washington, DC: U.S. Department of Education. Office of Educational Research and Improvement [Online]. Available: http://www.ed.gov.nationsreportcard

Campbell, J.R., Kelly, D.L., Mullis, I.V.S., Martin, M.O., & Sainsbury, M. (2001). *Framework and specifications for PIRLS assessment 2001*. Boston: PIRLS International Study Centre [Online]. Available: http://www.pirls.org

Elley, W.B. (1992). *How in the world do students read?* The Hague, The Netherlands: International Association for the Evaluation of Educational Achievement.

Elley, W.B. (1994). *The IEA study of reading literacy: Achievement and instruction in thirty-two school systems*. Oxford, England: Pergamon.

Lafontaine, D. (2000). From comprehension to literature: Thirty years of reading assessment. In *The*

INES compendium (pp. 51–66). Paris: Organisation for Economic Cooperation and Development.

Lundberg, I., & Linnakyla, P. (1993). *Teaching reading around the world.* The Hague, The Netherlands: International Association for the Evaluation of Educational Achievement.

Organisation for Economic Cooperation and Development. (1999). *Measuring student knowledge and skills: A new framework for assessment.* Paris: Author [Online]. Available: http://www.pisa.oecd.org

Organisation for Economic Cooperation and Development. (2001). *Knowledge and skills for life: First results of PISA 2000.* Paris: Author.

Owen, E., Stephens, M., Moskowitz, J., & Guillermo, G. (2000). From "horse race" to educational improvement: The future of international educational assessments. In *The INES compendium* (pp. 13–26). Paris: Organisation for Economic Cooperation and Development.

Postlethwaite, T.N., & Ross, K.N. (1992). *Effective schools in reading: Implications for educational planners.* The Hague, The Netherlands: International Association for the Evaluation of Educational Achievement.

Shiel, G., Cosgrove, J., Sofroniou, N., & Kelly, A. (2001). *Ready for life? The literacy achievements of Irish 15-year-olds with comparative international data.* Dublin, Ireland: Educational Research Centre.

Thorndike, R.L. (1973). *Reading comprehension education in 15 countries: An empirical study.* New York: Wiley.

Walker, D.W. (1976). *The IEA six subject survey: An empirical study of education in twenty-one countries.* New York: Wiley.

The Evils of the Use of IQ Tests to Define Learning Disabilities in First- and Second-Language Learners

Lee Gunderson and Linda S. Siegel

Joe Sun (pseudonym) immigrated from Hong Kong with his family when he was 11 years old. He struggled with school and failed nearly all of his classes. He had difficulty learning both English and the material presented in his academic classes. He received some English as a Second Language (ESL) help, but after 3 years of continued failure he was referred for assessment. It was found that Joe could not define words such as *thief* or *brave*, words that should be easy for most English-speaking students his age. When asked, he was unable to read easy words such as *rug*, *with*, *stove*, *ground*, and *airplane*. He read *even* as *eve*, *finger* as *fighter*, *size* as *sat*, *felt* as *fit*, and *lame* as *lem*. He was asked to read pseudowords, but he did so with great difficulty: *ift* was *ept*, *Nan* was *ang*, *Chad* was *chand*, and *ap* was *aip*. When asked, he spelled *correct* as *coright*, *him* as *her*, and *must* as *mucs*. He had great difficulty repeating two-syllable nonwords and could not delete initial and final phonemes. However, he did have outstanding visual–spatial skills.

The teachers in Joe's school were faced with a difficult and perplexing question, "Was Joe failing to learn because he was learning English as a second language (ESL), or was he learning disabled?" It is often difficult to determine which individuals are learning disabled when they are native speakers of a language. However, the task is considerably more complex when they are second-language (L2) learners.

There are students at all levels, kindergarten to university, who have difficulty learning. Indeed, the number of school-age students identified as learning disabled in the U.S. rose from 797,000 in 1976–1977 to 2,317,000 in 1993–1994 (Kavale & Forness, 1998). Many individuals find learning difficult or impossible for reasons that are not always clear to teachers. In many cases they may have some type of learning disability. That is, they may have significant difficulty in acquiring reading, spelling, writing, or mathematical skills. The U.S. National Joint Committee on Learning Disabilities (2000) published an expanded definition of learning disabilities first developed in 1994:

> Learning disabilities...[refer] to a heterogeneous group of disorders manifested by significant difficulties in the acquisition and use of listening, speaking, reading, writing, reasoning, or mathematical abilities. These disorders are intrinsic to the individual, presumed to be due to central nervous system dysfunction, and may occur across the life span. Problems in self-regulatory behaviors, social perception, and social interaction may exist...but do not by themselves constitute a learning disability. Although learning disabilities may occur...with other handicapping conditions (for example, sensory impairment, mental retardation, serious emotional disturbance), or with extrinsic influences (such as cultural differences, inappropriate or insufficient instruction), they are not the result of [them]. (National Joint Committee on Learning Disabilities, 2000)

Learning disabilities are not always outwardly visible; they must often be inferred. To

From *The Reading Teacher*, 55(1), 48–55. © 2001 by the International Reading Association.

determine whether an individual has a learning disability, school personnel are usually required by policy to administer an intelligence test (e.g., see Kavale & Forness, 1998). A student may be diagnosed as having a reading disability if there is a large and significant discrepancy between an IQ test score and reading achievement. The United States Department of Education (1977) established rules and regulations for detecting learning disabilities.

> A specific learning disability may be found if (1) the child does not achieve commensurate with his or her age and ability when provided with appropriate educational experiences, and (2) the child has a severe discrepancy between achievement and intellectual ability in one or more areas relating to communication skills and mathematical abilities. (p. 65083)

There are a number of different discrepancy-based models of disability involving IQ scores in use, and it has been argued for some time that they should be replaced by approaches based on grounded theories of learning (Willson, 1987). However, this discrepancy definition of learning disability continues to shape policy in many jurisdictions, including the United States (cf., Kavale & Forness, 1998), the United Kingdom (cf., United Kingdom Department for Education and Employment, 2000), and Canada (cf., British Columbia Ministry of Education, 1999). We have concerns about the use of intelligence tests to determine who is reading disabled and who is not. We are particularly concerned when the students speak a first (L1) or primary language other than English, are from backgrounds that are culturally different from the mainstream, or are from low socioeconomic backgrounds. We are convinced that these students are penalized because of the use of IQ tests. Indeed, we are certain that some students who should be identified as learning disabled are not, and some who are identified should not be. We believe that the use of IQ testing and the discrepancy concept is invalid and harmful, and is particularly destructive for those students who differ linguistically and culturally from the "norm." We agree with Strickland (1995) that students with a record of school failure, classified with labels ranging from "learning disabled" to "educably mentally retarded," are often deprived of educational opportunities because of those labels. In many cases students are being improperly labeled on the basis of the results of an IQ test.

What Role Does IQ Play in the Assessment of Learning Disabilities?

The intelligence test is one of the primary instruments used in the identification of learning disabilities. In many cases, an individual cannot be identified as learning disabled unless an IQ test has been administered. Federal law in the United States, for instance, indicates that a disability exists if "a child has a severe discrepancy between achievement and intellectual ability" (34 CFR 300.541). The U.S. Head Start program policy stipulates that a disability exists when "the child has a severe discrepancy between achievement milestones and intellectual ability in one or more...[area]" (45 CFR Part 1308, Section 1308.14 Eligibility criteria: Learning disabilities). As outlined in the U.S. Individuals with Disabilities Education Act (IDEA), a learning disability exists if the student has "an IQ of 70 or higher, and a severe discrepancy between intellectual ability and academic achievement in one or more areas" (1990, Section 1401).

In many jurisdictions, funding is not available for students who have not been administered an IQ test. We are convinced, however, that the presence of a discrepancy is not a necessary part of the definition of a learning disability and, furthermore, that it is not necessary to administer an IQ test to determine whether a learning disability exists.

Measuring Intelligence

The concept of "intelligence" should signify skills in reasoning, problem solving, critical thinking, and adaptation to the environment. Although this notion appears logical, it breaks down when one carefully examines the content of IQ tests. Typically they consist of measures of factual knowledge, definitions of words, memory recall, fine-motor coordination, and fluency of expressive language; they probably do not measure reasoning or problem-solving skills. They assess only what a person has learned, not what he or she is capable of doing. An IQ test is not culture free, because background is important, nor is it language free, because it requires knowledge of English.

In some subtests on an IQ test extra points are given for responding quickly, thereby putting a premium on speed. An individual with a culturally based slow, deliberate style may not achieve as high a score as an individual who responds more quickly. This is a problem that cannot be overcome by simply translating the test into a student's first language. In essence, IQ tests are based on the notion that scores do not represent a single entity but are a composite of many skills. (For an extended discussion of the content of IQ tests, see Siegel, 1989.)

It is argued that IQ tests are needed to measure the "potential" of an individual. This argument implies that there is some measure that can reliably predict how much an individual can learn and what can be expected of him or her. In this view IQ scores predict the limits of academic performance. A person with a low score is not expected to have high levels of academic skills, while one with high scores is. In other words, an IQ score is thought to estimate reliably how much knowledge an individual can be expected to acquire. However, there is evidence that this putative relationship is neither strong nor reliable. There are individuals who have low scores on IQ tests, less than 80 or 90, who also have average or above average scores on reading tests. Indeed, reading comprehension may be more influenced by background knowledge (e.g., Schneider, Körkel, & Weinert, 1989) or phonological skills (e.g., Siegel, 1993) than IQ scores.

Our perusal of the research for the purpose of writing this article revealed that the relationship between IQ scores and achievement, particularly in reading, varies greatly, but that in the typical case only about 20–25% of reading scores can be predicted accurately from IQ scores. In most cases, there appears to be no reliable relationship between IQ and reading scores. It should also be noted that parental income predicts achievement with the same level of accuracy. Should we decide on educational programs for students based on parental income? We hope the answer is no, and we think that it is equally inappropriate to use IQ in this way.

There is an additional problem with the use of IQ tests for individuals with learning disabilities. Most of these individuals have deficiencies in one or more of the component skills that are part of IQ tests and, therefore, their scores are an underestimate of their competence. It seems illogical to find that someone has deficient memory or language or fine-motor skills and then say that they are less intelligent because of the deficiency.

There is evidence to suggest that it is unnecessary to use an intelligence measure to define a reading disability. When children with reading disabilities are divided into groups on the basis of their IQ and compared on a variety of reading, language, memory, spelling, and phonological tasks, there are no differences in scores on the reading-related tasks (Siegel, 1988). The reading disabled group in this study was quite homogeneous in relation to reading-related skills, and administering an IQ test did not provide useful information about performance differences on reading-related tasks.

If individuals are poor readers but show no discrepancy between their IQ and reading scores, then they are not considered reading disabled. If they show this discrepancy they are said to have a reading disability. There are a significant number of studies that find no difference in reading, spelling, phonological, or even reading comprehension skills of learning disabled individuals with high and low IQ scores. Furthermore, there are no differences between disabled and poor readers on measures of the processes most directly related to reading (e.g., Siegel, 1988, 1992; Stanovich & Siegel, 1994; Toth & Siegel, 1994).

Siegel (1992) compared two groups of children who had low reading scores. One group, the disabled readers, had reading scores that were significantly lower that those that were predicted by their IQ scores, and the other group, the poor readers, also had low reading scores but these were not significantly lower than would be predicted by their IQ scores. On a variety of reading, spelling, and phonological tasks, there were no significant differences between these two groups in reading comprehension. These results have been replicated in a study of adults with reading disabilities (Siegel, 1998). It seems that there is no need to use IQ scores to predict the differences between the individuals traditionally called learning disabled and those who have equally poor achievement and lower IQ scores. IQ scores do not appear to predict who is able to benefit from remediation (Arnold, Smeltzer, & Barneby, 1981; Kershner, 1990; Lytton, 1967; Van der Wissel & Zegers, 1985; Vellutino et al., 1996). One study (Yule, 1973) found that reading-disabled children with lower IQ scores made more gains than reading-disabled children with higher scores. We agree with Lyon (1995), who stated,

> The assumption that a discrepancy between achievement and aptitude (typically assessed using intelligence tests) is a clear diagnostic marker for learning disabilities or can be considered a pathognomonic sign is at best premature, and at worst invalid. (Lyon, 1995, p. 12)

To this point we have argued that IQ tests are inappropriate for identifying disabilities, but our discussion has focused on their use with native English speakers. We turn now to the case of individuals whose first or primary language is not English.

Intelligence and Language

Researchers have explored the issues related to intelligence for nearly 100 years. Binet and Simon (1905), for instance, created a test they believed measured intelligence. Spearman (1904) developed the notion of "general intelligence," or the "g factor." One argument is that intelligence is innate and testable and that it does not necessarily require language. Unfortunately, intelligence tests are not language-free. They require an understanding of the language of the test and the testing process. Oller (1997) noted the following:

> To reform the use of IQ and other school testing procedures, it is essential to start calling "verbal IQ tests" *measures of **primary** language skills* [emphasis in original]. When they are applied to persons for whom the language of the test is not the primary language, they are *measures of **second** (or **nonprimary**) language skills* [emphasis in original]. If these changes are made, the absurdity of calling a normal person who has not yet learned a certain dialect of English "retarded," "learning disordered," "language impaired," "learning disabled," and the like, will be averted. (pp. 493–494)

Language-free or nonverbal IQ tests also require language (Oller, 1997). Oller argued that such tests "are measures of conceptual skills that are accessible only through proficiency in some particular language, usually the test-taker's primary language" (p. 494). He cautioned, further, that "the results of all 'nonverbal' tasks should be regarded with reasonable skepticism" (p. 494). The use of IQ tests to assess students whose primary language is different from the language of the test is dubious at best because it denies the relationship between language and culture. Indeed, we learn a language as members of particular cultures. We have concluded that

> The cultural factor must be considered in administering and interpreting any standardized tests, especially those that purport to measure intellectual ability. Memory, learning, perceiving, and problem solving cannot be measured except through content. And content is always culturally related. We must accept that intelligence tests measure the degree to which the individual's knowledge and skills enable him or her to function intelligently in a culture, rather than assessing pure intelligence in some way. (Siegel & Gunderson, in press)

English as a Second Language (L2) Students

The number of students for whom English is a second language continues to increase. As this number increases, so does the number of ESL students who have difficulty learning. Some have learning disabilities. The problem is to identify the learning disability when there are complex linguistic and cultural differences that confound the assessment process (Siegel & Gunderson, in press). We have found that

> culturally/linguistically diverse students may be seen as disabled (when, in fact, they are not), and therefore, identification as a student with special needs is inappropriate. Or, the gifts and talents of culturally and linguistically diverse students may be overlooked, which prevents them from receiving the services that would contribute to the development of their potentials. Or, students from linguistically and culturally diverse backgrounds may have genuine learning disabilities and need some special education assistance, but remain unidentified. (Siegel & Gunderson, in press)

We have come to the conclusion that the use of intelligence tests in general to identify learning-disabled students is inappropriate. To use them to identify learning disabilities for students who differ linguistically and culturally from the mainstream is particularly inappropriate. Unfortunately, as we have pointed out, such use of intelligence tests is widespread.

Intelligence Tests and Second Language

Second-language students may not receive access to help with their reading, spelling, writing, or arithmetic problems because of their performance on IQ tests. This is unfortunate, and a result of a failure to acknowledge that there is a serious discrepancy between the language of the test and the language of the student. IQ tests are wholly inappropriate for ESL students for a variety of reasons. ESL students vary in their knowledge of English, and the variance has important consequences for their performance on an IQ test. Language is complex. It includes phonological, syntactic, semantic, pragmatic, and background knowledge. A mature first-language speaker has learned the phonology —how to produce and understand the sounds— of his or her language. He or she can produce and comprehend grammatically acceptable utterances and communicate with other speakers of the same sociolinguistic group. The mature language speaker understands how to be polite, what language is appropriate for different contexts, how to take turns in a conversation, who to talk to and who to defer to, how to switch codes so that the language matches the situation, how to use intonation to produce meaning, who to respect, gender- and age-appropriate roles, who to look at and who not to look at, and how to react appropriately to different situations, including testing sessions. In essence, to do well in a testing situation, an individual must know a great deal about both the second language and the second culture (see Gunderson & Anderson, 2003).

Most ESL students do not possess the complex second-language and second-cultural knowledge required to succeed in such situations, and the individual doing the testing may not have the knowledge of the student's first culture or first language to be able to differentiate discrepancies from differences. Translating a test that has cultural biases into different languages does not eliminate the inherent difficulties related to cultural biases or scoring schemes that favor faster response times. IQ tests are simply wrong for identifying learning disabilities for ESL students.

IQ tests in different languages?

The Matthew Effect

One of the reasons for the inappropriateness of IQ tests is the "Matthew effect." Stanovich (1986, 1988a, 1988b) has conceptualized the Matthew effect as "the tendency of reading itself to cause further development in other related cognitive abilities such as intelligence such that 'the rich get richer and the poor get poorer'" (1986, p. 361). Certain minimum cognitive capabilities must be present to begin reading; however, once reading begins, the act of reading itself further develops these same cognitive capabilities. This relationship of mutual reinforcement is called the Matthew effect. This reciprocal relationship between reading and other cognitive skills is reflected in performance on IQ tests and, consequently, undermines the validity of using an IQ discrepancy-based criterion because children who read more gain the cognitive skills and information relevant to the IQ test and consequently attain higher IQ scores. Children with reading problems read less and, therefore, fail to gain the skills and information necessary to allow for the development of abilities measured by IQ tests.

As a result of the Matthew effect there will be a decline in IQ scores for disabled readers with increasing age, because vocabulary and knowledge increase as a result of experiences with print through the act of reading. In a cross-sectional study, Siegel and Himel (1998) found that the IQ scores and, in particular, vocabulary scores of older reading-disabled children were significantly lower than those of younger reading-disabled children. Similar declines in IQ and vocabulary were not noted for normally achieving readers, that is, children who showed age-appropriate reading skills. However, reading scores of the children with reading problems compared to chronologically age-matched children remained relatively constant with time so that there was not an overall decline in skills. Younger children were much more likely to be classified as disabled readers (as opposed to poor readers) than older children because of the "decline" in IQ scores that resulted from lack of print exposure.

The Matthew Effect and Second-Language Students

If the Matthew effect exists in English, it is likely that it exists for readers of other languages. A number of second-language researchers have found that immigrants with L1 reading backgrounds develop L2 reading faster than those without reading backgrounds (e.g., Collier, 1987; Cummins, 1979, 1984; Cummins & Swain, 1986). Immigrant students with 4 to 6 years of successful L1 literacy backgrounds have higher achievement levels than those who have little or no L1 reading experience (Gunderson & Clarke, 1998). These findings suggest the existence of a second-language Matthew effect. We paraphrase Stanovich by saying "the L1 rich will become the L2 rich."

Negative Consequences of IQ Test Use

The negative consequences of using an IQ test to define learning disability are quite serious. Many learning disabled children who need help, but do not meet the discrepancy definition, are not getting it. Berninger (1998) noted that only 44% of the children who met the criterion for low reading achievement also met the criterion for the IQ achievement discrepancy. This means that 56% of the children who need it do not get help for their learning problems, because they have low IQ scores. She also noted that only 36% who met the criterion for IQ achievement discrepancy also met the criterion for low achievement. This means that the remaining 64% are eligible for remedial help when they really do not have low achievement scores and do not need remedial help. The consequence of using IQ means that children with lower IQ scores, although not necessarily very low, will not receive the help that they need. Berninger stated that children with low IQ scores and low achievement "would benefit from support services" (1998, p. 535).

The fact that there is no difference in reading skill between children who have a discrepancy and children with the same kind of problems but with no discrepancy should be a clue that the IQ test is not really useful. In other words, IQ does not predict the ability to benefit from remediation. The IQ test is particularly insidious because in the present educational system children must often be administered an IQ test to determine whether they have a learning disability. Resources in most systems are quite limited, and the child must wait a long time although he or she is having difficulties in school. It would make much more sense to recognize these difficulties, whether or not an IQ test is done, and start remediation immediately. Teachers are in the best position to observe whether or not individual students have learning difficulties.

In many places in the world the type of help that children receive for their reading problems depends on their IQ, and children with higher IQ scores are more likely to receive the remediation that they need. The use of IQ to define reading disability seems fatally flawed because it is confounded by socioeconomic status and age. The implications seem clear. If the IQ-achievement discrepancy is used as a part of the definition of reading disability, and if reading-disabled and poor readers are treated differently by the school system, then children with lower IQ scores, even though they have serious reading problems, will not get the help that they need. Therefore, the use of IQ scores systematically discriminates against certain children. To help all children learn to read, teachers should recognize some of the difficulties inherent in making inferences about reading potential based on IQ scores and instead develop detailed analyses of reading, spelling, arithmetic, and writing skills. (See Siegel & Heaven, 1986, for a detailed discussion of these issues.)

The use of IQ tests with ESL or English-dialect students is inappropriate. There is no way that an IQ test can reliably measure intelligence, even if it exists and can be tested, when the student's first or primary language is different from the language of the test. The results are problematical. Indeed, they marginalize ESL students. They fail to identify true reading-disabled students. They are not able to differentiate a first-language learning problem from a second-language learning problem or from a general language learning problem. In summary, use of the IQ test may be harmful to the education of children because it often prevents those who really need help from getting it.

What Teachers Can Do

The IQ test as it is currently given does not provide much information about the child's achievement difficulties. A careful analysis of errors in reading, spelling, arithmetic tests, and in writing samples is more useful. Millions, perhaps billions of U.S. dollars are spent each year on IQ test administration and scoring. Teachers can and should trust their own observations and instincts. It is relatively easy to identify which children are having significant difficulties with reading, spelling, written work, and math, especially as they function in learning situations independently and in groups with other students. Teachers who believe particular students have learning difficulties can confirm their beliefs by the administration of standardized tests of letter recognition, word identification, and comprehension. Such tests are usually available in schools or school districts. A great deal of information is also available through the administration of an informal reading inventory. Analyses of students' production errors or miscues reveal a great deal about their skills. For example, does the child read the word *have* to rhyme with *gave* or *said* as *sayed* (rhyming with *maid*)? In this case, the child has not yet mastered the complex, often irregular pronunciation of English vowels. Does the child read *father* as *five* or *takes* as *tells*? These kinds of errors indicate that the child is paying attention only to the first letter and then guessing.

Students' spelling errors reveal information about their knowledge of phoneme–grapheme correspondences. Does the child spell *nature* as *nachure* or *education* as *educashun*? The student demonstrates a good knowledge of letter–sound correspondences, but a poor visual memory and a lack of understanding of the structure of English words. No English word ends in *-shun*, although *shun* is an English word. In English the orthography uses *-tion* or *-sion*.

It was concluded that Joe Sun (the student mentioned in the introduction) had a learning disability. The difficulty in making the determination was in separating errors he made related to influences from his first language, Cantonese, from those directly related to difficulties in reading English. Cantonese is an open-syllabic language without final consonant clusters (see Chang, 1987). Typically Cantonese speakers substitute glottal stops for final consonants and consonant clusters in English, such as /faI/ for /faIv/ (*fi* for *five*). These errors were not evident in Joe's reading nor were other second-language features. Indeed, the teacher's analysis of his errors suggested he had a learning disability.

If teachers were given the time and opportunity to administer individual achievement tests and to analyze the results, particularly the errors, students, teachers, and administrators would be helped more than by the administration of an IQ test. What will make the difference for the student is that he or she receives early instruction based on a thoughtful analysis of the student's needs and abilities. We will not recommend a particular method or approach because we agree with

Duffy and Hoffman (1999) who noted that "reading instruction effectiveness lies not with a single program or method, but rather, with a teacher who thoughtfully and analytically integrates various programs, materials, and methods as the situation demands" (p. 11). There is also no perfect IQ test or achievement test to determine a child's strengths and weaknesses. What is needed is that teachers be given the time, support, and staff development required to administer and interpret both holistic and standardized measures.

References

Arnold, L.E., Smeltzer, D.J., & Barneby, N.S. (1981). Specific perceptual remediation: Effects related to sex, IQ, and parents' occupational status; behavioral change pattern by scale factors; and mechanism of benefit hypothesis tested. *Psychological Reports, 49*, 198.

Berninger, V.W. (1998). Specific reading and writing disabilities in young children: Assessment, prevention, and intervention. In B. Wong (Ed.), *Learning about learning disabilities* (2nd ed., pp. 529–555). San Diego, CA: Academic Press.

Binet, A., & Simon, T. (1905). New methods for the diagnosis of the intellectual level of subnormals. *L'Annee Psychologique, 5*, 191–244.

British Columbia Ministry of Education. (1999). *Assessing disabilities* [Online]. Available: http://www.bced.gov.bc.ca/specialed/review/report/id.htm

Chang, J. (1987). Chinese speakers. In M. Sawn & B. Smith (Eds.), *Learner English: A teacher's guide to interference and other problems* (pp. 224–237). Cambridge, England: Cambridge University Press.

Collier, V.P. (1987). Age and rate of acquisition of second language for academic purposes. *TESOL Quarterly, 21*, 617–641.

Cummins, J. (1979). Cognitive/academic language proficiency, linguistic interdependence, the optimum age question and some other matters. *Working Papers on Bilingualism, 19*, 197–205.

Cummins, J. (1984). *Bilingualism and special education: Issues in assessment and pedagogy.* Clevedon, England: Multicultural Matters.

Cummins, J., & Swain, M. (1986). Linguistic interdependence: A central principle of bilingual education. In *Bilingualism in education* (pp. 80–95). New York: Longman Group UK.

Duffy, G.G., & Hoffman, J.V. (1999). In pursuit of an illusion: The flawed search for a perfect method. *The Reading Teacher, 53*, 10–16.

Gunderson, L., & Anderson, J. (2003). Multicultural views of literacy learning and teaching. In A.I. Willis, G.E. Garcia, R. Barrera, & V.J. Harris (Eds.), *Multicultural issues in literacy research and practice* (pp. 123–144). Mahwah, NJ: Erlbaum.

Gunderson, L., & Clarke, D.K. (1998). An exploration of the relationship between ESL students' backgrounds and their English and academic achievement. In T. Shanahan & F.V. Rodriguez-Brown (Eds.), *National Reading Conference Yearbook 47* (pp. 264-273). Chicago: National Reading Conference.

Kavale, K.A., & Forness, S.R. (1998). Covariance in learning disability and behavior disorder: An examination of classification and placement issues. In T.E. Scruggs & M.A. Mastropieri (Eds.), *Advances in learning and behavioral disabilities, Vol. 12* (pp. 1–42). London: JAI Press.

Kershner, J.R. (1990). Self-concept and IQ as predictors of remedial success in children with learning disabilities. *Journal of Learning Disabilities, 23*, 368–374.

Lyon, G.R. (1995). Toward a definition of dyslexia. *Annals of Dyslexia, 45*, 3–27.

Lytton, H. (1967). Follow up of an experiment in selection of remedial education. *British Journal of Educational Psychology, 37*, 1–9.

National Joint Committee on Learning Disabilities. (2000). *Learning disabilities: Issues on definition* (1990, January) [Online]. Available: http://www.ldonline.org/njcld/defn_91.html

Oller, J.W., Jr. (1997). Monoglottosis: What's wrong with the idea of the IQ meritocracy and its racy cousins? *Applied Linguistics, 18*, 467–507.

Schneider, W., Körkel, J., & Weinert, F.E. (1989). Domain-specific knowledge and memory performance: A comparison of high- and low-aptitude children. *Journal of Educational Psychology, 81*, 306-312.

Siegel, L. (1988). Evidence that IQ scores are irrelevant to the definition and analysis of reading disability. *Canadian Journal of Psychology, 42*, 201-215.

Siegel, L. (1989). Why we do not need IQ test scores in the definition and analysis of learning disability. *Journal of Learning Disabilities, 22*, 514–518.

Siegel, L. (1992). An evaluation of the discrepancy definition of dyslexia. *Journal of Learning Disabilities, 25*, 618–629.

Siegel, L. (1993). Phonological processing deficits as the basis of a reading disability. *Developmental Review, 13*, 246–257.

Siegel, L. (1998). The discrepancy formula: Its use and abuse. In B.K. Shapiro, P.J. Accardo, & A.J. Capute (Eds.), *Specific reading disability: A view of the spectrum* (pp. 123–135). Timonium, MD: York.

Siegel, L., & Gunderson, L. (in press). *Assessing the individual learning needs of students with linguistically and culturally diverse backgrounds.* Victoria, BC: British Columbia Ministry of Education.

Siegel, L., & Heaven, R. (1986). Defining and categorizing learning disabilities. In S. Ceci (Ed.), *Handbook of cognitive, social, and neuropsychological aspects of learning disabilities, Vol. 1* (pp. 95–121). Hillsdale, NJ: Erlbaum.

Siegel, L., & Himel, N. (1998). Socioeconomic status, age and the classification of dyslexics and poor readers: The dangers of using IQ scores in the definition of reading disability. *Dyslexia, 4*, 90–104.

Spearman, C.E. (1904). General intelligence: Objectively determined and measured. *American Journal of Psychology, 15*, 201–292.

Stanovich, K.E. (1986). Matthew effects in reading: Some consequences of individual differences in the acquisition of literacy. *Reading Research Quarterly, 21*, 360–407.

Stanovich, K.E. (1988a). Explaining the differences between the dyslexic and garden variety poor reader: The phonological-core variable-difference model. *Journal of Learning Disabilities, 21*, 590–604, 612.

Stanovich, K.E. (1988b). The right and wrong places to look for the cognitive locus of reading disability. *Annals of Dyslexia, 38*, 154–177.

Stanovich, K.E., & Siegel, L. (1994). Phenotypic performance profile of children with reading disabilities: A regression-based test of the phonological-core variable-difference model. *Journal of Educational Psychology, 86*, 24–53.

Strickland, K. (1995). *Literacy, not labels: Celebrating students' strengths through whole language.* Portsmouth, NH: Boynton/Cook.

Toth, G., & Siegel, L. (1994). A critical evaluation of the IQ-achievement discrepancy based definition of dyslexia. In K.P. van den Bos, L.S. Siegel, D.J. Bakker, & D.L. Share (Eds.), *Current directions in dyslexia research* (pp. 45–70). Lisse, The Netherlands: Swets & Zeitlinger.

United Kingdom Department for Education and Employment. (2000). *Special educational needs in England* [Online]. Available: http://www.dfee.org.uk

United States Department of Education. (1977). Definition and criteria for defining students as learning disabled. *Federal Register, 42:250*, 65083.

Van der Wissel, A., & Zegers, F.E. (1985). Reading retardation revisited. *British Journal of Developmental Psychology, 3*, 3–9.

Vellutino, F.R., Scanlon, D.M., Sipay, E.R., Small, S.G., Pratt, A., Chen, R., et al. (1996). Cognitive profiles of difficult-to-remediate and readily remediated poor readers: Toward distinguishing between constitutionally and experientially based causes of reading disability. *Journal of Educational Psychology, 59*, 76–123.

Willson, V.L. (1987). Statisical and psychometric issues surrounding severe discrepancy. *Learning Disabilities Research, 3*(1), 24–28.

Yule, W. (1973). Differential prognosis of reading backwardness and specific reading retardation. *British Journal of Educational Psychology, 43*, 244–248.

SECTION THREE

Gaining Perspective

- What are the goals of reading assessment?
- What do those goals reveal about your perspective on assessment?
- How do you react when the high-stakes test results for your school are reported? Is the reaction productive?
- What is the nature of your "assessment conversations" with other teachers? Do they promote achievement of your assessment goals?
- How can student perspectives affect your teaching and assessing?
- Is there a relationship between assessment and inquiry? If so, what is that relationship?
- How can you change or develop attitudes about assessment?

Because the topic of assessment has become a lightning rod for passionate beliefs and feelings, it is important for inservice and preservice teachers to understand many sides of the dialogue around this often contentious topic. According to Peter Johnston's article, what we as teachers say to one another about students and about achievement has potential to improve reading achievement. Amid the pressures of high-stakes testing, professionals can lose perspective on the importance of positive, solution-oriented dialogue. Johnston's ideas aim to help teachers focus their day-to-day assessment and professional dialogue on expanding notions about readers and achievement. Possibilities and problem solving can help reveal children's literate behaviors, whereas criticism creates tension and tends to reduce the richness of the instruction that teachers offer.

Kathleen A. Hinchman and Pamela A. Michel expand the circle of participants in the assessment "conversation" and include the students themselves. Seeking a way to align their assessment data and instruction with the readers' "social selves,"

Hinchman and Michel define a framework for child-centered literacy instruction. These researchers found that the student perspective humanizes the teaching and learning process. Literacy teaching becomes a social act, not purely academic, and far from prescriptive in its nature.

A broad perspective of literacy assessment helps professionals communicate with one another about this important topic. In his valuable and highly instructive article, Frank Serafini organizes assessment into three paradigms, each embodying a different assessment perspective: assessment as measurement, as procedure, and as inquiry. The paradigms can help professionals identify their own perspective and communicate using pragmatic language to choose, implement, and even defend a perspective on assessment.

Professional reading is a basic tool for growth and change. Bonita L. Wilcox provides a testimonial to the power of this tool and its ability to alter her perspective on assessment and to send her on a journey of changing her approach to classroom assessment. In that spirit, she and a team of reviewers (Lisa C. Schonberger, Deborah B. Kennedy, and Paul T. Kasunich) report on books on the topic of assessment that have been influential in their professional lives.

Additional Reading

- Coles, G. (2000). *Misreading reading: The bad science that hurts children*. Portsmouth, NH: Heinemann.
- Harvey, S., & Goudvis, A. (2000). *Strategies that work*. Portland, ME: Stenhouse.
- Krashen, S. (2004). False claims about literacy development. *Educational Leadership, 61*(6), 12–17.
- McQuillan, J. (1998). *The literacy crises: False claims, real solutions*. Portsmouth, NH: Heinemann.
- National Institute of Child Health and Human Development. (2000). *Report of the National Reading Panel. Teaching children to read: An evidence-based assessment of the scientific research literature on reading and its implications for reading instruction. Reports of the subgroups*. Washington, DC: U.S. Government Printing Office. (ERIC Document Reproduction Service No. ED444127)
- Popham, W.J. (2004). A game without winners. *Educational Leadership, 62*(3), 46–50.
- Routman, R. (1996). *Literacy at the crossroads: Crucial talk about reading, writing and other teaching dilemmas*. Portsmouth, NH: Heinemann.
- Routman, R. (1999). *Conversations: Strategies for teaching, learning, and evaluating*. Portsmouth, NH: Heinemann.
- Taberski, S. (2000). *On solid ground: Strategies for teaching reading k–3*. Portsmouth, NH: Heinemann.

Create a Statement of Reading Assessment Principles and Practices

Using the principles you have identified and revised for issues of equity and diversity, discuss your perspective on literacy assessment. Who influenced your perspectives? Do you value a measurement approach, as described by Serafini as one paradigm of assessment? Or, is your perspective one that values an eclectic mix? Does your perspective on assessment draw heavily from the needs of the individual learner? Does your perspective include growth and change, like Wilcox's? Do other teachers and conversation with them influence your perspective? Explain how and why you have adopted the perspectives you have. Then, review your principles and discuss them with your peers. Revise them once again to reflect your viewpoint on reading assessment.

Assessment Conversations

Peter Johnston

In theory, assessment is about gathering and interpreting data to inform action. In practice, data interpretations are constrained by our views of literacy and students, the assessment conversations that surround us, and the range of "actions" we can imagine. When I wrote this column a very capable kindergarten teacher explained to me why she had sent three students to be assessed for learning disabilities. She did so (a) because of pressure from first-grade teachers to retain students who were "not far enough along" and (b) because the administration opposed retention. Another teacher commented, "These children have such language deficits and there's no language in the home." A third teacher wished her faculty "could discuss retention and realistic expectations for grade levels without the nastiness and accusations." These assessment conversations are predictable fallout from a high-stakes testing environment and part of the reason for the International Reading Association's (1999) concerns about such practices. We cannot allow ourselves these conversations any more than we can allow their equivalents in our classrooms. They prevent learning, limit problem solving, and build unproductive relationships and identities.

There are better assessment conversations. First-grade teachers in a local high-poverty urban school asked me to their weekly grade-level meeting to help think through a problem. Each teacher had a group of children who seemed "unable to move from level E books," even though the students' journals indicated they had the necessary print knowledge. The teachers' systematic records and regular Wednesday afternoon (data-based) meetings allowed them to identify the problem. Their conversation assumed that each person was working hard to provide the best instruction for his or her students. This belief allowed them to describe the problem in terms of professional practice and children's progress, rather than student, community, or colleague deficiencies, and to seek collegial support for alternatives. The teachers drew on multiple sources of information and understood the advantage of other sets of eyes for overcoming the limitations of their own assessment lens, inviting one another (and me, an outsider) into their classrooms to seek more solutions.

These assessment strategies, documenting and collaboratively analyzing data, will help them achieve their goals of improving their teaching and reducing achievement differences among groups of students—the primary goals of assessment (International Reading Association & National Council of Teachers of English Joint Task Force on Assessment, 1994). These are also the stated goals of high-stakes testing. However, the tests provide no useful or timely information to help teachers accomplish such goals, and they encourage an interactional climate that can undermine them.

Assessment That Improves Learning

Noticing and recording literate knowledge and practice. Teachers' ability to make productive sense of (and record) children's literate behavior is the central component of assessment. This means, for example, noticing the strategies children use to figure out a word, and their appeals for verification. It means realizing that the appeals indicate they are monitoring their read-

From *The Reading Teacher*, 57(1), 90–92. © 2003 by the International Reading Association.

ing, and that the next step might be helping to integrate multiple cue sources. It means recognizing what a child's *kycke* (cake) indicates about his or her knowledge of phonemic structure (all sounds sequentially, if not conventionally, represented) and orthographic structure (predictable patterns—*ck*, marker *e*). This knowledge informs the moment-to-moment decisions of adaptive teaching—knowing what a child can almost do, can do independently or in collaboration, or understands incompletely. Recognizing these patterns focuses instruction. It also allows us to reflect an image of competence and agency by revealing to learners what they are doing well, and it balances the high-stakes testing central focus on attending to what less capable students are *not* doing well.

Assessment requires uncovering the sense children make of literacy and literacy instruction. For example, a fourth grader once explained to me that a good writer "writes fast" and good readers are "all the kids that are quiet...they just listen...they get chapter books." She said she doesn't converse with other students about their writing because she "wouldn't want to hurt their feelings" or to give them "things that you thought of in your head" because then they'd "probably have the same stories" (Johnston, Jiron, & Day, 2001, p. 226). These conceptions influence her engagement in classroom literate practices. Our goal is to teach children to view themselves as engaged readers and writers and to show them that literacy is more about social action and meaning making than about recognizing and writing words accurately (though it also involves that).

Revealing knowledge and practice. Noticing what children know and can do, and how they understand literacy, is easier when their literate learning is accessible (visible and audible). This means that children need to read and write a lot and to talk about doing so in ways that provide information about their development. We normalize conversations with questions like "What problems are you encountering today?" (assuming all readers and writers do encounter them). This raises the possibility of discussing solution strategies: "How did you solve that problem?" "How else could it be figured out?" "How did you know to do it that way?" Such discussions make children's confusions and strategic thinking accessible, providing evidence of their problem solving and stimulating a sense of literate agency. Collaborative literacy practices also make literate thinking available. When it is normal for children to ask questions of texts and engage one another with ideas about the texts they read and write, their comprehension processes are made accessible in a way they are not with retellings and closed questions.

Analyzing the learning context. To optimize instruction requires assessing the classroom learning environment. When a group of children fails to thrive in a classroom, it is likely that some aspect of instruction is not functioning optimally for those children—perhaps limited book access (physical access, time, difficulty, cultural relevance) or lack of instructional attention to independence-building strategies like cross checking. Frameworks derived from successful instruction can provide helpful assessment lenses (Allington & Johnston, 2002; Lyons, Pinnell, & DeFord, 1993). However, there is always the temptation to ascribe difficulties to limitations in children (e.g., language processing limitations, learning disabilities), particularly when we are under public accountability pressure. While such limitations can exist, there are good reasons to curb such explanations.

First, one-to-one adaptive instruction can generally overcome learning difficulties (Vellutino & Scanlon, 2002). Second, such limitations are too easily confused with cultural differences. Third, merely viewing children through a disability lens can diminish our teaching. For example, Lyons (1991) described a successful Reading Recovery teacher who was unsuccessful with one student. Detailed records of the boy's literate behavior did not help the teacher adapt instruction. She viewed the child as learning disabled and interpreted his data differently from that of other students, so her instructional responses maintained his disabling behaviors. When a colleague drew the discrepancies in interpretation and instructional interaction to her attention, the teacher altered her instruction and accelerated the student's learning.

Assessing a learning context is not easy. First, we run the risk of discovering a glitch in our teaching and feeling the burden of responsibility. Second, the same assumptions that underlie our teaching underlie our assessment, creating blind spots. Sometimes a different set of eyes and ears—a different perspective—is necessary to circumvent the unconscious assumptions we inevitably carry about different kinds of students. Sometimes the eyes might belong to trusted colleagues whose theories or cultural experiences are different. Sometimes video or audiotape provides sufficient distance to align our learning theories with our teaching practice.

Productive Assessment Conversations

Assessment to improve instruction requires active learning communities that sustain productive conversations about teaching and learning that are based on data. As in the classroom, the conversations cannot be about who is more or less competent but about how to make teaching, learning, and interpretations better. Just as we want children to ask questions of texts and engage with one another's ideas about those texts, we want our assessment data to produce these conversations about teaching and learning. As in the classroom, difference in perspective is critical; it produces the disjunctures that reveal what is taken for granted and allows us, in a trusting environment, to view literacy and instructional environments with depth of vision.

Our assessments of children, as we enact them in our classrooms, are part of the intellectual environment into which they will grow (Vygotsky, 1978). Therefore, the features of literate behavior on which we focus, and our interpretations of them, have consequences. We cannot afford assessment conversations that shrink our view of a child's promise and invite unproductive instructional practices and literate identities—or that reduce the richness of the literacy we teach, regardless of the pressures to do so.

References

Allington, R.L., & Johnston, P.H. (Eds.). (2002). *Reading to learn: Lessons from exemplary fourth-grade classrooms.* New York: Guilford.

International Reading Association. (1999). *High-stakes assessments in reading.* Retrieved March 20, 2003, from http://www.reading.org/pdf/high_stakes.pdf

International Reading Association & National Council of Teachers of English Joint Task Force on Assessment. (1994). *Standards for the assessment of reading and writing.* Newark, DE: Author; Urbana, IL: Author.

Johnston, P.H., Jiron, H.W., & Day, J.P. (2001). Teaching and learning literate epistemologies. *Journal of Educational Psychology, 93*(1), 223–233.

Lyons, C.A. (1991). Helping a learning disabled child enter the literate world. In D.E. DeFord, C.A. Lyons, & G.S. Pinnell (Eds.), *Bridges to literacy: Learning from reading recovery* (pp. 205–216). Portsmouth, NH: Heinemann.

Lyons, C.A., Pinnell, G.S., & DeFord, D.E. (1993). *Partners in learning: Teachers and children in Reading Recovery.* New York: Teachers College Press.

Vellutino, F.R., & Scanlon, D.M. (2002). The interactive strategies approach to reading intervention. *Contemporary Educational Psychology, 27,* 573–635.

Vygotsky, L.S. (1978). *Mind in society: The development of higher psychological processes* (M. Cole, V. John-Steiner, S. Scribner, & E. Souberman, Eds. & Trans.). Cambridge, MA: Harvard University Press. (Original work published 1934)

Reconciling Polarity: Toward a Responsive Model of Evaluating Literacy Performance

Kathleen A. Hinchman and Pamela A. Michel

> Reading is looking for the little words in the big words, and knowing enough words. Hey, you know I'm the third worst reader in my class. I know, because the other kids read books with more pages in them than I do.
> —Jason, age 8

Oral reading samples tell us that Jason can read simple books, sounding out one word at a time. His writing includes predictable, complete sentences with spelling that approaches phonetic appropriateness but that suggests confusion of some vowel sounds. School records indicate a history of ear infections and some difficulty with expressing himself orally. He is among the youngest of the third graders in his school. His parents did not graduate from high school, but they desperately want more education for Jason, and they are dismayed at his difficulties in learning to read and write.

Why is all this information helpful to us as literacy specialists? We believe that Jason's words are central to understanding his literacy learning and can help us to contextualize other observations. His words tell us that he is actively pursuing an understanding of reading and writing. He is developing a strategy for recognizing common syllable types within longer words, and he wants to know more sight words to help his reading fluency. His statement about his status suggests that he understands that reading is important in our culture, that he is valued in a certain way because of his lack of reading skill, and that it will be a problem if he does not learn to read very well. His words reflect the inferences he has been able to construct from available data, and his reading and writing efforts are additional signs of these insights. He does not know that he is enacting behaviors that are, unfortunately, somewhat expected, considering his age, medical background, gender, and parents' education backgrounds, although his parents' concern suggests that they have some understanding that he is fighting an uphill battle.

Instruction most suited to helping Jason would likely focus on enhancing his developing insights so that he can begin to see reading as a fluid, communicative process. Helpful teaching will also show him differences among vowels, tied to actual reading, so that meaning making is emphasized. We have some instructional ideas that may help Jason add to what he knows, but we will not be certain of their utility until we teach them and ask him how they are working. We then can refine instruction as we develop a relationship with him that is anchored in his point of view.

In this article we share a model of evaluating literacy that places students' understandings, like Jason's, in the foreground of assessment and instructional decision making. However, we argue against "throwing out the baby with the bath water"; that is, eliminating all the inferences that might be drawn from considering elements of the now widely criticized causal model of reading diagnosis. Instead, we argue for informing our interpretations of literacy learners' enact-

From *The Reading Teacher*, *52*(6), 578–587.

ments with a variety of data representing various perspectives and for interpreting these data critically, from the students' points of view. We propose testing our hypothetical explanations by teaching and asking students what they think—and then by carefully and respectfully listening to what they have to say.

Moving Away From the Causal Model

As teachers of literacy education courses at two institutions, we have tried to develop ways to help our specialists-in-training to organize their assessment and instructional decision making. Like that of many long-practicing specialists, our own training focused on the causal or "medical" models of diagnosis and remediation; we studied the large number of traits that have been thought to be significantly correlated with reading disability (Johnston & Allington, 1991). We learned to follow a cycle of determining reading status, contributing factors, and ways to establish learning (D. Sawyer, personal communication, July 1, 1978). The premise was that knowledge of the causes of reading disability should dictate treatment (Harris & Sipay, 1990).

To determine reading status, we used various tools, including informal reading inventories, norm-referenced reading tests, informal assessments of a variety of subskills, interest inventories, and observation. We qualified reports of reading level with qualitative analyses of reading behaviors. We tested for the possible presence of any of the correlates of reading disability (Harris & Sipay, 1990; McCormick, 1987). These included physical development, cognitive development, language development, social/emotional development, and educational background.

As Harris (1977) suggested, instructional recommendations within this paradigm were based on what the child could and could not do, working with or around the possible causes of initial failure. We acknowledged that our business was one of best guesses, to be validated within the context of ongoing diagnostic teaching and reflection (Lipson & Wixson, 1996). Our work was successful when our tentative conclusions allowed students to move forward or when they led us to new, refined guesses. Our experiences in elementary, secondary, adult, and clinical settings helped us to develop depth and range to our insights.

But defining instruction in terms of assessment can be risky. Many have recommended alternative models of assessment, generated from different epistemologies and resulting in more effective practices (Garcia & Pearson, 1994; Glaser & Silver, 1994; Wolf, Bixby, Glenn, & Gardner, 1991). We especially have found ourselves agreeing with the criticisms that suggested that such models of diagnosis were too easily interpreted in simplistic ways (Johns, 1992; Roller, 1996; Spear-Swerling & Sternberg, 1996). Our own experiences in schools confirmed the reports we read of the failure of such causal models within the contexts of school-based remedial programs (Johnston, 1992; Walmsley & Allington, 1995). Lipson and Wixson (1996) explained that students could be reduced to the sum of identifiable factors in a way that seemed to blame them for their lack of reading success and set them up for ongoing failure: "Poor John has an IQ of 70, so his outlook is limited as a reader," or "Mary's parents didn't read to her, and that's why she hasn't learned to read." Once teachers constructed such expectations, resulting instruction was not likely to have much impact (Allington & Li, 1990; McGill-Franzen, 1994; McGill-Franzen & James, 1990).

Making Sense of Students' Perspectives

Many researchers have looked at children's explanations for their reading. Early work in this area was most important because it recognized and valued children's perceptions of and actions related to reading. However, this work, like most work of its time, also assumed a causal model of reading. It judged children's responses according to researchers' notions of proficient reading, using structured questions to elicit responses that causality?

highlighted deficits in relation to these notions. As a result, it was suggested that children were confused about the purposes and nature of reading (Denny & Weintraub, 1963, 1966; Downing, 1969, 1970; Johns, 1972; Johns & Ellis, 1976; Oliver, 1975; Reid, 1966).

More recently, researchers have used alternative theoretical frameworks and methodologies to build on early insights regarding the importance of children's perceptions. These later studies added the collection of richer and more varied data, but interpretations of children's words began, instead, with the child's perspective. Children were represented in this more child-centered view as being able to describe components of reading in sophisticated ways that have meaning for them (Dahlgren & Olsson, 1986; Harste, Woodward, & Burke, 1984; Swanson, 1985). Our own research has found that many important insights are held by even the youngest participants in literacy instruction settings (e.g., Hinchman, 1998; Michel, 1994).

Age-specific experience with students' insights helps teachers hear and know how to respond to what students know. Such context-specific expertise is at the core of successful literacy intervention programs (e.g., Clay, 1993; Wasik & Slavin, 1993). However, most literacy specialists, including those with whom we work, are trained and certified for K–12 settings. They need approaches that allow them to make sense of many different types of literacy learners who come from backgrounds other than their own. As a result, and in keeping with recommendations for child centeredness, we encouraged our specialists-in-training to consider data that represented multiple, varied snapshots of students' literacy performance and insights. Such data included interviews, oral reading samples, classroom observations, retellings, responses to literature, and writing samples (Gillet & Temple, 1994; Roskos & Walker, 1993; Taylor, 1994). We encouraged them to organize their "kidwatching" (Goodman, 1985) through interactive portfolio construction (Tierney, Carter, & Desai, 1991). We asked them to consider the meanings of literacy that seemed most important from the children's varied social perspectives, especially those tied to such issues as gender, class, and ethnic background (Heath, 1983).

As we helped new literacy specialists to implement these techniques, we realized that they had difficulty orchestrating their work efficiently and effectively. At the same time, we heard them admiring the clarity with which we could talk to children and find instructional implications in their words. They were skeptical that they would ever be able to do the same, despite their in-depth study of methods, materials, and assessment. Their dismay led us to realize that we used our knowledge of the causal model as we carried on our own kidwatching. Yet many of them seemed to believe that if they chose to enact a child-centered pedagogy, they had to reject references to causality.

When we spoke with the most successful kidwatchers we knew, they too reported tacit reference to their previous training. Asking ourselves questions about the children's previous experiences helped us to know something about what to do next. The causal model helped in organizing our thinking, even as we talked the talk of child centeredness. We wanted to find a way to share our resolution of these perspectives with our students, and we came up with an alternative framework to do so.

An Alternative Framework

We think that insights regarding possible causality can be helpful when they are considered critically, in light of literacy learners' own explanations. To share this insight with other reading specialists, we developed a framework for organizing ongoing assessment and instruction, derived from Sawyer's causal model heuristic (personal communication, July 1, 1978), but grounded, instead, in an epistemology that is more concerned with interpretations of individuals' actions in social settings. Our model moves the literacy learner's point of view to the center of a critical analysis of all available data:

1. Collect the student's constructions, but from a variety of perspectives representing all that we can of the child's world;

2. Interpret the student's constructions, with a variety of perspectives in mind but grounded in the student's point of view; and
3. Mediate the student's constructions, while listening carefully for the student's ongoing interpretation of this mediation.

By using the term *constructions*, we mean to align our understanding of literacy learning with those, like Johnston (1992), who explained, "We make and order our knowledge of the world with language, and we do so in interaction with others. We each construct our versions of the world and live within these realities" (p. 6).

The understanding that communicative competence is derived from our participation in the social world is often referred to as social constructivism. This perspective suggests that readers' active construction of understandings of what and how they read is woven throughout with fibers of their social lives (Flippo, 1997; Spivey, 1997; Vygotsky, 1962). This notion is tied to the belief, common to interpretive qualitative research, that we constitute our social selves through our talk and actions (Schwandt, 1994). This view holds that we can better interpret others' perspectives by collecting varied, rich data from their day-to-day lives. Thus, we value children's expressions of their constructions while, at the same time, we recognize that these expressions represent only a part of their understanding. Moreover, we own responsibility for our interpretations of these data, and we realize that we have to check our inferences against ongoing observations and interactions.

Within our framework, we use many strategies to *collect* children's constructions and a sense of their worlds. One strategy involves systematic observation of students engaged in reading and writing in a variety of contexts. Another involves collecting artifacts of these actions, such as students' written stories, lists of books read, and names of favorite authors. Still another way to explore literacy learners' understandings is by inviting parents to collaborate, sharing insights of children's home reading and writing. We also collect the variety of school reports that might be available, including report cards, teacher anecdotes, and psychological testing. Most important, we ask children what they understand about their reading and writing through use of "listening questions" (Michel, 1994). These questions are nondirective and ongoing, with more listening than talking, and with children knowing that they can share insights that are important to them.

To *interpret* children's constructions, we consider what students say and do in light of what we know of their histories. We attend to traditional correlates of disability. At the same time, our concern for the individuals' perspectives calls our attention to the ways they may be enacting their gender-, ethnicity-, and class-related expectations. We ask what data are available to children, and by what means they have been interpreted. What cognitive and language processes are suggested by school reports, and how are these viewed by students and those who interact with them? What is the impact of any visual, auditory, or other physical difficulties? What instruction has been used to date, and how has it been perceived? What supports are offered by family literacy, and how do families perceive their children's needs? How do children perceive their own literacy histories, as well as the things others say about them?

To *mediate* children's constructions, we consider how to act on what we hear the children say to represent their perspectives. We then orchestrate activities to help them build on the data that we think they have available to them. We recognize and value their constructions as inferences that will be central to their development of more effective insights, at least with regard to written language literacy. We assume that they share our culture's desire for access to the literate world, but we try to be sensitive to the complicated ways this desire works for those of varying backgrounds. We try, too, to attend to our own sociocultural politics. That is, we try to attend to and disrupt our own tendencies to be most "successful" in our relations with children who are most like us (Dressman, 1997).

For validation, we turn to the children themselves, revising our guesses as the result of instruction and listening. We suggest that they develop strategies to put themselves in control of their development, recognizing and resisting the socially constructed expectations that narrow their choices. We see our work as an ongoing effort rather than as a simple cause-and-effect sequence, as many have previously interpreted the diagnostic–prescriptive model.

Our students have told us that they appreciate being able to organize their data collection and analysis in a way that encourages the consideration of multiple perspectives. This model allows them to collaborate with a variety of professional educators because they know how to listen, learn, and be critical of all the data that may be shared about a particular child. Although each child's story is a different one, the model gives us and our students a predictable place to start each new instructional journey toward responsive, child-centered literacy instruction.

Case Study: Chanise

We share the story of Chanise as an example of the way our alternative framework was applied to the tutoring of one child. Chanise came to tutoring as a 7-year-old girl who was entering second grade and reportedly having great difficulty in learning how to read.

Collecting Chanise's constructions. Chanise's tutor began their sessions by "casting a wide net" (Clay, 1993). She created an early lesson framework that was meant to involve Chanise in some reading and writing each day, engaging her in several print-related transactions and chances for conversation. This was meant to give her tutor a sense for what Chanise understood and could do as they had a chance to get to know each other.

Early in tutoring, Chanise was invited to listen to and talk about stories that she chose from a small collection of tutor-selected picture books. She was also invited to choose texts for shared reading with her tutor, initially from the most basic level of predictable books, and to start a dialogue journal with her tutor. She was asked to dictate language-experience stories into a tape recorder. These were typed and printed by her tutor for later reading. Finally, she was invited to participate in daily, multilevel themed inquiry with the other children who were enrolled in the tutoring program.

Chanise presented herself to us as an energetic and quick-thinking child. She engaged easily in general conversation, talking with her tutor about her day or her adventures with her mother, sister, and cousins. She enjoyed listening to stories, and she talked about them enthusiastically. After listening to one story, Chanise exclaimed, "That's a good book! Can we read that again?" She looked forward to attending group instruction, even though she rarely spoke to any of the adults or tutors who were present during these sessions. She especially enjoyed hands-on enactments of themes, such as the time when all the children were invited to help make ice cream.

When she was asked about her preferences, Chanise looked up at her tutor and said, "I like reading the stories where the words rhyme." She pointed to the predictable text that she had just reviewed and asked, "Can I take that home?" despite the fact that she was memorizing the words and not reading them conventionally. She was unable to listen to individual words and isolate the sound segments that made up these words. Chanise avoided answering those questions specifically related to reading or writing. She kept her backpack on, ready to leave, for the first 3 weeks of the program, saying "I don't want to do that work" whenever she was directly confronted with requests to engage in print-driven tasks.

Once Chanise resisted a task, she was firm in her resolve. She especially resisted any activity that involved particular letter–sound or word recognition, instead playing with magnetic letters during lessons designed to teach her to build words and explaining that such work was "too hard" or "dumb." She would say the names of most letters, confusing those that were visually similar. She would not write. When asked to write by her encouraging tutor, she often responded, "No way. Not today."

We also observed that in conversation Chanise often confused labels for objects that were somehow similar. For example, she called a vase a "lamp." She sometimes even invented words, calling an animal doctor a "pet-eranarian."

Chanise came to our program with thoroughly completed guardian information sheets. She lived in a local medium-sized city with her mother and a much-older sister who was also reported to have had difficulty learning to read. Her mother noted that Chanise had 12 ear infections by her first birthday, that she was diagnosed as asthmatic when she was 2-1/2 years old, and that she continued to have frequent colds and headaches.

Chanise began kindergarten at an urban public school but was transferred to a parochial school for most of kindergarten and half of first grade. She was withdrawn from this school when her mother was laid off from work. She then moved to another urban, public, multiaged, continuous progress classroom for the rest of first grade.

Chanise's mother brought us teacher reports, report cards, and standardized test scores. Chanise's initial literacy instruction reportedly had focused on sounding out words for word recognition. Her work in the new school was reported to have been anchored in the use of a literature-based literacy series and cooperative learning activities.

Her teacher in this last classroom reported that Chanise had difficulty working with the other children on literacy activities, disrupting others' work when she was not confident of being able to complete assigned tasks. Chanise reported to her mother that she could not concentrate in the new classroom. She asked to go back to kindergarten instead of on to second grade at the end of the school year.

Interpreting Chanise's constructions. From our efforts to collect Chanise's own insights, we knew that she knew much that would help her reading and writing development, despite her reluctance to share many specifics with us. She knew that she was not proficient at either reading or writing. On one occasion when asked to read, Chanise said, "I'm not really a good reader 'cause I can't read much stuff. I can't write the words either. It's hard when you don't know the words."

She was not yet easily matching voice to print, although her knowledge of letter names and willingness to rhyme suggested some phonological awareness. Her initial suspicions of her tutor and of our intent suggested that she was also not comfortable or confident that anyone was going to help her figure out how to do so. However, she was confident in her sense of story and in her sense of knowing what teachers do and why they do it, a knowledge that gave her the upper hand in early struggles with her tutor for control of the tutoring session. When Chanise was introduced to her tutor the first day, she turned to the person doing the introductions and said, "I'm not reading to her. I don't need her to help me read."

Chanise told us in direct and indirect ways that she was uncomfortable with tasks that were too difficult for her. When asked to read a poem, she said, "That's not a real book. I hate that story. It makes no sense. I'm tired," and she put her head down. We thought about what she told us in light of our knowledge of factors thought to contribute to written language acquisition. As a result, we realized that developing precision in the decoding of specific words could be a slow process for Chanise. It would need to be mediated with a focus on her strengths at remembering stories and attending to inflection in others' reading of stories. Her apparent difficulties with retrieving specific words from memory, evidenced in both our observations and school reports, may have complicated her ability to generalize understandings of letter–sound correspondence and her memory for sight words.

Chanise may also have been slow to warm up to the practicum setting for other reasons: She was a person of color entering a setting where most of the other children and all of the adults were white. Chanise may also have been slow to warm up because her frequent school transfers made her uncomfortable in school-like settings. These transfers are also likely to have contributed to inconsistency in instruction, augmented by her own confession that the last school had been particularly difficult to get used to. When describing her school, Chanise said, "I didn't learn anything there. None of the teachers thought I read good."

We understood that Chanise felt relatively powerless and frustrated, and we worried that her potent resistance would result in ongoing school failure. One day she hopelessly said, "I'm never going to learn to read. My sister couldn't read either." We felt that our first goal was to negotiate a situation where Chanise could achieve more success with regard to goals she shared with the adults who were important to her.

Mediating Chanise's constructions. If her tutor had built an instructional program that responded directly to information gleaned from school reports and observations without concern for Chanise's perspective, it may have resulted in instruction that represented a highly structured, explicit phonological awareness training with extra memory supports for her processing difficulties. On the other hand, if her tutor had built a program directly from Chanise's quite verbal general expressiveness, without considering the evidence suggesting difficulties with visual and auditory processing and expressive language, we might have expected Chanise to develop letter–sound insights with the same instruction and at the same rate as her peers. Instead, Chanise's words combined with our critical concern for others' reports provided us with insights that helped us to design a plan that could be further refined during teaching.

Given both the apparent and the possible in her perspective, her tutor designed instruction that was grounded in Chanise's sense of story. At first, her tutor was only able to elicit some participation in focused instructional activities with extrinsic rewards (e.g., systematic rewarding of tokens and points). After this initial somewhat strenuous negotiation for a tutoring space that both Chanise and her tutor found productive, Chanise was increasingly willing to "read" memorized language experience stories and leveled predictable books, and eventually the tokens were dropped. She and her tutor talked often about text selection, with Chanise favoring picture books with female main characters. She also really enjoyed listening to chapter books about African American characters.

Her tutor made certain that texts available to Chanise were easy enough for her to read with roughly 95% accuracy. Sometimes Chanise would attempt to read the texts independently, while at other times she insisted that the tutor read even often-read texts again to her so that she could "get the hang of it." She continued to recite the text without actually looking at the words, imitating well the language patterns and inflections of her tutor's voice. Sometimes she embellished the stories, making them more elaborate, saying, "I just made that up," with a giggle. She frequently referred to previously read stories or talked about characters and actions in connection with her own life as she made predictions regarding the contents of new texts. She also referred to her reading of particular words in previously read texts as she encountered these words in new texts.

Her enthusiasm propelled her to keep trying to read despite her difficulties with using letter–sound knowledge to determine unknown words, and her tutor encouraged her to continue to build on this strength. She loved to rhyme words, creating her own verses to match texts or for jumping rope. She would then use these word patterns to practice initial consonant substitution with magnetic letters. From this start, her tutor worked to develop more specific phonological awareness through practice in manipulating initial consonants and ending vowel–consonant patterns and in segmenting simple three-letter words (e.g., Ball & Blachman, 1991). Her tutor also pointed out other high-frequency words encountered in reading and writing, and she helped Chanise to build a word bank to help her review these words.

Although Chanise would dictate stories, eliciting writing remained a problem throughout the summer. However, her tutor discovered that Chanise would slowly type words she knew on a word processor if the tutor promised to run the spell checker quickly after the words were typed. The tutor used this strategy as a way to gain additional insights into Chanise's letter–sound knowledge. Her inventive spelling suggested good phonetic use of initial consonants and white space to mark word boundaries but mostly guesses with the middles and endings of words. The tutor ended up helping the spell checker, which couldn't identify these words, so that she could continue to gather Chanise's spelling samples.

By the end of a summer of daily tutoring, and after evolving efforts to interpret and mediate Chanise's constructions, Chanise's clinic portfolio consisted of writing samples, dictated stories, lists of books read and words learned, rhyming word and matching phrase games, dictated story retellings, interest inventories, and dictated reflections about tutoring sessions and progress made. Other important artifacts included running records and accompanying miscue analyses and anecdotal records of observations and instructional transactions. Chanise continued to have difficulty reading, yet she seemed to grow to enjoy coming to the program, and she grew in her ability to mimic the proficient reading of texts.

Chanise was an energetic girl who had some understandings that were necessary for beginning reading. She looked for herself in texts, and she seemed to appreciate instruction that allowed her to build on her sense of story. Within such contexts, she would engage in the kind of language manipulation that many have associated with emergent literacy. Her tutor tried to create an instructional setting that invited Chanise to be comfortable with her constructions and her competencies, and this made both of them more confident that the time they spent was worthwhile and productive.

Chanise completed second grade successfully with instructional supports commensurate with a learning disability in reading and written expression. The school's psychological evaluation suggested that Chanise had an average to high average IQ and both auditory and visual perceptual difficulties, as well as difficulties with expressive language. Teachers collaborated with Chanise's mother in implementing our clinic instructional recommendations. She continued to receive these supports and to attend the summer reading clinic for several years.

When last we received school reports, Chanise was reading materials appropriate for her grade level, although her reading lacked the fluency typical for her grade. She also continued to have some difficulty producing well-edited compositions, but she was becoming adept at composing on the computer and using the text editing features of a word processing program.

Conclusion

As teacher educators and as reading specialists, we knew that we benefited from our understandings of traditional diagnostic models as well as from insights derived from more current perspectives, and we wanted to share both ways of thinking with our students; we know that we are far from the first educators to propose using a variety of measures to assess literacy behaviors. However, many of our students came to us believing that if they chose to enact a child-centered pedagogy, they, in turn, had to reject references to causality. Our enthusiasm for children's perspectives, our understandings of causality, and our appreciation for social context helped us to develop this alternative framework that is grounded in a sense of literacy learners' construction of meaning but that does not ignore any available data.

Our framework complicates the notion that teaching should be derived from the application of generalized principles of literacy acquisition. Instead, it situates teaching as a collective social act, a conversation taking place within the context of a responsive relationship (Davis & Sumara, 1997; Phelan, 1997). We have found that repositioning our work in a less polarized fashion helps us to better organize our assessment and instruction. Our model has made it easier for us and our students to listen to children with a more critical ear that values what they have to say. We invite others who struggle with reconciling the differing positions in our field to consider our approach.

References

Allington, R., & Li, S. (1990, December). *Teacher beliefs about children who find learning to read difficult*. Paper presented at the annual meeting of the National Reading Conference, Miami, FL.

Ball, E., & Blachman, B. (1991). Does phoneme segmentation training in kindergarten make a difference in early word recognition and developmental spelling? *Reading Research Quarterly, 26*, 49–66.

Clay, M.M. (1993). *Reading Recovery: A guidebook for teachers in training*. Portsmouth, NH: Heinemann.

Dahlgren, G., & Olsson, L. (1986, April). *The child's conception of reading*. Paper presented at the annual meeting of the American Educational Research Association, San Francisco. (ERIC Document Reproduction Service No. ED 268 497)

Davis, B., & Sumara, D.J. (1997). Cognition, complexity, and teacher education. *Harvard Educational Review, 67*, 105–125.

Denny, T.P., & Weintraub, S. (1963). Exploring first graders' concepts of reading. *The Reading Teacher, 16*, 363–365.

Denny, T.P., & Weintraub, S. (1966). First graders' responses to three questions about reading. *The Elementary School Journal, 66*, 441–448.

Downing, J. (1969). How children think about reading. *The Reading Teacher, 23*, 217–230.

Downing, J. (1970). Children's concepts of language in learning to read. *Educational Research, 12*, 101–112.

Dressman, M. (1997). Preference as performance: Doing social class and gender in three school libraries. *Journal of Literacy Research, 29*, 319–362.

Flippo, R.F. (1997). *Reading assessment and instruction: A qualitative approach to diagnosis*. Fort Worth, TX: Harcourt Brace.

Garcia, G., & Pearson, P.D. (1994). Assessment and diversity. In L. Darling-Hammond (Ed.), *Review of educational research* (Vol. 20, pp. 337-391). Washington, DC: American Educational Research Association.

Gillet, J.W., & Temple, C.A. (1994). *Understanding reading problems: Assessment and instruction* (4th ed.). New York: Addison-Wesley.

Glaser, R., & Silver, E. (1994). Assessment, testing, and instruction: Retrospect and prospect. In L. Darling-Hammond (Ed.), *Review of educational research* (Vol. 20, pp. 393–419). Washington, DC: American Educational Research Association.

Goodman, Y. (1985). Kidwatching: Observing children in the classroom. In A. Jaggar & M.T. Smith-Burke (Eds.), *Observing the language learner* (pp. 9-18). Newark, DE: International Reading Association.

Harris, A.J. (1977). The reading teacher as a diagnostician. In E.A. Earle (Ed.), *Classroom practice in reading* (pp. 21-26). Newark, DE: International Reading Association.

Harris, A.J., & Sipay, E.R. (1990). *How to increase reading ability* (9th ed.). New York: Longman.

Harste, J., Woodward, V.A., & Burke, C. (1984). *Language stories and literacy lessons*. Portsmouth, NH: Heinemann.

Heath, S.B. (1983). *Ways with words: Language, life and work in communities and classrooms*. Cambridge, England: Cambridge University Press.

Hinchman, K.A. (1998). Reconstructing our understandings of adolescents' participation in classroom literacy events: Learning to look through other eyes. In D. Alvermann, K. Hinchman, S. Phelps, & D. Waff (Eds.), *Reconceptualizing the literacies in adolescents' lives* (pp. 173–192). Mahwah, NJ: Erlbaum.

Johns, J. (1972). Children's concepts of reading and their reading achievement. *Journal of Reading Behavior, 4*, 56–57.

Johns, J. (1992). *From traditional reading clinics to wellness centers* (Literacy Research Report No. 16). DeKalb, IL: Northern Illinois University.

Johns, J., & Ellis, D. (1976). Reading: Children tell it like it is. *Reading World, 16*, 115–128.

Johnston, P.H. (1992). *Constructive evaluation of literate activity*. New York: Longman.

Johnston, P.H., & Allington, R.L. (1991). Remediation. In R. Barr, M.L. Kamil, P.B. Mosenthal, & P.D. Pearson (Eds.), *Handbook of reading research* (Vol. II, pp. 984–1012). New York: Longman.

Lipson, M.Y., & Wixson, K.K. (1996). *Assessment and instruction of reading and writing disability: An interactive approach* (2nd ed.). New York: Scott, Foresman.

McCormick, S. (1987). *Remedial and clinical reading instruction*. Columbus, OH: Merrill.

McGill-Franzen, A. (1994). Compensatory and special education: Is there accountability for learning and belief in children's potential? In E.H. Hiebert & B.M. Taylor (Eds.), *Getting reading right from the start: Effective early literacy interventions* (pp. 13–35). Boston: Allyn & Bacon.

McGill-Franzen, A., & James, I. (1990, December). *Teacher beliefs about remedial and learning disabled readers*. Paper presented at the annual meeting of the National Reading Conference, Miami, FL.

Michel, P. (1994). *The child's view of reading: Understandings for teachers and parents.* Boston: Allyn & Bacon.

Oliver, M.E. (1975). The development of language concepts of preprimary Indian children. *Language Arts, 52,* 865–869.

Phelan, A. (1997). When the mirror cracked: The discourse of reflection in pre-service teacher education. In K. Watson (Ed.), *Dilemmas in teaching and teacher education* (pp. 169–178). London: Cassell.

Reid, J.F. (1966). Learning to think about reading. *Educational Research, 9,* 56–62.

Roller, C. (1996). *Variability not disability: Struggling readers in a workshop classroom.* Newark, DE: International Reading Association.

Roskos, K., & Walker, B. (1993). *Interactive handbook for understanding reading diagnosis: A problem-solving approach using case studies.* Columbus, OH: Merrill.

Schwandt, T.A. (1994). Constructivist, interpretivist approaches to human inquiry. In N. Denzin & Y. Lincoln (Ed.), *Handbook of qualitative research* (pp. 118–137). Thousand Oaks, CA: Sage.

Spear-Swerling, L., & Sternberg, R.J. (1996). *Off track: When poor readers become learning disabled.* Denver, CO: Westview Press.

Spivey, N. (1997). *The constructivist metaphor: Reading, writing, and the making of meaning.* New York: Academic Press.

Swanson, B.B. (1985). Listening to students about reading. *Reading Horizons, 22,* 123–128.

Taylor, D. (1994). *From a child's point of view.* Portsmouth, NH: Heinemann.

Tierney, R.J., Carter, M.A., & Desai, L.E. (1991). *Portfolio assessment in the reading-writing classroom.* Norwood, MA: Christopher-Gordon.

Vygotsky, L.S. (1962). *Thought and language.* Cambridge, MA: MIT Press.

Walmsley, S.A., & Allington, R.L. (1995). Redefining and refining instructional support programs for at-risk students. In R.L. Allington & S.A. Walmsley (Eds.), *No quick fix: Re-thinking literacy programs in America's elementary schools* (pp. 19–44). New York: Teachers College Press.

Wasik, B.A., & Slavin, R.E. (1993). Preventing early reading failure with one-to-one tutoring: A review of five programs. *Reading Research Quarterly, 28,* 179–200.

Wolf, D., Bixby, J., Glenn, J., & Gardner, H. (1991). To use their minds well: Investigating new forms of student assessment. In G. Grant (Ed.), *Review of educational research* (Vol. 17, pp. 31–75). Washington, DC: American Educational Research Association.

Three Paradigms of Assessment: Measurement, Procedure, and Inquiry

Frank Serafini

Different assessment frameworks have different intended audiences, are used for different purposes and use different procedures to collect information (Farr,1992). However, these are not the only differences. Each of these assessments may also involve different beliefs about the nature of knowledge, the level of teacher and student involvement, the criteria for evaluating student achievement, and the effects of these assessment frameworks on classroom instruction (Garcia & Pearson, 1994).

The differences between standardized, norm-referenced testing programs and classroom-based assessments have been written about extensively (Neill, 1993). However, as one begins to investigate the various assessment frameworks contained in the professional literature, the distinguishing features of these assessment frameworks, commonly referred to as performance-based, authentic, or classroom-based assessment, tend to overlap and blend.

Various assessment frameworks use similar procedures and data collection methodologies, and many of these "alternative" assessments do not adhere to traditional criteria of standardization, reliability, and objectivity (Linn, Baker, & Dunbar, 1991). This article is intended to help teachers and other concerned educators by providing a broader perspective concerning assessment frameworks or "paradigms" and how these assessments affect classroom practice.

Short and Burke (1994b) described three paradigms of curriculum. They suggested that curriculum could be viewed as Fact, as Activity and as Inquiry. In this description, curriculum as Fact refers to knowledge as a commodity that is "transferable" and exists separately from the "knower," whereas curriculum as Activity is concerned with the actual activities within the classroom, and curriculum as Inquiry is concerned with the process of creating knowledge in the classroom. As teachers begin to move from a teacher-directed curriculum, based on the transmission of "facts," to a student-centered curriculum, based on inquiry processes, the purposes of assessment and the methods used to collect information may need to be revisited.

In reference to Short and Burke's work, Heald-Taylor subsequently developed three paradigms for literature instruction (1996) and three paradigms for spelling instruction (1998). Heald-Taylor used Short and Burke's curricular paradigms to analyze literature and spelling instruction to help teachers understand their own perspectives, or paradigms, concerning literacy development and classroom practices. This article will look at the distinctions between these three paradigms and use the structure suggested by Short and Burke to shed light on the differences between the various assessment frameworks that operate in schools today.

Short and Burke originally developed these three paradigms to distinguish between the traditional models of curriculum development and an inquiry model. The traditional model, curriculum as Fact, is based on modernist or positivist perspectives of reality and epistemology (Elkind, 1997). From this perspective, knowledge is viewed as an objective commodity that can be transmitted from teacher to student and subsequently measured through standardized forms of assessment (Bertrand, 1991).

From *The Reading Teacher*, 54(4), 384–393. © 2000 by the International Reading Association.

In comparison, from a constructivist perspective—curriculum as Inquiry—knowledge is viewed as socially and cognitively constructed by humans as they interact with their environment (Fosnot, 1996). Knowledge is viewed as a construction and not a commodity that exists separately from the "knower." It is this shift from a positivist perspective to a constructivist perspective that underlies the differences in the assessment paradigms to be described in this article.

The curricular paradigms described by Short and Burke are purported to represent different philosophical views of reality, knowledge, and learning (Short & Burke, 1994a). However, in describing the differences between the three paradigms in assessment, one must also look at the level of student and teacher involvement, the methods used to gather information, the purposes or goals of the assessment framework, and the intended audiences for the results. Paralleling the structure used by Short and Burke, the three paradigms of assessment are entitled (a) assessment as measurement, (b) assessment as procedure, and (c) assessment as inquiry.

In this article, I will describe how the three assessment paradigms are similar and how they are different, using various writing assessments—specifically writing portfolios—to help distinguish between the different paradigms. Next, I will present several factors that I believe support teachers making a "paradigm shift" from assessment as measurement to assessment as inquiry. Finally, I will explain several pedagogical suggestions that teachers in transition are using to change their perspectives on assessment.

Assessment as Measurement

The first paradigm is assessment as measurement. As mentioned previously, this paradigm is closely associated with a positivist or modernist view of reality and knowledge. The primary instrument of this paradigm is the large-scale, norm-referenced standardized test. These standardized tests are designed to objectively measure the amount of knowledge that a student has acquired over a given time (Wineberg, 1997). A major concern for classroom teachers is whether these assessments provide the necessary information required to make day-to-day instructional and curricular decisions (Johnston, 1992).

In the assessment as measurement paradigm, knowledge is believed to exist separately from the learner, and students work to acquire it, not construct it. The student is seen as an empty vessel, a "blank slate," ready to be filled up with knowledge. Learning is viewed as the transmission of knowledge from teacher to student while meaning is believed to reside within the text, and only one interpretation or judgment is accepted in the standardized tests (Short & Burke, 1994b).

In this paradigm, objectivity, standardization, and reliability take priority over concerns of teacher and student involvement. In these tests, the role of the classroom teacher is scripted, scoring is done by computer, and the tests are kept secured to ensure fairness. The student's primary role in these standardized testing programs is that of test taker. In other words, there is little opportunity for self-evaluation or student reflection. The test is given and a score is tabulated. In this externally mandated form of assessment, classroom teachers have little or no input to the decision-making process and relatively little use for the results of these assessments in directing classroom and curricular decisions (Rothman, 1996).

Primarily, standardized tests are designed to compare large-scale educational programs and to provide accountability to public stakeholders (Murphy, 1997). These tests are used by school districts, state or provincial education departments, and other external stakeholders to rank and compare schools and children (Meier, 1994). Because of the high-stakes agenda associated with these standardized tests, such as funding decisions and school appropriations, they may become highly competitive (Kaufhold, 1995). These tests were not designed to support classroom instruction; rather, they were designed for large-scale educational and program evaluation (Taylor & Walton, 1997).

In the assessment as measurement paradigm, decisions about the information to be collected, and the means of evaluating this information, are usually determined by authorities outside the classroom. For example, writing ability is measured on standardized tests by means of multiple choice questions that focus primarily on issues of grammar, word choice, and spelling. The test items are designed to measure the amount of "writing knowledge" students have accumulated over their school experiences. These tests are also concerned with what a child has not learned or understood. In this way, standardized tests are concerned with deficits of knowledge as well as accumulations.

In this paradigm, portfolios or collections of authentic writing samples are not generally used to evaluate students' writing abilities. In fact, rarely will an actual example of student writing even be evaluated in a standardized testing program.

Assessment as Procedure

The assessment as procedure paradigm has elements of the assessment as measurement paradigm as well as the assessment as inquiry paradigm. In this paradigm, the primary focus is on the assessment procedures, not on the underlying purposes of the assessment program or the epistemological stance. Epistemologically, this paradigm is closely related to the assessment as measurement paradigm. Knowledge is still believed to exist independently from the learner; this knowledge can be transmitted to the student and eventually objectively measured.

The main difference between this paradigm and the assessment as measurement paradigm is that the procedures have changed to resemble qualitative data collection methods. However, even though the methods have changed, the underlying beliefs that student achievement can be objectively measured and that knowledge exists independently from the learner have not. In this way this paradigm has elements of the measurement and the inquiry paradigms.

Daly, a social philosopher, referred to a focus on procedures as "methodolatry" (as cited in Noddings, 1992). She described methodolatry as an overemphasis on the correct method of doing things, rather than a focus on the purposes for doing those things. This definition of methodolatry captures the essence of this paradigm very well. The assessment as procedure paradigm is primarily concerned with different methods for collecting data rather than new purposes or audiences for collecting this information.

In this paradigm, like the assessment as measurement paradigm, teachers and students are not directly involved in making decisions concerning the assessment procedures or the purposes for these assessments. The primary concern is with reporting information, albeit information gathered by new methods, to external stakeholders and not with directing classroom instruction (Cizek, 1998).

In Arizona, for example, many portfolio assessment projects were initiated by school district administrations in response to the state-mandated Arizona Student Assessment Program (ASAP). In response to the ASAP, many teachers were directed by their districts to keep portfolios of children's work as part of the state writing assessment. They were required to use a "generic rubric" to score each piece of writing in the student's portfolio and submit a final writing score for each student. This portfolio score would be in lieu of the ASAP performance-based test score. Teachers simply collected the student work, used the rubric to determine a score, and submitted the score to the state department. This was done because an authority outside the classroom directed them to do so.

Because of this situation, these portfolios often become an end in and of themselves. The portfolios were mandated and used to provide scores for the state department. Because of the external mandate, limited teacher input, and little or no staff development, these portfolios became a classroom activity, something teachers were required to administer, rather than a vehicle to promote student or teacher reflection or direct classroom decisions (Smith, 1991).

In this paradigm, the actual procedures for collecting student work, the activities themselves and not the purposes for collecting the student work, have taken priority. As a result of the ASAP, some teachers became more concerned with the type of folders to be used and the procedures for passing these portfolios on to the next grade level than with discussing the various ways these portfolios could be used to promote reflection and self-evaluation.

In the assessment as procedure paradigm, teachers are still being asked to objectively measure students' abilities and report information in numerical form to external audiences. They remain outside the decision-making process, barely involved in determining the purposes for these assessments.

Many of these "assessment as procedure programs" are destined to fail because they become an end in and of themselves. Classroom teachers have not been involved in the creation of these new methods, which are not intended to provide new insights to a child's learning. Teachers are simply burdened with another set of procedures given to them by their administration in order to provide scores for an external authority.

In effect, the procedure or method of collecting information in and of itself does not determine the assessment paradigm. This paradigm is a blend of two other paradigms. It is the purpose and the audience for these assessments, along with the epistemological stance and methods used to gather information, that helps determine the paradigm.

Assessment as Inquiry

In the assessment as inquiry paradigm, assessment is based on constructivist theories of knowledge (Fosnot, 1996), student-centered learning (Altwerger, Edelsky, & Flores, 1987), and the inquiry process (Short, Harste, & Burke, 1995). Here, the teacher uses various qualitative and quantitative assessment techniques to inquire about particular learners and their learning processes. It is a process of inquiry, and a process of interpretation, used to promote reflection concerning students' understandings, attitudes, and literate abilities.

Not only have the procedures changed for collecting information, but so have the levels of teacher and student involvement, the purposes of these assessments, the epistemological perspective, and the audiences for the information created. In the assessment as procedure paradigm, the changes were only at the pedagogical level, concerned with new information-gathering procedures. In comparison, within this paradigm the purpose of the assessments is a deeper understanding of individual learners in their specific learning contexts. The audience has also changed from external authorities to the teachers, parents, and students involved in the classroom.

Assessment, in this paradigm, is viewed as a social, contextually specific, interpretive activity (Crafton & Burke, 1994). Knowledge is believed to be constructed by the individual within the social contexts of the learning event, rather than being acquired solely through transmission or direct instructional techniques. In this paradigm multiple interpretations are encouraged, and each learner transacts with different texts and the world to create meanings (Rosenblatt, 1979).

Using assessment as inquiry, teachers are no longer simply test administrators. Rather, teachers and students are viewed as active creators of knowledge rather than as passive recipients (Wells, 1984). Instead of using tests to measure student abilities and compare children, teachers use these classroom-based assessment procedures to facilitate learning, direct curricular decisions, and communicate more effectively with students and parents (Serafini, 1995).

In this assessment as inquiry paradigm, it is believed there is no simple prescription for each student's ailment or a program that one can administer quickly and relatively effortlessly to eliminate inappropriate behaviors. Assessment is not viewed as an "objective" measurement process, intended for comparisons and prescriptions; rather, it is seen as a human interaction involving the human as the primary assessment instrument (Johnston, 1997). The differences between this paradigm and the assessment as procedure paradigm are in why teachers implement these procedures, not necessarily how these procedures are carried out. What is done with the information and for whom the assessments are conducted has also changed.

Instead of state or provincial education departments mandating a particular portfolio assessment program such as the ASAP example used earlier, teachers implement their own portfolio assessment process to collect samples of student work in order to make appropriate instructional decisions. These portfolios have become vehicles to promote reflection and student self-evaluation (Tierney, 1998). The methods used to collect information may be similar, but the purposes and the goals of the assessment as inquiry paradigm are quite different.

In this paradigm, portfolios are seen as a vehicle for promoting student and teacher reflection, self-evaluation, and goal setting. These portfolios are an ongoing collection of work used to understand a student's interests, abilities, needs, and values. The artifacts in the portfolios are not usually scored or used to compare children against their same-age cohorts; rather, students reflect upon the contents in order to understand their academic progress and to document their growth. This has been referred to as learner-referenced assessment (Johnston, 1997).

The work included in these portfolios has been created in a more authentic context, rather than in a testing situation (Bergeron, 1996). In this paradigm, classroom instruction does not stop in order to assess learning. Assessment is viewed as part of the learning process, not as separate from it.

Portfolios are noncompetitive and attempt to focus on students' strengths rather than their deficiencies (Murphy, 1997). The portfolios in this paradigm are used to uncover the possibilities for students, to understand each child as a whole, and to attempt to provide a window into a student's conceptual framework and ways of seeing the world.

Educational communities would look radically different if this were the dominant theory of assessment; however, standardized tests will not disappear tomorrow. This shift from assessment as measurement to assessment as inquiry will take time, resources, administrative support, and dialogue among interested educators. Viewing assessment as inquiry would shift the focus of assessment research and practices from the standardized testing programs to the classroom itself, where assessment may be of more service in helping teachers to improve classroom learning experiences (Serafini, 1998).

Supporting Teachers in Transition

The shift toward an inquiry-based assessment paradigm places different demands not only upon classroom teachers, but also on school administrations, staff development programs, and teacher education models. Making changes in a teacher's practice or educational belief system demands considerable time, research, and the opportunity for teachers to collaborate (Fullan, 1994). In general, teachers need time, support, and the opportunity to have a dialogue with colleagues. Teachers need time to read professional literature concerning assessment, engage in dialogue with other teachers in transition and have the chance to try these new procedures in a supportive, collaborative environment.

Time is already at a premium during the school day for classroom teachers. Paperwork, school site committees, staff meetings, large classroom enrollments, and shortened preparation periods all contribute to the inadequate amount of time allotted to professional development. Administrators and staff development specialists need to become more creative and supportive in finding time to help classroom teachers understand these new assessment procedures, read about their implementation, try them out in the classroom, and reflect on their progress.

Change can be threatening. Teachers, like other educators, need peer support when working through new ideas. A trusting environment where teachers can enter into open dialogue with one another is of primary importance. However, when teachers are allowed to voice their concerns and ideas, change may become less threatening.

By looking at the existing school structures and developing alternatives to the traditional school day, administrators may find new ways to create time for teachers to collaborate, research new assessment practices, and take the first step toward making a shift in their assessment beliefs and practices. When teachers and administrators come to value the changes necessary to move toward reflective practice and assessment as inquiry, it becomes easier for these groups to justify the time required to support these changes.

In making this shift, teachers will need to reevaluate not only the procedures used to generate information about their students, but also the purposes and audiences for the information collected. In this way it is a "paradigm shift," a new stance toward assessment and knowledge as well as a change in the actual procedures used (Cambourne & Turbill, 1997).

Making the Shift

In order to make this paradigm shift from assessment as measurement to assessment as inquiry, teachers need a supportive environment where administration and staff development programs provide time to collaborate with other educators, time to reflect, and the opportunity to work through the new purposes and procedures in the new assessment framework. The general support mechanism needs to be in place to allow teachers the time, dialogue, and collaboration necessary for change to occur.

Along with these general supports, specific changes in a teacher's practice and thinking may support a transition to this new paradigm. Teachers may want to consider the following ideas: (a) teachers as knowledgeable, reflective participants; (b) meaningful student involvement; and (c) negotiating criteria used to assess student performance. Each of these ideas will now be addressed in more detail, including some practical suggestions for teacher consideration.

Teachers as Knowledgeable, Reflective Participants

The teacher as a knowledgeable, reflective participant is the foundation for the assessment as inquiry paradigm. Rather than relying on testing agencies outside the classroom context to evaluate student progress, teachers in this paradigm assume an active role in the assessment process. This new role involves using observational strategies and other classroom-based assessment procedures to gather information about student achievement.

The information collected is then interpreted by teachers on the basis of their existing knowledge and experiences. Teachers reflect on and interpret classroom experiences and student performances to make decisions about curriculum and instruction, rather than relying solely on the interpretations or scores from an externally mandated test. The more extensive the teacher knowledge base, the more effective the interpretations and subsequent instructional decisions (Fenstermacher, 1994). When teachers assume an active role in the assessment process, the audience and purposes for these assessments shift from an external focus on comparison and student ranking to an internal focus on informing classroom practice (Tierney, 1998).

Traditionally, teachers were perceived as "program operators," and the knowledge they needed to be successful was based on how to implement prepackaged curriculum or present the lessons scripted for them in teacher manuals (Bullough & Gitlin, 1985). Subsequent traditional teacher education programs were developed around methods courses that explained how to deliver the curriculum. These notions of teacher as automated program delivery person become problematic in shifting to an assessment as inquiry paradigm.

Many teacher education programs have attempted to restructure their programs to develop teachers who assume an active, reflective role in curriculum and assessment decisions (Ross, 1989). The teacher as a reflective participant is a different stance than the transmission or direct instruction models still taught in some traditional teacher education programs (Zeichner, 1987). If teachers are going to make the transition from assessment as measurement to assessment as inquiry, they need to know more about observing learners, learn how to make curriculum decisions based on these observations, and increase their knowledge base concerning child development and learning processes.

In the assessment as inquiry paradigm, teacher participation means that not only do teachers administer the assessments, but they also have a voice in the decisions as to how, when, and for what purposes these assessments are being used. Teachers are no longer simply the test givers, but become critically involved, deciding which assessments generate the most useful information for their instructional purposes. These new assessments are not blindly accepted, but are judged on the type of information they create, the purposes for these assessments, and the needs of the audiences involved.

As reflective participants, teachers make a commitment to learn from past experiences. It is an intentional, systematic, and deliberate focus on why things occur and what effects these experiences have on student learning (Dewey, 1933). Reflection has been defined as "systematic enquiry into one's own practice to improve that practice and to deepen one's understanding of it" (Lucas, 1991, p. 85).

Reflective thinking is initiated by the perception of a problem (Dewey, 1933). It is this acknowledgement of uncertainty and "unsettledness" that initiates the inquiry process. In other words, in order to be reflective participants, teachers need to be able to discuss their doubts and inquiry questions without being seen as unknowing or incompetent. Being able to make one's practice "problematic" has been observed as a first step in this process (Valli, 1997). When teachers have no doubts about their practice or the programs they are using, reflection remains of minimal importance.

In working toward becoming knowledgeable, reflective participants in the assessment process, teachers have assumed the role of teacher-researcher to better understand the experiences and interactions in their classrooms (Cochran-Smith & Lytle, 1992). In doing so, teachers have become producers of research and knowledge as well as consumers (Richardson, 1994). By videotaping classroom events (Berg & Smith, 1996), observing peers at work in classrooms, and working in team teaching situations, teachers are opening up new avenues for dialogue and collaboration. This has allowed teachers the opportunity to become more reflective about their practice. Teachers also use journal writing as a way to help understand the perspectives and beliefs they bring to their practice and their effect on classroom events (Hubbard & Power, 1993).

Many teachers have used journal writing to create belief statements or platform statements about their philosophy of education in order to understand the expectations and hidden beliefs they bring to the assessment process (Kottkamp, 1990). In writing these statements, teachers have been able to "unpack" their values and biases and to distance themselves from their practice in order to critique it more effectively. The purpose of these procedures is to help teachers see their practice from a different, more critical perspective (Osterman, 1990).

Another way to help teachers make this shift is to support the development of teacher dialogue groups. When teachers come together to discuss educational issues that are relevant to their practice, change and growth become possible (Ohanian, 1994). Teacher-research groups (Queenan, 1988) and assessment-driven teacher dialogue groups (Stephens et al., 1996) help provide a structure for teachers to support one another through the change process. Through these dialogue groups, teacher-research groups, and journal writing, teachers are inquiring into the quality of the learning experiences provided for their students and the effectiveness of the decisions they make in their classroom.

Meaningful Student Involvement

The assessment as measurement paradigm has historically left students out of the assessment process (Bushweller,1997). Assessment has been something we do "to" students rather than "with" students. Schools administer standardized tests and send them off to be scored by external testing agencies; eventually the results of the tests are reported back. Through this traditional assessment as measurement paradigm, students and schools have come to rely on external testing agencies to judge their effectiveness and to document their educational progress. This lack of involvement has created passive recipients, not active participants, in the learning as well as the assessment process (Calfee & Perfumo, 1993).

In the assessment as inquiry paradigm, portfolios of student work, student-led conferences, learning response logs, and negotiated reporting procedures include the student in the assessment process (Tierney, Carter, & Desai, 1991). This new level of involvement helps students to accept more responsibility for their learning and to reflect on their own educational progress. Students need to be invited to participate in determining the criteria by which their work will be judged and then play a role in actually judging their work (Kohn, 1993).

Portfolios are used as a vehicle to promote reflection on students' academic progress as well as document their growth in various subject areas (Graves, 1992). Students collect work generated during the school year to evaluate their progress and set goals for their future learning experiences. Many times these portfolios are used in conjunction with student-led conferences where students share their portfolios and reflections with parents and other interested audiences. These portfolios have an authentic purpose and are a primary vehicle for supporting student reflection as well as student involvement in the assessment process.

Another way students are involved in the assessment process is through negotiated reporting configurations (Anthony, Johnson, Mickelson, & Preece, 1991). Students are invited to become intimately involved in the creation of their report cards in a negotiated process with both teachers and parents. This process may begin by allowing students to evaluate their efforts and performances, based on criteria negotiated between the teacher's perspective, the information contained in various standards documents, and the beliefs and values of the community. Opening up the criteria used to evaluate student work and inviting students to participate in the evaluation process helps students begin to feel a part of the assessment process, rather than as passive recipients of someone else's evaluation.

Another way of involving students in assessing their progress is through classroom-designed rubrics (Rickards & Cheek, 1999). Rubrics are negotiated forms of criteria explicitly written for particular classroom work and activities. Again, opening up the conversation to include students in the decisions about what criteria are used to evaluate their progress helps students become involved in the assessment process. When students become an active part of the assessment process, assessment becomes a process of inquiry rather than an external measurement reducing student performance and ability to a numerical score for comparative purposes.

Negotiating the Criteria Used to Assess Student Performance

The debate over what children should be taught and what they need to know in order to be successful adults has been going on in the United States for centuries (Bracey, 1995). This debate has been rekindled by many of the standards-based restructuring initiatives across the U.S. and other countries (Noddings, 1997). The creation of standards documents by state legislatures and federal education agencies, along with the standardized testing that usually accompanies these documents, has tended to restrict programs to the assessment as measurement paradigm, while at the same time supporting agendas tied to gatekeeping and exclusion (Tierney, 1998). These documents are written as general learning statements by people far removed from actual classrooms and students. The negotiation of educational criteria becomes a highly political issue and hence a highly controversial one (Shannon, 1996).

As educators, we just don't know all that students need to know, nor are we able to teach them everything we do know (Wiggins, 1989). The criteria used for assessing student performance should be open for negotiation and revision to adapt to our changing societal demands. Teachers and students should have a voice in what is taught, how this knowledge is eventually assessed, and what criteria are used for evaluation.

With all of these restructuring efforts, teachers have been bombarded with standards created by federal and state agencies, local school boards, and professional organizations like the

National Council of Teachers of English and the International Reading Association. Using these documents as guidelines, teachers may open the negotiations by writing detailed belief or platform statements concerning their expectations for student learning and behavior (Kottkamp, 1990). These platform statements provide a place to open up a discussion among parents, teachers and school officials about the experiences to be provided for students during the school year. By presenting their criteria to be negotiated, teachers open up a space for different voices to be heard concerning what is of value in education and what place particular content areas and learning processes are to have in the school curriculum.

As mentioned before, classroom rubrics designed with student and teacher input are an excellent vehicle for negotiation and involvement in the assessment process. Students and teachers come together to "unpack" their values and beliefs about education in order to expose these to discussion and negotiation. It is this process of negotiation that is of primary importance, not necessarily the actual documents that are created in the process (Boomer, 1991).

The items included on school district report cards and how amenable these cards are to change should also be open to negotiation. School report cards are a written statement about what the community deems valuable in education. If it is on the report card and it gets a grade, it is probably seen as important by that community. Even the amount of space designated for each subject area is a statement concerning how much value is placed upon that topic. The larger the space, it seems the more value is assigned to that particular subject or topic.

In negotiating the criteria used to assess student performance, educators should consider the "models of excellence" already available in the outside world that classroom teachers and students can use to judge the quality of the work done in schools. Possibly educators can look to various awards, such as the Newbery or Pulitzer prize for writing or the Nobel prize for science, in order to find criteria that are authentic and can be incorporated into the negotiation of student evaluation. What are the authentic models of criteria available for assessing student performance? Instead of school districts and education departments being the sole creators of these criteria of student progress, opening up the discussion to bring in multiple voices may create more authentic, more useful criteria.

No Quick Fix

When educators begin to acknowledge the complexity and the interpretive nature of the learning and assessment process, traditional assessment as measurement procedures become problematic. All assessments are interpretive; unfortunately teachers and students rarely become involved in large-scale testing programs' interpretations or dissemination of results. The assessment as inquiry paradigm offers teachers another perspective from which to understand the needs and abilities of their students, using different assessment methods for different purposes and audiences.

Making this shift from assessment as measurement to assessment as inquiry takes time, administrative support, collaboration, and the opportunity to engage in dialogue. Simply mandating new procedures for teachers to administer will not help teachers make this shift in assessment paradigms.

It is my hope that classroom teachers will begin to take an active role in the assessments used in their classroom. Teachers need to involve students in the assessment process in meaningful ways, become knowledgeable, reflective participants in the assessment process themselves, and negotiate the criteria used to evaluate academic performances. As educators, we need to acknowledge the complexity of the learning process and stop trying to find the quick-fix solutions to both educational and assessment issues. When assessment becomes a process of inquiry, an interpretive activity rather than simply the "objective" measure of predetermined behaviors, teachers will be able to use assessment to make informed decisions concerning curriculum and instruction in their classrooms.

References

Altwerger, B., Edelsky, C., & Flores, B. (1987). Whole language: What's new? *The Reading Teacher, 41*, 144–154.

Anthony, R., Johnson, T., Mickelson, N., & Preece, A. (1991). *Evaluating literacy: A perspective for change*. Portsmouth, NH: Heinemann.

Berg, M.H., & Smith, J.P. (1996). Using videotapes to improve teaching. *Music Educator's Journal, 22*(5), 31–37.

Bergeron, B. (1996). Seeking authenticity: What is "real" about thematic literacy instruction? *The Reading Teacher, 49*, 544–551.

Bertrand, J. (1991). Student assessment and evaluation. In B. Harp (Ed.), *Assessment and evaluation in whole language programs* (pp. 17–33). Norwood, MA: Christopher-Gordon.

Boomer, G. (Ed.). (1991). *Negotiating the curriculum: A teacher-student partnership*. Sydney, Australia: Ashton-Scholastic.

Bracey, G. (1995). *Final exam: A study of the perpetual scrutiny of American education*. Washington, DC: Technos Press.

Bullough, R.V., Jr., & Gitlin, A. (1985). Schooling and change: A view from the lower rungs. *Teachers College Record, 87*, 219–237.

Bushweller, K. (1997). Teach to the test. *The American School Board Journal, 184*, 20–25.

Calfee, R., & Perfumo, P. (1993). Student portfolios: Opportunities for a revolution in assessment. *Journal of Reading, 36*, 532–537.

Cambourne, B., & Turbill, J. (Eds.). (1997). *Responsive evaluation*. Portsmouth, NH: Heinemann.

Cizek, G. (1998). The assessment revolution's unfinished business. *Kappa Delta Pi Record, 34*, 144–149.

Cochran-Smith, M., & Lytle, S. (Eds.). (1992). *Inside/outside: Teacher research and knowledge*. New York: Teachers College Press.

Crafton, L., & Burke, C. (1994). Inquiry-based evaluation: Teachers and students reflecting together. *Primary Voices, 2*(2), 2–7.

Dewey, J. (1933). *How we think*. Chicago: Henry Regnery.

Elkind, D. (1997). The death of child nature: Education in the postmodern world. *Phi Delta Kappan, 78*, 241–245.

Farr, R. (1992). Putting it all together: Solving the reading assessment puzzle. *The Reading Teacher, 46*, 26–37.

Fenstermacher, G. (1994). The knower and the known: The nature of knowledge in research on teaching. In L. Darling-Hammond (Ed.), *Review of research in education, 20* (pp. 3–56). Washington, DC: American Educational Research Association.

Fosnot, C.T. (1996). Constructivism: A psychological theory of learning. In C.T. Fosnot (Ed.), *Constructivism: Theory, perspectives and practice* (pp. 8–33). New York: Teachers College Press.

Fullan, M. (1994). Why teachers must become change agents. *Educational Leadership, 50*, 12–17.

Garcia, G.E., & Pearson, P.D. (1994). Assessment and diversity. In L. Darling-Hammond (Ed.), *Review of research in education, 20* (pp. 337–391). Washington, DC: American Educational Research Association.

Graves, D. (1992). Portfolios: Keep a good idea growing. In D. Graves & B. Sunstein (Eds.), *Portfolio portraits* (pp. 1–12). Portsmouth, NH: Heinemann.

Heald-Taylor, B.G. (1996). Three paradigms for literature instruction in grades 3 to 6. *The Reading Teacher, 49*, 456–466.

Heald-Taylor, B.G. (1998). Three paradigms of spelling instruction in grades 3 to 6. *The Reading Teacher, 51*, 404–412.

Hubbard, R.S., & Power, B.M. (1993). *The art of classroom inquiry: A handbook for teacher researchers*. Portsmouth, NH: Heinemann.

Johnston, P.H. (1992). Nontechnical assessment. *The Reading Teacher, 46*, 60–62.

Johnston, P.H. (1997). *Knowing literacy: Constructive literacy assessment*. York, ME: Stenhouse.

Kaufhold, J.A. (1995). Testing, testing. *The American School Board Journal, 182*, 41–42.

Kohn, A. (1993). Choices for students: Why and how to let students decide. *Phi Delta Kappan, 75*, 8–20.

Kottkamp, R.B. (1990). Means for facilitating reflection. *Education and Urban Society, 22*, 182–203.

Linn, R., Baker, E., & Dunbar, S. (1991). Complex, performance-based assessment: Expectations and validation criteria. *Educational Researcher, 20*(8), 15–21.

Lucas, P. (1991). Reflection, new practices and the need for flexibility in supervising student teachers. *Journal of Higher Education, 15*(2), 84–93.

Meier, T. (1994). Why standardized tests are bad. In *Rethinking our classrooms: Teaching for equity and social justice* (pp. 171–175). Milwaukee, WI: Rethinking Schools Ltd.

Murphy, S. (1997). Literacy assessment and the politics of identity. *Reading and Writing Quarterly, 13*, 261–278.

Neill, M. (1993). A better way to test. *The Executive Educator, 15*, 24–27.

Noddings, N. (1992). *The challenge to care in schools.* New York: Teachers College Press.

Noddings, N. (1997). Thinking about standards. *Phi Delta Kappan, 79,* 184–189.

Ohanian, S. (1994). *Who's in charge? A teacher speaks her mind.* Portsmouth, NH: Heinemann.

Osterman, K. (1990). Reflective practice: A new agenda for education. *Education and Urban Society, 22*(2), 133–152.

Queenan, M. (1988). Impertinent questions about teacher research: A review. *English Journal, 77*(2), 41–46.

Richardson, V. (1994). Conducting research on practice. *Educational Researcher, 23*(5), 5–10.

Rickards, D., & Cheek, E., Jr. (1999). *Designing rubrics for K-6 classroom assessment.* Norwood, MA: Christopher-Gordon.

Rosenblatt, L.M. (1979). *The reader, the text, the poem.* Carbondale, IL: Southern Illinois University Press.

Ross, D. (1989). First steps in developing a reflective approach. *Journal of Teacher Education, 40*(2), 22–30.

Rothman, R. (1996). Taking aim at testing. *The American School Board Journal, 183,* 27–30.

Serafini, F. (1995). Reflective assessment. *Talking Points: Conversations in the Whole Language Community, 6*(4), 10–12.

Serafini, F. (1998). Making the shift. *Talking Points: Conversation in the Whole Language Community, 9*(2), 20–21.

Shannon, P. (1996). Mad as hell. *Language Arts, 73,* 14–18.

Short, K., & Burke, C. (1994a). *Creating curriculum.* Portsmouth, NH: Heinemann.

Short, K., & Burke, C. (1994b). *Curriculum as inquiry.* Paper presented at the Fifth Whole Language Umbrella Conference, San Diego, CA.

Short, K., Harste, J., & Burke, C. (1995). *Creating classrooms for authors and inquirers.* Portsmouth, NH: Heinemann.

Smith, M.L. (1991). Put to the test: The effects of external testing on teachers. *Educational Researcher, 20*(5), 8–11.

Stephens, D., Story, J., Aihara, K., Hisatake, S., Ito, B., Kawamoto, C., et al. (1996). When assessment is inquiry. *Language Arts, 73,* 105–112.

Taylor, K., & Walton, S. (1997). Co-opting standardized tests in the service of learning. *Phi Delta Kappan, 79,* 66–70.

Tierney, R.J. (1998). Literacy assessment reform: Shifting beliefs, principled possibilities, and emerging practices. *The Reading Teacher, 51,* 374–390.

Tierney, R.J., Carter, M.A., & Desai, L.E. (1991). *Portfolio assessment in the reading-writing classroom.* Norwood, MA: Christopher-Gordon.

Valli, L. (1997). Listening to other voices: A description of teacher reflection in the United States. *Peabody Journal of Education, 72*(1), 67–88.

Wells, G. (1984). *The meaning makers.* Portsmouth, NH: Heinemann.

Wiggins, G. (1989). The futility of trying to teach everything of importance. *Educational Leadership, 47,* 14–18.

Wineberg, S. (1997). T.S. Eliot, collaboration and the quandaries of assessment in a rapidly changing world. *Phi Delta Kappan, 79,* 59–65.

Zeichner, K. (1987). Preparing reflective teachers: An overview of instructional strategies which have been employed in preservice education. *International Journal of Education Research, 11,* 565–575.

Changing Attitudes on Assessment

Bonita L. Wilcox

As an English teacher for many years, I frequently carried home bundles of papers to correct. What an attitude I had! As if I could "correct" the thinking and writing of my students. I got the idea of correcting from my own English teachers' superficial correction of spelling and grammar, sorting and ranking our papers to assign grades. In my teacher preparation program, we never addressed the concept of correcting, but it was practiced by our professors, and we were readily influenced by these kinds of models.

When I went to graduate school I enrolled in an elective course, Assessments in English Education, and I read a book by Mina Shaughnessy, *Errors and Expectations* (1977). This was the beginning of an attitude adjustment on my concept of correcting. My understanding of writing assessment expanded, and I began to study and experiment with other kinds of assessments. I no longer avoided discussions on assessment, and I kept a close watch for new publications. One of my favorites is *Classroom Assessment Techniques* (Angelo & Cross, 1993), and it isn't about grading at all—it's about assessment as a tool for learning. When we see assessment as being helpful, our attitude begins to change.

A positive attitude toward assessment is important for teachers and for learners. Positive feedback encourages students to take the next step in their learning. If we think of assessment as a part of the scaffolding to get us to the next level, it lessens our fears and increases our confidence. Still, attitudes toward assessment have been difficult to change, especially since nearly all of us consider ourselves experts when it comes to assessing. We judge, misjudge, forejudge, prejudge, and pass judgments on ourselves, our students, our colleagues, our supervisors, and our spouses. We approve, support, and praise our work, our food, our thinking, and our situations. Or we disrespect, disapprove, and censure what others do and say.

More formally, we test extensively in schools, using IQ tests, achievement tests, placement tests, teacher-made tests, and career inventories. Some U.S. states test for minimum competencies. We use tests to get into school and to get out of school. We spend a lot of time and money with all this testing. Yet, these tests are rarely learning opportunities for students. Perhaps this emphasis on testing has contributed to negative feelings about assessment. Formal testing is summative and one-dimensional, quite different from multidimensional, formative assessment. Testing connotes criticism and scrutiny, judging, ranking, and sorting. Assessment, on the other hand, connotes process learning. As testing doesn't promote learning and assessment does, then why don't we do more assessing and less testing?

That is the question I asked myself years ago, and I'm still reading about and discussing this question as new thinking about assessment continues to fascinate me. The following books offer assessment strategies teachers can use to improve their instructional practice, to increase their own learning, and to enhance their programs.

Enhancing Professional Practice: A Framework for Teaching. Charlotte Danielson. 1996. Association for Supervision and Curriculum Development (120 N. Pitt Street, Alexandria, VA 22314, USA). ISBN 0-87120-269-7. Softcover. 140 pp. US$19.95.
Reviewed by Lisa C. Schonberger

According to Danielson, *Enhancing Professional Practice* is a guide for novice teachers through

From *The Reading Teacher*, 52(3), 294-297. © 1998 by the International Reading Association.

their initial classroom experiences, a structure to help experienced professionals become more effective, and a means to focus experienced professionals. I believe administrators involved in assessing teachers will also benefit from this book.

Charlotte Danielson has an impressive background in assessment. She is president of Princeton Education Associates in Princeton, New Jersey, and project coordinator for the South Brunswick Township Public Schools in Monmouth Junction, New Jersey. She has worked as a consultant on performance assessment for numerous states, school districts, and schools in the United States and other countries, as well as for Educational Testing Service. She has designed both assessment systems and training programs for assessors. Her work has encouraged assessment use in the service of learning by both teachers and students.

The author concentrates on four domains of teaching responsibility, which she titles planning and preparation, classroom environment, instruction, and professional responsibilities. Each domain contains several components. For example, under planning and preparation the six components are demonstrating knowledge of content and pedagogy, demonstrating knowledge of students, selecting instructional goals, demonstrating knowledge of resources, designing coherent instruction, and assessing student learning. These components are then rated using four levels of performance: unsatisfactory, basic, proficient, and distinguished.

To implement this model, data are collected from a variety of sources, such as detailed observations of the classroom, lessons, and written materials supplied by the teacher. The data are then organized to supply evidence for each component under the four domains. After data are compared to given examples under the four levels of performance, goal setting and action plans can be discussed and developed.

Another section of *Enhancing Professional Practices* focuses on creating a professional portfolio. It is full of practical ideas and models to follow. I have used portfolio assessment with preservice teachers, and I find this process exciting. The attention to actual data collected from a variety of sources over time versus the traditional checklist from a single observation by an administrator should convince educators and administrators alike to incorporate some ideas from this book into a school district's strategic plan for assessing teacher performance.

Teacher Self-Evaluation Tool Kit. Peter Airasian and Arlen Gullickson. 1997. Corwin Press, Inc. (2455 Teller Road, Thousand Oaks, CA 91320, USA). ISBN 0-8039-6517-6. Softcover. 82 pp. US$19.95.
Reviewed by Bonita L. Wilcox

Teacher self-evaluation, according to Airasian and Gullickson, must involve decision making and self-improvement. Reflecting and questioning are helpful as teachers make judgments about their own knowledge, performance, and beliefs, but opportunities for collaboration and professional growth are essential to improving one's practice. The authors write, "Teacher self-evaluation is evaluation of the teacher by the teacher and for the teacher" (p. 2), although they recognize the need for other forms of evaluation as well.

The self-evaluation process is presented in four easy steps: identify the problem, gather information, reflect and make a decision, and finally apply what you have learned. However, self-evaluation for the purpose of improving practice is rarely easy, and most of us seek input from colleagues, students, parents, and supervisors. Accountability necessitates many forms of teacher evaluation.

Poor student performance, a shift from authoritative to reflective evaluations, new state requirements, and constructivist models of teaching and learning have contributed to changing trends in teacher assessments. The authors stress the importance of a teacher's individual need for self-improvement. They also point out that teachers are the experts in the classroom, and significant changes occur at this level.

Chapter 3, entitled "What do we know about teacher self-evaluation?" may be disappointing to readers because the authors neglect to mention how extensive the use of portfolio assessment has become, especially in teacher preparation programs, and how this rapidly expanding body of literature indicates that teachers can and do monitor and manage their own professional development.

The heart of this text is found in Chapter 4, presenting 20 ready-to-use, or easy to adapt, self-assessment strategies. These examples result in tangible records for a teacher's total assessment package and also help teachers to become more aware of their strengths and weaknesses in practice. For example, if you wanted to get student feedback on a lesson just taught, you could stop and ask students to write The Minute Survey. Student responses to a question as simple as "How difficult would it be for you to solve this problem?" may indicate strengths or weaknesses in instructional practice. Addressing weaknesses actually strengthens an overall assessment package. Becoming aware of a problem is often the first step in solving it. The steps one implements to improve one's practice can be a positive addition to a teacher's assessment portfolio.

The book ends with an annotated source list for further investigation, a chapter on "Getting Started," which suggests starting small and building a support system, and finally, a section on resources with detailed descriptions for easy application.

Teacher Self-Evaluation Tool Kit would be useful to teachers at all levels of expertise. Whether the assessment focus is on accountability or has a higher purpose, such as improving one's practice, this book is sure to be helpful to teachers. An added bonus is that it will deepen our understanding of the procedures and benefits of doing our own classroom research.

Situating Portfolios: Four Perspectives. Kathleen B. Yancy and Irwin Wieser, Eds. 1997. Utah State Press (871 East 900 North, Logan, UT 84322, USA). ISBN 0-87421-220-0. Softcover. 416 pp. US$21.95.
Reviewed by Deborah B. Kennedy

This book is a collection of 24 essays by writing teachers and teacher-educators at all academic levels. The editors' goal is to "demonstrate a range—of voices, perspectives, and of contexts, unified not by one author-subject, but by a common interest in exploring, extending, and critiquing our use of a rich and complex teaching and evaluation tool" (p. 16).

The editors present this wide range of materials in four broad sections that are representative of various portfolios in relation to theory and power. Elbow and Belanoff's contribution begins the section with a historical perspective on the initiation of portfolios at the State University of New York at Stony Brook in 1983 as a response to demands for teaching/learning accountability. However, portfolio use resulted in an unpredictable impact on teaching practice. Instead of the assessment process driving instructional methods, those utilizing portfolios for student evaluations discovered that the teaching process was actually determining outcome assessment. As the authors suggest, "Teaching needs to be the dog that wags the tail of assessment rather than vice versa" (p. 32). The theory and power section of *Situating Portfolios* includes contributions about the current use of portfolios in evaluating student writing, a summary of Kentucky's state-mandated portfolio program, the creative aspects of multitask portfolio assessment, and the significance of faculty development in portfolio success across the curriculum.

A later section in *Situating Portfolios* examines teaching and professional development. This section investigates the use of portfolios in the preparation, evaluation, and self-reflection of preservice teachers. Yancey shares three of her students' portfolios that describe the relationship between curriculum and student experience. Burch suggests that portfolios may be a method to develop professional identity among student-teachers. Paulson and Paulson's piece is based on the self-reflection of 23 teachers involved in a staff development project designed to encourage and instruct participants regarding student portfolio development. The teacher-participants were given the task of creating their own portfolio and, by doing so, "constructed a personal concept of 'portfolio' and its place in learning and assessment" (p. 292). Perhaps this is the best approach to the challenge of gaining the active participation of teachers in districtwide portfolio assessment. Finally, Weiser suggests utilizing portfolios in practicum situations so that new teachers can focus on learning to teach rather than experiencing the anxiety that frequently accompanies evaluation.

The final section of the book presents an overview of the technological aspects of portfolios. Several authors present various looks into the hypertext nature of electronic portfolios. Contributors suggest the advantages and potential dangers of combining portfolios and computers. Electronic portfolios are in their infancy. One of the primary concerns is how to incorporate portfolios in a wide-scale assessment process using computers.

I found this collection to be a comprehensive, sometimes provocative look at the education trend of portfolio assessment. It would certainly serve as an excellent introduction to portfolio perspectives as well as a thought-provoking reflection for even the most seasoned portfolio expert. As the editors concluded in their introduction, "We hope that the ways portfolios have been situated in these essays will offer teachers at many levels and in a variety of instructional settings stimulus for their own reflection and practice and collaboration" (p. 17).

Program Evaluation: Alternative Approaches and Practical Guidelines. Blaine Worthen, James Sanders, and Jody Fitzpatrick. 1997. Longman Publishers (One Jacob Way, Reading, MA 01867, USA). ISBN 0-8013-0774-0. Softcover. 558 pp. US$53.55.
Reviewed by Paul T. Kasunich

As the pressure grew on educators to be held "accountable" for their teaching, a comprehensive work on the evaluation process was greatly needed. The difficult part was to find a book that explained the rationale, history, and future of educational evaluation in language that is concise and easy to understand. *Program Evaluation* accomplishes both tasks by never forgetting that the audience for this book is not statisticians, but teachers and administrators.

All three of the authors have extensive experience in evaluation methodology, development, implementation, and analysis. They want readers to learn the many alternative approaches to and guidelines for planning and conducting program evaluation. The reader begins the journey with an historical perspective on evaluation as a science, as well as an examination of the various arguments for alternative means of evaluation. Terms such as *quantitative*, *qualitative*, *formative*, and *summative* have been known to strike fear into the hearts of many teachers. The writers never forget their audience when explaining these terms, taking care to explain in great detail the concepts behind the terms. Additionally, excellent examples are utilized to illustrate the process by which these types of evaluation terms have become so popular.

I found this book to be extremely beneficial, particularly because evaluation approaches are examined for their strengths and weaknesses, the limitations of the particular approaches are highlighted, and examples of real studies are cited. These examples allow readers to begin to develop a critical eye toward the evaluation process and how decisions are made to implement certain evaluation projects. I suspect these examples will be of particular interest to classroom teachers who historically have had little or no voice in educational evaluation projects within their respective districts.

The authors also address the very real "political" aspects of the evaluation process such as ethical standards, potential biases, reporting structures, and the art of producing meaningful evaluation reports that address stakeholder concerns. One section of the book also highlights emerging problem areas, such as the need for meaningful assessment of nonprofit organizations.

I found *Program Evaluation: Alternative Approaches and Practical Guidelines* to be a highly informative work that will be a useful reference tool for many years to come. The crisp writing style, coupled with real-world examples of educational evaluation programs, provide an excellent resource for the experienced school administrator or classroom teacher. I highly recommend this text to anyone with an interest in the field of educational program evaluation. The authors have done a masterful job of producing a book that provides valuable explanations and examples of evaluations that all teachers will find enlightening.

Assessment Can Improve Teaching and Learning

Learning more about assessment has made me a better teacher. Effective assessment practices really did improve instruction and learning in my classroom. Reflections on teaching, input from students, and dialogue with colleagues often offered insight into more constructive ways to assess and to learn. Assessment is a powerful tool, and it can help or hinder our learning. Sometimes I failed to consider the impact my judgments had on students. I ranked and sorted with arrogance, as if I knew the grades I assigned were accurate and purposeful. I assessed students on what they already knew, rather than on what they should have learned from my lessons. Now I know that my students and I can benefit from a variety of assessment strategies.

Still, when I talk with my graduate students about how their first assignment will be assessed, I can sense their fears of evaluation as they wonder about how I will grade their papers and projects. What does she want? Will she like my work? How many errors will she discover? Will she understand what I meant? Will she take off for spelling? We can take the mystery out of assessment by sharing strategies with our students. We can help them to see that assessment is natural and necessary to their learning. I show students how to do rubrics. I ask them how they learn best. I tell them we are experimenting with alternative assessments, and I make sure that they notice when their learning increases. Perhaps the most important thing I do is share the books I read on best practices in assessment. I have just begun to read a new one entitled *Challenging the Mind, Touching the Heart* (Reineke, 1998). It begins with this quotation, "Instruction touches the mind; assessment touches the heart" (p. 1).

References

Angelo, T., & Cross, P. (1993). *Classroom assessment techniques* (2nd ed.). San Francisco: Jossey-Bass.

Reineke, R. (1998). *Challenging the mind, touching the heart*. Thousand Oaks, CA: Corwin Press.

Shaughnessy, M. (1977). *Errors and expectations*. New York: Oxford University Press.

SECTION FOUR

Negotiating the Influence of High-Stakes Testing

- What is high-stakes testing? How is this term defined and/or viewed differently by various stakeholders in schooling?
- Referring back to Serafini's article in Section Three, what paradigm of assessment fits with most high-stakes testing?
- What are the purposes for and uses of high-stakes tests? Do the ends (e.g., school accountability) justify the means?
- What are the pitfalls associated with high-stakes testing? How can you help avoid the pitfalls?
- How does high-stakes testing affect teaching? Learning?
- How can you help students, especially those who struggle with reading, prepare for high-stakes tests?
- How can you use high-stakes testing to inform your teaching (e.g., to address reading comprehension)?

Evident in the six articles in this section is concern about the effects of high-stakes testing on children. The authors, however, wade through the concerns and also diligently seek ways to help students succeed on tests, achieve durable and meaningful learning, and maintain student-centered learning communities.

In the first article, Loraine H. Phillips expresses concern about her son's anxiety at the thought of being retained if he did not pass the Texas Assessment of Academic Skills (TAAS). After conferring with school personnel, she realized the goal was for straight-A students like her son to achieve perfect TAAS scores, helping to raise the school's average score. She ascertains that there is fallout from high-stakes testing—such as emotional distress and loss of real learning due to time spent on test preparation—for *all* students. This, she concludes, is a very high price to pay for school accountability.

The TAAS is the focus of a study by James V. Hoffman, Lori Czop Assaf, and Scott G. Paris. They surveyed Texas teachers about this high-stakes test, a test that has been presented to the nation as an exemplar for all other high-stakes testing. Results indicate that the Texas teachers have many concerns about the test. The authors present valuable contextual knowledge about high-stakes testing and also provide guidance on how to negotiate the high-stakes testing movement.

Given the fact that testing pressures are increasing, what is a teacher to do? Jo Worthy and James V. Hoffman, along with three other educators, advise a colleague on this question. In order for students to do well on tests, the teacher is advised to be proactive. Practical recommendations aim to help students prepare for test taking but avoid allowing test preparation to dominate instruction.

Loraine Phillips's son, referred to in the first article in this section, was an "A" student and good reader. Yet he worried about passing the TAAS. The dilemma of good readers who have low expectations for their performance on reading tests is addressed by Patrick P. McCabe. Practical suggestions to raise students' self-efficacy for high-stakes reading tests are useful in planning classroom instruction and in preparation for taking high-stakes reading tests.

In their important and compelling research, Sheila W. Valencia and Marsha Riddle Buly describe patterns of performance among "garden variety" fourth-grade readers who failed a fourth-grade standardized reading test. The authors collected individualized data on 108 readers, whose reading performance is clustered into six patterns. The researchers profile a representative reader for each cluster, especially examining word identification, meaning (comprehension and vocabulary), and fluency (rate and expression). The research suggests that to succeed on these tests, readers require instruction and text that target their unique pattern of needs.

Also in response to low test scores, Kathleen M. Lawrence planned and implemented a unit of instruction for third and fourth graders on critical comprehension of informational texts. Teaching the students to understand that "all questions are not equal," she introduces them to a "student friendly" strategy for recognizing the varied demands of comprehension questions. Lawrence provides a model for raising test scores while also teaching readers to achieve durable learning.

Additional Reading

- Airasian, P.W. (1998). Symbolic validation: The case of state-mandated, high-stakes testing. *Educational Evaluation and Policy Analysis, 10*(4), 301–313.
- Amanda, S., & Rabinowitz, S. (2000). *The high stakes of "high stakes" testing.* Washington, DC: Office of Educational Research & Improvement. (ERIC Document Reproduction Service No. ED455254)
- Calkins, L., Montgomery, K., & Santman, D. (with Falk, B.). (1998). *A teacher's guide to standardized reading tests: Knowledge is power.* Portsmouth, NH: Heinemann.
- Chase, B. (1999). Don't get mad. Get ready! *NEA Today, 17*(6), 2.
- Duke, N.K., & Ritchhart, R. (1997). No pain, high gain standardized test preparation. *Instructor, 107*(3), 89–92, 119.
- Heubert, J.P., & Hauser, R.M. (1999). *High stakes: Testing for tracking, promotion, and graduation.* A report of the National Research Association, New Orleans, LA.
- Popham, W.J. (2001). *The truth about testing: An educator's call to action.* Alexandria, VA: Association for Supervision and Curriculum Development.
- Raphael, T.E. (1982). Question-answering strategies for children. *The Reading Teacher, 36*(2), 186–190.
- Shepard, L.A., & Dougherty, K.C. (1991). *Effects of high-stakes testing on instruction.* Paper presented at the annual meeting of the American Educational Research Association/National Council on Measurement in Education, Chicago. (ERIC Document Reproduction Service No. ED337468)

Create a Statement of Reading Assessment Principles and Practices

Do your assessment principles include the view that assessment must be linked to student achievement—to durable learning? Given the realities of high-stakes testing (emotional stress, pressure to teach to the test, test preparation), discuss how you can maintain your assessment principles and still help students succeed on standardized measures of school achievement. Do you need to revise your principles to encompass the testing realities?

Next, compose an instructional overview, with at least two lesson plans, addressing preparation for high-stakes testing. Include both academic and social–emotional factors in this instructional plan. You are encouraged to access your state and school district reading standards to identify target objectives. Or, if your state standards are not readily available, refer to the goals specified in the Lawrence article. Develop your overview and lessons based on one or more of those stated objectives.

Testing a Texas Mama

Loraine H. Phillips

Joe came home from his seventh day of third grade with some scary news. "Mom, if I don't pass TAAS in April, then I won't be able to go to the fourth grade," he cried. He was frightened, and I could not console him. I was confused by how a straight-A student could feel so unsure and wondered about the threat of repeating third grade looming this early in the school year.

Upon further investigation, I found good news and bad news. Actually, students in our Texas school district were not going to be retained that year for failure to pass the Texas Assessment of Academic Skills (TAAS). But according to Texas state law and the Texas Education Agency, the next year would be different. Every Texas third grader in 2002–2003 must submit to the new law that requires all third graders to pass the new Texas Assessment of Knowledge and Skills (TAKS) in reading to be promoted to the fourth grade (Texas Education Agency, 2002).

I scheduled conferences with the teacher, principal, and school counselor and explained the emotional impact of Joe's seventh day of third grade. I also asked questions about why they felt he might not pass the TAAS test. I was surprised by their responses.

First, they said that often very bright students take for granted that they will do well on a test and simply rush through it. But their ultimate point was that they expected Joe to be one of the students at the school to attain Academic Recognition status in reading, an honor on the state report resulting from a student's nearly perfect reading score. This would raise the school's average test score. Now I understood that their goal for Joe was not simply passing the reading test, but receiving a perfect score.

The TAAS practice sheets started coming home in Joe's folder. His grades on these worksheets were admirable. Daily TAAS work was a normal part of Joe's school experience.

Then the practice tests began. Joe worked through two full days of TAAS practice tests, which were administered to simulate the actual test day. I shared my concerns with the teacher and principal about all this time during the school day spent on TAAS. But the procedure was districtwide. The results? On one of the practice reading tests Joe reached what would be considered Academic Recognition status, with a perfect score of 100%. Then we waited for the official April testing date, while Joe still worked on TAAS reading practice sheets each day at school. Would Joe disappoint his teachers and his school if he did not make a perfect score on the reading test? For me, a 94% does not beg the draconian question, "Why not a 100%?" But in this testing climate, how would Joe respond?

As parents, what can we do about the high stakes associated with this reading assessment—the practice sheets day after day, the formal practice tests to predict scores, and the goal for some children to attain a perfect score for their school's average? First, continue discussions with teachers, school officials, and senior school district administrators regarding the impact of high-stakes testing on children, teachers, and their learning environment. Remind everyone, including students, that perfection is a dangerous goal for anyone, especially a child. Do not end the dialogue upon hearing the explanation that this is the state's way of holding schools accountable. Encourage teachers and school officials to seek alternatives for classroom assessment intended to improve instruction and student learning (International Reading Association, 1999).

From *The Reading Teacher*, 56(7), 676.

My son is not a "Lone Star" in Texas schools. Many children share his experience. But this Texas mama is going to keep talking about the high impact of high-stakes testing.

References

International Reading Association. (1999). *High-stakes assessment in reading: A position statement of the International Reading Association.* Newark, DE: Author.

Texas Education Agency. (2002). *Student success initiative: A parent guide to testing requirements.* Retrieved February 27, 2002, from http://www.tea.state.tx.us/curriculum/ssi.html

High-Stakes Testing in Reading: Today in Texas, Tomorrow?

James V. Hoffman, Lori Czop Assaf, and Scott G. Paris

State-mandated achievement testing has grown at an exponential rate over the past two decades. Prior to 1980 fewer than a dozen states in the United States required mandated standardized testing for students, but in 2000 nearly every state used high-stakes testing. Accountability through testing, for students, teachers, and administrators, is the key leverage point for policymakers seeking to promote educational reform. Policies surrounding educational testing have become political spectacles and struggles for both publicity and control (Smith, Heinecke, & Noble, 1999–2000). State-mandated standardized tests have become the centerpiece for standards-based reform and are "high stakes" because they are often used to make decisions about tracking, promotion, and graduation of students (Heubert & Hauser, 1999). Centralized control is achieved through explicit educational standards (e.g., state curriculum frameworks, performance standards), and standardized tests that allow comparisons of students' relative performance. Educators, caught between standards and tests, are left to "align" classroom practices to meet the demands that surround them. Policy makers, and the public to this point, have judged the impact of educational reform efforts through a comparison of outcomes (i.e., changes in test scores) over time. Despite cautions and caveats from testing experts, high-stakes tests have become the public benchmark of educational quality (Linn, 2000).

This design for educational reform is conceptually elegant and seductive to those who embrace rational planning models. Many of the "results" reported by the media to date suggest positive effects for this model of change. But is this the whole story of reform? We think not. How much of the "success" is an illusion that masks an intrusion of testing into good teaching. We think a lot. We are concerned about the hidden costs of standards-based reform efforts on teachers, on the curriculum, and on teacher education. We are concerned about the negative impact on students, especially low-achieving and minority students, who may be retained in grade or denied high school promotion because of poor test performance. In an effort to explore these issues, we conducted a survey of a selected group of educators in one state—Texas. We chose Texas because the accountability system and the standards-based reform effort there have been recognized as "a model" for other states to follow. Indeed, the press has dubbed the reform of education through accountability and high-stakes testing as the "Texas Miracle" (Haney, 2000). We begin with a brief history of the testing movement in Texas and then report the findings from our study. We conclude with suggestions to minimize the negative impact of high-stakes testing on students and teachers.

TAAS in Texas

What began in the era of minimum basic-skills testing as TABS (Texas Assessment of Basic Skills) has expanded over the past 25 years to become one of the most highly touted state education accountability systems in the United States. The main part of this accountability system is the TAAS (Texas Assessment of Academic Skills).

From *The Reading Teacher*, *54*(5), 482–492. © 2001 by the International Reading Association.

This criterion-referenced test focuses, for the most part, on the areas of reading, writing, and mathematics and is linked directly to the state-prescribed curriculum. The TAAS test is set within a broader set of indices that feed into the total accountability system. For example, districts also monitor such factors as dropout rates, the proportion of students assigned to special education, and graduation rates. Changes in TAAS performance are examined carefully in relation to patterns on this broader set of accountability measures. These other measures are used as checks to determine if any positive changes in test performance are the result of higher levels of student learning or the result of some other factors (e.g., high levels of exemption for low-performing students). In recent years, TAAS has been expanded to include more students, more grade levels, and more subject areas. Currently, the test is administered annually in the spring to all students in Grades 3 through 8 in reading and mathematics. Students in Grades 4, 8, and 10 are tested in writing. Grade 8 students also take tests in science and social studies.

As the amount of testing has increased, so have the consequences associated with student performance on TAAS. For students, high school graduation is dependent on successful performance on TAAS. For schools and districts, accreditation is dependent in large part on TAAS performance. For principals and teachers, performance ratings and merit raises are influenced by TAAS performance of their students. The state requires the reporting of TAAS data to individual schools with school improvement plans developed in consideration of student performance patterns. The high-stakes consequences were intended to increase the quality of both teaching and learning. It is important to recognize that the identification of the "achievement problem," as well as the identification of a solution through rigorous testing, were both politically inspired and imposed on educators (Berliner & Biddle, 1997).

TAAS scores increased consistently during the last decade across all areas tested and at every grade level. For example, the proportion of students passing TAAS rose from 55% in 1994 to 74% in 1997. Further, the "gap" in performance between minority students and white students has narrowed. Only 32% of the African American students passed the tests in 1994 as compared with 56% in 1997. The passing rates for Hispanics rose from 41% to 62% in the same period. Scores rose again in 1998 with an overall passing rate of 78%. Scores for African American students rose to 63% and for Mexican American students to 68% (Texas Education Agency, 1999). In the future, TAAS may be extended into the primary grades and included as part of high school course examinations. Perhaps the most controversial proposal is to use TAAS performance as a requirement for grade-level promotion.

The apparent success of the TAAS has attracted national attention and figured prominently in Texas Governor George W. Bush's presidential campaign. Because the TAAS model of testing and accountability may be adopted by other states, it is important to examine it critically. A comprehensive review of the TAAS was conducted by Haney (2000), a testing expert who was also an expert witness in a lawsuit against the TAAS. Haney concluded that claims about Texas education have been greatly exaggerated because of five fundamental problems with the TAAS. First, the TAAS has continuing adverse effects on African American and Hispanic American students. Compared with Caucasian students, minority students have significantly lower passing rates on the TAAS; they are more likely to be retained in grade; and they are less likely to graduate from high school. Second, the use of TAAS tests to control high school graduation is contrary to professional standards regarding the use of test scores.

Third, Haney (2000) argued that the passing score set on the TAAS is arbitrary and results in racial discrimination. He conducted a small study in which randomly selected adults were asked to examine the TAAS data and set the passing scores in a way that would maximize the differences between racial groups. Their passing scores were virtually identical to the scores set by the Texas Education Authority (TEA) leading to the conclusion that the passing scores were discriminatory, whether intended or not. Fourth, analyses of the psychometric data on the TAAS, and comparisons with the National Assessment of Educational Progress (NAEP) test results, cast doubt on the validity of the TAAS test scores. The apparent increases in TAAS scores are due to factors such as teaching to the test, higher retention and dropout rates for minority students, and exemption of minority students by increased placement in special education. Fifth, there are more appropriate ways to use TAAS scores, such as in sliding combination with high school grades, that would increase the validity and decrease the negative impact of TAAS scores. The judge who presided over the TAAS lawsuit was not persuaded that these problems invalidate the TAAS. He concluded that the TAAS does have discriminatory consequences for black and Hispanic students but is not illegal because it is educationally necessary (*GI Forum Image De Tejas v. Texas Education Agency*, 87 F. Supp. 667 [W.D.Tex. 2000]).

Teachers Respond to TAAS

While the legal and political implications of the TAAS attract headlines, teachers are left to implement instruction aligned with the TAAS. What is happening at the classroom level in response to the expansion of TAAS and the pressure to perform well on tests? In an effort to explore this issue, we conducted a survey of a selected group of teachers in Texas that focused on TAAS and its effects. Our primary goal was to examine the ways in which TAAS affects teachers, students, and instruction from the perspective of the professional educators in classrooms and schools who are most affected by TAAS. Our goal is to reveal some of the ways in which the pressures of high-stakes assessments may threaten or compromise excellence in teaching.

The Participants

All of the participants in this survey were members of the Texas State Reading Association (TSRA), an affiliate of the International Reading Association. The membership of this organization includes classroom teachers, reading specialists, curriculum supervisors, and others in leadership positions. Most of the members hold advanced degrees with a specialization in reading and extensive teaching experience. The complete membership mailing list, containing approximately 4,000 names, was obtained from TSRA headquarters. Using a random selection process, 500 individuals were initially identified (20% of the total membership) and sent survey questionnaires with self-addressed and stamped return envelopes. No incentives were offered to respond. After three weeks, a reminder letter was sent out to those who had not responded. Additional surveys, using the random selection process, were mailed until a total of 200 usable surveys were returned. In all, 750 surveys were sent out. The 200 surveys in the sample represent an overall return rate of 27% from 5% of the total membership. No biases were detected in the response rates based on geographical areas of the state. However, the sample is a select group of educators in Texas with both expertise and experience in the teaching of reading. The sample also includes many teachers who work primarily with students in circumstances of poverty. It may be that teachers who cared most about their profession or who felt most affected by the TAAS were more likely to respond to the survey, but there is no reason to believe that the views of these 200 educators are not representative of Texas teachers.

In general, survey respondents were older and more experienced than average classroom teachers in Texas. Sixty-six percent of the sample were over the age of 30, and 33% were between the ages of 40 and 60. Likewise, 63% had more than 10 years of classroom experience and 29% had more than 20 years' experience. This is not surprising given that our selection process focused on teachers with an active affiliation with a professional organization. It is also not surprising that most respondents worked in elementary schools (78%) that have predominantly minority students (81%) and serve low-income communities (72%) where the need for reading specialists is greatest and the funding sources for reading specialists most available. Only 16% of the respondents reported working in schools where the passing rate was over 90% on TAAS. The majority of those responding (51%) were working in schools with a past passing rate for students between 70% and 90%, and 32% were working in schools where the overall passing rate was less than 70%.

The Survey

The survey consisted of 113 items about the following topics: demographic information (12 items); general attitudes of the respondent (20 items); perceived attitudes of others (22 items); test preparation and administration practices (27 items); uses of scores (16 items); effects of the TAAS on students (11 items); and overall impressions about TAAS testing (5 items). Many of the items included in the survey were exact duplicates or slightly modified versions of items that appeared on the Urdan and Paris (1994) survey of teachers in Michigan and the Nolen, Haladyna, and Haas (1989) survey of teachers in Arizona. All of the items about attitudes focused directly on TAAS testing. The majority of items about attitudes required responses on a five-point scale: 1 = Strongly Disagree, 2 = Disagree, 3 = Agree, 4 = Strongly Agree, and 5 = Don't Know. All "5" responses were treated as missing data and ignored in calculating the average responses. The last five items contained an invitation for extended responses.

The Findings

The data from the 200 returned surveys were entered into a data file for item-level analyses. Subsequently, some composite scores were constructed combining items from sections of the questionnaire (e.g., general attitudes). Items were combined based on a priori decisions about face validity rather than factor analyses of the data. In the reporting of findings that follows, we will refer to data from individual items as well as combined items. Composite scores are reported using means and standard deviations, and individual items are reported using categories of responses and percentages. Lower mean scores indicate greater disagreement with the proposition in the item; higher mean scores indicate greater agreement. The qualitative analysis of comments on the final section of the survey focused on common themes among the responses. More than 80% of the respondents offered additional comments on the five items, and their comments reveal the depth of teachers' feelings regarding TAAS testing.

General attitudes and perceptions of others. To examine teachers' general attitudes about the TAAS, we created a composite score from the following four items.

- Better TAAS tests will make teachers do a better job. ($M = 1.8$; $SD = .75$)
- TAAS motivates students to learn. ($M = 1.6$; $SD = .71$)
- TAAS scores are good measures of teachers' effectiveness. ($M = 1.6$; $SD = .68$)
- TAAS test scores provide good comparisons of the quality of school from different districts. ($M = 1.9$; $SD = .76$)

Each item was asked in order to assess teachers' perceptions of the political intentions of the TAAS test. The average rating on the composite variable for these four items was 1.7, a rating between Strongly Disagree and Disagree, which suggests that teachers disagree with many of the underlying intentions of the TAAS.

Another composite variable was created with items related to the validity of TAAS as a measure of student learning. The four variables included in this analysis follow.

- TAAS tests accurately measure achievement for minority students. ($M = 1.6$; $SD = .73$)
- TAAS test scores accurately measure achievement for limited English-speaking students. ($M = 1.5$; $SD = .64$)
- Students' TAAS scores reflect what students have learned in school during the past year. ($M = 1.8$; $SD = .75$)

- Students' TAAS scores reflect the cumulative knowledge that students have learned during their years in school. (*M* = 2.1; *SD* = .84)

The average rating on the composite variable for these four items was also 1.7, suggesting that teachers challenge the basic validity of the test, especially for minority students and ESL speakers who are the majority of students in Texas public schools.

Contrast these general attitudes and beliefs regarding TAAS with the perception of the respondents that administrators believe TAAS performance is an accurate indicator of student achievement (*M* = 3.1) and the quality of teaching (*M* = 3.3). Also, contrast this with the perception of the respondents that parents feel TAAS reflects the quality of schooling (*M* = 2.8). The gaping disparity between the perceptions of teachers and their estimates of administrators' and parents' attitudes suggests an uncomfortable dissonance in attitudes about the TAAS. Although we cannot determine whether the perceptions of the respondents regarding administrators' and parents' attitudes are accurate or not, the overwhelming majority of the respondents question the assumptions, intentions, and validity of the TAAS test but believe that parents and administrators do not share their views.

A final composite variable for this section was constructed to capture additional stances toward TAAS that explore some extreme positions. This variable consisted of responses to the following four items.

- TAAS should be eliminated. (*M* = 2.8; *SD* = .97)
- TAAS tests take too much time from the regular curriculum. (*M* = 3.2; *SD* = .89)
- TAAS tests are overemphasized by administrators. (*M* = 3.5; *SD* = .74)
- TAAS testing is not worth the time and money spent on it. (*M* = 3.0; *SD* = .91)

The average rating on the composite variable for these four items was 3.0 (Agree), again reflecting a strong negative attitude toward TAAS.

Preparation and administration of the TAAS. The questions in this section of the survey focused on the amount of time and attention that teachers devote to preparing students to take the TAAS and the kinds of strategies teachers use to prepare students to take the test. Nearly all of the respondents indicated that preparation for TAAS begins more than a month before testing. Comments from respondents suggested that preparation occurs across the entire academic year reaching its peak in the months just before TAAS is administered. The responses reveal an average of 8 to 10 hours per week spent in TAAS preparation activities. TAAS preparation is required by principals, and the majority of respondents reported that principals encourage more time than is currently devoted. Direct preparation is only one point of impact on the curriculum. Respondents reported that teachers almost always plan their curriculum for the year to emphasize those areas that will be tested on TAAS. Although some reformers may regard this planning as a positive outcome, many teachers consider it to have a negative impact on the curriculum and their instructional effectiveness.

The line between what is acceptable and what is not acceptable in standardized test preparation and administration is not always clearly delineated. Respondents were asked to rate the frequency with which teachers in their schools engaged in various testing practices related to TAAS using the following scale: 1 = Never, 2 = Sometimes, 3 = Often, and 4 = Always. The actions of teachers described in Table 1 are arranged from commonly accepted as appropriate to those that could be questioned. Although only some of these practices fall clearly into a "cheating" category, many approach an unethical stance toward testing. All are capable of affecting test performance. Haladyna, Nolen, and Haas (1991) referred to such practices on a continuum of "test pollution" because they have the potential to enhance, when present, the scores of

Table 1
Reported practices related to test preparation and administration

Practices	Means
Demonstrate how to mark the answer sheet correctly.	3.2
Give general tips on how to take tests.	3.4
Tell students how important it is to do well on the test.	3.7
Use commercial test-preparation materials.	3.4
Have students practice with tests from previous years.	3.4
Encourage student attendance.	3.7
Reduce stress and anxiety by teaching relaxation.	2.4
Teach test-taking skills.	3.5
Teach or review topics that will be on the test.	3.5
Give students hints about answers.	1.2
Point out mismarked items to students.	1.3
Give some students extra time to finish.	2.6
Provide instruction during the test.	1.2
Allow students breaks for fatigue or stress.	3.0
Directly point out to students correct responses.	1.1
Change students' answers once they have been recorded.	1.1
Award prizes to students who do well/pass the test.	2.4

students in unethical ways. Such practices raise test scores without actually changing students' underlying knowledge or achievement so they give the spurious impression of educational improvement.

Haladyna et al. (1991) argued that as pressures increase to raise test scores, unethical testing practices will occur more often. Our data support this hypothesis. All of the practices noted in Table 1 were reported with greater frequency in schools that had a history of low TAAS performance. For example, the practice of rewarding students for doing well occurred at a reported mean level of 3.4 (Often +) in the schools with a history of low TAAS scores; whereas the practice was reported at a mean level of 1.9 (Sometimes –) in the schools with a history of high performance. In the lowest performing schools, the most blatant forms of "cheating" were reported at higher levels than in the schools with a history of high performance. The practices included giving hints about answers ($M = 1.7$), pointing out mismarked items ($M = 1.7$), providing instruction during the test ($M = 1.5$), and directly pointing out correct responses ($M = 1.5$). Although the frequency of these unethical practices is low even in the low-performing schools, the rates are consistent with previous findings (e.g., Haas, Haladyna, & Nolen, 1989; Nolen et al., 1989). The total combination of practices creates a disturbing scenario of teachers succumbing to pressures to raise test scores at any cost and the TAAS scores being contaminated by factors unrelated to students' abilities.

Effects on students. The items included in this section of the survey explored the impact of the TAAS on students and were borrowed directly from the surveys used in the Arizona and Michigan research cited earlier. The findings suggest the same patterns for TAAS as with other standardized tests. The data from our survey are displayed in Table 2. According to teachers, many students experience headaches and stomachaches while taking the TAAS. A surprising

Table 2
Effects of TAAS testing on students

Behavior	Reported frequency			
	Never %	Sometimes %	Often %	Always %
Truancy	40	52	5	3
Upset stomach	7	53	32	8
Vomiting	18	53	21	8
Crying	22	60	13	5
Irritability	12	50	30	8
Increased aggression	22	43	28	7
Wetting or soiling themselves	74	23	3	0
Headaches	8	45	33	14
Refusing to take test	53	37	7	3
Increased misconduct	29	42	23	6
Freezing up	12	54	25	9

number are anxious, irritable, or aggressive. The data are troubling because discomfort and illness during the TAAS undermine students' test performance, further polluting the scores and decreasing their validity. It seems likely that low-scoring students would be the ones most negatively affected, which puts at-risk students in more jeopardy during TAAS testing. We did not explore directly the effects of TAAS on student motivation or self-concept, although the negative effects of standardized tests, in particular on low-performing and minority students, have been clearly demonstrated (Paris, Lawton, Turner, & Roth, 1991).

Uses of TAAS. Two composite variables were created to summarize the uses of TAAS results. The first variable focused on how teachers use TAAS results by combining responses on the following items:

- To make decisions about curricula. (M = 3.2; SD = .74)
- To measure school or classroom effectiveness. (M = 3.1; SD = .76)
- To make decisions about how to group students. (M = 2.7; SD = .92)
- To identify students for remedial programs. (M = 3.0; SD = .86)
- To predict future performance. (M = 2.8; SD = .76)
- To diagnose learning problems for specific students. (M = 2.4; SD = .90)
- To assign students to low-track and basic classes. (M = 2.3; SD = 1.0)

Each of these items had been rated separately on a scale of 1 = Never, 2 = Sometimes, 3 = Often, and 4 = Always. The mean response for the composite variable for these seven items was 2.8 (SD = .62) suggesting that TAAS results are often used in these ways.

The second composite variable focused on the uses of TAAS results by school principals. Here we combined responses on the following items:

- To help teachers improve their instruction. (M = 2.8; SD = .86)

- To identify strengths and weaknesses of the curriculum. ($M = 3.0$; $SD = .75$)
- To evaluate teacher effectiveness. ($M = 3.0$; $SD = .80$)
- To evaluate school effectiveness. ($M = 3.3$; $SD = .73$)
- To evaluate the effectiveness of new programs. ($M = 2.9$; $SD = .82$)
- To recognize outstanding student or teacher performance. ($M = 2.8$; $SD = .98$)

The mean for the composite variable for these six items was 3.0 ($SD = .60$) suggesting that TAAS results are often used in these ways. None of the uses described in this section are surprising. What is a matter of concern is the extreme if not sole reliance on TAAS results as the data source in guiding planning, decisions, and actions.

Overall impressions on TAAS. This final section of the survey included five questions and teachers' comments about each topic. We provide the questions and responses below.

1. The results from TAAS testing over the past several years seem to indicate that scores are on the rise. Do you think this rise in test scores reflects increased learning and higher quality teaching?

Yes = 27%   No = 50%   Not Sure = 23%

Half of the respondents did not believe that the increases in TAAS scores were the result of higher levels of student learning. Their comments suggest that they believed the higher scores were the direct result of teaching to the test.

> "Teaching to the test and test-taking strategies."
>
> "Teaching to the format of the test."
>
> "Students know how to take the test because we practice ad nauseam."
>
> "Teachers are spending the school day teaching to the test."

Awareness of the objectives as well as better training and test practice materials were also given credit.

> "We have better training on how to prepare students."
>
> "We know what to expect on the test."

Many believed that TAAS is incapable of tapping the higher level learning that is taking place in schools.

> "TAAS does not require higher level thinking and does not allow for it."

Some teachers even suggested that the test is getting easier.

> "I think the tests are easier to make the legislators look better."

Some teachers raised the explanation of cheating.

> "There are a lot of teachers and administrators who know how to 'cheat' and get higher scores from kids...they don't want their school to score bad, so they cheat."

The results from the NAEP (Donahue, Voelkl, Campbell, & Mazzeo, 1999), as well as the results of the TEA's own national comparison study (Texas Education Agency, 1997), suggested that the improved scores in the area of reading are restricted to the TAAS test and that these increases are not reflected on the performance of Texas students on nationally standardized tests. Apparently, many respondents felt the same way because they indicated that the increases in test scores might be due to artificial causes such as teaching to the test, rather than increasing children's reading abilities.

2. It has been suggested that the areas not tested directly on the TAAS (e.g., fine arts) and other areas not tested at certain grade levels (e.g., science at the fourth-grade level) receive less and less attention in the curriculum. What do you feel about this assertion?

Very True = 49%   Somewhat True = 36%
Somewhat False = 8%   Totally False = 7%

The responses related to the second item indicate that there is considerable curriculum displacement due to TAAS because 85% of the teachers replied that "if it's not being tested, it's not being taught." These findings are consistent with those of Darling-Hammond and Wise (1985) who found that tested content was taught at the expense of untested content.

> "We were told by administration if it isn't tested don't spend the bulk of your time teaching it."
>
> "We hardly teach social studies and science."
>
> "There is no time to teach these subject areas because of TAAS."
>
> "At our school, third- and fourth-grade teachers are told not to teach social studies and science until March (after TAAS)."
>
> "The test has become the curriculum."
>
> "The principal told us not to be teaching social studies and science."
>
> "We only teach TAAS. The rest is just fluff. My social studies and science grades come from TAAS reading passages. Everything must be done in TAAS format."

3. It has also been suggested that the emphasis on TAAS is forcing some of the best teachers to leave teaching because of the restraints the tests place on decision making and the pressures placed on them and their students. Do you agree or disagree?

Strongly Agree = 42% Somewhat Agree = 43%
Disagree = 11% Strongly Disagree = 4%

The third item explored the consequences of high-stakes testing on teachers. Although teachers may not value the TAAS as much as parents and administrators, they are expected to teach to the TAAS and raise test scores. This leads to frustration and a desire to escape the pressures of the TAAS. Eighty-five percent of the teachers expressed agreement with the statement that some of the best teachers are leaving the field because of the TAAS.

> "People do not want to work in this type of environment."
>
> "I know of a great many (who are leaving), and I am also."

Some teachers described efforts to flee TAAS pressure without dropping out of teaching altogether.

> "I used to teach fourth grade, but now I teach first grade. I just don't want the pressure."
>
> "This is why I teach in a specialization area where TAAS is not tested."
>
> "It has dramatically shifted the purpose of teaching. We are 'required' to teach to the TAAS. I became a teacher to teach children."

4. TAAS is being recommended as the basis for making promotion decisions about students in some schools. What is your view regarding this policy?

Strongly Agree = 4% Somewhat Agree = 30%
Disagree = 36% Strongly Disagree = 30%

The use of TAAS as a requirement for high school graduation is a reality. The proposals for using TAAS to control grade-level advancement are widespread. A substantial majority (66%) of the respondents opposed the use of TAAS scores to make decisions about grade-level advancement.

> "If you have a poor instrument, then you will always make poor decisions."
>
> "TAAS + promotions = bull—."

Many commented on the logistical nightmare that would be created by such a policy.

> "Fourth grade will be huge. In my class alone I suspect 40% to fail."

Some expressed general dissatisfaction with retention as a solution to anything.

> "Retention doesn't work and research has shown this! We should be considering other areas to help, not the same old things that didn't work before."

Most of those responding, including those who seem to favor the use of TAAS in promotion decisions, suggest that multiple factors should be considered.

"I think it could support the decision on promotion, but it should not be the sole source for this decision."

"TAAS should be a factor in promotion decisions but not the sole criterion."

5. Do the informal assessments you currently make in your classroom provide you with a sufficient basis for good instructional decision making, or do TAAS results help you?

Informal assessments are sufficient = 43%
TAAS helps some = 52% TAAS helps a lot = 5%

This notion of multiple measures was confirmed by the respondents' answers. Many favored a combination of measures.

Discussion

The findings from this study are consistent with research on the negative effects of "high-stakes" assessments (e.g., Airasian, 1988; Madaus, 1988; Meisels, 1989; Paris, 1998; Shepard & Dougherty, 1991). The findings from this study are also consistent with two other studies of the TAAS. In one study, Gordon and Reese (1997) surveyed 100 Texas teachers (who were apparently graduate students in their program) about the impact of TAAS on teachers and students. Twenty individuals were also interviewed. Respondents reported that preparation for the TAAS was the main activity for months before the test and that there was a de-emphasis on teaching content that was not related to the TAAS. Of the 20 interviewed, 19 teachers felt that the TAAS was not an appropriate tool for evaluating students or teachers. Teachers reported that the TAAS was culturally biased and had deleterious impact on at-risk students. A second study conducted by Haney (2000) involved two surveys of secondary teachers in Texas. He summarized four similarities among the surveys administered in his study, the survey reported in this paper, and the Gordon and Reese (1997) study. All the similarities undermine effective teaching and learning.

1. Texas schools are devoting a huge amount of time and energy preparing students specifically for the TAAS.
2. Emphasis on TAAS is hurting more than helping teaching and learning in Texas.
3. Emphasis on TAAS is particularly harmful to at-risk students.
4. Emphasis on TAAS contributes to retention in grade and dropping out of school.

This study confirms the negative impact on teachers and students in Texas. The respondents to this survey, experts in reading and close to the classroom, reported that the TAAS does not measure what it purports, is unfair to minority students, is affecting instruction in negative ways, is leading both students and teachers to "drop out," and is being used in ways that are invalid. These educators would argue that the triumph of the Texas accountability system touted by politicians, bureaucrats, and test publishers should be challenged. The extensions of TAAS into more subject areas and into earlier grade levels are disturbing. More disturbing is the prospect that many state policymakers regard the TAAS as successful and want to expand the use of TAAS results for teacher evaluation and student promotion.

Today in Texas, Tomorrow?

The impact of Texas on textbooks, curriculum, and assessment across the United States is enormous and continues to expand. The Texas state curriculum, The Texas Essential Knowledge and Skills, is used to guide commercial textbook development and may become the de facto reading curriculum for a large part of the United States. As public recognition of the TAAS increases, it is likely to be emulated by other states too. When tests drive instruction, teachers become increasingly responsive to the demands of the tests and less considerate of the needs of the students in their classrooms. Instruction that conforms to high-stakes tests in content and format will become more patterned and predictable and less responsive and adaptive. Teachers and students deserve better, and the respondents to our survey recognize this. Our survey forms were filled with comments that revealed frustration, anger, and helplessness with respect to TAAS testing.

> "I am very sad that education has stooped to the low level of measuring performance with standardized testing and Texas has taken it even lower with their TAAS. We know what works in education—we just seem to ignore the research and keep on banging our heads against the 'TAAS wall' and 'retention walls.'"
>
> "Please support teachers more than ever. Our children are hurting more than ever. If there was ever a time to change, it is now. Give teachers back their classrooms. Let them teach and spend quality time with their students. They need us!"
>
> "I think TAAS is the biggest joke in Texas. I have never seen such an injustice."
>
> "I believe that TAAS interferes with the very nature of our job. The pressure from administrators to increase campus scores leaves teachers little time for real instruction. My heart breaks to see so many teachers 'just surviving.' I believe that our solution is just to support each other because the public has no real concept of the situation."
>
> "TAAS is ruining education in Texas! Help!"

What Can Be Done?

If we were totally fatalistic about the future of reading assessment, we would not have conducted this study, nor would we be writing this article. We believe there are actions to be taken within Texas and the United States to stem the tide of high-stakes assessments. As part of a profession of concerned reading educators, we suggest the following steps.

Provide data. Statistical claims regarding high-stakes assessments typically use data provided by those who control its design, administration, and data analysis. We are in desperate need of independent research that provides a critical analysis of the effects of high-stakes assessments on stakeholders from a variety of perspectives. Parents, teachers, and students should be surveyed about the high-stakes tests given by their districts.

Compare. There are a number of other states that have taken other paths to ensure educational accountability that are based on sound principles of assessment without the high-stakes pressure of TAAS. We need careful examination and comparison of the alternatives. Fair-Test (http://fairtest.org) offers a good example for how this kind of principled analysis can be conducted (Neill, 1999).

Advocate. Both individually and collectively, we must advocate for reasonable assessment of students in schools. The International Reading Association (1999) has taken a bold stance toward high-stakes assessment. Other national, state, and local organizations need to act similarly. We believe it is particularly important that student advocacy groups and parent groups become more active in voicing their concerns.

Challenge. The Mexican-American Legal Defense and Educational Fund (MALDEF) has taken the lead in challenging the TAAS test and its use as a graduation requirement in Texas as racially discriminatory. Despite a complex and lengthy court battle, the MALDEF suit was not successful. More challenges should be made, and the current efforts supported.

Explore alternatives. No one is opposed to accountability in education. We must demonstrate that the goals of accountability can be achieved through alternative testing. For example, states and districts could use a NAEP model in which only some sampled students are tested. This removes the onus of an individual score for students or teachers yet still provides an estimate of achievement by district or state. When high-stakes decisions are required about promotion, retention or graduation of students, or the quality of teaching, multiple measures should be used.

Don't be seduced. Silence prevails in educational circles with respect to TAAS-type testing because it is viewed as a necessary evil to achieve other goals. Recent pay raises for teachers in Texas have been negotiated in the context of accepting, if not embracing, high-stakes assessment. The words of the president of the National Education Association speak to this.

> [Our] colleagues in Texas...are dealing positively and creatively with standards-based instruction...I repeat, high standards and high stakes tests are here to stay. They have thrust us into a brave new world. By all means, let us be brave and affirmative in shaping this new world in the best interests of the children we serve. (Chase, 1999)

Similarly, some minority leaders have been silent on high-stakes testing because low performance is seen as a way of increasing the flow of money to needy schools. These are indefensible positions in the light of the negative effects of such tests on education.

It is easy to get discouraged by the TAAS frenzy and the political steamrollers of standards and testing. The political and economic forces supporting the movement are formidable. TAAS is approaching a hundred-million-dollar-a-year industry in direct costs alone (Brooks, 1998). Teaching to TAAS is far easier than teaching to students. Every good teacher who drops out opens a space for someone who might be more vulnerable to the pressures of high-stakes testing. We urge teachers to stay the course. Be creatively compliant and selectively defiant as it fits the learning needs of your students. As leaders in reading and literacy education, we have an important role to play in the appropriate use of high-stakes assessment. Our professional colleagues, the voices of those responding in our survey, are crying out for assistance and guidance. Their pleas are not just about themselves and their situation but the plight of the students they serve. Will we remain silent?

References

Airasian, P.W. (1988). Symbolic validation: The case of state-mandated, high-stakes testing. *Educational Evaluation and Policy Analysis, 10*, 301–313.

Berliner, D.C., & Biddle, B.J. (1997). *The manufactured crisis: Myths, fraud, and the attack on America's public schools*. White Plains, NY: Longman.

Brooks, P.A. (1998, December 16). Lawmaker proposes more-frequent TAAS testing. *Austin American Statesman*, p. B5.

Chase, B. (1999). Don't get mad. Get ready! *NEA Today, 17*(6), 2.

Darling-Hammond, L., & Wise, A. (1985). Beyond standardization: State standards and school improvement. *The Elementary School Journal, 85*, 315–336.

Donahue, P.L., Voelkl, K.E., Campbell, J.R., & Mazzeo, J. (1999). *NAEP 1998 reading: Report card for the nation and states*. Washington, DC: U.S. Department of Education.

Gordon, S.P., & Reese, M. (1997). High stakes testing: Worth the price? *Journal of School Leadership, 7*, 345–368.

Haas, N.S., Haladyna, T.M., & Nolen, S.B. (1989). *Standardized testing in Arizona: Interviews and written comments from teachers and administrators* (Tech. Rep. No. 89-3). Phoenix, AZ: Arizona State University, West Campus.

Haladyna, T., Nolen, S.B., & Haas, N.S. (1991). Raising standardized achievement test scores and the origins of test pollution. *Educational Researcher, 20*(5), 2–7.

Haney, W. (2000, April). *The myth of the Texas miracle in education*. Paper presented at the annual meeting of the American Educational Research Association, New Orleans, LA.

Heubert, J.P., & Hauser, R.M. (1999). *High stakes: Testing for tracking, promotion, and graduation*. A report of the National Research Council, Washington, DC: National Academy Press.

International Reading Association. (1999). *High-stakes testing in reading. A position statement of the International Reading Association*. Newark, DE: Author.

Linn, R.L. (2000). Assessments and accountability. *Educational Researcher, 29* (2), 4–15.

Madaus, G.F. (1988). The influence of testing on curriculum. In L.N. Tanner (Ed.), *Critical issues in curriculum: 87th yearbook of the National Society for the Study of Education* (pp. 83–121). Chicago: University of Chicago Press.

Meisels, S.J. (1989). High stakes testing in kindergarten. *Educational Leadership, 46*, 16–22.

Neill, M. (1999). Is high-stakes testing fair? *NEA Today, 17*(6), 6.

Nolen, S.B., Haladyna, T.M., & Haas, N.S. (1989). *A survey of Arizona teachers and schools administrators on the uses and effects of standardized achievement testing* (Tech. Rep. No. 89-2). Phoenix, AZ: Arizona State University, West Campus.

Paris, S.G. (1998). Why learner-centered assessment is better than high-stakes testing. In N. Lambert & B. McCombs (Eds.), *Issues in school reform: A sampler of psychological perspectives on learner-centered schools* (pp. 189–209). Washington, DC: American Psychological Association.

Paris, S.G., Lawton, T.A., Turner, J.C., & Roth, J.L. (1991). A developmental perspective on standardized achievement testing. *Educational Researcher, 20,* 12–20.

Shepard, L.A., & Dougherty, K.C. (1991). *Effects of high-stakes testing on instruction.* Paper presented at the annual meeting of the American Educational Research Association, Chicago. (ERIC Document Reproduction Service No. ED 337 468)

Smith, M.L., Heinecke, W., & Noble, A.J. (1999–2000). State assessment becomes political spectacle: Parts I–VIII. *Teachers College Record* [Online]. Available at http://www.tcrecord.org (ID Number: 10454)

Texas Education Agency. (1997). *Texas Student Assessment Program: Student performance results 1995–1996.* Austin, TX: Author.

Urdan, T.C., & Paris, S.G. (1994). Teachers' perceptions of standardized achievement tests. *Educational Policy, 8*(2), 137–156.

The Press to Test

Jo Worthy and James V. Hoffman

Visit any school, especially in the spring, and you'll probably hear talk about standardized tests. In some schools, this talk extends throughout the year as teachers and administrators wonder how best to prepare students for tests while maintaining meaningful instruction. In May we posed the following question:

> I am concerned about the increased focus on required testing. One concern is the instructional time used to prepare students. The test itself takes almost a week to complete, and some teachers start "practicing" for it weeks or even months in advance. I am on pins and needles waiting to hear the results because I know they will be seen as a reflection on my teaching and on my students' learning. I want my students to learn what they need to know, but I don't think "teaching to the test" is right. I would love to have some ideas from educators who have fought this battle. Do you know of ways that I can be an effective teacher while still helping my students to do well on the tests?

We received many thoughtful replies to the question. We selected three that reflect the range of ideas and professional experiences of the respondents. We learned from these authors that, while tests are inevitable, they do not have to dominate instruction.

Make the Test Serve the Student

The dilemma of how to be an effective teacher while still helping students to do well on "the test" is rapidly becoming an international one. As the global economy and the nature of literacy and its socioeconomic function continue to change, western society finds an outlet for its concerns in the so-called literacy crisis and alleged lack of basic skills. The standardized test, in one form or another, has become the instrument of choice for comparing present and past achievement ("things aren't what they used to be") and the potential of one nation with another. As educators, we realize that such tests are not neutral in origin or intent, in spite of their seeming objectivity and scientific nature. We also appreciate that standardized assessment narrows the curriculum, limits the body of knowledge available, objectifies the individuals who are our students, and places teacher and student alike in the grip of what Michel Foucault referred to as "one of the great instruments of power" (p. 196, *The Foucault Reader*, Paul Rabinow, Ed., Pantheon, 1984).

What can be done to use the power of this widespread policy in a beneficial way, to put a more positive spin on a potentially time consuming but mandatory experience? What counts is to make the test serve the needs of the students rather than merely those of the authority imposing it. One of my colleagues commented recently that the most that could be said for our annual standardized testing process was that learning to take a test was a useful life skill. Agreeing with many educators (e.g., Lucy Calkins, Kate Montgomery, and Donna Santman, *A Teacher's Guide to Standardized Reading Tests: Knowledge Is Power*, Heinemann, 1998) who believe that knowledge is power, we have begun to counter the power of the test while developing our students' learning without betraying professional ethics and obligations. Our aim is to focus on transferable skills.

Rather than practicing commercially published exercises, for example, I suggest encouraging students to analyze the type of reading passages presented on the test, and helping them

From *The Reading Teacher*, 53(7), 596–598.

appreciate the fact that the nature of some of them offers little opportunity for engagement. Expose them to factual items and other genres as well as the stories they enjoy. Help them to develop the skill of "getting inside the examiner's head" by presenting answers and asking for possible questions, with supporting proof, rather than vice versa. Model reading with an audience (the tester) and a purpose (what does he or she want to know?) in mind. Use critical literacy tools as test-taking life skills for all those future occasions when tests will be taken and questions asked whose answers are predetermined. Have students create cloze passages; if they "do" them themselves, they will understand the rationale behind them. Give immediate feedback on the successful use of these strategies, validating them and encouraging ongoing use by grade or report card commentary. The all-pervasive power of the test can be countered if we make aspects of it useful and relevant to future learning for life, encouraging our students to become active rather than passive participants.

Rita Armitage, deputy director, a learning center, Ottawa, Ontario, Canada

Develop Strategies for Success

Whether or not it is a worthwhile use of instructional time, whether or not they are authentic assessments, whether we like it or not, standardized, norm-referenced tests are having an incredibly powerful impact on U.S. schools right now. It is imperative for our students to know how to take a test. This does not mean, though, that teachers need to teach test preparation from the same philosophical base as those who wrote the tests.

I would highly recommend that the educator who posed the above question read *A Teacher's Guide to Standardized Reading Tests: Knowledge Is Power* by Lucy Calkins, Kate Montgomery, and Donna Santman. The authors point out that most teachers, regardless of how they teach, prepare their students for a standardized test in the same way—by repetitious practice completing multiple-choice worksheets in an environment that mimics the test-taking day. However, test practice is not the same as test preparation, so Calkins et al. maintain that teachers must create a test-taking curriculum that evolves from effective methods and structures that are used in student-centered, literature-based classrooms to teach reading and writing.

After reading *A Teacher's Guide to Standardized Reading Tests* my second-grade team and I developed materials and minilessons that taught test taking in a manner more compatible with our teaching practices and beliefs in how young children learn. Our students worked in pairs and small groups to read and discuss standardized tests as a genre of literature. The children learned to read the test as if it were a video game to beat or a scavenger hunt to win. As we analyzed tests, the second graders loved the challenge of finding the traps and tricks set by the Tricky Testmaster (Tricky T for short).

Together we developed strategies for reading and succeeding at this particular form of literature. A few of the strategies we had on our list were (a) find the answer on the page, not out of your life; (b) use "feather writing" to keep track of your thinking—write or underline so lightly that the computer cannot see it; (c) prevent "brain drain" by taking a "brain break"; (d) don't fall into the trap of thinking that there is a pattern to the answers; and (e) when it says "What is a good title?" remember it really means "What is the main idea?"

During testing week, the second graders were confident and excited about taking the test. They felt very prepared to beat Tricky T and actually thought that the test was fun. Now I wait with too many other teachers across the U.S. for our test scores to be returned, but while we wait we need to work toward educating legislators and the public about more authentic forms of assessment and methods of accountability. Let's hope the children of our students will have no idea what a standardized test is.

Meg Johnson, elementary teacher, Agua Caliente, Tucson, Arizona, USA

Be On the Learner's Side

"How can I be an effective teacher while still preparing my students to do well on the tests?" Just by asking the question you have taken the first step of separating the test from the life of the learner. Keep your eye on what feeds and what defeats the learner in the long run. Then intensify those elements that serve the life of the learner while also meeting the short-term goals of the test.

After the goals are put into perspective it's time to turn to the learner. The best way to figure out which tools will help your students the most, because you will have to choose, is to put yourself on the side of the learner. I heard Donald Graves once explain that he never gives his students an assignment that he does not also do himself. Putting oneself into the process—on the side of the writer, the reader, the learner—gives one information that is not available to the reviewer, evaluator, or judge. The creation of a work, the process of problem solving and making meaning, is a delicate process not easily uncovered by examining only the end product, the writing sample, or answers alone. Teachers of writing are better teachers if they are writers. Teachers of readers are stronger teachers if they allow themselves to be informed by their own experiences as readers.

Rather than working from the test backwards, as we tend to do, it is more productive in the long run to begin with the natural road of the learner. Rather than ask our students to practice writing to a prompt in order to learn to stay focused on a topic, we would make better use of our time to begin with the students' own pieces and help them experience the power of a focused piece. Then we can talk about the nature of writing to prompts and staying focused on a preselected topic. The students will already be armed with the understanding of what is to be accomplished, through experiences with their own works.

In order to help our students do well on tests designed outside our classrooms, we must first set them on the road to becoming self-satisfied, natural learners who engage in the process for its own reward. First a student must understand for himself or herself the value of reading and writing and thinking clearly. Only then will we be able to spend some reasonably small amount of time developing a specific understanding of what a test is meant to assess and how to use what one already knows in order to demonstrate that understanding in an artificial situation.

Karen Lewis, teacher, Palm Lake Elementary, Orlando, Florida, USA

Enhancing Self-Efficacy for High-Stakes Reading Tests

Patrick P. McCabe

Federal legislation in the United States (the No Child Left Behind Act of 2001) calls for annual testing in reading and other subject areas in grades 3 through 8. Ostensibly, the purpose of this law is to monitor educational progress and identify children who have fallen behind academically so that they can receive help. However, evidence suggests that neither retention nor social promotion has a significant impact on student achievement (Jenkins & Weldon, 1999; Roderick, Nagaoka, Bacon, & Easton, 2000; Thompson & Cunningham, 2000) and that, even with effective remediation, long-term negative effects of retention remain (Hauser, 2000).

Called "high-stakes" tests because the important decision about promotion to the next grade often depends heavily on standardized test scores, these measures and performance on them are critical to the lives of millions of children, parents, and teachers. They remain important despite recognition that reliance upon one measure —high-stakes tests—to determine promotion is problematic for many reasons. The alternative position is that multiple measures more accurately determine student ability and, therefore, provide a stronger "database" for such important decisions (American Educational Research Association, 2000; Ananda & Rabinowitz, 2000; Domenech, 2000; Gratz, 2000; Hoffman, Assaf, & Paris, 2001; Howe, 2000; Huber & Moore, 2000; International Reading Association, 1999; Kane, 2001; Lewis, 2000; Madaus & Clarke, 2001; Prystowsky, 2001; Smith & Fey, 2000; Villaire, 2001).

In order to more fully appreciate the effect of annual high-stakes testing, it helps to understand the perspective of students who read well but unfortunately do not do well on high-stakes tests of reading ability. Their reading scores reflect test anxiety to a large degree, rather than true reading ability. (Those who design and produce standardized tests call this "testing error.") According to Pintrich and Schunk (1996), as many as 25% of all elementary- and secondary-level children in the United States, about 10 million, have some degree of test anxiety, and about 10%, some 4 to 5 million, have a level of test anxiety considered high. Thus, while the stage has been set at the federal legislative level with the decision to test annually, a hypothetical but likely scenario in the cafeteria of an elementary school not far from Washington, D.C., reveals two teachers' trepidations and misgivings about high-stakes testing.

Mr. Wilson and Mrs. Parker (pseudonyms) are overheard discussing high-stakes testing. Mr. Wilson says,

> I do not know what to do with Lucinda. She reads so well and gets high grades on assignments, but she cannot take standardized tests. She tells me that she "freezes and cannot think clearly" when she sees those tests. I have practiced the test over and over with her with old tests to make her used to it, but still she does not do well. I also keep telling her to believe in herself and that she has the ability to do well on tests. But this does not seem to be working. I am so frustrated. She is really such a good reader, and I feel so bad for her. The test is just around the corner.

Mrs. Parker voices similar complaints about a student in her class; they finish the conversation feeling exasperated and without hope for their students.

From *The Reading Teacher*, 57(1), 12-20.

It is inevitable that, after test day, Mr. Wilson, Mrs. Parker, and many other teachers in U.S. schools will be disappointed in low scores of those students who read well and who usually do well on classroom assignments. Such students may even develop symptoms of learned helplessness, the feeling that there is little or nothing that can be done to improve their performance on tests. If unchecked, this perception of inadequacy will grow through the years and become a self-fulfilling prophecy; individuals who have such feelings doom themselves to less than optimal performance on tests critical to their lives. When they discuss testing, these children might say "I have always been that way, I just don't do well on tests," thus protecting their ego. The national testing mandate coupled with the poor test-taking ability of students like Lucinda dictates that teachers focus on students' test-taking skills, especially because the outcome is so critical. Instruction should strengthen such skills and help students develop a positive attitude toward taking these important tests.

Sources of Self-Efficacy

The degree to which an individual possesses and enacts the skills necessary to accomplish a particular task is called efficacy. A student is an efficacious reader to the degree that he or she enacts and implements skills necessary to successfully complete a particular reading task. Lucinda's efficacy for reading is high because, according to her teacher, she is an on-level reader. However, her perception of her efficacy—her self-efficacy—for doing well on a high-stakes reading test is low. Self-efficacy, the "Belief in one's capabilities to organize and execute the courses of action required to produce given attainments" (Bandura, 1997, p. 3), is task specific and may vary in relation to the task. An individual may have high self-efficacy for tennis but low self-efficacy for swimming, or high self-efficacy for reading during regular class sessions and low self-efficacy for reading on a test.

Self-efficacy develops as a result of feedback from family, school, and community interactions throughout the developmental continuum, and the interpretation and degree of attention given to each or all sources of feedback will depend upon individual cognitive and social experiences. The nature and effect of this feedback will vary, and therefore students in Mr. Wilson's class will have self-efficacy beliefs that differ in origin, strength, and generalizability across tasks.

For example, familial factors may affect how self-efficacy skills are learned and the degree to which they are sustained. Children who participate in activities that enable them to recognize their ability to accomplish a variety of tasks develop stronger feelings of self-efficacy than children who lack that opportunity (Bandura, 1997). The strength and development of self-efficacy will even vary within a family. "Different family structures—as reflected in family size, birth order, and sibling constellation patterns—create different social references for comparative appraisal of personal efficacy" (Bandura, 1997, p. 169). First-born children tend to have parents or caretakers as a reference or a model to measure their ability to accomplish a given task; children born thereafter tend to have siblings as perhaps a less than perfect reference or model. In another example, adults from individualistic cultures relied more upon individually based feedback to determine their level of self-efficacy; those from collectivistic cultures relied more upon group-based feedback (Earley, 1994; Earley, Gibson, & Chen, 1999).

Other cultural and familial dimensions that affect children's efficacy development and judgment include, but are not limited to, the role of authority, personal autonomy and perceived or actual social distance from relative power and control in the society, and degree of avoidance of uncertainty and ambiguity (Oettingen, 1995). Children from authoritative cultures or families may validate their efficacy by relying most upon verbal persuasion from teachers and other adults; those from cultures or families that are, or are perceived to be, disenfranchised in this society may rely most upon peer modeling and even distrust verbal persuasion from authority figures; and those from cultures or families most tolerant of ambiguity and uncertainty may rely most upon successes from enactive mastery experiences for efficacy judgments. These influences upon self-efficacy may operate to varying degrees independently or, more likely, in combination and underlie the need for different strategies or combinations of strategies that will be best for individual learners.

Self-efficacy is an important influence on motivation—the degree to which an individual will become engaged in and expend physical or mental energy in an activity. Mr. Wilson can help Lucinda realize that she has the ability to do well on standardized tests and thus reduce her test anxiety if he designs and implements a test-taking program that is consistent with the development of self-efficacy. Such a program should include opportunities for Lucinda to receive and evaluate feedback from the four principal sources of self-efficacy knowledge. According to Bandura (1997), these sources are enactive mastery, vicarious experiences, verbal persuasion, and physiological/affective state. "Any given influence, depending on its form, may operate through one or more of these sources of efficacy information" (p. 79). The four sections that follow provide a framework for a test-taking program structured around sources of self-efficacy beliefs. The length, focus, and intensity of such a program will and should vary according to the needs of the learner.

1. Enactive Mastery

The recognition that one has mastered a task as a result of personal effort provides strong feedback that one possesses the ability to succeed. This knowledge, in turn, has a significant effect on the development of self-efficacy. "Enactive mastery experiences are the most influential source of efficacy information because they provide the most authentic evidence of whether one can muster whatever it takes to succeed" (Bandura, 1997, p. 80). The following suggestions to enhance enactive mastery should be kept in mind when creating and selecting material for use in test-taking lessons.

Use test-like material. Selection and use of test-like material that facilitates enactive mastery is critical because it provides unequivocal and convincing feedback to students like Lucinda that they possess the skills necessary to be successful. For a number of reasons, some children may have had more opportunities to experience mastery than others; therefore, the amount of mastery experiences necessary before a student is able to recognize that he or she has a particular skill will vary. When Lucinda realizes that her responses to questions on test-like material are consistently correct, she has strong, irrefutable evidence of an authentic nature attesting to her ability to succeed at taking tests.

When material used is inappropriate to learner needs and does not allow for mastery, frustration and negativity often develop; learners likely will become convinced that they really cannot accomplish the task at hand, in spite of contrary exhortations by teachers and others. As a result, perceptions of self-efficacy weaken or fail to develop. Test anxiety can be reduced when practice sessions incorporate material that resembles the actual test. "Clarifying test format and content establishes structure for students; this structure, in turn, reduces test anxiety and leads to higher achievement for all students, particularly those of low ability" (Eggen & Kauchak, 1997, p. 545).

The appropriate use of previously administered tests allows the student to become familiar with the test format. When this is not possible, material that looks like the actual test, including font size, number of columns (if any), amount and nature of questions and answers (multiple-choice, open-ended), method of recording answers (separate page, bubble sheets with choices running vertically or horizontally), and "packaging" of the test material (thickness of test booklet) should be developed and used. Success with instructional material that has the same or similar format as the actual high-stakes test will be more likely to enable the student to generalize his or her recognition of success to the actual high-stakes test than material with dissimilar format.

Perceived efficacy generalizes from one task to another to the degree that the tasks are similar

(Bandura, 1997). Individuals with low self-efficacy hesitate to or may never apply learned skills in situations that differ or appear to differ from that in which the skill was learned. During an instructional session, a student might successfully answer questions based on a passage formatted with no columns but falter when presented with reading material written in two or three columns. He or she might perceive the task of answering questions based on material written in columns as new, unfamiliar, and intimidating and, therefore, might not generalize learned skills.

Use short, manageable selections. Students with poor test-taking self-efficacy may be overwhelmed when presented with a test booklet containing many pages of material. (Although they are usually warned against speaking once the testing has begun, an involuntary reaction of many students to this situation is an audible groan as lengthy test booklets are received or opened.) In order not to overwhelm Lucinda during initial test-taking instructional sessions designed to enhance self-efficacy, Mr. Wilson should create or use few pages with a minimal number of questions based on short, manageable text. Short, manageable selections provide more frequent opportunities for mastery than longer selections. As success with relatively short portions of test-like material is achieved, material length can be gradually increased without damaging self-efficacy. (The decision about the amount of material to use initially is, of course, made by the teacher after considering the nature of the student. Even though they may have the same reading ability, in initial sessions designed to enhance test-taking self-efficacy some students may be comfortable reading a passage and then responding to three questions, while others may be comfortable answering five questions after reading the same passage.)

Use easy "test" material. If Lucinda has a sixth-grade reading ability level, for example, test-like material that resembles the format of the test and that is written at an approximately fourth-grade level may be appropriate to use when developing self-efficacy. The goal of using easy material is to provide "fail-proof" mastery experiences for Lucinda that result in evidence of ability to succeed. Cunningham and Allington (1999) noted the critical importance of experience with easy material to the development of reading ability. Students feel successful when they have a sense of accomplishment, and material that is easy to read allows the student to experience success. (A rule of thumb to determine "easy" material is 99% decoding accuracy and 90% comprehension.) Students become discouraged, frustrated, and intimidated and may not attempt the task when material is hard to read.

Use "unrelated" passages. Students customarily read narrative or expository text consisting of a number of related paragraphs developed around a theme or subject. In narrative material, the plot and the characters are developed around a theme with a beginning, middle, and end. In expository material, the information is usually presented around a subject or focus, such as the French Revolution, westward expansion, or the causes of earthquakes. However, high-stakes tests of reading ability may consist of either narrative or expository excerpts, each of which may be unrelated to the other. If unprepared for the disjointed, unconnected reading material of some tests, students with low test-taking self-efficacy may be unable to apply recently acquired test-taking skills and, as a result, may become frustrated and unable to respond correctly to questions they have the ability to answer. Instructional material in the form of short, unrelated passages should be included during "test prep" sessions so that Lucinda can experience mastery with reading unrelated passages and will persevere in spite of frustration resulting from the lack of "relatedness" of the passages on the high-stakes test.

2. Vicarious Experiences

Vicarious experiences (observations and comparison to the actions or skills of others) provide feedback attesting to an individual's level of competence, allowing him or her to determine the degree to which a particular skill is possessed. "Efficacy appraisals are partly influenced by vicarious experiences mediated through modeled attainments" (Bandura, 1997, p. 86). For example, when judging one's skills in throwing a ball or swimming, comparison with peers and others may provide evidence that one possesses the desired skill level. In Lucinda's case, however, comparison with other, better-performing peers' performance on tests will be counterproductive to the development of her perceived self-efficacy. Therefore, Mr. Wilson should structure vicarious experiences that are consistent with enhancing Lucinda's self-efficacy for test taking and avoid those that are not helpful. The following suggestions should be implemented to enhance test-taking self-efficacy through vicarious experiences.

Model test taking. "Demonstrations that model critical thought processes enhance student learning and performance" (Johnson, 1998). Listening to a respected model as he or she shares his or her thoughts—called metacognitive modeling—while responding to test questions will help students like Lucinda. "Models who express confidence in the face of difficulties instill a higher sense of efficacy and perseverance in others than do models who begin to doubt themselves as they encounter problems" (B.J. Zimmerman & J. Ringle, as cited in Bandura, 1997, p. 88). "Modeling that conveys effective coping strategies can boost the self-efficacy of individuals who have undergone countless experiences confirming their personal inefficacy" (Bandura, 1997, p. 87).

When modeling the process of answering a question, Mr. Wilson might say something like the following as he responds to an item on a "mock" test:

> First, I think about what I have just read. Next, I read all the questions. Then, I read the first question carefully. I think about my answer before I read the choices. Then I go to the answer choices to see which one matches my answer. Let's see. This answer [pointing to one] cannot be correct. I know that it is really wrong so I will eliminate that one. That leaves me with three other possibilities. This one [pointing] cannot be right either because it has the wrong idea. That leaves me with two more answer choices. I think this one is correct because it matches my answer. Now, I think I have the answer, but I will read the last answer choice anyway to make sure. No, that last answer choice does not match my answer. So I will select the third choice for my answer.

(This is one possible script; obviously, alternative wording may be more effective for other students.) By sharing his thinking as it relates to answering questions on the mock test, Mr. Wilson enables Lucinda to experience, albeit vicariously, his thought processes. Lucinda's self-efficacy will be enhanced because she may realize either that she already knows the strategy modeled or has just learned a strategy that will help her do well on tests. In either case, as a result of observing a proficient, respected model take a test, there is a positive impact on her perception of her ability to take tests.

Work with peers. Other students may also be role models for Lucinda, articulating the processes used to respond to test questions as they perform the task, much like Mr. Wilson in the example above. However, there is evidence that students sometimes benefit more from peer models than from adult models (D.H. Schunk & A.R. Hanson, as cited in Bandura, 1997, p. 98); therefore, Mr. Wilson should give careful consideration to personal characteristics of members of Lucinda's group. He should know and recognize those personal characteristics valued by Lucinda that are present in other children because "Self-efficacy appraisals are often based not on comparative performance experiences, but on similarity to models in terms of personal characteristics that are assumed to be predictive of performance capabilities" (J.M. Suls & R.L. Miller, as cited in Bandura, 1997, p. 98). When nurturing Lucinda's self-efficacy, it is important to include group peers who possess characteristics or abilities she seems to value. If she seems to prefer friends who are similar to her in age, sex, economic or social group, or physique, those characteristics should be included when selecting group members and when modeling is involved. (Obviously, criteria for group membership may vary depending on the purpose.)

3. Verbal Persuasion

This refers to verbal feedback to convince the learner that he or she has been successful. When a teacher congratulates a student for succeeding on a task because he or she practiced or studied, self-efficacy is likely to be enhanced; when a teacher does not use pedagogically appropriate verbal feedback, self-efficacy does not develop as easily. "Persuasory efficacy attributions have their greatest impact on people who have some reasons to believe that they can produce effects through their actions" (Bandura, 1997, p. 101), and to be most effective such comments should heighten this awareness. Coupled with successful enactive mastery experiences, verbal persuasion can bolster feelings of self-efficacy. The following guidelines for verbal persuasion can be implemented when seeking to improve test-taking performance and perceptions of self-efficacy.

Attribute success to personal effort. Attribution refers to the realization that personal effort, not luck, chance, or another factor, has affected results. Some students who have low self-efficacy for the testing situation do not feel they can change an outcome, even with effort, and often exclaim, "This is just the way I am." It is the role of the teacher to help students understand that their effort will affect outcome, even in a testing situation, and that they do have the power to change the results.

Exhortations to succeed by saying to a student "You can do it" are vague and unspecified and do not adequately connect results to task-specific personal action. When complimenting a student on a task well done, the teacher should be sure to use words that help the learner realize that his or her effort caused the results and that it was not just a matter of chance. Herschell, Greco, Filcheck, and McNeil (2002) referred to this as "labeled praise." It is better, for example, to say "Lucinda, you were successful on that activity because you studied" than to say "Lucinda, you did very well on that activity." The latter comment is less effective because it does not attribute the cause of the success to Lucinda's effort studying. Attributing success to "hard work" has similarly deflating results because the individual is made to understand that only through a lot of effort is success possible. This realization tends to discourage students.

Use charts and graphs to make students aware of progress. Although nonverbal, feedback such as charts and graphs indicating progress can also be valuable in persuading the student that he or she can successfully complete the particular task. "Moreover, to ensure progress in personal development, skilled efficacy builders encourage people to measure their successes in terms of self-improvement rather than in terms of triumphs over others" (Bandura, 1997, p. 106). Displays that compare earlier successful attempts at a task with later ones can be powerful, tangible indicators to convince individuals of their capability. Feedback given in a visual display has an advantage over nonvisual feedback because a bar graph or a line graph can illustrate an immediately recognizable pattern. A line that ascends on a graph immediately and unmistakably indicates a trend (usually positive) and becomes a historical archive of the results of effort expended. There is evidence that nonverbal, visual displays are significant when helping at-risk students monitor their acquisition of skills (Johnson, 1998).

4. Physiological/Affective State

When Lucinda complained of an inability to think clearly and of "freezing" when confronted with a high-stakes reading test, she was attending to and relying mostly upon feedback information of a physiological/affective nature. "By conjuring up aversive thoughts about their ineptitude and stress reactions, people can rouse themselves to elevated levels of distress that produce the very dysfunction they fear" (Bandura, 1997, p. 107). A physiological/affective state can also be related to one or all of the three previous sources of efficacy information. Successful enactive mastery of a task, recognition of insight gained from vicarious experiences, and appropriate verbal persuasion all provide information to the individual that he or she has or can acquire the competence necessary to complete a particular task. This, in turn, may affect the physiological state of the learner by lowering the level of tension felt in relation to that task and increasing positive feelings. Because there is evidence that reduction of stress results in improved reading ability (Carter & Russell, 1985; Ignoffo, 1988; Margolis, 1990; Margolis & Pica, 1990; Zenker & Frey, 1985), one goal of Mr. Wilson's test-taking program for Lucinda should be to help her depend less on negative feedback from a physiological and affective source.

Bower (1981) suggested that mood is stored in memory along with the memory of the associated event. In this theory, the feeling of happiness experienced as a result of being successful in a task is connected to and stored along with the memory of the task. Therefore, when Lucinda consciously or subconsciously recalls learned test-taking skills, she will also activate the mood state in which those skills were learned. The recalled mood state will, in turn, influence—bias—her judgment of her efficacy. "Mood-biased recollection can similarly affect people's judgments of their personal efficacy" (Bandura, 1997, p. 111). If the mood was pleasant when Lucinda acquired the test-taking skills, then her perception of her skills at recall during the high-stakes test will be positive; if the mood was unpleasant, her perception of her skills will be negative. The following suggestions should be implemented with the others mentioned in this article to ensure that self-efficacy for taking tests will be enhanced.

Create a pleasant atmosphere conducive to learning. One obvious suggestion is to create a pleasant environment and atmosphere for the learner so that a positive mood is first created during learning and then recalled along with the test-taking strategies during the actual high-stakes test. Personal teacher characteristics that affect student mood and learning may vary according to students' and teachers' cultural mores. Characteristics include, but are not limited to, smiling, empathetic listening, voice moderation, frequent use of student's name, appropriate and reassuring facial gestures, affirmative head nodding, and general attentiveness. When positive environmental factors exist during stress-free instructional sessions, the learner will implement the strategy taught with little stress. If a student acquires a skill despite stress caused by an unpleasant, disruptive learning environment, the anticipation of implementing that skill will be accompanied by the memory of stress (Bower, 1981).

Schedule practice testing sessions optimally. It is not prudent to schedule test-taking practice sessions between activities the student finds distasteful. Anxiety developed during the previous activity and anticipated with the subsequent activity may affect performance and, therefore, self-efficacy. There is some evidence that learning schedule (time of day, length of instructional session, and other factors) affect students' ability to learn in different ways (Johnson, 1998).

While this difference is not true for all students, if Lucinda dislikes chemistry and swimming, for example, it may be counterproductive to place the test-taking activity designed to enhance her self-efficacy between those two activities. Negative mood developed as a result of frustration during chemistry class together with anticipated anxiety during swim class will influence mood during the test-taking session. The resulting negative mood associated with the sandwiched test-taking session will be recalled along with the test-taking skill taught.

Simulate testing conditions. Herschell et al. (2002) noted, "In any testing situation, special attention should be given to the structure of the environment" (p. 141). To the degree possible, the teacher should prepare the child for the testing situation by conducting instructional sessions in the same room in which the high-stakes test will be taken. The degree to which the learning environment is consistent with the testing environment is the degree to which self-efficacy can easily be generalized.

While this may be feasible in most cases and will help the students feel more comfortable when taking the actual high-stakes test, other variables beyond the control of the teacher and outside the walls of the classroom, such as noisy construction work, sirens of emergency vehicles, activated car-theft alarms, and lightning storms, are difficult if not impossible to prevent. Therefore, one suggestion to prepare the student to manage the negative effect on mood (stress, annoyance, anger) of these unanticipated distractions is to gradually introduce extraneous noise variables such as playing a radio first at a low volume then slightly louder, moving a chair or two, writing on the chalkboard, or gently dropping a book or pencil during the practice testing.

Another testing condition that could negatively affect Lucinda's mood and provide negative physiological feedback (disorientation, discomfort) severe enough to cause her to fail to generalize self-efficacy developed during practice test-taking sessions is an unexpected change in the testing room. Therefore, whenever possible, it is advisable to arrange the test-taking instructional sessions in the room designated for the test as well as in other rooms likely to be used on high-stakes test day. In this way, Lucinda will be less likely to be distracted by an unfamiliar environment and fail to generalize her test-taking self-efficacy.

Gradually introduce time. Standardized tests are timed. This means that the struggling reader needs to work against (or with) the clock, a stressful situation for many students. Not only is getting the correct answer important, but successful completion of the task within a specified period also becomes a significant factor in performance. This stress will be heightened if Lucinda discovers a question that requires more time to answer than expected. Therefore, in order to enhance and sustain readers' high-stakes test-taking self-efficacy, teachers should introduce time as a factor. For example, Mr. Wilson should start with an untimed situation and, depending upon Lucinda's cognitive skills and affective disposition, gradually reduce the time available to complete the task. Some readers will be comfortable initially when given 10 minutes to complete a given task; others may need 20 minutes. When the time limit is planned and implemented carefully, Lucinda and students like her will be better able to ignore stress caused by time limitations when taking the high-stakes test.

A "Can Do" Attitude

In summary, the four sources of self-efficacy outlined provide a framework for developing and evaluating efforts to enhance student achievement on and self-efficacy for high-stakes tests. Mr. Wilson's goal is to help Lucinda acquire appropriate test-taking skills and pay more attention to positive feedback from enactive mastery, vicarious experiences, and verbal persuasion, while extinguishing or minimizing any negative feedback from physiological/affective sources.

Although there is no guarantee of success on high-stakes tests, even when the strategies and principles I've discussed are included, instructional programs that either ignore or fail to take full advantage of these sources of feedback information deprive students of the opportunity to change "can't do" into "can do." Approaching a high-stakes test with low self-efficacy will further feed a self-perpetuating cycle of learned helplessness and guarantee less than optimal results. Approaching a high-stakes test with a positive attitude that includes strong self-efficacy will not guarantee success, but it is certainly a step in the right direction.

References

American Educational Research Association. (2000, July). *High-stakes testing in preK–12 education: A position statement of the American Educational Research Association*. Washington, DC: Author.

Ananda, S., & Rabinowitz, S. (2000). *The high stakes of "high-stakes" testing*. Washington, DC: Office of

Educational Research and Improvement. (ERIC Document Reproduction Service No. ED455254)

Bandura, A. (1997). *Self-efficacy: The exercise of control.* New York: Longman.

Bower, G. (1981). Mood and memory. *American Psychologist, 36*, 129–148.

Carter, J., & Russell, H. (1985). Use of EMG biofeedback procedures with learning disabled children in a clinical and an educational setting. *Journal of Learning Disabilities, 18*(4), 213–216.

Cunningham, P., & Allington, R. (1999). *Classrooms that work: They all can read and write.* New York: Longman.

Domenech, D. (2000). My stakes well done. *School Administrator, 57*(11), 16–19.

Earley, P. (1994). Self or group? Cultural effects of training on self-efficacy and performance. *Administrative Science Quarterly, 39*(1), 89–117.

Earley, P., Gibson, C., & Chen, C. (1999). "How did I do?" versus "how did we do?" Cultural contrasts of performance feedback use and self-efficacy. *Journal of Cross-Cultural Psychology, 30*, 594–619.

Eggen, P., & Kauchak, D. (1997). *Educational psychology: Windows on classrooms* (3rd ed.). Upper Saddle River, NJ: Merrill.

Gratz, D.B. (2000). High standards for whom? *Phi Delta Kappan, 81*, 681–687.

Hauser, R. (2000). *Should we end social promotion: Truth and consequences.* Madison, WI: Tests, Measurement, and Evaluation Clearinghouse. (ERIC Document Reproduction Service No. ED445015)

Herschell, A.D., Greco, L.A., Filcheck, H.A., & McNeil, C.B. (2002). Who is testing whom? Ten suggestions for managing the disruptive behavior of young children during testing. *Intervention in School and Clinic, 37*(3), 140–148.

Hoffman, J., Assaf, L., & Paris, S. (2001). High-stakes testing in reading: Today in Texas, tomorrow? *The Reading Teacher, 54*, 482–492.

Howe, H. (2000). High-stakes trouble. *American School Board Journal, 187*(5), 58–59.

Huber, R., & Moore, C. (2000). Educational reform through "high-stakes testing": Don't go there. *Science Educator, 9*(1), 7–13.

Ignoffo, M. (1988). Improve reading by overcoming the "inner critic." *Journal of Reading, 31*(4), 704–708.

International Reading Association. (1999, January). *High-stakes assessments in reading: A position statement of the International Reading Association.* Newark, DE: Author.

Jenkins, J.M., & Weldon, J. (1999). Reflection on retention and social promotion. *International Journal of Educational Reform, 8*(3), 308–311.

Johnson, G. (1998). Principles of instruction for at-risk learners. *Preventing School Failure, 4*(2), 167–174.

Kane, M. (2001, April). *The role of policy assumptions in validating high-stakes testing programs.* Paper presented at the annual meeting of the American Educational Research Association, Seattle, WA. (ERIC Document Reproduction Service No. ED454251)

Lewis, A. (2000). *High-stakes testing: Trends and issues.* Washington, DC: Office of Educational Research and Improvement. (ERIC Document Reproduction Service No. ED450183)

Madaus, G., & Clarke, M. (2001). *The adverse impact of high-stakes testing on minority students: Evidence from 100 years of test data.* Washington, DC: Office of Educational Research and Improvement. (ERIC Document Reproduction Service No. ED442806)

Margolis, H. (1990). Relaxation training: A promising approach for helping exceptional learners. *International Journal of Disability, Development and Education, 37*(3), 215–234.

Margolis, H., & Pica, L. (1990). *The effects of audiotaped progressive muscle relaxation training on the reading performance of emotionally disturbed adolescents.* (ERIC Document Reproduction Service No. ED331032)

Oettingen, G. (1995). Cross-cultural perspectives on self-efficacy. In A. Bandura (Ed.), *Self-efficacy in changing societies* (pp. 149–176). New York: Cambridge University Press.

Pintrich, P., & Schunk, D. (1996). *Motivation in education: Theory, research and applications.* Englewood Cliffs, NJ: Prentice Hall.

Prystowsky, R. (2001). Testing...testing...this doesn't seem to be working. *Paths of Learning: Options for Families & Communities, 8*, 55–57.

Roderick, M., Nagaoka, J., Bacon, J., & Easton, J.Q. (2000). *Update: Ending social promotion—Passing, retention, and achievement among promoted and retained students, 1995–1999.* Chicago: Consortium on Chicago School Research. (ERIC Document Reproduction Service No. ED451300)

Smith, M., & Fey, P. (2000). Validity and accountability in high-stakes testing. *Journal of Teacher Education, 51*(5), 334-344.

Thompson, C.L., & Cunningham, E.K. (2000). *Retention and social promotion: Research and implications for policy* (ERIC Digest No. 161). Washington, DC: Office of Educational Research. (ERIC Document Reproduction Service No. ED449241)

Villaire, T. (2001). High-stakes testing: Is it fair to test students? *Our Children, 26*(7), 5-7.

Zenker, E., & Frey, D. (1985). Relaxation helps less capable students. *Journal of Reading, 28*, 42-44.

Behind Test Scores: What Struggling Readers *Really* Need

Sheila W. Valencia and Marsha Riddle Buly

Every year thousands of U.S. students take standardized tests and state reading tests, and every year thousands fail them. With the implementation of the No Child Left Behind legislation (www.ed.gov/nclb/landing.jhtml), which mandates testing all children from grades 3 to 8 every year, these numbers will grow exponentially, and alarming numbers of schools and students will be targeted for "improvement." Whether you believe this increased focus on testing is good news or bad, if you are an educator, you are undoubtedly concerned about the children who struggle every day with reading and the implications of their test failure.

Although legislators, administrators, parents, and educators have been warned repeatedly not to rely on a single measure to make important instructional decisions (Elmore, 2002; Linn, n.d.; Shepard, 2000), scores from state tests still seem to drive the search for programs and approaches that will help students learn and meet state standards. The popular press, educational publications, teacher workshops, and state and school district policies are filled with attempts to find solutions for poor test performance. For example, some schools have eliminated sustained silent reading in favor of more time for explicit instruction (Edmondson & Shannon, 2002; Riddle Buly & Valencia, 2002), others are buying special programs or mandating specific interventions (Goodnough, 2001; Helfand, 2002), and some states and districts are requiring teachers to have particular instructional emphases (McNeil, 2000; Paterson, 2000; Riddle Buly & Valencia, 2002). Furthermore, it is common to find teachers spending enormous amounts of time preparing students for these high-stakes tests (Olson, 2001), even though a narrow focus on preparing students for specific tests does not translate into real learning (Klein, Hamilton, McCaffrey, & Stecher, 2000; Linn, 2000). But, if we are really going to help students, we need to understand the underlying reasons for their test failure. Simply knowing which children have failed state tests is a bit like knowing that you have a fever when you are feeling ill but having no idea of the cause or cure. A test score, like a fever, is a symptom that demands more specific analysis of the problem. In this case, what is required is a more in-depth analysis of the strengths and needs of students who fail to meet standards and instructional plans that will meet their needs.

In this article, we draw from the results of an empirical study of students who failed a typical fourth-grade state reading assessment (see Riddle Buly & Valencia, 2002, for a full description of the study). Specifically, we describe the patterns of performance that distinguish different groups of students who failed to meet standards. We also provide suggestions for what classroom teachers need to know and how they might help these children succeed.

Study Context

Our research was conducted in a typical northwestern U.S. school district of 18,000 students located adjacent to the largest urban district in the state. At the time of our study, 43% were students of color and 47% received free or reduced-

From *The Reading Teacher*, 57(6), 520–531. © 2004 by the International Reading Association.

price lunch. Over the past several years, approximately 50% of students had failed the state fourth-grade reading test that, like many other standards-based state assessments, consisted of several extended narrative and expository reading selections accompanied by a combination of multiple-choice and open-ended comprehension questions. For the purposes of this study, during September of fifth grade we randomly selected 108 students who had scored below standard on the state test given at the end of fourth grade. These 108 students constituted approximately 10% of failing students in the district. None of them was receiving supplemental special education or English as a Second Language (ESL) services. We wanted to understand the "garden variety" (Stanovich, 1988) test failure—those students typically found in the regular classroom who are experiencing reading difficulty but have not been identified as needing special services or intensive interventions. Classroom teachers, not reading specialists or special education teachers, are solely responsible for the reading instruction of these children and, ultimately, for their achievement.

Data Collection and Assessment Tools

Our approach was to conduct individual reading assessments, working one-on-one with the children for approximately two hours over several days to gather information about their reading abilities. We administered a series of assessments that targeted key components of reading ability identified by experts: word identification, meaning (comprehension and vocabulary), and fluency (rate and expression) (Lipson & Wixson, 2003; National Institute of Child Health and Human Development, 2000; Snow, Burns, & Griffin, 1998). Table 1 presents the measures we used and the areas in which each provided information.

To measure word identification, we used two tests from the 1989 Woodcock-Johnson Psycho-Educational Battery–Revised (WJ–R) that assessed students' reading of single and

Table 1
Diagnostic assessments

Assessment	Word identification	Meaning	Fluency
Woodcock-Johnson–Revised			
Letter-word identification	X		
Word attack	X		
Qualitative Reading Inventory–II			
Reading accuracy	X		
Reading acceptability	X		
Rate			X
Expression			X
Comprehension		X	
Peabody Picture Vocabulary Test–Revised			
Vocabulary meaning		X	
State fourth-grade passages			
Reading accuracy	X		
Reading acceptability	X		
Rate			X
Expression			X

multisyllabic words, both real and pseudowords. We also scored oral reading errors students made on narrative and expository graded passages from the 1995 Qualitative Reading Inventory–II (QRI–II) and from the state test. We calculated total accuracy (percentage of words read correctly) and acceptability (counting only those errors that changed the meaning of the text). Students also responded orally to comprehension questions that accompanied the QRI–II passages, providing a measure of their comprehension that was not confounded by writing ability. To assess receptive vocabulary, we used the 1981 Peabody Picture Vocabulary Test–Revised (PPVT–R), which requires students to listen and point to a picture that corresponds to a word (scores of 85 or higher are judged to be average or above average). As with the comprehension questions, the vocabulary measure does not confound understanding with students' ability to write responses. Finally, in the area of fluency, we assessed rate of reading and expression (Samuels, 2002). We timed the readings of all passages (i.e., QRI–II and state test selections) to get a reading rate and used a 4-point rubric developed for the Oral Reading Study of the fourth-grade National Assessment of Educational Progress (NAEP) (Pinnell et al., 1995) to assess phrasing and expression (1–2 is judged to be nonfluent; 3–4 is judged to be fluent).

Findings

Scores from all the assessments for each student fell into three statistically distinct and educationally familiar categories: word identification (word reading in isolation and context), meaning (comprehension and vocabulary), and fluency (rate and expression). When we examined the average scores for all 108 students in the sample, students appeared to be substantially below grade level in all three areas. However, when we analyzed the data using a cluster analysis (Aldenderfer & Blashfield, 1984), looking for groups of students who had similar patterns across all three factors, we found six distinct profiles of students who failed the test. Most striking is that the majority of students were not weak in all three areas; they were actually strong in some and weak in others. Table 2 indicates the percentage of students in each group and their relative strength (+) or weakness (–) in word identification, meaning, and fluency.

The Profiles

We illuminate each profile by describing a prototypical student from each cluster (see Figure) and specific suggested instructional targets for each (all names are pseudonyms). Although the instructional strategies we recommend have not

Table 2
Cluster analysis

Cluster	Sample percentage	English Language Learner percentage	Low socioeconomic status percentage	Word identification	Meaning	Fluency
1–Automatic Word Callers	18	63	89	+ +	-	+ +
2–Struggling Word Callers	15	56	81	-	-	+ +
3–Word Stumblers	17	16	42	-	+	-
4–Slow Comprehenders	24	19	54	+	+ +	-
5–Slow Word Callers	17	56	67	+	-	-
6–Disabled Readers	9	20	80	- -	- -	- -

Prototypical students from each cluster

Cluster 1–Automatic Word Callers (18%)

Word identification	Meaning	Fluency
+ +	–	+ +

Tomas

Word identification = ninth grade (WJ-R)
> fourth grade (QRI-II)
= 98% (state passages)
Comprehension = second/third grade
Vocabulary = 108
Expression = 3
Rate = 155 words per minute
Writing = proficient

Cluster 2–Struggling Word Callers (15%)

Word identification	Meaning	Fluency
–	–	+ +

Makara

Word identification = fourth grade (WJ-R)
< second grade (QRI-II)
= 75% (state passages)
Comprehension = < second grade
Vocabulary = 58
Expression = 2.5
Rate = 117 words per minute
Writing = below proficient

Cluster 3–Word Stumblers (17%)

Word identification	Meaning	Fluency
–	+	–

Sandy

Word identification = second grade (WJ-R)
= second-grade accuracy/third-grade acceptability (QRI-II)
= 80% accuracy/99% acceptability (state passages)
Comprehension = fourth grade
Vocabulary = 135
Expression = 1.5
Rate = 77 words per minute
Writing = proficient

Cluster 4–Slow Comprehenders (24%)

Word identification	Meaning	Fluency
+	+ +	–

Martin

Word identification = sixth grade (WJ-R)
> fourth grade (QRI-II)
= 100% (state passages)
Comprehension = > fourth grade
Vocabulary = 103
Expression = 2.5
Rate = 61 words per minute
Writing = proficient

Cluster 5–Slow Word Callers (17%)

Word identification	Meaning	Fluency
+	–	–

Andrew

Word identification = seventh grade (WJ-R)
> fourth grade (QRI-II)
= 98% (state passages)
Comprehension = second grade
Vocabulary = 74
Expression = 1.5
Rate = 62 words per minute
Writing = not proficient

Cluster 6–Disabled Readers (9%)

Word identification	Meaning	Fluency
– –	– –	– –

Jesse

Word identification = first grade (WJ-R)
< first grade (QRI-II)
< 50% (state passages)
Comprehension = < first grade
Vocabulary = 105
Writing = not proficient

been implemented with these particular children, we base our recommendations on our review of research-based practices (e.g., Allington, 2001; Allington & Johnston, 2001; Lipson & Wixson, 2003; National Institute of Child Health and Human Development, 2000), our interpretation of the profiles, and our experiences teaching struggling readers. We conclude with several general implications for school and classroom instruction.

Cluster 1—Automatic Word Callers

We call these students Automatic Word Callers because they can decode words quickly and accurately, but they fail to read for meaning. The majority of students in this cluster qualify for free or reduced-price lunch, and they are English-language learners who no longer receive special support. Tomas is a typical student in this cluster.

Tomas has excellent word identification skills. He scored at ninth-grade level when reading real words and pseudowords (i.e., phonetically regular nonsense words such as *fot*) on the WJ–R tests, and at the independent level for word identification on the QRI–II and state fourth-grade passages. However, when asked about what he read, Tomas had difficulty, placing his comprehension at the second-grade level. Although Tomas's first language is not English, his score of 108 on the PPVT–R suggests that his comprehension difficulties are more complex than individual word meanings. Tomas's "proficient" score on the state writing assessment also suggests that his difficulty is in understanding rather than in writing answers to comprehension questions. This student's rate of reading, which was quite high compared with rates of fourth-grade students on the Oral Reading Study of NAEP (Pinnell et al., 1995) and other research (Harris & Sipay, 1990), suggests that his decoding is automatic and unlikely to be contributing to his comprehension difficulty. His score in expression is also consistent with students who were rated as "fluent" according to the NAEP rubric, although this seems unusual for a student who is demonstrating difficulty with comprehension.

The evidence suggests that Tomas needs additional instruction in comprehension and most likely would benefit from explicit instruction, teacher modeling, and think-alouds of key reading strategies (e.g., summarizing, self-monitoring, creating visual representations, evaluating), using a variety of types of material at the fourth- or fifth-grade level (Block & Pressley, 2002; Duke & Pearson, 2002). His comprehension performance on the QRI–II suggests that his literal comprehension is quite strong but that he has difficulty with more inferential and critical aspects of understanding. Although Tomas has strong scores in the fluency category, both in expression and rate, he may be reading too fast to attend to meaning, especially deeper meaning of the ideas in the text. Tomas's teacher should help him understand that the purpose for reading is to understand and that rate varies depending on the type of text and the purpose for reading. Then, the teacher should suggest that he slow down to focus on meaning. Self-monitoring strategies would also help Tomas check for understanding and encourage him to think about the ideas while he is reading. These and other such strategies may help him learn to adjust his rate to meet the demands of the text.

Tomas would also likely benefit from additional support in acquiring academic language, which takes many years for English-language learners to develop (Cummins, 1991). Reading activities such as building background; developing understanding of new words, concepts, and figurative language in his "to-be-read" texts; and acquiring familiarity with genre structures found in longer, more complex texts like those found at fourth grade and above would provide important opportunities for his language and conceptual development (Antunez, 2002; Hiebert, Pearson, Taylor, Richardson, & Paris, 1998). Classroom read-alouds and discussions as well as lots of additional independent reading would also help Tomas in building language and attention to understanding.

Cluster 2—Struggling Word Callers

The students in this cluster not only struggle with meaning, like the Automatic Word Callers in Cluster 1, but they also struggle with word identification. Makara, a student from Cambodia, is one of these students. Like Tomas, Makara struggled with comprehension. But unlike Tomas, he had substantial difficulty applying word identification skills when reading connected text (QRI–II and state passages), even though his reading of isolated words on the WJ–R was at a fourth-grade level. Such word identification difficulties would likely contribute to comprehension problems. However, Makara's performance on the PPVT–R, which placed him below the 1st percentile compared with other students his age, and his poor performance on the state writing assessment suggest that language may contribute to his comprehension difficulties as well—not surprising for a student acquiring a second language. These language-related results need to be viewed with caution, however, because the version of the PPVT–R available for use in this study may underestimate the language abilities of students from culturally and linguistically diverse backgrounds, and written language takes longer than oral language to develop. Despite difficulty with meaning, Makara read quickly—117 words per minute. At first glance, this may seem unusual given his difficulty with both decoding and comprehension. Closer investigation of his performance, however, revealed that Makara read words quickly whether he was reading them correctly or incorrectly and didn't stop to monitor or self-correct. In addition, although Makara was fast, his expression and phrasing were uneven and consistent with comprehension difficulties.

Makara likely needs instruction and practice in oral and written language, as well as in constructing meaning in reading and writing, self-monitoring, and decoding while reading connected text. All this needs to be done in rich, meaningful contexts, taking into account his background knowledge and interests. Like Tomas, Makara would benefit from teacher or peer read-alouds, lots of experience with independent reading at his level, small-group instruction, and the kinds of activities aimed at building academic language that we described earlier, as well as a more foundational emphasis on word meanings. Makara also needs instruction in self-monitoring and fix-up strategies to improve his comprehension and awareness of reading for understanding. Decoding instruction is also important for him, although his teacher would need to gather more information using tools such as miscue analysis or tests of decoding to determine his specific decoding needs and how they interact with his knowledge of word meanings. Makara clearly cannot be instructed in fourth-grade material; most likely, his teacher would need to begin with second-grade material that is familiar and interesting to him and a good deal of interactive background building. At the same time, however, Makara needs exposure to the content and vocabulary of grade-level texts through activities such as teacher read-alouds, tapes, and partner reading so that his conceptual understanding continues to grow.

Cluster 3–Word Stumblers

Students in this cluster have substantial difficulty with word identification, but they still have surprisingly strong comprehension. How does that happen? Sandy, a native English speaker from a middle class home, is a good example of this type of student. Sandy stumbled on so many words initially that it seemed unlikely that she would comprehend what she had read, yet she did. Her word identification scores were at second-grade level, and she read the state fourth-grade passages at frustration level. However, a clue to her strong comprehension is evident from the difference between her immediate word recognition accuracy score and her acceptability score, which takes into account self-corrections or errors that do not change the meaning. In other words, Sandy was so focused on reading for meaning that she spontaneously self-corrected many of her decoding miscues or substituted words that preserved the meaning. She attempted to read every word in the reading selections, working until she could figure out some part of each word and then using context clues to help her get the entire word. She seemed to over-rely on context because her decoding skills were so weak (Stanovich, 1994). Remarkably, she was eventually able to read the words on the state fourth-grade reading passages at an independent level. But, as we might predict, Sandy's rate was very slow, and her initial attempts to read were choppy and lacked flow—she spent an enormous amount of time self-correcting and rereading. After she finally self-corrected or figured out unknown words, however, Sandy reread phrases with good expression and flow to fit with the meaning. Although Sandy's overall fluency score was low, her primary difficulty does not appear in the area of either rate or expression; rather, her low performance in fluency seems to be a result of her difficulty with decoding.

With such a strong quest for meaning, Sandy was able to comprehend fourth-grade material even when her decoding was at frustration level. No doubt her strong language and vocabulary abilities (i.e., 99th percentile) were assets. As we might predict, Sandy was more than proficient at expressing her ideas when writing about her experiences. She understands that reading and writing should make sense, and she has the self-monitoring strategies, perseverance, and language background to make that happen.

Sandy needs systematic instruction in word identification and opportunities to practice when reading connected text at her reading level. She is clearly beyond the early stages of reading and decoding, but her teacher will need to determine through a more in-depth analysis precisely which decoding skills should be the focus of her instruction. At the same time, Sandy needs supported experiences with texts that will continue to feed and challenge her drive for meaning. For students like Sandy, it is critical not to sacrifice intellectual engagement with text while they are receiving decoding instruction and practice in below-grade-level material. Furthermore, Sandy needs to develop automaticity with word identification, and to do that she would benefit from assisted reading (i.e., reading along with others, monitored reading with a tape, or partner reading) as well as unassisted reading practice (i.e., repeated reading, reading to younger students) with materials at her instructional level (Kuhn & Stahl, 2000).

Cluster 4—Slow Comprehenders

Almost one fourth of the students in this sample were Slow Comprehenders. Like other students in this cluster, Martin is a native English speaker and a relatively strong decoder, scoring above fourth-grade level on all measures of decoding. His comprehension was at the instructional level on the fourth-grade QRI–II selections, and his vocabulary and writing ability were average for his age. On the surface, this information is puzzling because Martin failed the fourth-grade state test.

Insight about Martin's reading performance comes from several sources. First, Martin was within two points of passing the state assessment, so he doesn't seem to have a serious reading problem. Second, although his reading rate is quite slow and this often interferes with comprehension (Adams, 1990), results of the QRI–II suggest that Martin's comprehension is quite strong, in spite of his slow rate. This is most likely because Martin has good word knowledge and understands that reading should make sense, and neither the QRI–II nor the state test has time limits. His strong score in expression confirms that Martin did, indeed, attend to meaning while reading. Third, a close examination of his reading behaviors while reading words from the WJ–R tests, QRI–II, and state reading selections revealed that he had some difficulty reading multisyllabic words; although, with time, he was able to read enough words to score at grade level or above. It appears that Martin has the decoding skills to attack multisyllabic words, but they are not yet automatic.

The outstanding characteristic of Martin's profile is his extremely slow rate combined with his relatively strong word identification abilities and comprehension. Our work with him suggests that, even if Martin were to get the additional two points needed to pass the state test, he would still have a significant problem with rate and some difficulty with automatic decoding of multisyllabic words, both of which could hamper his future reading success. Furthermore, with such a lack of automaticity and a slow rate, it is unlikely that Martin enjoys or spends much time reading. As a result, he is likely to fall further and further behind his peers (Stanovich, 1986), especially as he enters middle school where the amount of reading increases dramatically. Martin needs fluency-building activities such as guided repeated oral reading, partner reading, and Readers Theatre (Allington, 2001; Kuhn & Stahl, 2000; Lipson & Wixson, 2003). Given his word identification and comprehension abilities, he most likely could get that practice using fourth-grade material where he will also encounter multisyllabic words. It is important to find reading material that is interesting to Martin and that, initially, can be completed in a relatively short time. Martin needs to develop stamina as well as fluency, and to do that he will need to spend time reading short and extended texts. In addition, Martin might benefit from instruction and practice in strategies for identifying multisyllabic words so that he is more prepared to deal with them automatically while reading.

Cluster 5—Slow Word Callers

The students in this cluster are similar to Tomas, the Automatic Word Caller in Cluster 1. The difference is that Tomas is an automatic, fluent word caller, whereas the students in this cluster are slow. This group is a fairly even mix of English-language learners and native English speakers who have difficulty in comprehension and fluency. Andrew is an example of such a student. He has well-developed decoding skills, scoring at the seventh-grade level when reading words in isolation and at the independent level when reading connected text. Even with such strong decoding abilities, Andrew had difficulty with comprehension. We had to drop down to the second-grade QRI–II passage for Andrew to score at the instructional level for comprehension, and, even at that level, his retelling was minimal. Andrew's score on the PPVT–R, corresponding to first grade (the 4th percentile for his age), adds to the comprehension picture as well. It suggests that Andrew may be experiencing difficulty with both individual word meanings and text-based understanding when reading paragraphs and longer selections. Like Martin, Andrew's reading rate was substantially below rates expected for fourth-grade students (Harris & Sipay, 1990; Pinnell et al., 1995), averaging 62 words per minute when reading narrative and expository selections. In practical terms, this means he read just one word per second. As we might anticipate from his slow rate and his comprehension difficulty, Andrew did not read with expression or meaningful phrasing.

The relationship between meaning and fluency is unclear in Andrew's case. On the one hand, students who realize they don't understand would be wise to slow down and monitor meaning. On the other hand, Andrew's lack of automaticity and slow rate may interfere with comprehension. To disentangle these factors, his teacher would need to experiment with reading materials about which Andrew has a good deal of background knowledge to eliminate difficulty with individual word meanings and overall comprehension. If his reading rate and expression improve under such conditions, a primary focus for instruction would be meaning. That is, his slow rate of reading and lack of prosody would seem to be a response to lack of understanding rather than contributing to it. In contrast, if Andrew's rate and expression are still low when the material and vocabulary are familiar, instruction should focus on both fluency and meaning. In either case, Andrew would certainly benefit from attention to vocabulary building, both indirect building through extensive independent reading and teacher read-alouds as well as more explicit instruction in word learning strategies and new words he will encounter when reading specific texts (Nagy, 1988; Stahl & Kapinus, 2001).

It is interesting that 50% of the students in this cluster scored at Level 1 on the state test, the lowest level possible. State guidelines characterize these students as lacking prerequisite knowledge and skills that are fundamental for meeting the standard. Given such a definition, a logical assumption would be that these students lack basic, early reading skills such as decoding. However, as the evidence here suggests, we cannot assume that students who score at the lowest level on the test need decoding instruction. Andrew, like others in this cluster, needs instruction in meaning and fluency.

Cluster 6—Disabled Readers

We call this group Disabled Readers because they are experiencing severe difficulty in all three areas—word identification, meaning, and fluency. This is the smallest group (9%), yet, ironically, this is the profile that most likely comes to mind when we think of children who fail state reading tests. This group also includes one of the lowest numbers of second-language learners. The most telling characteristic of students in this cluster, like Jesse, is their very limited word identification abilities. Jesse had few decoding skills beyond initial consonants, basic consonant–vowel–consonant patterns (e.g., *hat*, *box*), and high-frequency sight words. However, his knowledge of word meanings was average, like most of the students in this cluster, which suggests that receptive language was not a major problem and that he does not likely have limited learning ability. With decoding ability at the first-grade level and below, it is not surprising that Jesse's comprehension and fluency were also low. He simply could not read enough words at the first-grade level to get any meaning.

As we might anticipate, the majority of students in this cluster were not proficient in writing and scored at the lowest level, Level 1, on the state fourth-grade reading test. It is important to remember, however, that children who were receiving special education intervention were not included in our sample. So, the children in this cluster, like Jesse, are receiving all of their instruction, or the majority of it (some may be getting supplemental help), from their regular classroom teachers.

Jesse clearly needs intensive, systematic word identification instruction targeted at beginning reading along with access to lots of reading material at first-grade level and below. This will be a challenge for Jesse's fifth-grade teacher. Pedagogically, Jesse needs explicit instruction in basic word identification. Yet few intermediate-grade teachers include this as a part of their instruction, and most do not have an adequate supply of easy materials for instruction or fluency building. In addition, the majority of texts in other subject areas such as social studies and science are written at levels that will be inaccessible to students like Jesse, so alternative materials and strategies will be needed. On the social–emotional front, it will be a challenge to keep Jesse engaged in learning and to provide opportunities for him to succeed in the classroom, even if he is referred for additional reading support. Without that engagement and desire to learn, it is unlikely he will be motivated to put forth the effort it will take for him to make progress. Jesse needs a great deal of support from his regular classroom teacher and from a reading specialist, working together to build a comprehensive instructional program in school and support at home that will help him develop the skill and will to progress.

Conclusions and Implications

Our brief descriptions of the six prototypical children and the instructional focus each one needs is a testimony to individual differences. As we have heard a thousand times before, and as our data support, one-size instruction will not fit all children. The evidence here clearly demonstrates that students fail state reading tests for a variety of reasons and that, if we are to help these students, we will need to provide appropriate instruction to meet their varying needs. For example, placing all struggling students in a phonics or word identification program would be inappropriate for nearly 58% of the students in this sample who had adequate or strong word identification skills. In a similar manner, an instructional approach that did not address fluency and building reading stamina for longer, more complex text or that did not provide sufficient reading material at a range of levels would miss almost 70% of the students who demonstrated difficulty with fluency. In addition to these important cautions about overgeneralizing students' needs, we believe there are several strategies aimed at assessment, classroom organization and materials, and school structures that could help teachers meet their students' needs.

First and most obvious, teachers need to go beneath the scores on state tests by conducting additional diagnostic assessments that will help them identify students' needs. The data here demonstrate quite clearly that, without more in-depth and individual student assessment, distinctive and instructionally important patterns of students' abilities are masked. We believe that informal reading inventories, oral reading records, and other individually tailored assessments provide useful information about all students. At the same time, we realize that many teachers do not have the time to do complete diagnostic evaluations, such as those we did, with every student. At a minimum, we suggest a kind of layered approach to assessment in which teachers first work diagnostically with students who have demonstrated difficulty on broad measures of reading. Then, they can work with other students as the need arises.

However, we caution that simply administering more and more assessments and recording the scores will miss the point. The value of in-depth classroom assessment comes from teachers having a deep understanding of reading processes and instruction, thinking diagnostically, and using the information on an ongoing basis to inform instruction (Black & Wiliam, 1998; Place, 2002; Shepard, 2000). Requiring teachers to administer grade-level classroom assessments to all their students regardless of individual student needs would not yield useful information or help teachers make effective instructional decisions. For example, administering a fourth-grade reading selection to Jesse, who is reading at first-grade level, would not provide useful information. However, using a fourth- or even fifth-grade selection for Tomas would. Similarly, assessing Jesse's word identification abilities should probably include assessments of basic sound/symbol correspondences or even phonemic awareness, but assessing decoding of multisyllabic words would be more appropriate for Martin. This kind of matching of assessment to students' needs is precisely what we hope would happen when teachers have the knowledge, the assessment tools, and the flexibility to assess and teach children according to their ongoing analysis. Both long-term professional development and time are critical if teachers are to implement the kind of sophisticated classroom assessment that struggling readers need.

Second, the evidence points to the need for multilevel, flexible, small-group instruction (Allington & Johnston, 2001; Cunningham & Allington, 1999; Opitz, 1998). Imagine, if you will, teaching just the six students we have described, who could easily be in the same class. These students not only need support in different aspects of reading, but they also need materials that differ in difficulty, topic, and familiarity. For example, Tomas, Makara, and Andrew all need instruction in comprehension. However, Tomas and Andrew likely can receive that instruction using grade-level material, but Makara would need to use easier material. Both Makara and Andrew need work in vocabulary, whereas Tomas is fairly strong in word meanings. As second-language learners, Tomas and Makara likely need more background building and exposure to topics, concepts, and academic vocabulary as well as the structure of English texts than Andrew, who is a native English speaker. Furthermore, the teacher likely needs to experiment with having Tomas and Makara slow down when they read to get them to attend to meaning, whereas Andrew needs to increase his fluency through practice in below-grade-level text.

So, although these three students might be able to participate in whole-class instruction in which the teacher models and explicitly teaches comprehension strategies, they clearly need guided practice to apply the strategies to different types and levels of material, and they each need attention to other aspects of reading as well. This means the teacher must have strong classroom management and organizational skills to provide small-group instruction. Furthermore, he or she must have access to a wide range of books and reading materials that are intellectually challenging yet accessible to students reading substantially below grade level. At the same time, these struggling readers need access to grade-level material through a variety of scaffolded experiences (i.e., partner reading, guided reading, read-alouds) so that they are exposed to grade-level ideas, text structures, and vocabulary (Cunningham & Allington, 1999). Some of these students and their teachers would benefit from collaboration with other professionals in their schools, such as speech and language and second-language specialists, who could suggest classroom-based strategies targeted to the students' specific needs.

The six clusters and the three strands within each one (word identification, meaning, fluency) clearly provide more in-depth analysis of students' reading abilities than general test scores. Nevertheless, we caution that there is still more to be learned about individual students in each cluster, beyond what we describe here, that would help teachers plan for instruction. Two examples make this point. The first example comes from Cluster 1—Automatic Word Callers. Tomas had substantial difficulty with comprehension, but his scores on the vocabulary measure suggested that word meanings were likely not a problem for him. However, other students in this cluster, such as Maria, *did* have difficulty with word meanings and would need not only comprehension instruction like Tomas but also many more language-building activities and exposure to oral and written English. The second example that highlights the importance of looking beyond the cluster profile is Andrew, our Slow Word Caller from Cluster 5. Although we know that in-depth assessment revealed that Andrew had difficulty with comprehension and fluency, we argue above that the teacher must do more work with Andrew to determine how much fluency is contributing to comprehension and how much it is a result of Andrew's effort to self-monitor. Our point here is that even the clusters do not tell the entire story.

Finally, from a school or district perspective, we are concerned about the disproportionate number of second-language students who failed the test. In our study, 11% of the students in the school district were identified as second-language learners and were receiving additional instructional support. However, in our sample of students who failed the test, 43% were second-language learners who were not receiving additional support. Tomas and Makara are typical of many English-language learners in our schools. Their reading abilities are sufficient, according to school guidelines, to allow them to exit supplemental ESL programs, yet they are failing state tests and struggling in the classroom. In this district, as in others across the state, students exit supplemental programs when they score at the 35th percentile or above on a norm-referenced reading test—hardly sufficient to thrive, or even survive, in a mainstream classroom without additional help. States, school districts, and schools need to rethink the support they offer English-language learners both in terms of providing more sustained instructional support over time and of scaffolding their integration into the regular classroom. In addition, there must be a concerted effort to foster academically and intellectually rigorous learning of subject matter for these students (e.g., science, social studies) while they are developing their English-language abilities. Without such a focus, either in their first language or in English, these students will be denied access to important school learning, will fall further behind in other school subjects, and become increasingly disengaged from school and learning (Echevarria, Vogt, & Short, 2000).

Our findings and recommendations may, on one level, seem obvious. Indeed, good teachers have always acknowledged differences among the students in their classes, and they have always tried to meet individual needs. But, in the current environment of high-stakes testing and accountability, it has become more of a challenge to keep an eye on individual children, and more difficult to stay focused on the complex nature of reading performance and reading instruction. This study serves as a reminder of these cornerstones of good teaching. We owe it to our students, their parents, and ourselves to provide struggling readers with the instruction they really need.

References

Adams, M.J. (1990). *Beginning to read: Thinking and learning about print*. Cambridge, MA: MIT Press.

Aldenderfer, M., & Blashfield, R. (1984). *Cluster analysis*. Beverly Hills, CA: Sage.

Allington, R.L. (2001). *What really matters for struggling readers*. New York: Longman.

Allington, R.L., & Johnston, P.H. (2001). What do we know about effective fourth-grade teachers and their classrooms? In C.M. Roller (Ed.), *Learning to teach reading: Setting the research agenda* (pp. 150–165). Newark, DE: International Reading Association.

Antunez, B. (2002, Spring). Implementing reading first with English language learners. *Directions in Language and Education, 15*. Retrieved October 15, 2003, from http://www.ncela.gwu.edu/ncbe pubs/directions

Black, P., & Wiliam, D. (1998). Assessment and classroom learning. *Assessment in Education, 5*(1), 7–74.

Block, C.C., & Pressley, M. (2002). *Comprehension instruction: Research-based best practices*. New York: Guilford.

Cummins, J. (1991). The development of bilingual proficiency from home to school: A longitudinal study of Portuguese-speaking children. *Journal of Education, 173*, 85–98.

Cunningham, P.M., & Allington, R.L. (1999). *Classrooms that work* (2nd ed.). New York: Longman.

Duke, N.K., & Pearson, P.D. (2002). Effective practices for developing reading comprehension. In A.E. Farstrup & S.J. Samuels (Eds.), *What research has to say about reading instruction* (pp. 9–129). Newark, DE: International Reading Association.

Echevarria, J., Vogt, M.E., & Short, D. (2000). *Making content comprehensible for English language learners: The SIOP model*. Boston: Allyn & Bacon.

Edmondson, J., & Shannon, P. (2002). The will of the people. *The Reading Teacher, 55*, 452–454.

Elmore, R.F. (2002, Spring). Unwarranted intrusion. *Education Next* [Online]. Retrieved March 21, 2003, from http://www.educationnext.org

Goodnough, A. (2001, May 23). Teaching by the book, no asides allowed. *The New York Times*. Retrieved March 21, 2003, from http://www.nytimes.com

Harris, A.J., & Sipay, E.R. (1990). *How to increase reading ability* (9th ed.). New York: Longman.

Helfand, D. (2002, July 21). Teens get a second chance at literacy. *Los Angeles Times*. Retrieved March 21, 2003, from http://www.latimes.com

Hiebert, E.H., Pearson, P.D., Taylor, B.M., Richardson, V., & Paris, S.G. (1998). *Every child a reader: Applying reading research to the classroom*. Ann Arbor, MI: Center for the Improvement of Early Reading Achievement, University of Michigan School of Education. Retrieved March 21, 2003, from http://www.ciera.org

Klein, S.P., Hamilton, L.S., McCaffrey, D.F., & Stecher, B.M. (2000). What do test scores in Texas tell us? *Education Policy Analysis Archives, 8*(49). Retrieved March 21, 2003, from http://epaa.asu.edu/epaa/v8n49

Kuhn, M.R., & Stahl, S.A. (2000). *Fluency: A review of developmental and remedial practices* (CIERA Rep. No. 2-008). Ann Arbor, MI: Center for the Improvement of Early Reading Achievement, University of Michigan School of Education. Retrieved March 21, 2003, from http://www.ciera.org

Linn, R.L. (2000). Assessments and accountability. *Educational Researcher, 29*(2), 4–16.

Linn, R.L. (n.d.). Standards-based accountability: Ten suggestions. *CRESST Policy Brief, 1*. Retrieved March 21, 2003, from http://www.cse.ucla.edu

Lipson, M.Y., & Wixson, K.K. (2003). *Assessment and instruction of reading and writing difficulty: An interactive approach* (3rd ed.). Boston: Allyn & Bacon.

McNeil, L.M. (2000). *Contradictions of school reform: Educational costs of standardized testing*. New York: Routledge.

Nagy, W.E. (1988). *Teaching vocabulary to improve reading comprehension*. Urbana, IL: ERIC Clearinghouse on Reading and Communication Skills and the National Council of Teachers of English.

National Institute of Child Health and Human Development. (2000). *Report of the National Reading Panel. Teaching children to read: An evidence-based assessment of the scientific research literature on reading and its implications for reading instruction* (NIH Publication No. 004 769). Washington, DC: U.S. Government Printing Office. Retrieved March 21, 2003, from http://www.nationalreadingpanel.org

Olson, L. (2001). Overboard on testing. *Education Week, 20*(17), 23–30.

Opitz, M.F. (1998). *Flexible grouping in reading*. New York: Scholastic.

Paterson, F.R.A. (2000). The politics of phonics. *Journal of Curriculum and Supervision, 15*, 179–211.

Pinnell, G.S., Pikulski, J.J., Wixson, K.K., Campbell, J.R., Gough, P.B., & Beatty, A.S. (1995). *Listening to children read aloud*. Washington, DC: U.S. Department of Education.

Place, N.A. (2002). Policy in action: The influence of mandated early reading assessment on teachers' thinking and practice. In D.L. Schallert, C.M. Fairbanks, J. Worthy, B. Malock, & J.V. Hoffman (Eds.), *Fiftieth yearbook of the National Reading*

Conference (pp. 45–58). Oak Creek, WI: National Reading Conference.

Riddle Buly, M., & Valencia, S.W. (2002). Below the bar: Profiles of students who fail state reading tests. *Educational Evaluation and Policy Analysis, 24*, 219–239.

Samuels, S.J. (2002). Reading fluency: Its development and assessment. In A. Farstrup & S.J. Samuels (Eds.), *What research has to say about reading instruction* (pp. 166–183). Newark, DE: International Reading Association.

Shepard, L.A. (2000). The role of assessment in a learning culture. *Educational Researcher, 29*, 4–14.

Snow, C.E., Burns, M.S., & Griffin, P. (Eds.). (1998). *Preventing reading difficulties in young children.* Washington, DC: National Academy Press.

Stahl, S.A., & Kapinus, B.A. (2001). *Word power: What every educator needs to know about vocabulary.* Washington, DC: National Education Association Professional Library.

Stanovich, K.E. (1986). Matthew effects in reading: Some consequences of individual differences in the acquisition of literacy. *Reading Research Quarterly, 21*, 360–407.

Stanovich, K.E. (1988). Explaining the difference between the dyslexic and garden-variety poor reader: The phonological-core variable-difference model. *Journal of Learning Disabilities, 21*, 590–612.

Stanovich, K.E. (1994). Romance and reality. *The Reading Teacher, 47*, 280–290.

Red Light, Green Light, 1-2-3: Tasks to Prepare for Standardized Tests

Kathleen M. Lawrence

Since the mid-1990s, Vermont students in grades 4, 8, and 10 have been required to take the New Standards Reference Exam in the English Language Arts as part of the statewide Comprehensive Assessment Plan. This national test is aligned with Vermont's Framework of Standards and Learning Opportunities, and it includes four parts: Reading for Basic Understanding, Reading Analysis and Interpretation (which includes a written component—a text-based essay), Independent Writing, and Conventions: Usage, Spelling, and Punctuation. The exam yields two types of information: (a) How students perform against particular standards for language arts, and (b) what students need in terms of instruction to achieve the standard in particular areas.

Early test results for the elementary school where I used to work as a librarian were disappointing. Despite our best efforts to provide a workshop environment with students actively engaged in the writing process (selecting topics, writing, conferring, revising, sharing, and evaluating their work) we were still faced with assessments outside of our own portfolio system that focused on the product. Of particular concern (with 70% or more of our students in need of improvement) were skills such as "proving assertions using evidence from the text, examining a text critically, and organizing a text-based essay." These are, in fact, life skills that we want our students to have and be able to demonstrate. It was clear that we needed to strengthen our teaching in reading analysis and interpretation and in writing effectiveness.

As a staff, then, we looked to the data to inform our instruction. What would we need to do to increase student performance on such tests? I decided to explore with students the demands that are placed upon them as writers in the artificial setting of a testing situation and to give them some strategies for meeting those demands. My plan, which will be the focus of this article, was the design and implementation of a 10-week unit for our third and fourth graders using QARs (Question-Answer-Relationships) (Raphael, 1982) to integrate reading and writing tasks. My objectives for the unit were as follows:

1. Increase comprehension of informational text.
2. Help students effectively respond to short-answer questions about a text they've read.
3. Help students recognize and locate textual evidence that supports statements they write about what they have read.
4. Provide students with practice writing a balanced essay on demand, within a time limit, and to a specific prompt.

It was important to me to have minimal disruption to the daily writing workshop block, so lessons for this unit were designed to take place just twice a week for 30 minutes during the writing support times I provided to each class. I made it clear to the students that we would be engaged in a different approach to a written essay, an approach that would be expected of them on the writing test. Students would work without the luxury of a self-selected topic and without

From *The Reading Teacher*, 55(6), 525–528. © 2002 by the International Reading Association.

the benefits of peer and teacher conferences and multiple drafts. Initially we worked as a whole class. I shared what I was working on with our special educator, and she was able to provide additional support to students in her case load outside of the class writing periods.

Types of Questions

After sharing my objectives with the students, I emphasized the following points in my first lesson:

1. When faced with a reading or writing test, students should read the questions first. This helps them know what to look (or listen) for in a text before reading it. It engages the brain and heightens awareness of particular details that may prove helpful later.
2. All questions are not equal. (This is the central theme for QARs.) Questions can be easy to answer with a few words or phrases from the text, or a bit more challenging if an answer is implied in the reading or composed of details from different parts of the text. Some questions demand more from the student by asking for opinions or connections to the reader's life.

Duke and Ritchhart (1997) recommended color coding the different types of questions that students might be asked on practice tests that help prepare them for standardized assessments. Therefore I introduced the notion of QARs with a traffic light analogy. (See Figure 1.) Using an overhead projector I displayed a picture of a traffic signal with a green, yellow, and red light. I pointed out that green-light questions are the simplest kind of question to answer, because you

Figure 1
QAR questions

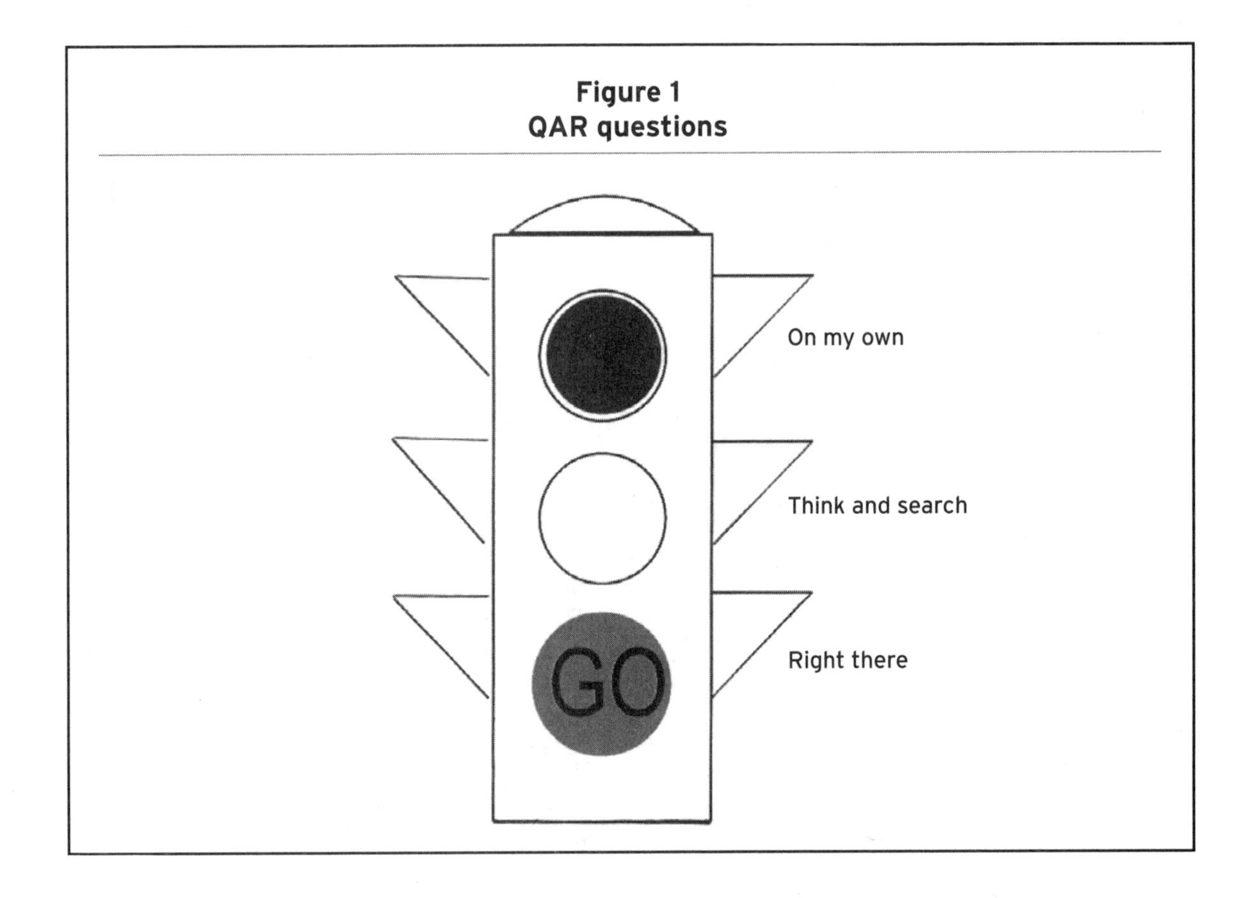

can *go* right to one spot in the text and the answer will be *right there*. These, of course, are the most basic types of questions, requiring literal comprehension.

Next I introduced yellow-light questions. After asking students what drivers are supposed to do when they see a yellow light, we agreed that for some questions it's necessary to *slow down and proceed with caution*. These are the *think and search* kind of questions, requiring the reader to slow down and look in more than one place in the text to assemble an answer (e.g., "In what three ways are pigs like people?" or "How do you know that the DeSotos worked as a team?"). The words to help build the answer are in the text as with green-light questions, but they are in several locations and may be more implicit than explicit.

Finally I talked about what I called the red-light questions. These questions require the reader to *stop* and to think hard about what the passage shows (textual information) and what the student already knows (prior knowledge). What is needed for an answer cannot be found solely in the text, though textual evidence is still critical. I emphasize to students that as a reader I must develop the answer *on my own*. Students must show a clear understanding of what was read, but elaborate upon and embellish using their own experiences and prior knowledge (e.g., after reading an informational article about westward expansion in the United States students are asked to "Pretend you are one of the older Sager children. Now that you've safely reached the Oregon Territory, write a journal entry or a letter to a friend back home. Give your impressions of the journey, as well as some of your feelings as you settle into your new life."). I pointed out that other red-light questions may ask students to offer an opinion based upon information presented (e.g., "Do you think it was wise for the DeSotos to treat the fox? What advice would you have given them, and why?"). It becomes clear that these red-light questions take more time and energy to answer, requiring students to move beyond the boundaries of the text on the page.

As Cunningham and Allington (1994) suggested, before trying these strategies with a longer published text we practiced with some short paragraphs that were school- or classroom-related. (Using the names of some of your students in these passages can be motivating as well.) When I felt confident that the class was comfortable with the language and concepts for QARs we proceeded to the next step—reading a longer text and answering related questions, one of which would require an essay.

A variety of texts, both fictional and informational, were chosen so that students practiced reading for information as well as reading for pleasure. Choosing texts of high interest is critical. Picture books (especially folk tales and biographies) work well with this whole-class model, but I also developed lessons around expository text found in quality periodicals such as *Appleseeds*, *Cricket*, *Ranger Rick*, *Faces*, and *Cobblestone*. (An added bonus for me as librarian was the increased student exposure to some of these excellent magazines; interest in them as choices during library sign-out times rose slightly as a result of this unit.)

Implementing QARS for Writing Essays

When I began the lesson for a particular day I showed the book or periodical from which that day's text would come and perhaps shared a bit of background information. I then reminded students of the first strategy we talked about for reading and writing tasks, and we looked at the questions for that text up on the overhead before I read. At this point I simply encouraged students to keep those questions in mind as they listened to the passage and to identify (for themselves) those parts of the text that would help answer the questions as we went along. Their listening is purposeful, and this helps to keep students engaged.

After reading the text aloud, we returned to the questions on the overhead and first identified the types of questions (green light, yellow light, red light) they had been asked to answer. I usually gave five questions per reading passage, with a mixture of all three types. We color-coded these using overhead transparency markers and then decided as a group which ones we'd answer first. Students generally chose to answer the green-light questions first because they're the simplest, and I pointed out that that can be a good strategy in a testing situation.

Next the text was put up on the overhead. For articles or short stories from a magazine, newspaper, or similar source, transparencies are easily made from the source itself. However, when using a picture book biography, folk tale, or longer story, I recommend preparing transparencies of the text alone without illustrations. (Parent volunteers who like to type at home can be most helpful with this task.) I do this for a number of reasons. Students are asked to focus on the content of the text in order to provide evidence and answer questions thoughtfully. I find that it is easier to maintain that focus at this point by proceeding without illustrations. Viewing just the text also allows me to use just one or two transparencies in most cases so there are fewer distractions at the overhead projector, switching and flipping from one page to the next. It's also easier for students to find patterns among questions and answers and to get a better sense of how different types of text are constructed when they can view most paragraphs at a glance.

We proceeded to answer each question in turn, orally first, moving from easiest (green light) to most challenging (red light). We highlighted (with the appropriate colored marker) relevant portions of the text that offered proof or details for our answer. Visually, with just one or two transparencies for students to look at, it became clear that for some questions we could go right there to find what was needed, for others we had to think and search in several paragraphs to assemble what we needed, and that for some we had to stop and think about what we read and what we already knew in order to formulate an answer.

Finally, we moved to putting our thoughts into writing. We returned to the overhead that listed the questions, and I asked students to "give me some words" to answer the questions thoughtfully and completely. Several students typically contributed to each question's answer. Using their words, I acted as scribe at the overhead. This provided a great opportunity to reinforce and model sentence structure, punctuation, grammar, and effective word choices. In addition, the longer text-based essay for our red-light question requires careful attention to skills such as prewriting and brainstorming, organizing information into paragraphs, making transitions between paragraphs, elaborating with details, summarizing, and writing powerful leads and satisfying conclusions.

A Student-Friendly Model

The first year I implemented this unit I began it in January and we finished shortly before the April testing dates. (Recently, however, teachers have begun using this student-friendly model for QARs early in the fall and building upon it in their reading program.) During our last few sessions I moved from the whole-class model to an individual model in order to simulate for students the testing situation and to see how they would respond once the whole-group supports were removed. Another possibility is to move gradually from whole-group to partners or small groups and then to an individual model. Closure for the unit came in our very last session with a review of the strategies taught for QARs and some reminders about test taking. (See Figure 2.)

Test scores in the school have slowly begun to improve, and students now have additional tools to help them to analyze what they read, articulate thoughts about what they read, and support their statements with evidence from the text. One of our third- and fourth-grade teachers now challenges students in book groups to generate the red-light, green-light, and yellow-light questions themselves, and lively discussion often follows.

Teachers who wish to create units similar to the one discussed here are reminded to do the following:

1. Use a variety of texts and a variety of questions. (You may even want to include a multiple-choice question in several lessons for test-taking practice if your students are unfamiliar with that format.)
2. Read and reread the texts you've chosen before each lesson. You'll save valuable

Figure 2
Test-taking tips for students

1. Read the questions before you read the passage so you know what you'll be looking for before you read.
2. Take notes, underline, and so on as you read along.
3. Remember that all questions are not equal. They range from easy to challenging and require different responses. Evidence from the text may be found in more than one place. The reader may have to offer a personal connection or opinion.
4. Answers to questions about the setting of the story can usually be found toward the beginning of the passage, the problem in the middle, the solution toward the end.
5. Plan your writing before you begin to write. It is time well spent.
6. Show what you know. Relax about it.
7. Remember that human beings are going to read your work. Use everything you know about good writing so that your work is interesting to read.

time at the overhead if you can quickly locate relevant bits of textual evidence that students are likely to point out.

3. Enlist parent volunteers if necessary to type reading passages and create overhead transparencies.
4. Move from the whole-class model to an individual model in stages as you feel students are ready.
5. Use your time at the overhead as an opportunity to reinforce elements of the writing process (e.g., brainstorming, prewriting, webbing), the writer's craft (e.g., leads, conclusions, effective word choices and sentence patterns), and technical accuracy (e.g., grammar, usage, mechanics).

Today's climate of high-stakes testing is just one more reason for teachers of reading and writing to continue their best teaching efforts on behalf of their students. QARs can be a part of any literacy program designed to help students become strategic, independent readers and competent writers. The student-friendly model described here is easy to implement and can be customized for any classroom and grade level. Though originally designed as a response to low test scores, it became an integral part of the literacy program.

References

Cunningham, P., & Allington, R.L. (1994). *Classrooms that work: They can all read and write*. New York: HarperCollins.

Duke, N.K., & Ritchhart, R. (1997, October). Standardized test preparation. *Instructor*, pp. 89–92.

Raphael, T.E. (1982). Question-answering strategies for children. *The Reading Teacher, 36,* 186–190.

SECTION FIVE

The Assessment-Instruction-Assessment Cycle

- How do you know when a reader is struggling? Succeeding? Developing effective reading behaviors?
- How does assessment serve to help you analyze and understand what is happening with readers?
- What assessment practices do you use in the assessment–instruction–assessment cycle?
- What professional knowledge is required to interpret reading assessment data and respond effectively to assessment data?
- What type of information on readers can be obtained through the use of anecdotal records? Is this information "scientific" enough to report to colleagues, parents, and others?
- How can you use conferences to collect data about students? What are the advantages or disadvantages of using conferences for this purpose?
- What role can informal reading inventories (IRIs) play in a classroom assessment system? Can IRIs be used on a broader scale and supply annual assessment data to political stakeholders?
- How can you use miscue analysis to provide information about readers?

The seven articles chosen for this section reveal that there are no shortcuts for understanding readers' behaviors or for being responsive to readers' needs. Knowledge about the reading process and readers and systematic observation are professional requirements for successful assessment and instruction.

Karen R. West developed a literacy assessment plan in harmony with her approach to instruction in her kindergarten classroom. To achieve this harmony, she matched her choice of assessment tools, such as anecdotal notes and checklists, with curricular staples, such as calendar, read-aloud, writing workshop, shared reading, centers, and Drop Everything And Read (DEAR). Ultimately using the assessment data to "build a descriptive story of each students' learning," West reports on her cycle of assessment and evidence-based teaching.

Anecdotal record assessment (ARA) is the practice of observing and documenting readers' behaviors for analysis and instructional decision making. Paul Boyd-Batstone describes a pragmatic, standards-based approach for documenting, organizing, interpreting, and using anecdotal records. This highly instructive article demystifies this authentic assessment tool and illuminates the value of being a skilled "kid-watcher."

Using reading conferences as her central practice for teaching and assessing, Sharon Ruth Gill reveals how she demonstrates strategies to readers *in situ*—at the readers' point of need. Gill collected anecdotal notes during her conferences with Amy, one of her students, and used them to document Amy's choice of texts, effective and ineffective reading behaviors, degree of fluency, miscues, orchestration of the reading process, and teacher assistance. Gill has grounded her teaching and assessing in Ken Goodman's explanation of "how reading happens"—the psycholinguistic view of reading. She provides an excellent summary of this view of reading and brings this view to life as she tells the story of "reading with Amy."

Teachers use IRIs to diagnose reading difficulties, to document individual growth, to uncover readers' behaviors, as a graphic tool for reporting to parents, and to guide instructional decisions. In their article on IRIs, Scott G. Paris and Robert D. Carpenter explain that most IRIs are designed to assess oral reading accuracy, comprehension, and sight word vocabulary. Assessment data derived from this assessment tool are used by skilled teachers to instruct students to develop productive reading.

Can IRIs be used to assess annual reading progress on a statewide scale and still provide teachers with formative assessment information? Teachers want assessment information that empowers their teaching, and political forces push for assessment results that report reading achievement. Scott G. Paris reports on work by the Center for the Improvement of Early Reading Achievement that resulted in identifying ways that IRIs or other leveled texts can be legitimately used to assess reading growth and report annual progress on a statewide scale. IRIs by Beaver (1997) and Leslie and Caldwell (2001) are referred to in this article, but are only two examples of numerous choices available to teachers.

Classroom Reading Miscue Analysis (CRMA) is a tool based on the work of Ken and Yetta Goodman. Lynn K. Rhodes and Nancy L. Shanklin explain that CRMA differs from most miscue analysis procedures because teachers record observations of a reader during reading, rather than from a taped reading. This highly instructive article offers steps on conducting CRMA and a teacher-friendly form for organizing the information from a CRMA session. The CRMA procedure and form are an excellent source to "provide teachers with a framework for understanding the reading process" but also for informing instruction and providing feedback to students and parents.

Although the article by Rita A. Moore and Karen L. Brantingham reports on the work of a Title I teacher, classroom teachers will value learning about this application of miscue analysis. The authors implemented Retrospective Miscue Analysis (RMA) to teach Nathan, a third-grade boy, to become empowered as a reader. Supported by retrospective discussions with the teacher about his reading, Nathan learned to listen to himself and adopt reading strategies that promoted his comprehension and confidence as a reader. He also grew to understand the nature of the reading process and ultimately changed from a less effective to a more effective reader.

Additional Reading

- Beaver, J. (1997). *Developmental reading assessment.* Glenview, IL: Celebration Press.
- Billmeyer, R. (2001). *Capturing all of the reader through the Reading Assessment System: Practical applications for guiding strategic readers.* Alexandria, VA: Association for Supervision and Curriculum Development.
- Calhoun, E. (2004). *Using data to assess your reading program.* Alexandria, VA: Association for Supervision and Curriculum Development.
- Chaleff, C.D., & Ritter, M.H. (2001). The use of miscue analysis with deaf readers. *The Reading Teacher, 55*(2), 190–200.
- Clay, M. (1993). *An observation survey of early literacy achievement.* Portsmouth, NH: Heinemann.
- Dewitz, P., & Dewitz, P.K. (2003). They can read the words, but they can't understand: Refining comprehension assessment. *The Reading Teacher, 56*(5), 422–435.
- Goodman, Y.M. (1996). Revaluing readers while readers revalue themselves: Retrospective miscue analysis. *The Reading Teacher, 49*(8), 600–609.
- Hill, B.C., Norwick, L., & Ruptic, C. (1998). *Classroom based assessment.* Norwood, MA: Christopher-Gordon.
- Hornsby, D., Sukarna, D., & Parry, J. (1986). *Read on: A conference approach to reading.* Portsmouth, NH: Heinemann.
- Leslie, L., & Caldwell, J. (2001). *Qualitative reading inventory* (3rd ed.). New York: Longman.
- Rhodes, L.K., & Nathenson-Mejia, S. (1992). Anecdotal records: A powerful tool for ongoing literacy assessment. *The Reading Teacher, 45*(7), 502–509.

Create a Statement of Reading Assessment Principles and Practices

Thus far, you have developed a refined set of principles to guide your assessment planning. Additionally, you have composed an overview and two lessons, compatible with your principles, to help students succeed on high-stakes tests. Now, turn your attention specifically to classroom assessment to complete these two tasks.

First, choose one of the assessment processes presented in one of the articles in this section. Carry out the process with a group of students. To do so, plan your implementation carefully, make notations as you implement, and reflect on what you learned about the readers and on the assessment–instruction–assessment cycle. For example, for a minimum of one week, use Boyd-Batstone's article on anecdotal record keeping and observe one or two students' actions relative to your instructional goals. Use his forms to support your efforts, and refer back to his article as you reflect on your success. As you engage in this exercise, maintain a written record of your experiences. Share the forms you maintained and your written record with a colleague. Discuss what you learned and how your assessment plan is affecting your principles.

Second, like the teachers in the introduction to the book, make a list of required and choice assessment tools used in your school or district (see reproducible provided). Discuss those tools with a colleague. Which tools inform your teaching? Which tool could you use more effectively to support readers' growth? Consider having a colleague conduct a peer observation of you as you engage in this assessment. Discuss the observation and determine how you will modify your assessment–instruction–assessment cycle.

Required Assessment Tools	Choice Assessment Tools

Noticing and Responding to Learners: Literacy Evaluation and Instruction in the Primary Grades

Karen R. West

In this article, I describe a program that effectively enables me to reach my kindergarten students. As a consequence, the children in my class show dramatic growth, particularly in their reading and writing development. I am able to individualize the classroom instruction more effectively due to my increased focus on and awareness of each child's progress. My program, which includes parents, is instrumental in helping me become a more effective primary teacher.

I am working to clarify my beliefs about literacy and learning, so that my curriculum and instruction are congruent. As suggested by Cambourne (1994), the evaluation tools I use need to match my instruction. So too, suggests the International Reading Association in a 1988 resolution on assessment, "Reading assessment must reflect advances in the understanding of the reading process" (as cited in Rhodes & Shanklin, 1993, p. 43).

Anders (in press) suggests a stance on learning theory may be aligned with one of the three major models of reading: traditional subskills model, eclectic model, or a whole language transactive model. We may believe language is learned piece by piece or that we learn language more holistically based on the surrounding context. Our beliefs relate to how we work in our classrooms.

My historical perspective on reading education has guided the development of my program. My stance towards holistic instruction and evaluation has been evolving, even from my early years as a general music teacher. I have been developing and refining my beliefs on learning through many years of teaching, talking, risk taking, reflecting, college coursework, and sharing language with my preschool son.

I now believe in and attempt to practice holistic instruction. I am working to develop holistic ways of evaluating learners' growth. Turbill (1994) suggests that such an "everyday model of evaluation" includes "opportunities to observe, interact, intervene, and participate in whatever is being evaluated" (p. 12). I want instruction and evaluation to be in meaningful authentic contexts.

I begin by describing various evaluation events that are integrated throughout curriculum and across instruction. Next I discuss the importance of planning to write and reflect each day. Further, I describe the organization and management of the evaluation tools and data. Finally, I look at how the students in my classroom benefit from this approach and what the program means for students, parents, and teachers.

Evaluation Throughout the Curriculum

Evaluation is ongoing throughout the entire day. While engaged in learning, children show us what their capabilities are and what they are attempting to learn. As children are involved in learning events, I record information and hy-

From *The Reading Teacher*, 51(7), 550–559. © 1998 by the International Reading Association.

pothesize about their learning. Goodman (1985) tells us of the value of kidwatching: "Through observing the reading, writing, speaking, and listening of friendly, interactive peers, interested, kidwatching teachers can understand and support child language development" (p. 9).

In other words, I look closely to find out what kids know in a variety of contexts. I work to see and hear what the children notice about literacy each day. For example, when I look at students' written work, miscues "often signal that the child is reaching out to some new facet of written expressions, and that he needs help towards some new learning" (Clay, 1975, p. 35). I analyze their learning both in process and as products, and I work to respond in ways that support and challenge their learning. One way to look at evaluation and instruction is by progressing through our daily classroom activities.

Greetings/calendar. Students get daily routines going, such as the pledge of allegiance, calendar, and other responsibilities. During the calendar discussion, I notice things about our calendar leader. Does she have one-to-one voice-print match? Does she move left to right and from the top down on a calendar text? I also look at the whole group and notice who is actively engaged and who appears to need some guidance or redirection. As I notice these specific details, I jot down a few notes on my lesson plan clipboard or sticky notes. These notes are rewritten and expanded at the end of the day.

Sometimes I share my observations with the students right away. For example, one day Alan pointed out that we forgot to read the days of the week. So we read the list in Spanish, then in English. I asked, "What day is today?" Several children chimed out "Friday." "How do you know?" Ryan told us, "You have to read down, down, down...." Beth explained, "'Cause it goes, Monday, Tuesday, Wednesday, Thursday, and *Friday*!" Matt also explained his logic, "Friday's next to Sunday...I mean Saturday." Each student shared different logic. All responses were accepted and valued. "Oh, so there are a lot of different ways to find out what day it is?" "Yeah!"

Read aloud. The next activity on a typical morning is a read-aloud session. When I read literature to my class, kids are actively involved in the story. Many students have ideas and questions they want to share. Through their comments and questions, some students may, for example, connect a story to their lives, connect a book to another book, notice specific details in illustrations, question the author as to "why" a character did or said something, laugh and enjoy the story (evidence that they are comprehending), share their knowledge to increase others' understanding of the story, or spontaneously dramatize a part of the story.

When I am reading a story, I make mental notes of students who volunteer and share ideas. Later in the day I write about students whose comments were unusual or stood out in some way. These students are sharing some of their thinking processes, and they are also teaching their peers different ways to think about stories.

When we go to the library, and the librarian reads aloud, or when a parent visits our class to read, I have a greater opportunity to observe students. I focus on the students and record my observations on paper immediately. It is much easier to record data when someone else is reading a book aloud.

I have developed a grid system to take notes during these times (see Figure 1). The librarian reads to the children, they get to enjoy the story, and I observe the students. Each time I observe kids as they respond to a story, their responses are unique. The categories are different for every grid; they evolve based on the children's particular responses of the day. It is through students' conversation that I am able to evaluate their thinking and also encourage others to do the same.

Writer's workshop. Our writer's workshop has four parts: (a) model writing, (b) sharing student journal entries, (c) journal writing, and (d) writing conferences.

Model writing is used to focus learners on one or two specific aspects of print. It is an instructional activity but also helps me find out what students know. The main teaching points

Figure 1
A grid helps record students' thoughtful responses to literature, to be used for evaluation purposes

	Jean	James	Stefeny	Dallas	Ryan	Jimmy	Matt	Beth	Steve	Sally	Brenda	Susie
Responds to adult's questions	X	X X	X	X X		X	X	X		X X	X	
Comments or interprets					XX X				X			
Connects book to life												X
Asks a question									X			
Makes a prediction										X	X	
Shares back-ground info							X					
Tangent?												X

come from me; others occur spontaneously from the kids. As I demonstrate by writing a journal entry on a large chart tablet, students are invited to support my thinking and writing. As kids provide an appropriate letter or sound, or take a risk or remind me to leave a space between two words, I make a mental note or write comments about students' specific shared learnings. As students help me with my work, I evaluate their understanding while I am instructing. Model writing is a good place for whole-group instruction that is based on observations and evaluations made about students' understandings during journal writing or guided reading and writing.

For example, I encourage kids to write stories on their own. In journals, I have seen that several students write words they have memorized. I acknowledge this strategy, but I also want children to take risks and figure out some letters that represent other words they want to write. Beginning writers don't need to write every letter of every word, but I want them to realize that they can write one or two letter sounds for each word they are writing.

My model writing lesson has several parts: (a) I draw the picture, and students make predictions about my story based on their perceptions of my drawing; (b) I tell a brief story to go with my picture; (c) Kids volunteer letter sounds to write for each word. The students then do the writing; (d) As I point to the writing, the children read the text. We discuss how we don't have to have every single letter to figure out the word. As the school year progresses, we also look for patterns in the writing, which leads us to specific teaching points.

Sharing student journal entries is another way to prepare for writing. Bobbi Fisher (1991) suggests we validate students' efforts as writers by encouraging them to share their work. Students who choose to share a journal may display their work in the classroom or talk about it with the whole class. All class members are invited to share comments and questions or tell what they notice about the writer's work. During this time students and teacher are evaluating and instructing. We can learn from each other about what makes a good journal entry.

We all look at the individual's work and try to understand what s/he is doing as a writer. Then we respond in a positive, supportive manner. Students become better equipped to self-evaluate and inform their own writing development.

In addition to sharing single journal entries, at times we share a complete portfolio. One writing sample from each month of the school year is stapled together. We look briefly at a collection. I ask the children, "What do you notice about Sally's writing?" Everyone looks to see how her writing has changed from August to January. Several students share their thoughts. Lane makers a very powerful insight when he tells us, "She's making more connections with letters and sounds." Lane knows how to recognize literacy development. He is evaluating Sally's work and instructing his peers.

Journal writing occurs after we have evaluated one another's writing or had a model writing lesson. This is a time for each child to work independently at a level that is personally appropriate. Everyone is responsible for drawing, writing his or her name, and writing a story. I expect to see different things from different students.

Writing conferences start once children are on task. I work individually with three to five students each day. I ask the child to "Tell me about your work" and the conference begins from there. I may write the child's dictation, or we may do some dialogue or shared writing; the child then reads back the written text. With more opportunities for us to work together, each child gains more self-confidence, takes more writing risks, and builds on those letter sounds he or she already knows.

As we confer, I record bits of information as to what stood out about the work, any special comments made by the child, and letters and sounds that the child used appropriately in his/her writing. I also suggest to the child a strategy that might be tried next time. Later that day, these brief comments, which I write on sticky notes, are transferred to each student's individual record page of writing observations.

My teaching responses are grounded in evidence from children's journal work. I must support and challenge each child in relation to the unique strengths and weaknesses that are in evidence both in that journal entry and those from the days and months beforehand.

During a particular writing conference, Beth and her peers began seeing, hearing, and talking about her literacy strengths. Beth and I were doing some collaborative writing to put together the text she had dictated for her drawing. She had already written down words she knew (names of people in her family). During this conference, some classmates overheard and commented, "Beth knows a lot!" "She's really smart!" "Beth knows a lot of her letters and sounds!" Students initiated this conversation, and I agreed with them. Beth beamed with pride because classmates were commenting about her strengths as a writer.

In another example, Matt's mom came in to visit. I opened my evaluation notebook to the anecdotal records section. I found a recent entry about Matt's writing. I was immediately reminded that he had invented the spelling for *cyclops*, and it was very recognizable to adults. I shared this with his mother and commented that this was one of the first times he had invented spelling on his own. Since his mom's visit, Matt has continued to take more risks and use invented spellings in his journal.

Shared reading. Each day, after we complete writer's workshop, we regroup with shared reading activities that take many forms. In a whole group, all learners are able to successfully participate when we read chorally. We may read big books or poetry, sing songs, or chant. We focus on enjoying the text; then I draw students into the print for one or two specific teaching points. This procedure was initially developed by Don

Holdaway (1979) to accommodate students' wide range of language and literacy abilities. Shared reading mimics the parent–child home reading situation.

Shared reading is a good place to connect evaluation with instruction. Students share what they know, instructing one another. I can observe and evaluate what children are noticing, plan future lessons to help clarify misconceptions, and lead them further in their literacy development.

After reading, I often ask, "Who wants to show what they know?" Children's contributions give me evidence of their current development. I keep track of their comments and elaborate on my notes at the end of the day. I don't try to recall everything that is contributed by all the children. I stay alert for comments from children who have been struggling or have not been showing much development, or those who seem to be noticing something unusual.

For example, we chorally read *Sing a Song* (Melser, 1980). After we read together, kids start to make some observations. "There's a *s*. And another *s*. There's lot of them!" remarks Ryan. I notice that he is locating specific letters in the context of the story. Early in the year, he had a low letter identification score, but now Ryan is showing me that he is ready to look more closely at specific letters.

Centers. Learning centers are where I enhance students' literacy development within content area learning. Four to 7 students, grouped heterogeneously, work at each of the 4 or 5 different centers in the classroom. Centers may include math, social studies, science, computer use, and art. A balance of independent and collaborative learning is structured into the centers.

During center time I work with a group at a guided reading center, which provides me a rich opportunity to see specific reading behaviors in action. At the guided reading center we reread a familiar book. Then the group is introduced to a new predictable book. We look at the front cover and title. I ask students to tell me what they know about the topic or predict what the book may be about. We also look at a few pages together, perhaps noticing some illustration details, and I draw out more of the students' background knowledge.

Then I ask the students to read and solve problems along the way. I encourage them to think about the story as they read. I also ask them to read together and listen to one another. They solve problems as they read the text chorally for the first time. When they hesitate, I remain silent for several seconds, giving them opportunities to do the reading work without me. If they continue to struggle, I ask questions to guide their thinking. I use questions like, "What would make sense?" "What would sound right?" "What's happening in the story?" "What can the picture tell you?" "What would make sense and look right?" As a last resort, I read the word. After the children read through the text together, I ask for a volunteer to read the book aloud for the group.

During the group choral reading and the individual rereading, I have the opportunity to watch and listen to what the readers are showing me they can do. Sometimes I come into a guided reading session with some specific information I want to find out. I ask for specific information such as: "Show me the front cover" or "Show me a capital letter." In addition to these specific questions, students lead the way, and I write down what they show me as they read: left-to-right progression on a page; one-to-one voice and print match; reading with expression; miscues, which the group can talk about as we become more aware of the language systems and strategies being used; attitude and interest in reading; and more.

In one experience, Jean and I were preparing for her to read *Zoo-Looking* (Fox, 1986) to her mom after school. Jean had read this book for the first time that morning at our guided reading center. I asked Jean, "Could I read it with you, or do you want to read it yourself?" She quickly responded, "I want to read it myself!" She continued to demonstrate her confidence, motivation, and interest in reading, as she worked through this 16-page text. She kept the story intact and read with high-quality miscues. Jean, her mom, and I talked about how well she read and made sense of the story. Both Jean and her mom appeared extremely proud.

I take brief notes during these guided reading sessions. At the end of the week, the recorded information will be transferred to checklists. Other notes become brief narrative anecdotes about children's reading growth and risk taking. (I'll explain more about checklists and anecdotes later.) All these notes are collected into an evaluation binder. I look at these notes to see how children appear to be progressing as readers and how I can plan the next guided reading session to give more support and challenge as it is needed.

Choice time. During this time, students choose an activity, materials, and peers with whom they wish to work. Some of our activity areas include two computer workstations, book and tape center, chalkboard, building blocks, sand table, art, housekeeping, games, math manipulatives, classroom library, piano, and rhythm instruments. Some choices are available throughout the year; others come and go or evolve as the need arises.

Choice time is another opportunity for evaluation and instruction. I can hold individual conferences, provide minilessons for a small group, or introduce a new activity that we'll all be doing within the next few days. I can sit back and observe the students in action, take field notes, and evaluate children when they are involved in an activity of their choice. I observe how they work in this situation, as compared to a task that I structure. Choice time gives me the opportunity to be more informal with kids. We can get to know one another as we talk, play, and learn together.

For example, one day Craig and I were talking about how all the people in the class are teachers. I mentioned that it's good to ask kids for help too, not just the adults. He didn't seem to agree with me. Then I reminded him how he responds when we share stories—he frequently asks questions, shares ideas, and makes connections. I told Craig he helps others learn how to think about stories. He smiled and said, "I know!" Craig is beginning to realize that he is a teacher, and his classmates are teachers, too. By evaluating Craig's active response to books and by helping Craig see his strengths, I was able to instruct him to use peers as resources, just as they might use him as a resource.

Drop Everything And Read. The last thing we do each day is Drop Everything And Read (DEAR) time. Students choose whatever materials they wish to read and are encouraged to read with a buddy or by themselves if they prefer. Some students will be quite comfortable reading a book independently; others will be more effective if they work with a classmate. I believe that by offering students the choice of reading alone or with peers, they will become more motivated and successful than if I had not offered any choices.

Another option for me at this time is to have individual reading conferences. Students who choose to may read a book for me; then we talk about and enjoy the story, and we discuss some strategies the child is using. We also talk about ways to improve on what the reader is already doing. During this time, I may do an informal miscue analysis, and I take notes during the time the child is reading. I tell the child, "I am going to write down some good things that I see and hear you doing, so we can go back and talk about a few of them after you read." Most children seem to thrive on this individual attention, and it gives everyone a chance to read, read, read.

Sometimes I hypothesize about what a student is doing with a particular miscue. When a student reads something that does not appear in the written text, I have an opportunity to find out about the child's thinking.

For example, Brenda read from *All of Me* (Butler, 1989): "You can see my eyes." The text actually was "See my eyes."

Brenda's insertion of two words suggests several things. She appeared to construct meaning from the sentence. When she added the two words, the meaning of the text was not changed significantly. She knew it would be logical and sound right to read "You can see my eyes." (She actually inserted "You can" in five pages of an eight-page book.) It is possible that this patterned language text was too "simple" a text structure to offer much support or information. After all, we generally don't speak in three-word sentences once our personal oral language development is more complex. Her focus and strengths appeared to be in the area of making meaning and using syntax. These are two very positive forces for a reader to bring to a text.

By noticing Brenda's strengths, I can plan instruction. She appears to need instructional support that will help integrate her use of semantics and syntax with the graphophonic cueing system. This will influence book selection, teaching points, and guiding questions for individual work with Brenda and also in small-group and whole-class lessons.

During DEAR time each child is encouraged to build up a collection of books they can read independently. I ask students to read a book for any adult in the classroom and show that they can read the text on their own. As a child reads a book successfully (the meaning of the story is kept intact, even though some of the words may not have been read exactly as printed), the book then goes into their personal book boxes. In these cut-off, empty cereal boxes, they build a collection of stories they can read.

I look in book boxes for patterns or learning trends. Maybe a child is reading and collecting pattern books with two-word sentences. I need to encourage this reader to work with more complex sentence structures. Maybe another student's book box is empty. I need to find some books that will give this reader some immediate success.

Finding Time to Write and Reflect

At day's end, I sit down at my desk and pull out my stack of anecdotal records. I write brief anecdotes for the five different students I had selected to focus on for the day. I write these anecdotal records in about 15 minutes each day.

I choose children to focus on each morning. Before students arrive I look through my stack of anecdotal papers (a loose-leaf page for each child) to see which children I have not written about yet that week. Students whose progress is not yet "documented" go onto the top of my stack. Of these children, I consider those that (a) I don't know very well, (b) I have less information on than I would like, (c) seem to be somewhat quiet in class, (d) approach me less frequently than many of their peers, (e) may be at a plateau or struggling in their literacy development, and (f) are a concern and a challenge for me.

These children become my priority for the day. I choose to watch and learn from them so that I may find out more about them as individual learners. I don't ignore students who are successful. My focus is on the children I have preselected, yet ultimately whatever happens within the context of the classroom determines who I write about. Anyone who stands out in some way may be a candidate for a narrative anecdote.

Over the course of the week, I have written about and observed each child at least once. These anecdotes could be about any part of the curriculum, including social development. I think of the child and about what s/he seemed to notice about literacy that day, took a risk about, had a strong successful experience with, or shared with a classmate or the entire class. It may be something that I remember from a read-aloud session, the computer lab, or free-choice playing or learning. Every anecdote is different! Here are two examples:

> Dec. 7 Art Center—Kathleen and her committee (Ryan, Matt, and Steve) were very successful with a pattern chain today. They talked over their plan and were very cooperative as they created their "AABC" chain.
>
> Dec. 12 Whole group—Read Aloud—Lane was making predictions for the story *Milk and Cookies* (Asch, 1982). He continues to show interest and creativity in sharing ideas connected to books. "They have a chair like ours!" He was talking about the rocking chair we have in our classroom.

Over time, I simply compile stories about each child. Rhodes and Nathenson-Mejia (1992) suggest that anecdotes in narrative form are "a natural and easy way to impart information about students' literacy progress" (p. 503). Throughout our curriculum I am getting to know students better. I am creating a data bank that I will reread, reflect on, and use to look for patterns indicating growth and needs for specific instructional support. Responsibilities and relationships between and among students, parents, and teachers become clarified and strengthened with this evaluation and instruction model (see Figure 2).

Managing the Data

It is important to keep various evaluation instruments organized and easily accessible. I use a binder, clipboards, self-adhesive mailing address labels, sticky notes, and portfolios.

The binder is organized by sections: checklists, daily anecdotes, writing observations, library read-aloud observations, guided reading notes, reading conference information, letter identification (Clay, 1979), math evaluation charts, and observation notes describing students in various settings. This organization seems to work well for day-to-day use. For conferences,

Figure 2
Evaluation and instruction connections strengthen relationships between and among teachers, students, and parents

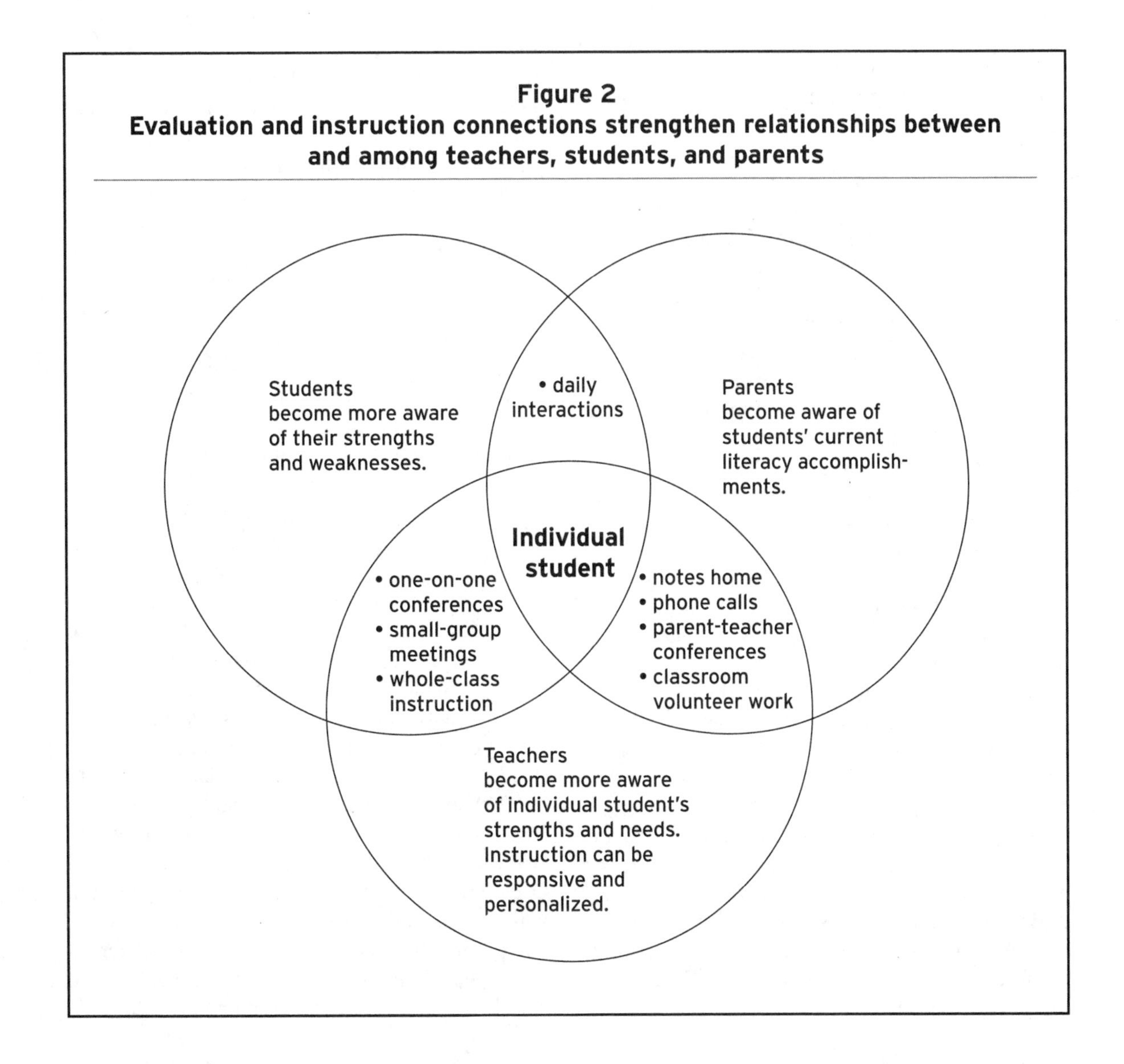

the binder is reorganized to have one section for each child, so all the information is in one place.

I created my own set of literacy checklists after having used and read about many others. They have several purposes. The items on the checklists serve as markers of literacy behaviors that I expect to see in my students. This helps guide my observations. I also keep written records of what children are accomplishing in other areas. By creating my own checklists, I am sure these markers reflect my beliefs about literacy development. The five lists I currently use include (a) attitudes and motivation toward stories, (b) bookhandling and print awareness, (c) directionality, (d) emergent strategies and strategy use, and (e) evidence of letters and sounds used in guided writing.

Each checklist is further subdivided into different facets of literacy that I believe to be important in students' development. I use these checklists to remind myself of the various kinds of reading and writing development that occur and to create a concise record of students' literacy behaviors. As Church (1994) points out, checklists are primarily developed and used "to sharpen the teachers' observational and listening skills rather than serve as the kind of checklist tool we used to use to determine whether the child measured up or not" (p. 259).

The information I record on the checklists comes from various settings. I transfer what I learn about students throughout the day. Much of this information comes from the guided reading sessions and the reading and writing conferences.

Writing conferences lead me to become organized with other materials. At the beginning of the week, I prepare a clipboard with several strips of mailing address labels. I have written each child's name across the top of a label. When I confer with a writer, I write brief comments; later I transfer the labels into individual student's writing pages, which are kept on loose-leaf paper in my evaluation binder. As the week progresses, I see which children I need to confer with, making sure to meet with each child at least once a week. The information I collect during writing conferences guides my planning for future model writing sessions.

The next tool in my evaluation notebook is a letter identification task. Children engage in this summative task several different times during the year. (For a more complete explanation, see Clay, 1979, pp. 23–27, 119.) Individually, I give the student a chart of letters, which appear in random order. I ask the child to point and tell me what s/he knows. I record the responses, whether it is an alphabetic response (*s*), letter sound (*sssssss...*), word (*snake*), or incorrect response. This tool helps me notice growth, strengths in recognizing upper or lower case letters, or confusions such as *b/d* or *u/n*. These assessments also inform instructional decisions for those students who need further focus in letter recognition. I use this tool about two or three times a year with each child, as needed, to show growth from the baseline data.

I also look at students' math development. I have developed a one-page chart on which I can record math abilities and growth over the year. This chart is largely based on the *Math Their Way* program (Baratta-Lorton, 1976). I record information about each child with various math tasks two or three times throughout the year, in order to document growth and inform instruction.

The final section in my notebook is baseline information. At the beginning of the year I want to get a sense of each child in various classroom settings. I consciously choose to observe children in various contexts in our classroom. For approximately the first 3 weeks of school, I record information about children in these settings: (a) read aloud, (b) choral reading and shared reading, (c) model writing, (d) journal writing, (e) independent or buddy reading, (f) listening and reading along with a story on tape, (g) free choice, (h) computer, and (i) sign-in sheet.

I keep one sheet for each child, and I work to "see" each child in several different settings. This tool, an adapted form of Marie Clay's "roaming around the known" as described by Marks and O'Flahavan (1994), has given me a baseline from which each student shows growth in literacy development. In Anne's case, I used this observation sheet to help me get to know her, as she joined our classroom midway into the first quarter.

We also have writing portfolios, based on a model described by Bobbi Fisher (1991). Once a week students choose their "best work" to add to their portfolio. Each child then files his or her writing into a hanging file folder, which is in a plastic crate. Students and visitors always have access to these files. These portfolio entries show strong evidence of children's growth over the school year. Portfolio collections and any of the above-mentioned evaluation records are powerful documents to share with parents at conferences.

All these data sources help me to build a descriptive story of each student's learning. Through triangulation of these sources, my understanding becomes more integrated, valid, and complete. This understanding affects my perception of myself as a professional, the instruction I offer my students, and my relationship with both my students and their parents.

Conclusions

Through my program of literacy evaluation and instruction, I make sound instructional decisions based on information I collect about individual students. Powerful connections occur between and among students, parents, and teacher. This model helps me understand and analyze complex interrelationships.

Children learn more about their strengths and strategies as learners. I work to understand students' efforts, commend them, and respond in ways that support and challenge future growth. Students also learn how they can support one another's learning. As I continue to refine this program, I anticipate that my students will show me more clear evidence of their literacy development.

Parents and I communicate about learners' strengths and needs in ways that are comfortable, such as conversations, brief notes, or phone calls. I share anecdotal information with parents, and it is well received. Parents learn about their child's specific literacy development and classroom curriculum and instruction.

Finally, due to this lens of evaluation, I believe I am a better teacher. I select and develop evaluation and instruction tools and techniques. The big decisions are guided by interpreting children's learning based on the interconnection of evaluation and instruction. As I learn more about literacy development, my beliefs evolve yet remain the backbone of my program. My students' literacy development is powerfully evident, and I am confident in my teaching.

Special thanks to Dr. Patty Anders for insightful revision support and *RT* reviewers for specific and constructive editorial comments.

References

Anders, P. (in press). *The theory-practice connection in reading instruction.* Boston: Allyn & Bacon.

Baratta-Lorton, M. (1976). *Math their way.* Menlo Park, CA: Addison-Wesley.

Cambourne, B. (1994). Why is evaluation of learning such a "hot" issue? What's the problem? In B. Cambourne & J. Turbill (Eds.), *Responsive evaluation: Making valid judgments about student literacy* (pp. 1-8). Portsmouth, NH: Heinemann.

Church, J. (1994). Record keeping in whole language classrooms. In B. Harp (Ed.), *Assessment and evaluation for student centered learning* (pp. 231-266). Norwood, MA: Christopher-Gordon.

Clay, M. (1975). *What did I write?* Portsmouth, NH: Heinemann.

Clay, M. (1979). *The early detection of reading difficulties* (3rd ed.). Portsmouth, NH: Heinemann.

Fisher, B. (1991). *Joyful learning: A whole language kindergarten.* Portsmouth, NH: Heinemann.

Goodman, Y. (1985). Kidwatching: Observing children in the classroom. In A. Jaggar & M. Smith-Burke (Eds.), *Observing the language learner* (pp. 9–18). Newark, DE: International Reading Association.

Holdaway, D. (1979). *Foundations of literacy.* Portsmouth, NH: Heinemann.

Marks, T., & O'Flahavan, J. (1994). *A study of two first-grade teachers "roaming around the known" with their students* (Reading Research Rep. No. 9). Athens, GA: National Reading Research Center.

Rhodes, L., & Nathenson-Mejia, S. (1992). Anecdotal records: A powerful tool for ongoing literacy assessment. *The Reading Teacher, 45,* 502-509.

Rhodes, L., & Shanklin, N. (1993). *Windows into literacy: Assessing learners K–8.* Portsmouth, NH: Heinemann.

Turbill, J. (1994). Getting a nut and bolt with the same thread: Matching evaluation theory with language learning theory. In B. Cambourne & J. Turbill (Eds.), *Responsive evaluation: Making valid judgments about student literacy* (pp. 9–15). Portsmouth, NH: Heinemann.

Children's Books Cited

Asch, F. (1982). *Milk and cookies*. New York: Parents Magazine Press.

Butler, A. (1989). *All of me*. Ill. S. Heinrich. Crystal Lake, IL: Rigby.

Fox, M. (1986). *Zoo-looking*. Ill. R. McRae. Gostard, NSW, Australia: Ashton Scholastic.

Melser, J. (1980). *Sing a song*. Ill. D. Gardiner. Bothwell, WA: The Wright Group.

Focused Anecdotal Records Assessment: A Tool for Standards-Based, Authentic Assessment

Paul Boyd-Batstone

A tension exists between macrolevels and microlevels of assessment, according to Valencia and Wixson (2000), yet there is common ground. In the current U.S. educational environment, standards-based measures dominate assessment (Johnston & Rogers, 2002). Yet, over the past two decades, qualitative measures for assessment purposes, and observational records in particular, have expanded considerably (Bird, 1986; Fishman & McCarthy, 2000). On a macrolevel, content standards arguably supply systematic criteria for quantitative measures to report trends and establish policy. On a microlevel, qualitative measures such as rubrics, student profiles, and anecdotal records provide measures that fill in the gaps to give teachers immediate information to plan for instruction. The purpose of this article is to describe a technique for anecdotal records assessment that uses the lens of content standards for an initial focus. As a classroom teacher and as a teacher educator, I sought to develop a teacher-friendly, standards-based way to address recording, managing, and using anecdotal records for authentic assessment purposes. I call the system focused anecdotal records assessment (ARA).

Why Anecdotal Records Assessment?

Observational notes as a technique for recording a child's natural literacy experiences emerged from qualitative research (Emerson, Fretz, & Shaw, 1995; Guba & Lincoln, 1982; Lofland, 1971; Patton, 1990). Applying observational techniques for classroom-based, ongoing assessment has been called a variety of names such as alternative, informal, or authentic assessment (Cole, Ryan, & Kick, 1995; Reutzel & Cooter, 2004; Tierney, 1999). I prefer the term *authentic assessment*, as opposed to *alternative assessment*, because it is not defined by a juxtaposition to standardized assessment. Authentic assessment is defined by the active role the teacher plays in classroom-based assessment of actual literacy experiences. Taking observational notes allows the teacher to record a wide range of authentic experiences and even unintended outcomes of literacy development. These notes are used to record objective and subjective information as well as affective information, such as levels of engagement, curiosity, and motivational factors (Baker, Dreher, & Guthrie, 2000; Wigfield, 1997). With focused ARA, content standards initially frame the field of vision to guide observation; however, it is not designed to preclude the observation and recording of a full range of experiences related to reading and the language arts.

Being a teacher calls for skilled techniques in observing children, recording, and managing authentic assessment data. Recording observational data "explicitly depends on the human expert" (Johnston & Rogers, 2002, p. 381), the kid watcher (Goodman, 1978), and the sensitive

From *The Reading Teacher*, 58(3), 230–239. © 2004 by the International Reading Association.

observer (Clay, 1993). In other words, the one closest to the classroom experience is in a unique position to see and communicate a reliable and valid instructional perspective of the child. Rhodes and Nathenson-Mejia (1992) identified anecdotal records as a powerful tool for literacy assessment. Miller-Power (1996) argued that systematic, daily recording of children's actions was essential to generate focused instructional planning. Anecdotal records in particular have been used as one of multiple tools in authentic literacy assessment (Pils, 1991; Valencia, Au, Scheu, Kawakami, & Herman, 1990). Anecdotal records assessment is an essential component in the development and interpretation of student portfolios (Klenowski, 2002; Valencia, 1998). In addition, Rollins-Hurely and Villamil-Tinajero (2001) used observational records to assess the language proficiency of English learners.

A fundamental purpose of assessment is to communicate what the child knows and is able to do. Teacher-generated, anecdotal records provide an insider's perspective of the child's educational experience (Baumann & Duffy-Hester, 2002; Cochran-Smith & Lytle, 1990). This perspective is vital to communication with the child and the child's family about academic progress. Anecdotal records also facilitate assessment conversations (Johnston, 2003) as educational professionals describe their observations of student learning and consider ways to develop appropriate strategies to build on strengths and address academic needs. The more focused the observational records, the more helpful they can be in making daily decisions about instructional approaches.

A Collection of Techniques

Focused ARA employs content standards to initially focus observations. It uses several techniques for recording standards-based notes and a simple format for managing multiple records. It also supplies a way to analyze records and a place to address instructional recommendations. To more fully answer the question of what focused ARA is, I discuss each component of the process of standards-based, anecdotal records assessment in a problem-and-solution format. The five components to be addressed are as follows: observing children in instructional settings, maintaining a standards-based focus, making anecdotal records, managing anecdotal records, and using anecdotal records for assessment.

1. Observing Children in Instructional Settings

In attempts to record observations of children, two problems emerge: limited time and how to compose quality records. This two-fold challenge is illustrated by the following example. Each week, I observe teachers working with groups of students. They may be leading a discussion of a children's book. They are excited by the adrenaline rush they get when students authentically respond to reading. The students are making personal connections to the story and insightful comments, and they are asking probing questions. The lesson comes to a close just as the recess bell rings. The class files out the door to play. The student teacher desperately needs a bathroom break. Now what?

Observations must be recorded before the moment is lost to short-term memory. There is no time. The teacher draws a blank and is confronted with a host of perplexing questions: What should I write? How do I start? How did what I saw match up with content standards? What do I do with the information? How can I record information that will be readily accessible in the future? If I write one note about the students, how can I avoid rewriting the notes in each of their files? The observational data is at risk of being lost.

Observing children requires planning and preparation. In order to address the time constraints of the classroom, select which students to observe ahead of time. Avoid attempting to observe everybody all at once. I recommend dividing the students into four groups with five to seven in each group. Monday through Thursday of each week, observe a different group. On Fridays, observe the students who were absent or require further observation. In other words, the teacher focuses on only a handful of students to observe each day. This simple organizational technique can keep the teacher from drowning in anecdotal record taking. Another way to address time constraints is the use of adhesive computer address labels for writing the records (Rhodes & Nathenson-Mejia, 1992). Prior to observing, write the current date and the student's initials on each label. All that the teacher carries, then, are five to seven dated and initialed blank labels. I also recommend carrying a few extra labels just in case it becomes necessary to write further observations. Selecting students and preparing the labels for recording observations will save valuable time, but having tools in place is only part of the solution. Prior to observation, one needs to establish a focus.

2. Maintaining a Standards-Based Focus

Reality is complex. When confronted with myriad situations that take place during instruction, it is easy for the teacher to become distracted and neglect to observe actions directly related to the subject of instruction. Think of how experienced photographers approach taking pictures. They are experts at drawing the eye to a subject and, prior to entering the studio, will sketch a series of poses to establish a dominant focus for the pictures. In contrast, inexperienced photographers often take pictures without realizing that the foreground or background images create significant distractions.

In much the same way with anecdotal record taking, teachers require a dominant focus to avoid being distracted by disruptive or unusual behaviors, personality differences, and so forth. This is not to exclude important information about a student that a teacher should note. There are a number of tools for inventory and survey of developmental levels, interests, unique qualities, and affective aspects of the reading process (for a comprehensive listing, see Reutzel & Cooter, 2004). But, in order to train the eye for observing instructional experiences related to content standards, a dominant focus must be established. Teachers already do this with lesson planning; therefore, it follows to use the selected content standard for observational purposes.

Establishing a content standard focus has several advantages. First, it directs the attention of the teacher to persistently observe what students know and do with regard to specific instructional content. (Consequently, the teacher resists distraction in a given moment of instruction.) Second, the verbs in well-written content standards facilitate composing observational data. The verbs initiate the focus for observation.

The field of vision for observation is set by the verbs found in each standard. Are the students, for example, *identifying* vocabulary or *matching* words to pictures? Are they *asking* clarifying questions or *retelling* the story? Borrowing the key verbs from the content standard saves time with on-the-spot composing of anecdotal records. The teacher is not wasting time trying to think of what to record because, prior to instruction, the content standard was selected and the key verbs noted. The verbs in Table 1 were extracted from the California Reading/Language Arts Framework for California Public Schools (1999) Content Standards and organized according to various facets of reading and language arts. (This is not an exhaustive list.)

The focus, initially established by the content standards, guides observation for assessment. This is not to advocate a rigid and narrow field of vision. Experienced teachers observe and record multiple features of student performance at a glance. However, using a selected content standard as a point of reference ensures that an instructional focus is maintained during an observation period.

3. Making Anecdotal Records

Following instruction, write specific anecdotal records on adhesive address labels that have been dated for reference. Once records are taken, the labels are peeled off and then pasted to a specially designed form—one per child. Maintaining a key with a listing of the selected standards is highly recommended. The standards key

Table 1
Meaningful verbs for writing anecdotal records

Strategies	Listening	Writing	Reading	Speaking
Uses (strategies)	Distinguishes	Writes	Blends	States
Organizes	Determines	Prints (legibly)	Reads	Describes
Generates	Recognizes	Spells	Tracks	Shares (information)
Classifies	Identifies	Illustrates	Decodes	Recites
Compares	Responds	Capitalizes	Follows words	Represents
Contrasts	Asks	Defines	Rereads	Relates
Matches	Questions	Indents	Uses references	Recounts
Plans	Clarifies	Describes	Studies	Retells
Provides	Discerns	Summarizes	Highlights	Reports
Connects (ideas)	Analyzes	Organizes		Concludes
Arranges	Follows directions			Quotes
Supports	Reacts			Delivers
Confirms	Points out			Requests
Selects	Points to			Asks
Chooses	Gestures			Indicates
Demonstrates				Confirms
Presents				
Clarifies				

provides a place to record and collect selected standards for future analysis of the anecdotal records (see Table 2).

Writing quality anecdotal records is facilitated by keeping in mind the following considerations: Write observable data, use significant abbreviations, write records in the past tense, support records with examples as evidence, don't use the C-word (*can't*), and avoid redundancy.

Write observable data. In order to ensure writing quality records, there are several questions that clarify the word choice for observable data. First, close your eyes and ask yourself these questions: Does the wording tell me what the student is doing? Do I see the child matching words to pictures? Is that an observable action? Conversely, a favorite phrase from the lexicon of expressions commonly used by educators is "on task." If you close your eyes and try to imagine what "on task" looks like, you draw a blank.

Two more questions deal with quantitative data: How many and how much? What you can count can be observed. How many words were spelled correctly? How many times did the student self-correct? How much time did the student read independently? Conversely, avoid using phrases that imply an embedded interpretation, such as "a lot," "a few," or "many times."

Some words are very tricky, such as *know* and *understand*, and yet they are essential to instruction. The reality is that one cannot directly observe the inner process of acquiring knowledge or understanding. These words are conclusions drawn from a composite of a student's demonstration of a skill or expression of summarizing or synthesizing concepts. We realize that a student has gained understanding by observing related actions. Children demonstrate their knowledge or understanding by responding to questions or performing a task. Note the difference in these kinds of records:

> Observable: "Wrote 3 sentences," "Read for 5 minutes," "Misspelled 6 words," "Defined vocabulary," or "Answered 2 comprehension questions."

Table 2
Anecdotal records standards key

1 Date: Standard	2 Date: Standard:
3 Date: Standard	4 Date: Standard:
5 Date: Standard	6 Date: Standard:
7 Date: Standard	8 Date: Standard:

> Not observable: "Wrote a few sentences," "Read a lot," "Misspelled words many times," "Knew vocabulary," or "Understood the story."

Use significant abbreviations. Table 3 provides some helpful abbreviations to speed the writing of records.

Write records in the past tense. Remember that the moment after an event takes place, it moves into the past. Knowing to write records in the past tense streamlines the composing process. There is less need to consider how to conjugate verbs. Maintaining the past tense makes for consistent and more accurate records.

Support records with examples as evidence. Include an example of what the student did. Any time the observer can cite a specific example, the record will more accurately generate a clear recommendation for instruction (e.g., "WA *picture* 3 different ways—*pitur*, *pictr*, *piture*"). Examining the record triggers a recommendation for, *r*-controlled word lessons.

Don't use the "C-word." There is a temptation to use the word *can't* when attempting to record an observation about what the student did *not* do. It is much more accurate to simply state that the student did not do a particular task than to imply that the student is unable to perform the task by writing *can't*. Note the difference in the following statements: "Can't write a five-line poem" versus "Did not write a five-line poem." The first statement is not an observation but an indictment against the student, whereas the latter expresses what did not happen, without implying a lack of ability on the student's part.

Use the null sign ø for a negative. Attempting to quickly report what was not observed proves cumbersome. It takes too many words to explain what was expected versus what was observed. A rapid way to state what was not seen is to preface the record with a null sign or the capital letter *N*. Then write the observational statement so that it reads like this: "ø—asked observational questions" or "N—identified past tense irregular verb." The record states what was expected to be seen; only the sign places it in the negative.

Avoid redundancy. A frequent problem in writing anecdotal records is including needless repetition when the implication is obvious, such as "the student retold the story" or "the student

Table 3
Helpful abbreviations

Abbreviation	Meaning	Example
ID	Identified	ID main idea
X	Times	Misspelled *tried* 3Xs
→	To or in relation to	Matched picture → words (see next example)
T	Teacher	Retold story → T
S(s)	Student(s)	Read to 4 Ss for 5 minutes
RA	Read alone	RA → 2 minutes
RT	Read with teacher	RT → 2 paragraphs
RS	Read with another student	RS entire book
SC	Self-corrected	Wrote *unitid* SC→ *united*
WA	Wrote alone	WA 3 sentences
WT	Wrote with teacher	WT 4 paragraphs
WS	Wrote with another student	WS 7 sentences
def	Defined	def 6 terms correctly
Δ (delta sign)	Changed	Δ initial focus in writing
N or ø (null sign)	Did not observe	ø clarifying questions

identified the main character." There is no need to repeat the subject. The ARA form clarifies who is being observed. The same cautionary note applies to rewriting the student's name multiple times. We have all been taught to write complete sentences with a subject and a predicate; however, for the sake of time, it is not necessary. With focused ARA, the subject is already identified on the label by initials. There is no need to write his or her name again, and the fact that the subject is a student is implied in the process. Rather than initiating writing with a subject, begin with a key verb: "Matched picture to vocabulary."

4. Managing Anecdotal Records

Using adhesive computer address labels to record observations has several advantages (Rhodes & Nathenson-Mejia, 1992). The size forces the writer to economize. I repeat the following mantra each time I attempt to write anecdotal records: "Lean is clean; wordy is dirty." The value of an assessment can easily be lost in a deluge of words. Succinct writing clarifies the entire process. Another advantage of using these labels is that, unlike sticky notes, the adhesive holds the labels firmly in place on ARA student forms for access later.

A single-page ARA student form is shown in Table 4. The form has several design features to facilitate managing records. There is room for up to eight observational records, and then there is a section for sorting observations into strengths or needs. After that, there is space for instructional recommendations based upon the child's identified strengths and needs. The final section is a boxed area for noting any special needs accommodations. The teacher prepares a binder with an ARA student form for each child in the class. After anecdotal records are taken and at a convenient time during the day, the teacher simply sticks a computer address label in the appropriate box for each child. Once a child's form is filled, it is ready for an analysis of strengths and needs and instructional recommendations.

5. Analysis of Anecdotal Records

Anecdotal records assessment is informed by comparing the standards to the child's performance. The standards also inform the selection

Table 4
Anecdotal records assessment form

Student's name ______________________ Evaluator's name ______________________

1	2
3	4
5	6
7	8

Assessment statement

Summary of records: ______________________

Recommendation of next steps: ______________________

Accommodation for special needs:

of strategies and activities for instructional recommendations. Periodically, analyze the compiled records for each student. The time between analyses may vary according to your own academic calendar. Consider analyzing the records every six to eight weeks. This is when the anecdotal records standards key (see Table 5) becomes useful. It is difficult to remember the various standards that were selected to guide observation over a period of weeks. Therefore, the anecdotal records standards key reminds the teacher of specific standards.

Reference each standard as you comb through the anecdotal records. Decide whether or

Table 5
Anecdotal records standards key

1 Date: 9/26 Standard: Concepts about print. Identify author, illustrator, and book features.	2 Date: 9/30 Standard: Comprehension. Ask for clarification and explanation of stories and ideas. Organization and delivery of oral communication: Retell stories, including characters, setting, and plots.
3 Date: 10/3 Standard: Vocabulary and concept development. Identify simple multiple-meaning words.	4 Date: 10/10 Standard: Written and oral English-language conventions. Grammar: Identify and correctly use various parts of speech, including nouns and verbs, in writing and speaking.
5 Date: 10/17 Standard: Writing applications. Write a brief narrative based on their experiences.	6 Date: 10/21 Standard: Writing applications. Write a brief narrative based on their experiences. Spelling: Spell frequently used, irregular words correctly.
7 Date: 10/28 Standard: Vocabulary and concept development. Use knowledge of individual words in unknown compound words to predict their meaning. Vocabulary and concept development: Identify simple, multiple-meaning words.	8 Date: 11/5 Standard: Writing applications. Write a brief narrative based on their experiences. Punctuation: Use appropriate ending punctuation marks.

not the student met the standard. Code the records as follows: Mark the records with an *S* to indicate an area of strength in comparison with the appropriate standard; mark the records with an *N* to indicate an area of need in relation to the standards. The records occasionally note a point of information that is neither a strength nor a need, such as the student's home language. Points of information are coded with an *I* (see Table 6). In addition, you may want to expand the range of coding to include anomalies or unique features with a *U*, or affective components of reading with an *A*. ARA is adaptable to the needs of the teacher.

Once the records are coded for strengths, needs, or information, simply list an abbreviated summary of the strengths and the needs in the space provided below the records. Separating the records into strengths and needs allows the teacher to summarize what patterns are being exhibited by the student. The summary also helps clarify and generate appropriate instructional recommendations.

Recommendations

Once the anecdotal records are summarized in terms of strengths and needs, student-specific recommendations can be made. In essence, the teacher is customizing instruction and support for the individual. To be effective and practical, the recommendations should be task oriented. New teachers have the most difficulty with this

Table 6
Anecdotal records

Student's name: Julia V. (pseudonym)	Evaluator's name: (Teacher)
1 9/26 J.V. S ID book's author, illustrator, title S ID copyright, year, publisher I Eng. learner = Spanish	2 9/30 J.V. S Asked clarifying questions S Retold beginning of story N MisID main character
3 10/3 J.V. S Classified vocab. words in self-generated categories	4 10/10 J.V. N Did not distinguish adjectives from verbs S Provided descriptive words to chart poem
5 10/17 J.V. Absent	6 10/21 J.V. N Wrote 2 paragraphs S Used cluster diagram as a prewriting organizer S SC 3 words writing *libary*, *troubel*, and *litle*
7 10/28 J.V. S Used *aerodynamic* in sentence N Matched 2 out of 5 vocab. words to definition	8 11/5 J.V. N Wrote 1 paragraph narrative w/assistance N No ending punctuation in 2 sentences

Assessment statement

Summary of records (Strengths): Asks clarifying questions; retells story beginnings; generates categories to classify words; uses descriptive words; uses prewrite organizers, self-corrects writing

(Needs): Misidentifies characters; parts of speech; writes 1 or 2 paragraphs with assistance; matching words to definitions; ending punctuation

Recommendation of next steps (Strengths): Continue to read books with her; encourage "who, what, why, how" questions; develop primary/secondary categories for words; use tree diagrams as a prewrite tool for more complex organization

(Needs): Character study and story mapping; compose cinquain poems to learn parts of speech; encourage 3 to 5 paragraph writing; match key vocab. to pictures; review ending punctuation rules

Accommodation for special needs:

N/A

part of the process. It is not uncommon to see recommendations written as teacher strategies rather than student activities. A common trap these teachers fall into is to recommend a word wall to address any number of needs related to literacy development without specifying what the child is to do. To me, it sounds like something akin to "Take two word walls and see me in the morning." Without a task associated to the strategy, the recommendation can be meaningless.

Remember to write recommendations with the children's parents in mind. What would you say to parents? They would need specific tasks to do with their children, like sorting words into families of *-ar*, *-er*, *-ir*, *-or*, *-ur*. Providing task-oriented recommendations based upon the content standards clarifies the recommendations and ensures the practicality of the activity.

A quality assessment is like a well-woven fabric. Components are all interrelated. Looking at the assessment, one can see (a) how the observations are standards based, accurately coded, and summarized in terms of strengths and needs and (b) how the selection of specific recommendations is the outcome. The relationships between components are strong. In other words, with focused ARA the recommendations are the direct result of the observation and analysis. The technique represents a complete process in observation and assessment.

Applications

There are three primary applications of focused ARA: formative assessment for determining instruction that matches the strengths and needs of the students, summative assessment for conferring with families about a child's progress, and a combination of both formative and summative assessment for consultation with a support staff.

Using and maintaining focused ARA generate substantive teacher observations as formative assessment for instructional planning. In contrast to standardized testing, which is far removed from the classroom setting, focused ARA utilizes the insights of an observant teacher to provide quality instruction. The process is based upon classroom experience, performance, and content standards. It allows the teacher to design instruction built upon individual strengths and needs. Focused ARA underlines the fact that standards-based performance assessment requires a relationship with the student to match strategies and activities to strengths and needs. The recommendations are tailored to the student.

The focused ARA is a useful tool for summative assessment. It outlines teacher comments to cite observations, summarize strengths and needs, and provide well-thought-out recommendations. When reporting a child's progress in a parent conference, focused ARA can be used to cite how a child performed to meet content standards on specific dates and how the teacher planned to address strengths and needs. Summarizing strengths establishes a positive note. Parents see from the outset that the teacher is advocating on behalf of their child. Summarizing needs follows naturally and provides the foundation for individualized recommendations. In the case of special needs, the focused ARA allows for addressing accommodations.

Prior to developing an alternative plan for instruction, support staff such as administrators, specialists, counselors, and school psychologists often ask to see a record of six weeks of interventions. Focused ARA meets that requirement in an organized fashion, providing evidence of student performance and teacher recommendations. This kind of information organized on a single sheet of paper can be invaluable to collaboration with the entire support system at a school site.

In Sum

In an educational environment that attributes significant weight to standardized measures for assessment, focused anecdotal records assessment provides teachers with an authentic tool to record observations in light of content standards. As part of a regular observational rhythm in the classroom, the teacher can manage records, analyze observational data, and provide standards-based recommendations. The system facilitates communication between the children, their families, and educational professionals participating in the assessment process. Focused ARA is a tool to work common ground across authentic and standardized assessment.

References

Baker, L., Dreher, M.J., & Guthrie, J.T. (2000). *Engaging young readers: Promoting achievement and motivation*. New York: Guilford.

Baumann, J., & Duffy-Hester, A. (2002). Making sense of classroom worlds: Methodology in teacher research. In M. Kamil, P. Mosenthal, P.D. Pearson, & R. Barr (Eds.), *Methods of literacy research* (pp. 77–98). Mahwah, NJ: Erlbaum.

Bird, L. (1986). The art of teaching: Evaluation and revision. In K. Goodman, Y. Goodman, & W. Wood (Eds.), *The whole language evaluation book* (pp. 15–24). Portsmouth, NH: Heinemann.

California Reading/Language Arts Framework for California Public Schools. (1999). Sacramento, CA: State Department of Education.

Clay, M. (1993). *An observation survey of early literacy achievement*. Auckland, New Zealand: Heinemann.

Cochran-Smith, M., & Lytle, S.L. (1990). *Insider/outsider: Teacher research and knowledge*. New York: Teachers College Press.

Cole, D., Ryan, C.W., & Kick, F. (1995). *Portfolios across the curriculum and beyond*. Thousand Oaks, CA: Corwin Press.

Emerson, M., Fretz, R., & Shaw, L. (1995). *Writing ethnographic fieldnotes*. Chicago: University of Chicago Press.

Fishman, S., & McCarthy, L. (2000). *Unplayed tapes: A personal history of collaborative teacher research*. Urbana, IL: National Council of Teachers of English.

Goodman, Y. (1978). Kidwatching: Observing children in the classroom. In A. Jagger & M.T. Smith-Burke (Eds.), *Observing the language learner* (pp. 9–18). Newark, DE: International Reading Association.

Guba, E., & Lincoln, Y. (1982). *Effective evaluation*. San Francisco: Jossey-Bass.

Johnston, P. (2003). Assessment conversations. *The Reading Teacher*, *57*, 90–92.

Johnston, P., & Rogers, R. (2002). Early literacy development: The case for "informed assessment." In S.B. Neuman & D.K. Dickinson (Eds.), *Handbook of early literacy research* (pp. 377–389). New York: Guilford.

Klenowski, V. (2002). *Developing portfolios for learning assessment*. London: Routledge/Falmer.

Lofland, J. (1971). *Analyzing social settings*. Belmont, CA: Wadsworth.

Miller-Power, B. (1996). *Taking note: Improving your observational note taking*. York, ME: Stenhouse.

Patton, M.Q. (1990). *Qualitative evaluation and research methods*. Newbury Park, CA: Sage.

Pils, L. (1991). Soon anofe you tout me: Evaluation in a first-grade whole language classroom. *The Reading Teacher*, *45*, 46–50.

Reutzel, D.R., & Cooter, R. (2004). *Teaching children to read: From basals to books*. Columbus, OH: Merrill/Prentice Hall.

Rhodes, L., & Nathenson-Mejia, S. (1992). Anecdotal records: A powerful tool for ongoing literacy assessment. *The Reading Teacher*, *45*, 502–509.

Rollins-Hurely, S., & Villamil-Tinajero, J. (2001). *Literacy assessment of second language learners*. Boston: Allyn & Bacon.

Tierney, R. (1999). Literacy assessment reform: Shifting beliefs, principled possibilities, and emerging practices. In S. Barrentine (Ed.), *Reading assessment: Principles and practices for elementary school teachers* (pp. 10–29). Newark, DE: International Reading Association.

Valencia, S. (1998). *Literacy portfolios in action*. Fort Worth, TX: Harcourt College.

Valencia, S., Au, K.H., Scheu, J.A., Kawakami, A.J., & Herman, P.A. (1990). Assessment of students' own literacy. *The Reading Teacher*, *44*, 154–156.

Valencia, S., & Wixson, K. (2000). Policy-oriented research on literacy standards and assessment. In M.L. Kamil, P.B. Mosenthal, P.D. Pearson, & R. Barr (Eds.), *Handbook of reading research* (Vol. 3, pp. 909–935). Mahwah, NJ: Erlbaum.

Wigfield, A. (1997). Motivations, beliefs, and self-efficiency in literacy development. In J.T. Guthrie & A. Wigfield (Eds.), *Reading engagement: Motivating readers through integrated instruction* (pp. 14–33). Newark, DE: International Reading Association.

Reading With Amy: Teaching and Learning Through Reading Conferences

Sharon Ruth Gill

While acrimonious debate about the best methods for teaching reading has long occupied our field, we know very little about how children learn to read. In 1991, Juel stated, "We clearly lack a comprehensive model of reading acquisition, one that would incorporate the various psychological, social, and instructional components that contribute to the process of learning to read" (p. 759). While acknowledging the importance of research on teaching methods, Juel echoed Gibson and Levin's (1975) assertion that "all the talk is of what the teacher does or should do and not of what happens or should happen in the child" (as cited in Juel, 1991, p. 761). Juel asserted that in order to understand the acquisition of literacy we must shift our focus from what the teacher does to the "processes, traits or skills *the child* actually learns as he or she becomes literate" (p. 761).

Yet much current research seems once again devoted to descriptions of method, using effective teachers as "an informative source of knowledge about highly effective teaching" rather than looking to "theory...or basic research...for guidance about reading instruction" (Wharton-McDonald et al., 1997, p. 518). While these studies are important, we must also continue to build theory by conducting research on children learning to read.

Bissex (1991) argued that case studies are especially appropriate for learning about learners. Studies of individual children learning to read provide contextualized data that could help us understand more about the psychological, social, and instructional components of reading acquisition. Moreover, primary teachers are in a unique position to observe and document this process. The emerging field of teacher research recognizes the value of "systematic, intentional inquiry by teachers about their own school and classroom work" (Cochran-Smith & Lytle, 1993); similarly, Yetta Goodman (1985) described the insights into child language development that "can emerge only from kidwatching based on a sound knowledge of language and language learning" (p. 13). Such ecologically valid studies are needed to produce a grounded theory (Strauss & Corbin, 1990) of reading acquisition, one that is based upon data grounded in the reality of children learning to read. This article will describe a teacher-research study of the reading acquisition of one second-grade student.

Two Paradigms of Reading Acquisition

Juel (1991) identified two paradigms of reading acquisition based on two very different theoretical perspectives on reading. In the first paradigm, which reflects modular theories and theories of automatic processing, fluent readers are seen as making use of *maximal* amounts of the graphic information. Therefore, attaining rapid word recognition, or automatic decoding, is seen as the goal in beginning reading (LaBerge & Samuels, 1974).

From *The Reading Teacher*, 53(6), 500–509. © 2000 by the International Reading Association.

In the second paradigm, which reflects a psycholinguistic view of reading, fluent reading is described as making *minimal* use of the graphic information through a cyclical process of predicting, sampling the graphic information, and confirming predictions (Weaver, 1994). Readers make predictions based on four cueing systems: syntactic (what they know about the English language), semantic (making sense based on the context), pragmatic (using what they know about the world), and graphophonic (using letter–sound relationships). Smith (1988) described this process as a trade-off between visual (graphophonic) and nonvisual (semantic, syntactic, and pragmatic) information: "The more prior knowledge a reader can bring to bear about the way letters go together in words...[and] the way words go together in grammatical and meaningful phrases...the less visual information is required to identify words" (p. 155). From this model, one can conclude that the hurdle in beginning reading would be learning to balance visual and nonvisual information. Little has been written about how beginning readers learn to make this trade-off, however.

Both my teaching and my research were guided by a sociopsycholinguistic view of reading. The social and instructional context of Amy's reading and her use of visual and nonvisual information were the primary frames I used to observe and describe her reading development.

The Reader

Amy was a bright, articulate, and outgoing second grader. She liked books and poems, listened eagerly when being read to, and joined in enthusiastically during shared book experience. She often brought books to school that had been read to her at home. Yet when Amy and I met for our first reading conference during the first week of school, I noticed that she was struggling as a reader. I wondered why Amy, who was not a student who would be considered at risk and whose oral language use was excellent, was lagging behind in her reading development.

During our first conference, Amy chose the poem "I Know an Old Lady Who Swallowed a Fly," which we had read that morning during shared book experience, and which she remembered from first grade. I quickly noticed that Amy was not reading from the text, but was reciting the poem from memory. When she faltered, she did not use the text to help her. During our next conference, Amy chose a much shorter text, a First Start Easy Reader containing only 34 words, with which she again struggled. I realized that Amy was trying to find texts with which she could have success; Amy wanted to be a reader.

Doake (1985) described the high expectations of books and reading and the great pleasure and satisfaction derived by children who have been read to at home. These early positive experiences with books, Doake said, lay the foundation for the powerful drive to gain independent access to such experiences. Amy seemed to have this drive; I felt sure that with the supportive curriculum of my classroom, which included one-on-one conferences when I would demonstrate strategies and encourage meaning making, Amy would successfully learn to read. I decided to use these reading conferences to observe, document, and reflect upon Amy's development as a reader in order to meet two goals: to help Amy succeed as a reader and to learn about the process of reading acquisition.

The Context

Reading conferences are meetings between individual students and their teacher, during which the student may talk about what he or she is reading, retell the story, or read aloud to the teacher. The teacher supports the reader by demonstrating or suggesting strategies at the point of need, taking over if the reading is too difficult, or simply talking about the book with the student. Conferences give teachers opportunities to assess students' reading as well as to provide individualized instruction (Gill, 1996). Rhodes and Dudley-Marling (1996) described reading conferences as one-on-one meetings that help students make sense of text as they read. Teachers help students find what interests them, set their own purposes, and use strategies for making meaning. Conferences also provide students with someone to "think with" about the book (p. 167). Although Hornsby, Sukarna, and Parry's (1986) "conference approach" to reading emphasizes group conferences, individual conferences are described as opportunities to give students close attention, to help them select books, to evaluate students' reading, or to give "injections of enthusiasm" (p. 65). Thus individual reading conferences can provide opportunities for increasing students' interest and motivation, for discussions about books, and for instruction and assessment.

Reading conferences were one component of my second-grade classroom curriculum, which also included reading aloud to students, shared book experiences, and an extended daily period of sustained silent reading. Skills and strategies were demonstrated in context each morning during the shared book experience activity. For example, during choral reading of poems or Big Books, I often masked entire words or parts of words, demonstrating that when we come to a word we don't know we can use strategies such as reading on, thinking about what would make sense, and looking at what the word starts with. Often a particular phonic element or spelling pattern (such as the rime *-ight*) would be introduced as we listed rhyming words from our reading and thought of similar words to add to the list. Brief lessons on conventions of print such as punctuation and grammar might also be included as we found examples in our readings.

An extensive classroom library and my reading aloud twice each day encouraged my students to become readers; 30 to 45 minutes per day of sustained silent reading (SSR) allowed them to read texts of their own choosing and also provided time for reading conferences. While I spent some of our SSR time reading myself, I also used this time to meet with two to three students per day, often very briefly with my better readers and at greater length with students who needed more support.

Data Collection and Analysis

I collected data on Amy's reading through anecdotal notes taken during our reading conferences over 4 months, from late August through December. These notes documented texts she chose to read, behaviors, degree of fluency, miscues, and any other indications of Amy's use of cueing systems and reading strategies, along with notes about how I assisted her. I later added reflections, which often supplied more information about the text or the reading situation, my thoughts about particular miscues or other behaviors, and often my developing hypotheses about Amy as a reader.

The following is a conference note from late September (slashes are used to set off words from the texts and Amy's miscues):

> Conference note 9/28: Big Book: *A Farm's Not a Farm*. This book had been read many times by the class in shared book experience. Very fluent. Pointed out *-ing* and then she read /oink/. Knew the *-ing* sound but didn't read it. Excellent reading!
>
> Big book: *Who's in the Shed*? Had been read by class. Had no trouble reading /howling/ and /growling/. They make more sense than in situation above! Excellent.
>
> *Reflections*: It's interesting that Amy pointed out *-ing* and identified it (we had been talking about *-ing* during shared book experience with the book) but she read /oink/ instead of /oinking/. The text says "oinking, oinking, oinking" to describe the sounds of the pigs, when "oink, oink, oink" is what you expect. Amy was using syntactic cues—what a story should sound like. This text is rhyming and repetitive and by this time very familiar to Amy. In *Who's in the Shed*? she used her knowledge about *-ing* when it made sense to her. This might indicate that she is giving precedence to nonvisual cues, because when what she decoded did not make sense to her, she abandoned the decoded word and went with meaning! This text helped her use nonvisual cues and meaning-making strategies, because of its predictability. The text makes the difference—what strategies she will use. Compare text and strategies!

Qualitative data analysis techniques were used in analyzing the conference notes and reflections (Miles & Huberman, 1984; Strauss & Corbin, 1990). Conference notes and reflections were coded, and data were organized into three major categories: Amy's choice of texts, Amy's use of reading strategies, and roles of the teacher. Clear patterns were evident in Amy's choice of texts over the 4-month period, and by plotting the first observations of various strategies I was able to see patterns in Amy's developing strategy use and the interplay between text choice and strategies (see Table).

Patterns in Text Choice

Several patterns emerged relating to the texts that Amy chose, both for her own reading and when she read aloud to me. From the beginning Amy seemed to strive for successful reading experiences and chose texts that she could read fluently. She spent little time with books with which she could not make meaning.

Familiar Texts as Scaffolds

Amy initially had success only with very familiar texts. During the second phase, she continued to read these, but often would try an unfamiliar book. In the third phase, she chose books I had read aloud, and she continued to try unfamiliar texts as well. Finally, Amy no longer needed the scaffolding provided by familiar books and launched herself completely into reading unfamiliar books.

Phase 1. During our first conference in early September, Amy chose a memorized text to read to me—a text with which she could feel successful. In the absence of other familiar texts, however, Amy next chose several First Start Easy Readers (published by Troll, 1970), a series of books containing a limited number of words repeated often to help develop word recognition and interest in reading. These books had few words per page and severely controlled vocabulary and sentence length; they looked "easy." Having no success with these texts, however, Amy settled on *The Giving Tree* (Silverstein, 1964), a book that had been read to her at home and in first grade and that she enjoyed. Amy brought *The Giving Tree* to five conferences between September 11 and September 21. *The Giving Tree* does not have controlled vocabulary or sentence length.

Many beginning reading texts are written with the assumption that short words and sentences are easier to read than longer ones. Written to comply with readability formulas, they use often-repeated sight words and words that are assumed to be easily decodable. The language of such texts has been labeled "primerese" (Simons & Ammon, 1989), and such texts have

Amy's text choices and strategies

Date	Text choice	Strategy use
Sept. 1–8	First Start Easy Readers	Focus on sounding out: avoidance behaviors, picture clues; waiting/asking; using first letter; syntactic cues
Sept. 11–21	Repeated readings of *The Giving Tree*	
Sept. 28–Oct. 5	Repeated readings of *The Giving Tree* and of familiar poems and Big Books from shared book experiences	Focus on making meaning: memory of text; self-correcting for meaning; syntactic, semantic, and pragmatic cues; reading on; reading with expression
Oct. 6–21	Repeated readings of familiar poems/books plus new stories	
Oct. 22–Dec. 7	Repeated readings of familiar poems/books plus new stories	Integration of strategies; development of new visual strategies: decoding by analogy
Dec. 10–16	New stories	

been attacked because they violate children's knowledge and expectation of the way that language works (Brennan, Bridge, & Winograd, 1986; Gourley, 1978; Simons & Ammon, 1989). Amy's success with *The Giving Tree* at the same time that she could not get through a primerese text like *Sticky Stanley* supports such allegations, as well as Ken Goodman's assertion that "authentic, sensible and functional language is easiest to read and to learn to read. When we tamper with narrative language, try to control the vocabulary, or tinker with texts to lower their readability levels, we make them less predictable, less cohesive, and less interesting and that makes them harder to read" (1982, p. 40).

Between September 28 and October 5 Amy continued her reliance on familiar texts, alternating *The Giving Tree* with poems and Big Books that were highly predictable and very familiar to her from our shared book experiences. She read these texts with great success and fluency and continued to improve on *The Giving Tree*.

Phase 2. During the next phase, which occurred between October 6 and 21, Amy chose very familiar texts from shared book experiences and something new to her as well. I noted this "something familiar then something new" routine in her own reading during this time as well as in the texts she brought to our conferences. Successful reading also marked this period, although Amy did occasionally choose a text that proved too difficult for her. In these cases, I asked her if she would like me to take a turn reading, and I often took over the reading to ensure a positive reading experience.

Phase 3. During the third phase, October 22–27, Amy had less need for previous experience with texts. During this period she no longer reread books and poems from shared book experiences, but instead often chose books that I had read aloud to the class. Completely new texts were mixed in with these somewhat familiar texts during this period. I considered all of Amy's readings successful during this period, and noted her growing success with unfamiliar texts.

Phase 4. Finally, during the last week of the study in mid-December, I noted that Amy chose completely unfamiliar books for her reading.

Aesthetic Factors

In addition to familiarity, aesthetic factors were also important for Amy. "The emotional response," as Frank Smith (1988, p. 177) reminded us, "is the primary reason most readers read." Amy certainly found some kind of emotional or aesthetic satisfaction in her readings of *The Giving Tree*, which is a story of a parent–child relationship between a boy and a tree. We cannot always see the elements of books that appeal to children or affect them in some way, but *The Giving Tree* drew Amy to read it again and again.

Amy's enjoyment of our poems from shared book experiences was also a motivating factor. She reread them often during SSR, sometimes pointing to each word with my pointer as though she were the teacher. Other texts connected with Amy's personal experiences, as I noted with her reading of *Just Going to the Dentist*, which she told me she liked because she was getting braces soon.

Predictability

Finally, Amy often chose texts with elements of predictability (see Rhodes, 1981). Most of the texts we read during shared book experience activities were either poems or Big Books with repetition, rhyme or rhythm, and a close match between text and illustrations. She abandoned "easy readers" with severely controlled vocabularies early on, but returned to them during Conference 31 in early December when her use of strategies and her new ability to integrate visual and nonvisual cues allowed her to read *Maxwell Mouse*, a First Start Easy Reader, successfully.

Patterns in Strategy Use

Amy extended her repertoire of strategies for using both visual and nonvisual cues during the 4-month period of the study. While we can only hypothesize about the strategies a reader uses, careful observation of the readers' miscues and other behaviors provides us with a window on the reading process (Goodman, 1973). During a brief period of unsuccessful attempts to read easy readers, Amy was unable to apply her knowledge of letter–sound correspondences, used few nonvisual strategies, and exhibited behaviors that indicated her discomfort (wiggling in her seat, pulling her hair). While engaging in repeated readings of familiar texts, however, Amy developed a number of nonvisual strategies as she focused on making meaning.

Nonvisual strategies. When she began reading familiar texts, Amy used her memory of them as a major strategy, but quickly developed other strategies for making meaning. By Conference 5 I noted evidence that Amy was self-correcting for meaning; by Conference 14 she was reading on to help identify an unknown word, using expression to help create meaning, and thinking metacognitively about her own reading.

Visual strategies. Amy certainly knew a great deal about letter–sound relationships, but was often unable to apply this knowledge successfully. During our first conference, she read, "I Know an Old Lady" from memory alone, ignoring voice-to-print matching. When her memory faltered, she was unable to find her place in the poem. During Conference 4 I noted her unsuccessful attempts to sound out the word *sit*: "St—...st—." In several other conferences I noted that Amy was unsuccessful when attempting to sound out words, such as *fall* and *cook* in Conference 25. Miscues in Conference 30 show that as late as December 4 she had not mastered phonics rules for vowel sounds (she read "lot" for *let* and "wiss" for *wise*).

Amy developed other visual strategies, however, including the use of spelling patterns or rimes. In Conference 22, I noted that Amy "knew *bright*, *light*, etc. (*bright* was in one of our chart poems)." During Conference 31 on December 7 (see below), Amy read "sleep toucht" for *sleep tight*. As I began to remind her to think of other words she knew that contained this pattern, she quickly remembered: "Night and light! So it sounds like...tight!" This supports Moustafa's (1997) conclusion that, rather than using letter–sound correspondences, children decode unfamiliar words by analogy with the onsets and rimes in words they already know.

Integrating visual and nonvisual strategies. The notes from the last three conferences illustrate Amy's growth in strategy use, and show that by the end of the study Amy was integrating visual and nonvisual information.

> 12/7. *Maxwell Mouse*. Had not read before. /Home swarten home/ corrected to /home sweet home/. /Whou made that noise/ corrected to /who made that noise/. Read /sleep toucht/. I said, "That's a word that's spelled like..."—she interrupted me and said "night and light! So it sounds like...tight!"
>
> 12/10. *Itchy Itchy Chicken Pox*. I had not read this aloud. A rhyming book, few words per page. Asked for /between/ my toes. *The Show and Tell Frog*. Never read before or read aloud. She told me, "I've never read this before so you'll have to tell me how I do." Aware of her own reliance on familiarity! /I'm ready here/ corrected to /I'm right here/. Good expression! Stopped and said, "That doesn't make sense!" Good comprehension—retold the story.
>
> 12/16. *Just Going to the Dentist*. Stopped and said, "That doesn't make sense!" and reread. /Put a big on me/ corrected to /Put a bib on me/. /Spit in the s- s- sink?/ Drawing on picture clues or background knowledge. I helped her read on, "I closed my eyes and *blank* to ten" and then she filled in *blank*. Good expression. Interested because she is going to get braces.

These notes show that Amy was monitoring her own meaning making ("That doesn't make sense!") and had an awareness of her previous dependence on familiar texts ("I've never read this before so you'll have to tell me how I do."). In addition, she seemed to have found her own way to integrate the visual and nonvisual strategies she had been developing: She made a first guess based on visual clues, then self-corrected immediately for meaning (using nonvisual cues).

The data also suggest that visual cues took precedence over meaning on texts that were unfamiliar, controlled, or written at a more difficult level than other texts Amy was reading. Familiar texts, however, allowed Amy to use and develop meaning-making strategies as well as strategies for dealing with visual information.

Roles of the Teacher

The analysis of the conference notes showed three teacher roles: collaborator, demonstrator, and observer/assessor.

Collaborator. In order to maintain an informal, sharing atmosphere, I often collaborated in the reading of some of the texts. Telling Amy an unknown word or taking over part or all of the reading if it became too difficult allowed the conferences to remain a positive, successful experience for her. Thus the conferences provided a risk-free environment in which Amy served as an apprentice. Waterland (1985) described an apprenticeship approach to reading in which children are invited to "Come and read with me" and students are supported "in whatever contribution they are able to make" (p. 29).

Demonstrator. The conferences provided natural opportunities for me to demonstrate strategies such as the following:

- reading on
- rereading
- using picture clues
- using context clues
- looking at what the word starts with
- looking at parts of the word.

I often helped Amy with difficult words by reminding her of similar words in the text, in other texts she had read, or around the classroom.

Comments such as, "Hmm...I didn't quite understand that, did you? Let's try this part again," provided demonstrations of monitoring strategies, such as monitoring one's own meaning making and being aware of one's own use and coordination of cues. Schwartz (1997) suggested that the development of monitoring strategies has largely been ignored in beginning reading instruction.

Demonstrations may play a crucial role in literacy development. Cambourne (1988) and Smith (1988) both identified demonstrations as one of the necessary conditions for language learning. Demonstrations show the learner "This is how something is done" (Smith, 1998, p. 190); literacy demonstrations show students specific strategies that readers and writers use in reading or writing whole texts (Cambourne, 1988). In my classroom, strategies that were introduced and demonstrated during shared book experience were reinforced and extended during the reading conferences, providing individualized instruction in strategy use at the student's point of need.

Observer/assessor. Careful observations of reading behaviors allow us to "infer the types of cues and strategies children use. Given these tentative theories of processing, we can then support their efforts to extend the set of cues they attend to and strategies they use as they read" (Schwartz, 1997, p. 42). As described here, reading conferences allowed me to informally assess many aspects of Amy's reading, including the use of cueing systems and strategies, fluency, interest, and knowledge of letter–sound correspondences. Examples of miscues provided information about areas of strength and weakness, and discussions about the book allowed me to informally assess comprehension. The following conference note illustrates the variety of types of information gained during one conference.

> 10/7 *My Mother Is Lost.* "I've never read this before so I'll need some help." Figured out *crowded* from the picture. Read "/Holded/ his mom's hand." Figured out *stared* from meaning. "Pocketbooks /hit/ (banged) him on the head." Did well as I encouraged her to use the picture clues and make sense. /very/ for /even/. Uses expression to help make sense: "She's not lost. YOU'RE lost."

This brief conference note provided information about Amy's text choice and use of reading strategies (looking at pictures, substituting words that made sense, using expression) as well as an indication of metacognition. Prior to this point she had chosen familiar books and relied on familiarity with the texts to help her make meaning; her comment reveals her consciousness of this strategy.

The reading conferences described in this study provided time for me to observe and assess Amy's reading strategies and behaviors, they allowed me to provide demonstrations of reading strategies at her point of need, and they ensured that she would have successful reading experiences.

A Self-Extending System

Repeated readings of favorite texts scaffolded Amy's development and integration of both visual and nonvisual strategies. The development of the ability to integrate visual and nonvisual strategies coincided with fluent, successful reading of unfamiliar material, and by the end of the study her text choices showed that she no longer needed the scaffolding of familiar texts. She seemed to have developed what Clay (1991) called a self-extending system. With her focus on making meaning, her ability to self-monitor, and her ability to integrate visual and nonvisual cues, each reading experience will teach her more about reading, and the texts themselves will become her reading teachers (Meek, 1988).

The Role of Repeated Readings in Reading Acquisition

In 1997 *The Reading Teacher* reprinted S. Jay Samuels's (1979) article "The Method of Repeated Readings," which is considered a classic in the field of reading. Samuels's method involved students in "rereading a short, meaningful passage until a satisfactory level of fluency is reached" (1997, p. 377). While fluency was defined as both accuracy of word recognition and reading speed, speed was emphasized in Samuels's method. The original article presented a number of studies that indicated positive results from repeated readings, and in his author notes accompanying the 1997 reprint Samuels summarized the results of nearly 200 studies on the topic:

- Repeated readings result in a high degree of accuracy and speed with the practiced text.
- Fluency is transferred to other portions of the text that were not specifically practiced.

Samuels also reported that repeated reading is the most universally used remedial reading technique, and in her introduction to the reprint Dowhower called the method "amazingly enduring" and "extremely effective" (Samuels, 1997, p. 376).

Samuels's method was based on the theory of automatic information processing (LaBerge & Samuels, 1974). According to this theory, becoming fluent in reading means becoming automatic at decoding. The beginning reader's attention is believed to be on decoding and is therefore not immediately available for comprehension, while the fluent reader decodes text automatically, without attention, enabling attention to comprehension. According to automaticity theory, then, repeated readings provide practice that allows word-recognition skills to become automatic.

The data in the current study, however, support a psycholinguistic perspective on the role of repeated readings. Psycholinguistic theorists suggest that attending to each letter or word of a text overloads the visual system (Smith, 1973), leading to halting, nonsensical word calling. However, by providing children with text that is highly familiar and therefore predictable, repeated readings lessen the visual load and increase the nonvisual information. Because the text is familiar, students can use their memory of it to help them make meaning with only a minimum of visual information. This allows students to keep meaning making at the forefront as they develop strategies for using both visual and nonvisual information and for integrating the two. The reader is able to select elements of the visual information to focus on and begin to analyze (as Amy did with *-ight* words), constructing knowledge about the way that print works while in the process of meaningful reading.

Teacher Roles in Reading Conferences

Reading conferences may be more important than has heretofore been recognized. Teacher roles that may support students' literacy development include making assessments that are critical to good instruction, demonstrating strategies at the point of need, and providing successful reading experiences. Guthrie and Wigfield (1997) concluded that when children believe they can be successful readers, and when they are "intrinsically motivated to read and find personal meaning" in their reading, they are more likely to read (p. 17).

Toward a Theory of Reading Acquisition

Amy learned to read in the context of a supportive classroom community. Daily reading and rereading of predictable texts, in-context skill and strategy lessons during shared book experiences, extended periods of time for reading and rereading texts of her own choosing, and individualized instruction and collaborative reading during reading conferences all seem to have contributed to her success. Although a number of studies have described supportive environments for literacy learning, little work has been done to show *how* children learn reading skills and strategies within this environment. Weaver (1984) asserted that reading is not only a psycholinguistic process but a sociopsycholinguistic one: "The reader-text transaction occurs within a social and situational context.... That is, a variety of social and situational factors influence how the person reads and what the reader understands" (p. 29). Amy's story helps illuminate the process of reading acquisition from a sociopsycholinguistic perspective.

References

Bissex, G. (1991). Small is beautiful: Case study as appropriate methodology for teacher research. In D.A. Daiker & M. Morenberg (Eds.), *The writing teacher as researcher* (pp. 70–75). Portsmouth, NH: Heinemann.

Brennan, A., Bridge, C., & Winograd, P. (1986). The effects of structural variation on children's recall of basal reader stories. *Reading Research Quarterly, 21*, 91–103.

Cambourne, B. (1988). *The whole story*. New York: Scholastic.

Clay, M.M. (1991). *Becoming literate: The construction of inner control*. Portsmouth, NH: Heinemann.

Cochran-Smith, M., & Lytle, S. (1993). *Inside/outside: Teacher research and knowledge*. New York: Teachers College Press.

Doake, D. (1985). Reading-like behavior: Its role in learning to read. In A. Jaggar & M.T. Smith-Burke (Eds.), *Observing the language learner* (pp. 82–98). Newark, DE: International Reading Association.

Gill, S.R. (1996, April). Integrating assessment and instruction through reading conferences. *Primarily Yours*.

Goodman, K. (1973). Psycholinguistic universals in the reading process. In F. Smith (Ed.), *Psycholinguistics and reading* (pp. 21–27). New York: Holt, Rinehart & Winston.

Goodman, Y. (1985). Kidwatching: Observing children in the classroom. In A. Jaggar & M.T. Smith-Burke (Eds.), *Observing the language learner* (pp. 9–18). Newark, DE: International Reading Association.

Gourley, J. (1978). This basal is easy to read—or is it? *The Reading Teacher, 32*, 174–182.

Guthrie, J.T., & Wigfield, A. (1997). *Reading engagement: Motivating readers through integrated instruction*. Newark, DE: International Reading Association.

Hornsby, D., Sukarna, D., & Parry, J. (1986). *Read on: A conference approach to reading*. Portsmouth, NH: Heinemann.

Juel, C. (1991). Beginning reading. In R. Barr, M.L. Kamil, P. Mosenthal, & P.D. Pearson (Eds.), *Handbook of reading research* (Vol. 2, pp. 759–788). Mahwah, NJ: Erlbaum.

LaBerge, D., & Samuels, S.J. (1974). Toward a theory of automatic information processing in reading. *Cognitive Psychology, 6*, 293–323.

Meek, M. (1988). *How texts teach what readers learn*. Exeter, England: The Thimble Press.

Miles, M., & Huberman, A. (1984). *Qualitative data analysis*. Beverly Hills, CA: Sage.

Moustafa, M. (1997). *Beyond traditional phonics*. Portsmouth, NH: Heinemann.

Rhodes, L. (1981). I can read! Predictable books as resources for reading and writing instruction. *The Reading Teacher, 34*, 511–518.

Rhodes, L.K., & Dudley-Marling, C. (1996). *Readers and writers with a difference*. Portsmouth, NH: Heinemann.

Samuels, S.J. (1979). The method of repeated readings. *The Reading Teacher, 32*, 408–409.

Samuels, S.J. (1997). The method of repeated readings. *The Reading Teacher, 50*, 376–381.

Schwartz, R.M. (1997). Self-monitoring in beginning reading. *The Reading Teacher, 51*, 40–48.

Simons, H., & Ammon, P. (1989). Child knowledge and primerese text: Mismatches and miscues. *Research in the Teaching of English, 23*(4), 380–398.

Smith, F. (1973). *Psycholinguistics and reading*. New York: Holt, Rinehart & Winston.

Smith, F. (1988). *Understanding reading*. Hillsdale, NJ: Erlbaum.

Strauss, A., & Corbin, J. (1990). *Basics of qualitative research*. Newbury Park, CA: Sage.

Waterland, L. (1985). *Read with me: An apprenticeship approach to reading*. Gloucester, England: The Thimble Press.

Weaver, C. (1994). *Reading process and practice* (2nd ed.). Portsmouth, NH: Heinemann.

Wharton-McDonald, R., Pressley, M., Rankin, J., Mistretta, J., & Ettenberger, S. (1997). Effective primary-grades literacy instruction = Balanced literacy instruction. *The Reading Teacher, 50*, 518–521.

Children's Books Cited

Gordon, S. (1970). *Maxwell mouse*. Mahwah, NJ: Troll Associates

MacCarone, G. (1992). *Itchy itchy chicken pox*. New York: Scholastic.

Mayer, M. (1998). *Just going to the dentist*. New York: Golden Books.

Myers, B. (1970). *My mother is lost*. New York: Scholastic.

Oppenheim, J. (1992). *The show and tell frog*. New York: Bantam Doubleday Dell.

Parks, B. (1989). *A farm's not a farm*. Crystal Lake, IL: Rigby.

Parks, B. (1989). *Who's in the shed?* Crystal Lake, IL: Rigby.

Silverstein, S. (1964). *The giving tree*. New York: Harper & Row.

Sticky Stanley. (1970). Mahwah, NJ: Troll Associates.

FAQs About IRIs

Scott G. Paris and Robert D. Carpenter

Assessing children's reading development is more important than ever—not just because test scores are visible indices of educational accountability that are reported in newspapers but because teachers use many types of assessment to inform their daily instruction. The connections between reading assessment and instruction may be strongest in primary grades for beginning readers when the variability among children's reading skills is large. That is when children benefit most from individualized instruction, and it's the time when teachers can use assessment to diagnose individual difficulties. As a consequence, researchers, publishers, and policymakers have created many new types of early reading assessments. This, in turn, has required teachers to learn more about reading assessment tools and how to use them. In this column we provide essential information for teachers, arranged in a question–answer format, about one type of early reading assessment—informal reading inventories, or IRIs.

What Is an IRI?

Informal reading inventories were designed more than 50 years ago to assess multiple aspects of children's reading skills in authentic situations (i.e., children reading texts with teachers in classrooms). Today, there are increasing numbers of IRIs created by commercial publishers and state education departments in the United States. As children read text, teachers observe their strengths and weaknesses, ask questions to probe their understanding and knowledge, and record quantitative and qualitative information. The assessments are informal and diagnostic because the IRI administration is tailored to each student and because the observations do not emphasize uniform or comparative data. IRIs usually include assessments of oral reading accuracy based on running records (Clay, 1993) or miscue analyses (Goodman & Burke, 1972). Many IRIs include grade-level word lists (i.e., sight vocabulary), comprehension questions, and retelling rubrics. Most include graded word lists and reading passages from preprimer through middle school levels. Some include procedures for assessing prior knowledge, listening comprehension, repeated readings, or silent reading.

Who Should Administer an IRI?

Teachers of K–3 can derive the greatest benefits from informal reading inventories because the skills that are assessed most often focus on decoding skills necessary for fluent oral reading. Teachers of grades 4–8 may find the oral reading assessments in IRIs useful with struggling readers. When students can read fourth-grade passages independently, IRIs can be used to assess silent reading and comprehension. Even teachers with English as a Second Language students and adult literacy learners may find IRIs helpful because of their focus on early development of reading skills, regardless of the age of the learner. However, we must emphasize that the primary value of any IRI is based on teachers' observations and insights about individual readers, so the data are not as useful when collected and interpreted by someone else.

Why Should I Use an IRI?

The most important reason for using informal reading inventories with beginning readers is to

From *The Reading Teacher*, 56(6), 578–580. © 2003 by the International Reading Association.

diagnose children's difficulties so that extra instruction can be directed toward the skills they lack. Too often, early reading difficulties go undetected until grades 2 or 3, a situation exacerbated historically by large classes in primary grades, little time for individual student assessment, and few available assessment tools for teachers (Snow, Burns, & Griffin, 1998). Early detection can lead to early remedial help in a variety of reading skills. Another important reason for using IRIs is to document growth in children's reading. IRIs are authentic, daily, quick, immediate, flexible, teacher controlled, and student centered—all positive characteristics of classroom assessments (Paris, Paris, & Carpenter, 2002). IRIs can provide useful information to students about their progress, to parents about achievement and skills that need improvement, and to teachers about appropriate instruction and texts to provide—all positive consequences for stakeholders.

Which IRI Should I Use?

Teachers often choose informal reading inventories based on familiarity, which may be influenced by the faculty and educators with whom they studied, by the fit with local literacy curricula and assessments, or by administrative mandate. Familiarity is important because it implies professional training to use and interpret the IRI, and teacher competence is crucial for effective IRI assessment. When teachers can choose an IRI, they should select one that fits their assessment purposes and the skills of their students. If oral reading rate and accuracy are the main assessment goals, then IRIs with measures of comprehension and retelling are less important. If using authentic books rather than abbreviated text is important, or if comparing reading skills across genres is important, teachers can choose specific IRIs with these features. Because administrators recognize the value of uniform data collected in IRIs, there is a trend to prescribe the selection and use of IRIs within districts and states. This trend may turn IRIs into increasingly formal and high-stakes assessments, but it does not diminish the value of IRIs for teachers' daily insights.

When Should I Administer an IRI?

Informal reading inventories can be given to children whenever teachers have time and whenever the information can be useful. At the beginning of the school year, IRIs provide immediate information about children's fluent reading, and they help to identify children with very good or very poor reading skills. Beyond initial screening for problems and placement in instructional groups and materials, IRIs at the beginning of the year provide baseline information about annual growth for each child. Thus, some schools encourage teachers to give IRIs before school begins or in the first weeks of the year. These schools also want to collect IRI data at the end of the year to assess individual student progress. Those data can provide summative information about the relative growth and achievement of students—information useful to administrators as well as parents, students, and future teachers. Finding time to administer IRIs is a common concern. Skilled teachers often organize their instruction to allow assessments to be staggered throughout the day. Then several students can be assessed individually for 10–20 minutes every day. Some schools solve the "time crunch" problem with teacher release time during the day, rotating subs, assessment days before the school year begins, team teaching (one teacher can assess students individually while one manages the other student groups), and instructional assistants to free teachers for one-on-one time.

How Do I Administer an IRI?

Every informal reading inventory manual provides detailed information for assessment that should be followed for uniform assessment procedures. One general problem is selecting appropriate text levels, and we recommend three practices to help solve it. First, use your background knowledge of the child to select a text level that can be read independently. Second, without such information, use graded word lists as a rough index of an appropriate text level. Third, administer several difficulty levels to allow students to read a range of easy to challenging texts. Two or three passages can usually be administered in 15 minutes, but testing should stop before students get bored or frustrated.

Another general problem is deciding which skills to observe and record. Some IRIs are designed to provide quick and simple measures, such as the number of words read correctly in a minute or the percentage of words read correctly on a standard passage. These are quick assessments that yield quantifiable data. Some IRIs provide no information on comprehension and other reading skills. We think that rate and accuracy measures may provide useful information on beginning readers only, and the measures should not be used alone for diagnostic or summative purposes. We think that IRIs permit simultaneous collection of oral reading accuracy, rate, prosody, retelling, and comprehension that are all informative, so we advocate collecting multiple indicators of children's reading skills.

Another general problem involves data collection. Some IRIs have paper formats for texts and answer forms, some use actual books, some require stopwatches and calculations of accuracy rates, and some involve tape recording for later analyses. Teachers may find all these procedures time-consuming. However, some IRIs can be administered with hand-held computers. This may provide a technological breakthrough that saves teachers' time, reduces dependence on paper copies, automates quantitative calculations of performance, and facilitates reports for students and classrooms over repeated assessments.

Are Data From IRIs Valid and Reliable?

The validity and reliability of informal reading inventory data depend on uniform administration and scoring procedures. In one research project, identical passages from the Qualitative Reading Inventory–3 (Leslie & Caldwell, 2001) or Developmental Reading Assessment (Beaver, 1997) were given to students in grades 2 and 3 by teachers and researchers a few weeks apart. Both IRIs showed positive and significant test–retest reliability (Paris, Pearson, Carpenter, Siebenthal, & Laier, 2002). The same evaluation project also revealed significant concurrent validity in the correlations between the Gates-MacGinitie Reading Tests and scores from the Qualitative Reading Inventory and Development Reading Assessment on word identification and reading comprehension. These correlations ranged from .48–.90, indicating acceptable concurrent validity. Most commercial IRIs are based on acceptable levels of reliability and validity. Thus, the data derived from IRIs can be used to assess individual growth and to document reading achievement when the instructions in the IRI manuals are followed carefully.

How Are the Data Reported?

Informal reading inventory data for oral reading accuracy, rate, and comprehension are usually reported by text level. For example, Joe read a level X passage in the fall with 95% accuracy and 75% comprehension, and he read a level Z passage in the spring with 92% accuracy and 80% comprehension. However, it is difficult to compare data concerning student growth or achievement across texts that vary in difficulty (see Paris, 2002). One solution to this problem is to determine if students can read grade-level texts at frustration, instructional, or independent levels. The levels can be calculated separately or on a combination of different measures for accuracy and comprehension. Another solution is to calculate scaled scores to compare performance across text levels. We prefer this method because it allows comparisons of progress over time and text levels and also because it can be incorporated into hand-held computers. Whether IRI data are reported by teachers anecdotally, by reference to levels of reading proficiency, or by scaled scores, they can show how students' different reading skills change over time across passages and books that vary in difficulty.

How Is Information From IRIs Used?

Teachers can use informal reading inventory data immediately to alter their teaching so that students are not drilled on skills already mastered or neglected on skills that are a struggle. Text difficulty, curricular materials, and genres can be modified. Even instructional grouping and peer assistance can be revised according to the results of IRI assessment. Students may be enlisted to monitor their own performance with certain skills, to seek help at home, or to enroll in additional tutoring programs. All of these options reveal the connections between improved assessment and improved instruction. IRI data can also be reported to teachers and parents in notes, forms, charts, reports, or conferences. Data aggregation, analyses, and reporting are made easy when the IRI data are collected on hand-held computing devices. Of course, principals can aggregate the data for school reports or professional development activities so that IRI assessments have credibility among teachers and parents and are not regarded as "low-stakes" tests. As one teacher said, "I used the test reports at my conferences and I thought they were very helpful. I could show the parents exactly what their child needed and tell them how we were addressing that in the classroom."

What Are the Limitations of IRIs?

No single assessment should ever be used exclusively. Informal reading inventory data should be considered in light of other evidence about children's reading development. The fact that passages in all IRIs vary in difficulty, length, and familiarity can influence children's oral reading fluency and comprehension, so multiple passages should be used. Likewise, there is no single way to assess comprehension and recall. Asking children questions about text or prompting them to retell passages can lead to different estimates of their understanding. Certainly, question difficulty varies by passage and item as does children's willingness to retell a story that they and the teacher obviously just read. Perhaps the major limitation of IRIs is the time required to administer, score, and interpret them. Practice, professional development, and peer support can all help teachers to use reading assessments more effectively. For additional information, see Lipson and Wixson (2003).

IRIs Are Excellent Tools

Informal reading inventory data on oral reading fluency and comprehension are most informative about children's reading during initial skill development and when the information is used in combination with other assessments. Assessments of prerequisite skills for fluent oral reading such as children's vocabulary, letter–sound knowledge, phonological awareness, beginning writing, understanding of text conventions, and book-handling skills may augment IRIs with valuable information. Thus, IRIs provide developmentally sensitive assessments for beginning and struggling readers when fluency and understanding are growing quickly and when teaching focuses on specific reading skills. IRIs are excellent tools for combining both diagnostic and summative assessments in an authentic format for teachers and students.

References

Beaver, J. (1997). *Developmental reading assessment*. Glenview, IL: Celebration Press.

Clay, M.M. (1993). *An observation survey of early literacy achievement*. Portsmouth, NH: Heinemann.

Goodman, Y.M., & Burke, C.L. (1972). *Reading miscue inventory*. New York: Robert C. Owen.

Leslie, L., & Caldwell, J. (2001). *Qualitative reading inventory–3*. New York: Addison Wesley Longman.

Lipson, M.Y., & Wixson, K.K. (2003). *Assessment and instruction of reading and writing difficulty*. Boston: Allyn & Bacon.

Paris, S.G. (2002). Measuring children's reading development using leveled texts. *The Reading Teacher, 56*, 168–170.

Paris, S.G., Paris, A.H., & Carpenter, R.D. (2002). Effective practices for assessing young readers. In B. Taylor & P.D. Pearson (Eds.), *Teaching reading: Effective schools and accomplished teachers* (pp. 141–160). Mahwah, NJ: Erlbaum.

Paris, S.G., Pearson, P.D., Carpenter, R.D., Siebenthal, S., & Laier, B. (2002). *Evaluation of the Michigan Literacy Progress Profile (MLPP). Final Report: Year 1*. Lansing, MI: Department of Education.

Snow, C.E., Burns, M.S., & Griffin, P. (Eds.). (1998). *Preventing reading difficulties in young children*. Washington, DC: National Academy Press.

Measuring Children's Reading Development Using Leveled Texts

Scott G. Paris

Many educational and political forces are pushing the assessment of children's reading skills to younger ages. These pressures make it increasingly important to design, choose, and use early reading assessments wisely, because the results measure proficiency and progress and are carefully watched by parents, teachers, administrators, and policymakers. Some people suggest that young children should be given the same kinds of tests as older children (i.e., silent reading followed by multiple-choice questions in a group-administered test). However, many teachers believe that such assessment is inappropriate for children in primary grades and that the tests do not provide useful information for classroom teachers. That is why many districts and states have designed individually administered reading assessments for children who are beginning to read. These tests usually cover letter knowledge, phonological awareness, word recognition, and oral-reading fluency. The tests are diagnostic for individual children and are used flexibly by teachers. Reading educators endorse both outcomes.

The people who might be most surprised by this trend are the educators who created early reading assessments as formative evaluations for teachers. For example, Clay's Observation Survey (1993) was one of the first batteries of early literacy assessments, popularized in Reading Recovery and adapted by many educators, but it was never intended as a summative measure of reading growth. Instead, the Observation Survey was designed to help teachers provide effective instruction, as were many other innovative assessments in New Zealand and Australia. Likewise, the many varieties of Informal Reading Inventories (IRIs) in the United States were designed to provide teachers with information about young children's developing oral-reading fluency, retelling, and comprehension. Three popular examples of IRIs are the Qualitative Reading Inventory–3 (Leslie & Caldwell, 2001), the Basic Reading Inventory (Johns, 1997), and the Developmental Reading Assessment (Beaver, 1997). Because they provide text of different levels and genres, along with procedures for collecting miscues, running records, and retellings, these IRIs are regarded as authentic for young children and appropriate for teachers. The authors of these diagnostic assessments must be surprised to see districts and states adapting IRIs as high-stakes measures of early reading.

Michigan, like many other states in the past few years, has created a battery of early literacy assessments for children in K–3, soon to be K–5, called the Michigan Literacy Progress Profile (MLPP). The MLPP is a collection of assessment tasks that are intended to be diagnostic, authentic, brief, and easily used by classroom teachers. Assessments gained visibility and importance when Michigan passed legislation requiring annual documentation of reading progress in grades 1–5, and the MLPP was accepted as one form of documentation. Standardized tests were also possible, but Michigan teachers and administrators preferred assessment of individual students with a flexible battery of tasks identified as either milestone or enabling skills. Some of those assessment tasks are similar to IRIs, and, indeed, commercial IRIs can be

From *The Reading Teacher*, 56(2), 168-170. © 2002 by the International Reading Association.

used to collect data on word identification, oral-reading accuracy, fluency, comprehension, and retelling. Michigan's goals (i.e., to assess children's reading progress annually in grades 1–5 and to provide teachers with formative assessment tools) and Michigan's problems (i.e., what data to collect and how to report and use it) are characteristic of the problems confronting other states. The purpose of this column is to share some insights the Center for the Improvement of Early Reading Achievement has gained about solving those problems.

The Measurement Problem

The main problem with using IRIs for measuring reading growth is that running records and miscue analyses are gathered on variable levels of text that are appropriate for each child. Thus, comparing a child's reading proficiency at two time points (or comparing various children to one another over time) usually involves comparisons of different passages and text levels so that changes in children's performance are confounded by differences in passage or level difficulty. For example, imagine that Joe is given an IRI in the fall and reads a second-grade level text with 98% accuracy, answers 75% of the comprehension questions, and has a retelling score of 4 on a four-point rubric. Then, in the spring, he reads a third-grade level passage with 94% accuracy, answers 50% of the questions correctly, and has a retelling score of 3 on the same rubric. Is he showing growth in reading? Some might say he is reading more difficult text, while others might say each measure is lower than the corresponding measure with the easier text. The bottom line is that we cannot tell if or how much Joe has progressed in reading from fall to spring. There might be additional data on reading rate or enabling skills, such as word recognition, to support the interpretation that Joe is really reading much (or not much) better than in the fall, but the data are hopelessly confounded and therefore make poor summative assessments.

In addition, it is worth noting that most IRI systems for text levels are imperfect. The differences among passages at each level are often large, and the differences between successive levels are usually ordinal (i.e., each is more difficult than the previous one) but not of equal interval (i.e., the difference between level A and B may not be the same as the difference between level B and C). Thus, IRIs provide poor measurement scales. Indeed, the bases for levels of passage "difficulty" are unclear and can include vocabulary, decodable words, prior knowledge, and comprehension. Some inventories include passages with various genres and forms, but they are seldom balanced or equated. Finally, anyone who has used IRIs knows that some comprehension questions seem peculiar, and some retelling schemes and rubrics are difficult to use. Nevertheless, many districts do not have the resources or expertise to create better materials, and so the commercial inventories are used. The difficulty of the problem should not lead educators to abandon authentic, leveled texts for assessments, nor should it lead educators to embrace standardized, normative tests. There are several possible solutions to the measurement problem beyond the simple profile descriptions usually reported from IRIs and early assessments. The common theme among the solutions that I offer is that they promote comparability of measurement scales despite text variability.

Some Solutions

Solution 1. The easiest solution is to use the *same* texts during each test and to measure increases in reading rate, accuracy, fluency, comprehension, and retelling on the texts. Most educators would predict little confounding due to specific memory for texts read 3 to 12 months earlier, but they would agree that the differences in reading identical texts clearly show improvement over time. Those measures of improvement can be compared across children even if different children read different passages. For example, Joe might have increased his reading comprehension from 50% to 75% while Mary increased hers from 50% to 100% of the questions—a larger increase even if they read different texts at different levels. This solution requires the least expertise in statistics to calculate, and it is straightforward to explain. It is also easy to report to parents and can be used directly for accountability—teachers can calculate how many children improved and how much on each measure. Annual reports can be prepared that show the percentages of children who improved their reading of the same texts. On the positive side, multiple measures of reading performance can be obtained; on the negative side, districts may worry about teachers who are tempted to use the test passages in classroom instruction.

Solution 2. Choose *specific* texts for testing because they have been scaled for their linear ordinal and interval properties (i.e., each text is the same number of units more difficult than the one before it according to measurement procedures). However, this is difficult to do and establishing the scales is time-consuming, especially across different measures such as oral-reading accuracy and comprehension. Again, test security is an issue. Thus, educators may want to create a pool of possible texts for testing or just counterbalance a few texts by testing periods. These procedures minimize and control confounding across text levels, but the problems of differential interest, difficulty, and ease of understanding among passages may still persist. Michigan uses a few selected passages each year to assess reading achievement among 4th, 7th, and 10th graders in the Michigan Educational Assessment Program (MEAP), and students frequently complain about idiosyncratic effects of specific passages.

Solution 3. Create categorical reporting variables that can be compared across different texts and levels. For example, it is common practice for IRIs to identify levels of oral-reading accuracy as Frustration (below 89%), Instructional (90–94%), and Independent (95–100%). The data for comprehension and retelling can also be reported for these three categories, and the categorical evaluations can be reported independently for each measure or conjointly. Then the same categorical evaluations can be reported across text levels for all students. One district in Michigan combines measures of oral-reading accuracy and comprehension to derive a single set of levels to describe a child's reading performance as Frustration, Instructional, or Independent. For example, a child might have to read a grade-level passage at 95% or higher oral-reading accuracy *and* answer at least 75% of the comprehension questions correctly to be classified as an Independent reader. (The specific criteria for each category may vary among districts or states.) The district can report each child's annual reading progress according to one of the categories on a text that is at, below, or above grade level, and those data can be compared across testing periods. For example, a district might report that 40% of its second graders were at the Independent level of reading on texts at or above grade level in the fall but that 65% were at that level in the spring. Thus, growth is measured and reported by categories of reading proficiency according to grade-level texts. Then children's reading proficiency is reported as Frustration, Instruction, or Independent, or according to rubrics, benchmarks, progress maps, levels, bands, or other developmental systems. All of these systems are forms of criterion-referenced assessment so that individual performance can be compared to a standard.

Solution 4. Create unitary scales of difficulty by multiplying performance (i.e., raw scores) by some index of text difficulty. For example, if a district has determined that the passages used in grades 1–5 vary in difficulty by a specific readability formula, it might multiply children's oral-reading accuracy or comprehension scores by the readability score to obtain a weighted score on a uniform scale. The same procedure can be used to multiply reading scores by Degrees of Reading Power difficulty scores, Lexile scores, or other indices of text complexity. The end result is a single quantitative scale on which children's reading of different passages can be compared. The basis of weighting the levels may be debated, but the outcome allows comparisons on a common scale.

Solution 5. To assess reading growth in summer school programs in Michigan, we devised a sophisticated statistical procedure (Paris et al., 2004). We used Item Response Theory (IRT) analyses to scale all the reading data from more than 1,000 children on different passages and different levels of the Qualitative Reading Inventory–3 (Leslie & Caldwell, 2001) so scores could be compared on single scales of accuracy, comprehension, retelling, and so forth. This solution requires a large number of cases and passages, more than 300 children (preferably more than 1,000) with multiple texts read by each child. IRT analyses calculate each child's performance by taking into account the relative difficulty of the passages and then creating difficulty scales based on the performance of just that group of children on just those passages (Embretson & Reise, 2000). The scale values and standard deviation can be set in the IRT model, and then all students' scores can be calculated on the same scale—whether it is 0–100, or 200–800, or some other range.

Item Response Theory is the same analysis used in calculations of scaled test scores such as the Scholastic Assessment Test, Graduate Record Examination, or the National Assessment of Educational Progress. In Michigan, it is similar to the procedures used to calculate MEAP scores for reading. In addition to comparisons of children on different passages and different text levels, IRT analyses allow statistical procedures such as comparisons of performance across multiple time points (i.e., growth) and calculation of the relations among the various reading measures across passages. It is by far the most sophisticated and powerful solution for measuring reading growth with leveled texts, but it requires a large sample of children reading multiple levels of texts. It also requires statistical expertise that may be unavailable in some districts.

The beauty of IRT is that it offers a rigorous statistical procedure for analyzing conventional reading data derived from Informal Reading Inventories and leveled-text assessments. IRT analyses of IRI data may also help to prevent externally imposed standardized testing in primary grades that are less aligned with classroom practices. Thus, teachers can use authentic assessments for what they were designed while administrators can use the same data for summative assessments that measure reading growth. In this manner, classroom-administered reading assessments can be diagnostic guides for teachers and can also provide accountability to parents. Many reading educators view this as a more desirable solution than using separate tests for formative and summative assessments, because the latter doubles the number of assessments given to children and creates the potential for mismatch between what teachers assess and what counts for accountability measures.

Final Comments

Teacher-administered assessments empower teachers to understand and use the assessment information diagnostically for individual children. Professional development activities can then focus on helping teachers to administer reading assessments appropriately and to use the results diagnostically for each child. These solutions to the problems of IRIs are not intended to make commercial IRIs into high-stakes tests. Districts can use any set of leveled texts from their own curriculum for assessment of children's oral-reading fluency and comprehension. It is clear that educators must discern new ways to integrate instruction and assessment, but these measurement suggestions might help demonstrate how authentic assessments can also be used to measure reading growth and report annual progress.

This research was conducted as part of CIERA and under the Educational Research and Development Centers Program, PR/Award Number R305R70004, as administered by the Office of Educational Research and Improvement, U.S. Department of Education. The contents of the study described here do not necessarily represent the positions or policies of the National Institute on Student Achievement, Curriculum, and Assessment, the National Institute on Early Childhood Development, or the U.S. Department of Education, and you should not assume endorsement by the federal government of the United States.

References

Beaver, J. (1997). *Developmental reading assessment*. Glenview, IL: Celebration Press.

Clay, M.M. (1993). *An observation survey of early literacy achievement*. Portsmouth, NH: Heinemann.

Embretson, S.E., & Reise, S.P. (2000). *Item response theory for psychologists*. Mahwah, NJ: Erlbaum.

Johns, J.L. (1997). *Basic reading inventory* (7th ed.). Dubuque, IA: Kendall/Hunt.

Leslie, L., & Caldwell, J. (2001). *Qualitative reading inventory-3*. New York: Addison Wesley Longman.

Paris, S.G., Pearson, P.D., Cervetti, G., Carpenter, R., Paris, A.H., DeGroot, J., et al., (2004). Assessing the effectiveness of summer reading programs. In G. Borman & M. Boulay (Eds.), *Summer learning: Research, policies, and programs* (pp. 121-142). Mahwah, NJ: Erlbaum.

Miscue Analysis in the Classroom

Lynn K. Rhodes and Nancy L. Shanklin

Miscue analysis examines students' use of language cues and strategies, permitting a powerful "window onto the reading process" (Goodman, 1965). When strategies and cues are used ineffectively, comprehension is affected. With this in mind, Denver area Coordinators/Consultants Applying Whole Language (CAWLs) developed an instrument to help teachers efficiently gather miscue data. This instrument, the Classroom Reading Miscue Assessment (CRMA), has been successfully used in several Denver area school districts for four purposes: (a) to provide teachers with a framework for understanding the reading process, (b) to aid teachers in instructional planning, (c) to help students evaluate their own reading progress, and (d) to provide information to parents and policymakers about students' reading progress. (CAWLs consists of Chapter 1, language arts, and reading coordinators from area school districts and university consultants. The group has met monthly for the last five years.)

As CAWLs worked on developing the instrument, we tried to keep administration time to a minimum by trusting in trained teacher judgment. As a result, we chose to use Likert scales as part of the instrument. We decided to trade off the depth, detail, and extensive quantification of data available from elaborate, formalized miscue analysis procedures for a more manageable, yet still informative, version of miscue analysis. The group believed this was necessary if the benefits of miscue analysis were to be realized in more classrooms.

Procedures

It takes about 10–15 minutes to administer the CRMA to an individual student. (See the sample CRMA on the next page.) Many teachers collect data on one or two students per day, using time allocated for sustained silent reading, Readers' Workshop, special classes, recess, or planning periods.

A key difference between the CRMA and most miscue analysis procedures is that CRMA miscue data are obtained without audiotaping the student's reading. Instead, the teacher records observations about the data heard "live" in the process of reading.

When selecting a passage for the CRMA, choose a whole text that has a sense of completeness such as a chapter, section of a content book, or whole story. The text should be one that the student has not read previously. The passage should be about 300–500 words long. Passages that use natural language patterns, have strong narrative or expository structures, and contain pictures or diagrams are best. The text should be challenging enough that the student will make miscues that allow the teacher to observe the student's reading strategies but not so difficult that it causes the student to be frustrated. A reasonable rule of thumb is that the reader should not make more than one meaning-disrupting miscue in every 10 words.

Begin the assessment session with a statement like the following: "I would like you to read this passage aloud. If you come to a word you don't understand, do what you would normally do if you were reading alone. When you finish reading, I'll ask you to retell all you can remember. When we are all finished, I'll share with you what I found out about your reading."

If a student asks for assistance during the reading, the teacher should gently remind the student "Remember, do what you would if you were by yourself" or "Remember, we are pretending

From *The Reading Teacher*, *44*(3), 252–254.

Classroom Reading Miscue Assessment
Developed by Coordinators/Consultants Applying Whole Language

Reader's name ______________________ Date ______________________

Grade level assignment ______________________ Teacher ______________________

Selection read: ____

I. What percent of the sentences read make sense?

	Sentence by sentence tally	Total
_____ Number of semantically acceptable sentences		
_____ Number of semantically unacceptable sentences		

_____ % Comprehending score: $\frac{\text{Number of semantically acceptable sentences}}{\text{Total number of sentences read}} \times 100$ TOTAL ___

II. In what ways is reader constructing meaning?	Seldom	Sometimes	Often	Usually	Always
A. Recognizes when miscues have disrupted meaning	1	2	3	4	5
B. Logically substitutes	1	2	3	4	5
C. Self-corrects errors that disrupt meaning	1	2	3	4	5
D. Uses picture and/or other visual clues	1	2	3	4	5
In what ways is reader disrupting meaning?					
A. Substitutes words that don't make sense	1	2	3	4	5
B. Makes omissions that disrupt meaning	1	2	3	4	5
C. Relies too heavily on graphic clues	1	2	3	4	5

III. If narrative text is used:	No		Partial		Yes
A. Character recall	1	2	3	4	5
B. Character development	1	2	3	4	5
C. Setting	1	2	3	4	5
D. Relationship of events	1	2	3	4	5
E. Plot	1	2	3	4	5
F. Theme	1	2	3	4	5
G. Overall retelling	1	2	3	4	5

If expository text is used:	No		Partial		Yes
A. Major concepts	1	2	3	4	5
B. Generalizations	1	2	3	4	5
C. Specific information	1	2	3	4	5
D. Logical structuring	1	2	3	4	5
E. Overall retelling	1	2	3	4	5

that I'm not here." The teacher should not help unless absolutely necessary to keep the reader involved because it is important for the teacher to uncover the student's repertoire of strategies used during independent reading. This information is invaluable for planning instruction.

As the student reads the text, the teacher determines each sentence to be semantically acceptable or unacceptable. To accomplish this, the teacher considers whether each sentence makes sense after self-corrections are taken into account. For example, if a student read the sentence *Marie decided to paint her new home* as *Marie decided to paint her new house*, it would be semantically acceptable. On the other hand, if the child read the sentence as *Marie decided to paint her new horse*, it would be semantically unacceptable.

By dividing the number of semantically acceptable sentences by the total number of sentences read, a comprehension (in-process comprehension) score may be figured. This provides an index of the degree to which the student constructs meaning effectively while reading. These data are recorded in Part I of the CRMA assessment form. Proficient readers will have a comprehension score of approximately 80% or above, adequate readers 60–80%, and poor readers 60% or below. These procedures and scoring guides are the same as those found in the Goodman, Watson, and Burke (1987) *Reading Miscue Inventory: Alternative Procedures*.

While tallying semantic acceptability, a teacher can also make general observations about the student's strategy and cue use. After the student finishes reading the text, record these observations in Part II of the CRMA form.

Next, the teacher listens to the student's unaided retelling of the story. Once the student is finished, ask "Is there anything else you can remember?" Finally, the teacher can use question probes to assess information not recalled spontaneously. Record observations about the retelling in Part III of the CRMA form, using the appropriate narrative or expository descriptors.

For the purpose of instructional planning, it is sufficient for the teacher to be internally consistent in determining ratings. If the instrument is to be used across classrooms or aggregated for policymaking purposes, practice scoring sessions need to be held. In these sessions, teachers listen to tapes of a variety of readers, carefully rating and discussing a student's reading and retelling in order to achieve a common understanding of criteria and consistency across teachers.

Collecting and Analyzing Data for Different Purposes

To inform instruction. The primary purpose of the CRMA is to inform instruction by providing data which allow a teacher to make instructional decisions for specific students. Thus, the CRMA may be used to observe a student's reading at any time in the year when more specific information is needed. For example, a teacher could use the CRMA with those students whose progress is of most concern, to observe students reading various types of text, or to check students' progress at particular intervals (e.g., at the end of each grading period).

To communicate progress to parents. CRMA data allow a teacher to communicate to parents specific information regarding their child's reading progress. Teachers might also choose to audiotape students' reading of the same text at intervals throughout the year and let parents listen to the tape. Then the teacher and parents can witness the development of the effective use of reading strategies and text cues.

To respond to policymakers' requests for data. Educators are increasingly interested in performance data to supplement or replace norm-referenced tests. CRMA data may be aggregated to provide administrators with information to help make policy decisions such as the focus of staff development, allocation of resources, and special program needs.

The CRMA helps teachers gather important instructional information by providing a framework for observing students' oral reading and their ability to construct meaning. It is an alternative assessment tool many have found to be informative and easy to use.

Refer to the following resources for more information about miscue analysis procedures:

Allen, P.D., & Watson, D.J. (Eds.). (1976). *Findings of research in miscue analysis: Classroom implications*. Urbana, IL: ERIC/National Council of Teachers of English.

Goodman, K.S. (1965). A linguistic study of cues and miscues in reading. *Elementary English, 42*, 639–643.

Goodman, Y., Watson, D., & Burke, C. (1980). *Reading strategies: Focus on comprehension*. New York: Richard C. Owen.

Goodman, Y., Watson, D., & Burke, C. (1987). *Reading miscue inventory: Alternative procedures*. New York: Richard C. Owen.

Nathan: A Case Study in Reader Response and Retrospective Miscue Analysis

Rita A. Moore and Karen L. Brantingham

Nathan (pseudonym), a third-grade boy attending a large urban public elementary school in the midwestern United States, was a troubled reader who read at preprimer level based on results from Leslie and Caldwell's (1988) Qualitative Reading Inventory (QRI). This six-month case study in Retrospective Miscue Analysis (RMA) was conducted by two teacher researchers: Karen, Nathan's Title I reading teacher (second author), and Rita, a university professor (first author). Title I is a federally funded program for at-risk students in the United States. The purpose of our work was to investigate the use of RMA with Nathan, for whom traditional approaches to reading had little success.

Nathan was not as confident as some children who believe they are good readers even if they struggle. Nathan told Karen that he was not a very good reader and that he felt "bad" when it was his turn to read aloud in his classroom, explaining, "I don't know the words a lot of the time and the rest of the kids have to wait on me." Nathan had received special services for reading instruction since first grade, and his lack of progress remained a puzzle to his teachers. Mrs. Parker (pseudonym), Nathan's classroom teacher, described him as a gregarious, friendly youngster who struggled with reading. She said, "He often omits words and hurries through his reading. He lacks confidence and motivation" (Teacher's note, November 20, 2000).

The RMA process enables readers to discuss the underlying logic of their miscues. Our goal as teacher-researchers was to explore patterns in Nathan's miscues as well as his responses to the miscues. Ultimately, we wanted to help him realize that miscues are attempts to construct meaning from text. When we began the study, Nathan relied almost completely on sound–symbol relationships when decoding text; but, unfortunately, his graphophonic skills were very weak. We were interested in the potential of RMA to help struggling readers like Nathan adapt or adopt a variety of word-solving strategies by finding out "how words work" in written language and learn to view miscues as a reader's efforts to make sense of text (Pinnell & Fountas, 2000, p. 78).

We hoped that the RMA discussions with Nathan would broaden his understanding of reading, strengthen his comprehension, and increase his confidence as a reader. At the beginning of the study, Rita asked Nathan, "What do you think reading is?" He squirmed nervously, then replied, "Getting the words right, you know, sounding them out." Midway through the study, patterns of Nathan's responses to text showed his increasing awareness that reading was a meaning-making process. At the end of the study, Rita again asked Nathan, "What do you think reading is?" He grinned with confidence and stated, "making sense and you can have miscues."

Instructional Background for RMA

Miscue analysis, based on the early work of Ken and Yetta Goodman (Y. Goodman, 1996) and

From *The Reading Teacher*, 56(5), 466–474.

others, has a long history of helping teachers better understand the reading process, but it does not involve the reader in a discussion of his or her own miscues. Retrospective Miscue Analysis (RMA) is "an instructional strategy that invites readers to reflect on their own reading process" (Y. Goodman, p. 600) by examining and discussing selected miscues with one or more RMA partners.

> Miscues are unexpected responses cued by the reader's knowledge of their language and concepts of the world.... When expected and unexpected responses match, we get few insights into this process. When they do not match and a miscue results, teachers have a "window on the reading process." (Y. Goodman, p. 600)

Research shows that readers use a combination of semantic (meaning), syntactic (grammar), and graphophonic (sound/symbol) cuing systems to acquire meaning from print (K. Goodman, 1996). Viewing patterns of miscues within the context of the printed text helps readers and teachers understand what cuing systems the reader consistently relies upon and their effectiveness.

We found that encouraging Nathan to discuss the reasoning behind his miscues in an informal, risk-free setting led to rich discussions about vocabulary and word-solving strategies. This was particularly evident in talking about miscues of substitution. By examining what are called *high-level* miscues (miscues that do not interfere with making sense of text) as well as *low-level* miscues (miscues that create barriers to meaningful comprehension) readers are encouraged to see their reading as a strategic, problem-solving process over which they have control and to which they always bring some information and skill (Goodman, Watson, & Burke, 1987). They are also encouraged to appreciate their own mistakes as a part of the learning process—no miscue is without value.

Research Questions

Our inquiry was designed according to guidelines for action research for teachers (Arhar, Holly, & Kasten, 2001). The questions, procedures, and findings presented in this article are intended to be useful to reading specialists or classroom teachers who wish to gain insight on how to reach struggling readers like Nathan. Our work began with the following questions:

- What reading strategies did Nathan adapt or adopt as a result of RMA?
- How was Nathan's ability to construct meaning affected by RMA?
- What impact did the RMA sessions have on Nathan's attitude toward and confidence in reading?

Nathan: A Case Study in RMA

Nathan was 8 years old and in the third grade. He was of mixed European and Hispanic heritage, and he came from a blended family of several siblings and cousins. English was the primary language spoken in the home, but Spanish was also spoken. Nathan had received special services in reading for three years, including regular attendance at summer school; however, at the beginning of the study his instructional reading level was preprimer. Past and present reading interventions were ineffective with Nathan. Worst of all, he was discouraged and unhappy with his reading, and these feelings were beginning to adversely affect his classroom behavior. Nathan attended an inner-city magnet school for grades K–5. The school's multiethnic population is largely composed of socioeconomically disadvantaged children like Nathan.

Data Sources

Our data sources included the following: (a) the Burke Reading Perceptions Interview (Goodman, Watson, & Burke, 1987), (b) audio taped, transcribed miscue session readings, (c) videotaped, transcribed RMA sessions, (d) the Elementary Reading Attitude Survey (McKenna & Kear, 1990), (e) the Qualitative Reading Inventory (QRI; Leslie & Caldwell, 1988), and (f) double-entry field notes.

To determine pre- and poststudy measures of reading proficiency, Karen administered the QRI to Nathan. The Elementary Reading Attitude Survey and the Burke Reading Perceptions Interview were given to measure pre- and poststudy confidence and attitude as well as to provide insight on Nathan's perceptions of reading.

Selecting Miscues for RMA Discussion

To examine Nathan's oral reading and retelling responses, approximately once every two weeks (depending on school schedules and Nathan's attendance), Karen administered a reading miscue inventory to Nathan based on published procedures (Goodman et al., 1987). This served as a preparatory step toward the follow-up RMA conversation. The purpose of the miscue analysis was to generate miscues for discussion with Nathan during the RMA session held approximately two weeks later.

The miscue sessions, lasting from 15 to 20 minutes, were conducted with only Nathan and Karen present. Karen or Rita prepared transcripts of complete stories or nonfiction pieces—a copy for Karen and one for Nathan. These were approximately 240–280 words in length and at least one level above Nathan's instructional reading level in order to elicit strong miscue patterns. We used complete selections so that Nathan's responses and comprehension would not be affected by incomplete text.

After Nathan finished the standard miscue procedures of oral reading and retelling, Karen listened to the session and coded the transcript using the following system: Substitutions are written above the text; omissions are circled; insertions are indicated with a caret; *RM* indicates a repeated miscue; *$* indicates a nonword; *P* indicates a five-second pause; *SC* indicates a self-correction; *R* indicates a repetition of text; *AC* is an abandoned miscue; and *RR* indicates repeated words (Goodman et al., 1987).

Karen also assessed Nathan's retelling of the text according to procedures outlined by Goodman and Marek (1996) in which characters, events, and themes were preselected as benchmarks of successful retelling. Prior to the reading, Karen highlighted important aspects of the reading on her transcript. When Nathan mentioned something different, Karen determined if his response was reasonable, then gave him comprehension credit for his answer. This approach strongly values student response, even if the response is different from that of the teacher. A few days later, Rita listened to the audiotaped reading and verified Karen's markings and comprehension percentages for the retelling. The miscues and a synopsis of the retelling were then transferred to an RMA organizer based on a model developed by Goodman and Marek. The RMA organizer (see Figure) provided a framework for RMA.

RMA Discussions

To organize for RMA discussions, we studied patterns in Nathan's syntactic, semantic, and graphophonic miscues previously recorded on the RMA organizer. We also kept a double-entry journal in response to both the miscue sessions and the RMA sessions. The journal was an effort to reduce possible distortion of data through personal interpretation; we did not read each other's comments until we finished writing our own. One to two weeks following the miscue session, we conducted a 30-minute RMA discussion with Nathan using guidelines developed by Goodman and Marek (1996). These were informal discussions about miscues that were puzzling, interesting, or representative of Nathan's use of specific reading strategies.

During RMA, we listened to Nathan's previously audiotaped reading, stopping the tape to discuss previously selected miscues from the organizer. Nathan followed along with the original text and often corrected himself. This led to rich RMA discussions about why he recognized the word the second time. During these discussions, we worked to boost Nathan's confidence as a reader by directing his attention to reading strategies he used most effectively; one of which was substitution of placeholders for unfamiliar words.

RMA session organizer

Reader:________________________

Date:________________________

Text:________________________

	Text	Miscue as read	Notes	Graphophonic (beginning/middle/end)	Syntactic	Semantic	Self-correction (+ or –)
1							
2							
3							
4							
5							
6							
7							
8							
9							

Note. Adapted from Goodman and Marek (1996).

Placeholders may be high- or low-level miscues. We define *placeholders* as substituted words that are often graphophonically similar to the text: They are a reader's best guess until the author provides more information. For example, in the first session, Nathan used a placeholder for the text, "lady." He read "Larin" instead of "the lady," saying, "It's a name." Later, in the retelling, he talked about the "lady who sang." During RMA, we always discussed Nathan's placeholders in the context of graphophonic, semantic, and syntactic knowledge by asking questions like, "Does that word make sense? Why? How is your placeholder similar to the text? What do you know about the sound of ____?" For example, "Larin" looks like "lady." Nathan's use of a proper noun for a noun phrase was syntactically acceptable but only partially semantically acceptable. These were authentic, learner-centered conversations about language and reading in which Nathan was an important participant.

To our delight, Nathan rapidly became empowered as a reader. In the third RMA discussion, he smiled and said that the way he read the sentence "sounded better" than the author's version. In miscue session four, Nathan read *out of* instead of *out* and substituted *when* for *where* because, as he explained during RMA, "it makes more sense that way."

Rereading text proved to be a very useful strategy for Nathan. For example, during one miscue session, he skipped the word *husband* and went on to read, "and his wife." He immediately reread "his wife" and went back to correctly pronounce "the husband and his wife." When asked during RMA how he knew *husband*, Nathan responded: "I knew it was husband because he had a wife." At the end of each RMA discussion, we listened to Nathan's taped retelling and discussed details that might be added to it now that we had reread the story.

Interpreting the Data

To ensure trustworthiness of findings, data used to measure Nathan's developing reading proficiency were triangulated using the following three sources: (a) results of Nathan's progress in retelling comprehension, (b) the degree to which Nathan used effective reading strategies, and (c) pre- and poststudy QRI scores. In addition, to assess Nathan's growing confidence and positive attitude we compared results from the teacher interviews conducted at the beginning and end of the study with the Elementary Reading Attitude Survey (McKenna & Kear, 1990) as well as pre- and poststudy Burke Reading Perception Interviews (Goodman et al., 1987).

What Reading Strategies Did Nathan Adapt or Adopt as a Result of RMA?

To answer this question, we decided to look at the miscue sessions and RMA discussions in sequence, thus charting Nathan's development as a reader. The first two sessions clearly showed Nathan's budding understanding of the role of syntax in language, the value of placeholders, and his awareness of chunking, or looking for familiar word parts in unfamiliar text. For example, although Nathan had little background knowledge to bring to the first two reading selections, he shared some insightful comments about how he problem solved. In *Harry and the Lady Next Door* (Zion, 1960) Nathan read *string* for *siren*, later explaining during RMA that he looked for familiar chunks to help him select a placeholder. To Karen's surprise, he read *engine* correctly during this early miscue session, so in RMA, she asked him how he had known the word. Nathan replied, "I've heard a fire engine." Almost in the same breath, he looked at both of us and self-corrected his earlier miscue exclaiming, "Oh! It's siren!"

During the second miscue session, Nathan read a passage about whales and fish from the QRI. Consistently, he read *willies* for *whales* and never really seemed to understand the text. During RMA, Nathan looked at the picture and said with obvious relief, "It's about whales!" He remembered that his class was studying whales: "They have flippers and are born alive in the water. We learned about that." Of course, we took this opportunity to discuss the value of picture clues, and later Nathan added many details to his original retelling. During the third miscue session, Nathan read *grows* instead of *glory* in a story about a flower called a snow glory (Rylant, 1987). When Rita asked him if that made sense to him, Nathan said, "Yes, like a flower grows." Obviously, prior knowledge influenced word choice and provided us with the chance to discuss how good readers relate what they know to what they are reading.

The fourth miscue session was a breakthrough in reading fluency and showed Nathan making important decisions as a reader. He read with expression and used repetition (rereading and confirming) to aid in his comprehension and fluency, which created more self-corrections than ever before. When Karen commented on his fluency, Nathan proudly announced, "I read it like they'd say it!" His retelling score was over 67% in a text with an approximate reading level of 2.5. The self-corrections revealed his growing use of graphophonic, semantic, and syntactic cues to derive meaning. He self-corrected *head* for *hand* saying, "it made more sense," and *brought* for *both* because, as he explained, "there wasn't two of them." In addition, in this reading, we noticed a strong influence of both dialect and colloquialism on pronunciation, which was something not readily apparent when Nathan was still reading choppily in preprimer or first-grade text. For example, on this miscue tape he read *roun* for *round* and *had* for *and*, explaining during RMA that "they *had* someone do something." We were also pleasantly surprised when Nathan's use of miscue terminology surfaced during the fourth RMA. He pointed out to us his "self-corrections" and "smart miscues."

The fifth miscue session highlighted Nathan's growing use of critical-thinking skills. Karen had presented him with a rather difficult story in which the main character stutters. Nathan problem solved his way through the text, puzzled by the unfamiliar representation of the dialogue of one who stutters; however, in his retelling he says that the main point of the story is that the boy has "some kind of problem. I think he's short." During his RMA session, he figured out the word *stutter*, but not until he reexamined the written dialogue did he exclaim, "He must talk like that!" These are complex word-solving and comprehension strategies that Nathan was exploring with few prompts from his RMA partners. We asked if he had ever heard anyone stutter and Nathan said he had not. Once again, we were reminded of the power of prior knowledge.

By the sixth and seventh miscue sessions, Nathan became more selective in the kind of reading strategy he used. He effectively used the placeholder strategy for fluency and comprehension, and utilized repetition or rereading for checking word solving and comprehension. During RMA, Nathan thoughtfully explained his substitution of *forms* for *frames*: "I read it that way because frames didn't make sense to me." In the story, the beekeeper works with bee frames (Maguiness, 1997). The word *forms* was a reasonable and meaningful substitution that showed Nathan using the language cueing systems simultaneously. In addition, in the last two miscue sessions, he omitted very few words and continued to demonstrate his new awareness of intonation and expression in oral reading.

How Was Nathan's Ability to Construct Meaning Affected by RMA?

The second research question explored the effects of RMA on Nathan's developing comprehension. The degree to which Nathan read for meaning was analyzed in two ways. First, we looked at Nathan's ability to construct meaning based on the number and types of miscues he made using a formula developed by Vacca, Vacca, and Gove (2000) in which self-corrections (SC) are added to semantically acceptable miscues (SAM) to get the number of acceptable miscues (AM). These AM are then divided by the total number of miscues to determine the reader's effective use of reading strategies. Above 60% is highly effective; 40% is moderately effective; 15% and above is somewhat effective. During the first miscue session, the degree of meaning registered at 44% at first-grade level. During the final session it registered 61% at third-grade level. The jump in these percentages within higher reading levels revealed Nathan's growing use of high-level miscues, or those that were semantically acceptable. The growing number of SAMs was due to Nathan's increased ability to rely on a variety of reading strategies compared to his earlier reliance on graphophonic cues. Table 1 charts Nathan's progress in the construction of high-level miscues.

Scores from the QRI corroborated his improvement. At the end of May, Nathan's instructional reading level measured through comprehension questions and word recognition on the QRI was at second-grade level (85% proficiency). His retelling scores ranged between 85% and 90% on two third-grade level passages from the QRI, which is consistent with his ability to construct meaning through the use of high-level miscues.

In addition, following each miscue session, Nathan's developing comprehension was evaluated according to the number of details he discussed during his miscue retelling and how well he explained them. For example, in *A Treeful of Pigs* (Lobel, 1979) he never quite interpreted the underlying moral of the story, which is that pigs will not bloom on trees no matter how enterprising the farmer. He did, however, acknowledge that the farmer's wife is not lazy like the farmer—a higher level interpretative detail. According to retelling scores, Nathan moved from 40% comprehension of first-grade reading material at the beginning of the study to 83% comprehension of third-grade reading material at the end of the study (see Table 2).

Table 1
Effective use of reading strategies during each miscue analysis

Session/text (grade level)	SAM	SC	Total miscues	Effectiveness
1. *Harry and the Lady Next Door* (1.5)	8	3	25	44%
2. *Whales and Fish* (2.0)	6	0	35	17%
3. *Henry and Mudge in Puddle Trouble* (2.5)	10	3	23	56%
4. *A Treeful of Pigs* (2.5)	9	2	18	61%
5. *Glue Fingers* (3.0)	10	2	29	41%
6. *The Little Spider* (3.5)	13	8	30	70%
7. *The Beekeeper* (3.0)	15	2	28	61%

Note. To calculate the reader's effectiveness in use of reading strategies, SC (Self corrections) + SAM (Semantically acceptable miscues) = AM (Acceptable miscues). Acceptable miscues/Total miscues = Effectiveness. Above 60% is highly effective; 40% is moderately effective; 15% and above is somewhat effective (Vacca, Vacca, & Gove, 2000, p. 542).

Table 2
Estimates of Nathan's Retelling Comprehension During Miscue Session

Session/text (Reading level)	Numbers of details chosen as criteria	Number of details Nathan retold and explained	Percentage of details retold and explained
1. *Harry and the Lady Next Door* (1.5)	5	2	40%
2. *Whales and Fish* (2.0)	5	1	20%
3. *Henry and Mudge in Puddle Trouble* (2.5)	6	5	83%
4. *A Treeful of Pigs* (2.5)	6	4	67%
5. *Glue Fingers* (3.0)	6	4	67%
6. *The Little Spider* (3.5)	6	4	67%
7. *The Beekeeper* (3.0)	6	5	83%

What Impact Did the RMA Sessions Have on Nathan's Attitude and Confidence in Reading?

Data from our field notes as well as the Elementary Reading Attitude Survey (McKenna & Kear, 1990) provided strong indications that Nathan's attitude and confidence in reading had changed. Beginning in March, Nathan's regular classroom teacher said she was "thrilled" with his new reading confidence, ability, and motivation (Teacher's note, April 12, 2000). Nathan's behavior improved as well. Mrs. Parker told Karen that Nathan was no longer reluctant to volunteer to read in class or to participate in class discussions. He became very interested in informational texts and in looking words up in the glossary.

We corroborated this anecdotal data with Nathan's full-scale percentile ratings on the Elementary Reading Attitude Survey (McKenna & Kear, 1990), which went from the 38th percentile in mid-November to the 84th percentile in mid-April. In addition, responses from the Burke Reading Interview (Goodman et al., 1987) showed that prior to the study, Nathan did not consider himself a good reader. In the exit interview, however, he described himself as a "pretty good" reader who "wants to get better." In addition, Nathan changed his definition of reading from "sounding out words" to "getting meaning from books."

Reflections on Teaching and Learning: "It's a Smart Miscue"

Every miscue and follow-up RMA session was a learning experience about language and reader response for us as well as for Nathan. We found it critical to the RMA discussion to honor Nathan's responses and help him talk about his reasoning during word solving. We learned that open-ended questions like, "What were you thinking about when you read that word? If you could change the story, what would you do? Why do you think you remembered that one thing and not another? What strategy did you use to read that word?" expedited this process.

In just a few months, Nathan grew increasingly proud of his ability to discern a "smart miscue" (Y. Goodman, 1996). One day, during reading class, Nathan was listening to another classmate read. She miscued, substituting another word that did not alter the meaning of the sentence. Another classmate immediately corrected her. Nathan looked squarely at the "corrector" and said, "It's a smart miscue. It didn't change the meaning." A few days later the "corrector" miscued and proudly announced to the group, "My word made more sense than the author's." Nathan smiled at Karen who winked back, and everyone kept on reading. Nathan went on to the fourth grade and, while still enrolled in his Title I reading class, was a participant in weekly group RMA sessions with two of his classmates.

While listening to previously recorded text during RMA, Nathan became skilled in correcting his own miscues and in adding details to his retelling from the previous miscue session. Most important, he became increasingly aware of reading as a meaningful process in which he could rely on a variety of strategies to help him read. Substitutions and repetition proved to be Nathan's strongest strategies for eliciting meaning from text, but when he was first interviewed about how he would figure out an unknown word, he simply said "sound it out." At the end of the study during the follow-up Burke Reading Perceptions Interview (Goodman et al., 1987), Nathan responded to the same question saying he might "go back and take a running start, read it again, or skip it and go on." Although in the interview Nathan did not mention substitutions, he was using the substitution strategy as a way of letting himself read on without losing appreciable meaning, and his placeholders were becoming increasingly acceptable. Instead of omitting words or rushing to be finished, Nathan now worked hard to make sense of his reading.

From our work with Nathan, we found RMA to be a powerful tool in crafting and guiding reading instruction. As a reading specialist, Karen always included minilessons in graphophonic, syntactic, and semantic self-monitoring in her instruction, but as the study progressed she began to draw from what she was learning during RMA to develop lessons for Nathan as well as other students. These lessons focused more clearly on use of language cues in reading. For example, she spent more class time on prediction and rime when discussing graphophonic cues because she had learned that Nathan was increasingly proficient at recognizing word "chunks" that were graphophonically similar.

We also affirmed our belief in valuing a reader's response to miscues (RMA) as a way of supporting developing and potential reading strengths. Nathan's use of placeholders provided Karen with the idea of holding small-group RMA discussions in her Title I class in which she and Nathan's classmates discussed the kind of words they chose when they miscued and why they did or did not make sense in the story. To introduce this strategy, Karen read a segment of text to the children, deliberately miscuing several times, thus giving them the opportunity to learn to talk about miscues in a safe way. In both Karen's class and in the RMA discussions with Nathan, miscues were discussed within a nonthreatening context of exploring the thinking behind the miscue.

We would like to conclude this article with something very important that Nathan taught us. Nathan coined a term, which we have since used in other reading instruction settings, called "okay" miscues. Nathan sometimes discussed his use of placeholders as okay miscues. An okay miscue, according to Nathan, does change the meaning of the sentence somewhat, but it also gives the reader just enough meaning to keep going. In Nathan's case, the use of an okay miscue often led to his accurately solving the word later in the text or during the retelling. It is the reader's best guess until the author gives more information leading to more accurate word solving.

During RMA Nathan steadily expanded his explanations and brainstorming about the nature of his miscues. These were almost always related to how he connected prior experience to the reading. Early research from Rosenblatt (1978) and Ken Goodman (1969, 1996) provided evidence that readers construct personal meaning from text based on prior knowledge. Emphasis on the reader's strengths builds confidence and gives the teacher a place to start with instruction. That emphasis gave Nathan the confidence to trust his miscues, challenge the author's text, and create as much meaning as possible from each reading. "Sounding out the word" was no longer his sole approach to reading. Newly adopted strategies that he called "checking the word" (repetition), "skipping the word and reading on," "stopping to think" aloud about the text when he needed to do so, and "using placeholders" gave him new power as a reader.

When Nathan was encouraged to use reading strategies that worked for him, he became empowered as a reader, a learner, and a person. He better understood his own reading process, used more effective reading strategies for word solving and comprehension, and became a more confident reader. Nathan began to articulate new knowledge in socially appropriate and influential ways in Karen's classroom and as a newly confident member of his regular classroom.

References

Arhar, J., Holly, M.L., & Kasten, W. (2001). *Action research for teachers*. Columbus, OH: Merrill Prentice Hall.

Goodman, K. (1969). Linguistics in a relevant curriculum. *Education, 89*, 303–306.

Goodman, K. (1996). *Ken Goodman: On reading*. Portsmouth, NH: Heinemann.

Goodman, Y. (1996). Revaluing readers while readers revalue themselves: Retrospective miscue analysis. *The Reading Teacher, 49*, 600–609.

Goodman, Y., & Marek, A. (1996). *Retrospective miscue analysis: Revaluing readers and reading*. Katonah, NY: Richard C. Owen.

Goodman, Y., Watson, D., & Burke, C. (1987). *Reading miscue inventory: Alternative procedures*. New York: Richard C. Owen.

Leslie, L., & Caldwell, J. (Eds.). (1988). *Qualitative reading inventory*. New York: HarperCollins.

McKenna, M., & Kear, D. (1990). Measuring attitude toward reading: A new tool for teachers. *The Reading Teacher, 43*, 626–639.

Pinnell, G.S., & Fountas, I. (2000). *Word matters*. Portsmouth, NH: Heinemann.

Rosenblatt, L. (1978). *The reader, the text, the poem*. Carbondale, IL: Southern Illinois Press.

Vacca, J.L., Vacca, R.T., & Gove, M.K. (2000). *Reading and learning to read* (4th ed.). New York: HarperCollins.

Nathan's Reading Selections

Beames, M. (1990). *The little spider*. Auckland, New Zealand: Shortland Publications.

Christopher, M. (1975). *Glue fingers*. Boston, MA: Little, Brown.

Leslie, L., & Caldwell, J. (Eds.). (1988). Whales and fish. In *Qualitative reading inventory* (pp. 157–158). New York: HarperCollins.

Lobel, A. (1979). *A treeful of pigs*. New York: Greenwillow.

Maguiness, J. (1997). *The beekeeper*. Crystal Lake, IL: Rigby.

Rylant, C. (1987). *Henry and Mudge in puddle trouble*. New York: Bradbury Press.

Zion, G. (1960). *Harry and the lady next door*. New York: Harper & Row.

Involving Students in Assessment

- How do students know when they are achieving success as readers and writers?
- What are some ways for students to participate in the assessment process, and what are the benefits of student participation?
- What assessment practices support student participation in the assessment process?
- What is the purpose of a portfolio? How can portfolios serve the purposes of providing assessment data and involving students in the assessment process?
- How can you move from teacher-led to student-led parent–teacher conferences?
- What are the benefits of co-constructing performance rubrics with students?
- What is performance assessment, and how can students contribute to the process of performance assessment?

The four articles in this section are intended to help inservice and preservice teachers learn how teachers build assessment partnerships with students, promoting students' responsibility for their own learning. For example, Ann M. Courtney and Theresa L. Abodeeb relate the story of partnering with second-grade students to create portfolios that "help learners see how they think, feel, work and change" over time. Teacher-collected diagnostic data on students, student-selected work samples, and co-constructed learning goals combine to depict student progress. As students are taught to reflect on the contents of their portfolio, they are able to describe their own progress as readers. The portfolio becomes a core tool to engage students in taking responsibility for their own learning.

JoAnn V. Cleland sheds more light on how teachers support students to become assessment partners using portfolios. From the first week of school up to the week of parent–teacher conferences, students learn to take responsibility for documenting and articulating their progress as readers. Teachers introduce a scaffold called an "I Can Chart" to help build the skills students need to state what they have learned as readers and to use the chart to develop the language needed to set goals and to explain their progress to parents.

To achieve success, students can be taught to articulate and recognize the attributes of successful work. Mary Jo Skillings and Robbin Ferrell provide an explanation of how one teacher removed the "mystery" of successful work by coconstructing rubrics with students—ultimately aiming to teach them how to achieve their best performance.

John T. Guthrie, Peggy Van Meter, and Ann Mitchell provide a model of performance assessment in which students are assessed based on active learning tasks while engaged in an integrated unit of study on owls. Meaningful and practical rubrics are used to describe the performance of students as they engage in essential learning tasks such as selecting and reading text to learn information about the topic. Performance assessment elevates students' ongoing engagement with each task since "learning by doing" and "appraisal" are "acted out together."

Additional Reading

- Ainsworth, L., & Christinson, J. (1998). *Student generated rubrics: An assessment model to help all students succeed.* Palo Alto, CA: Dale Seymour Publications.
- Bergeron, B.S., Wermuth, S., & Hammar, R.C. (1997). Initiating portfolios through shared learning: Three perspectives. *The Reading Teacher, 50*(7), 552–562.
- Flippo, R.F. (2003). *Assessing readers: Qualitative diagnosis and instruction.* Portsmouth, NH: Heinemann.
- Hansen, J. (1998). *When learners evaluate.* Portsmouth, NH: Heinemann.
- Lewin, L., & Shoemaker, B.J. (1998). *Great performances: Creating classroom-based assessment tasks.* Alexandria, VA: Association for Supervision and Curriculum Development.
- Stiggins, R. (1997). *Student-centered classroom assessment.* Columbus, OH: Merrill.
- Tierney, R.J., Crumpler, T.P., Bertelsen, C.D., & Bond, E.L. (2003). *Interactive assessment: Teachers, parents, and students as partners.* Norwood, MA: Christopher-Gordon.
- Valencia, S.W., & Place, N. (1993). Literacy portfolios for teaching, learning and accountability. In S.W. Valencia, E.F. Hiebert, & P.O. Afflerbach (Eds.), *Authentic reading assessment* (pp. 134–167). Newark, DE: International Reading Association.
- Vizyak, L. (1994/1995). Student portfolios: Building self-reflection in a first-grade classroom. *The Reading Teacher, 48*(4), 362–364.

Create a Statement of Reading Assessment Principles and Practices

Refer to the assessment tools chart you created at the end of Section Five. Now that you have read about how teachers draw students into the assessment process, select one of your practices to develop into an assessment partnership with students. Consider starting small, but specifically. For example, if your practices chart indicates you use rubrics to assess literature response projects, plan specific steps on how you can engage a group (or the entire class) of students to co-construct a rubric. Or, you might incorporate an I Can Chart into your literacy instruction. Consider having each student photocopy or scan a page from a text and place it in the portfolio. Then, help students use the text and the I Can Chart to explain what they can do as readers.

Refer back to your assessment principles and consider how partnering with students on assessment fits with them. Are you developing a strong relationship between your principles and your practices?

Diagnostic-Reflective Portfolios

Ann M. Courtney and Theresa L. Abodeeb

What is a portfolio and how is it implemented? The answer is as diverse as the number of professionals you ask because the word *portfolio* means different things to different people. A portfolio can be as simple as a collection of students' best work or as complex as an alternative assessment procedure. It can be used as a "learning strategy" (Porter & Cleland, 1995) or an elaborate test. A portfolio may become an ongoing part of the daily curriculum or something that is used only the last week of a grading period. Some states and school systems mandate the keeping of individual portfolios for evaluation purposes. Portfolios change their faces and composition with each practitioner and classroom because teachers and students choose to include varying samples of work and assessment tools. Thus, implementing portfolios becomes a journey of discovery for both students and teachers.

Kinds of Portfolios

Tierney, Carter, and Desai (1991) see portfolios "as systematic collections by students and teachers that could help both consider effort, improvement, processes, and achievement across a diverse range of texts that were read or written" (p. x). They also suggest reflection to "illuminate students' strengths, needs and progress" (p. 41). Valencia and Place (1994) detail the process of assessing portfolios according to a scoring rubric. Rief (1991) sees portfolios as "students' stories of who they are as readers and writers, rich with evidence of what they are able to do and how they are able to do it" (p. 133). Hill and Ruptic (1994) define a portfolio as "an organized collection of student work and self-reflections that helps paint a portrait of the whole child. The systematic process of collecting, selecting, and reflecting upon learning is what makes a portfolio dynamic and meaningful" (p. 21). In the Hill and Ruptic text, fifth graders collectively define a portfolio as "a colorful collection of a person's work that shows his/her thoughts, interests, efforts and goals in many different environments. Portfolios help learners see how they think, feel, work, and change over a period of time. The collections are really important to the learner" (p. 32). The concept of portfolios is stretched and pulled into many images. However, unifying these images is the view of portfolios as collections and reflections of a learner's work over time.

This article describes the methods we are currently using to introduce and construct portfolios in a second-grade classroom. We will discuss the preparation process, diagnosis, the collection and sorting process, goal setting, reflection, and student sharing.

The diagnostic-reflective portfolios we describe involve the teacher in a rich collaboration with each student. The teacher collects diagnostic data that, together with work samples and goals for learning, give an in-depth, accurate portrayal of students' progress. The student and the teacher reflect upon these goals alone and together in order to understand the student's individual learning processes. This type of portfolio assists all children in becoming critical thinkers who understand their own literacy and literacy learning. The aim of diagnostic-reflective portfolios is to help children become aware of the learning strategies they use to construct meaning. This is achieved in teacher–student discussions about the process of collection, selection, and assessment of what has been learned.

From *The Reading Teacher*, 52(7), 708-714.

Portfolios can reveal that students are consistently growing as readers and writers. This is apparent in the students' demonstrations and by their reflective responses about their work that indicate self-awareness of their individual growth. Practice and experience establish the framework for students to think about what they know, what they want to know, how they know, and what specific goals and strategies are needed to increase their proficiency.

The Professionals

Theresa is a second-grade classroom teacher, and I (Ann) am a college professor and a teacher researcher in Theresa's classroom. Together, we have been working with portfolios for the past 5 years. At the beginning of our investigation, each of us constructed our own personal, reflective portfolio. This enabled us to better understand the process through which students would progress. Our portfolios became the models for our students' development. Since then, we have changed and grown immensely; so too have the portfolios. We find that using portfolios requires continual re-evaluation and refinement, resulting in an ever changing and evolving portfolio that develops more fully as it is implemented.

Theresa's students read and write stories of their own choosing during reading and writing workshops. Theresa and I share the same holistic theory of the reading and writing process and believe in looking at the strategies readers and writers use to construct meaning. Theresa continually teaches children to use the three language cueing systems (semantic, syntactic, and graphophonic) as they construct meaning in reading and writing.

At first, we wanted to assess the implementation of portfolios in her classroom. Gradually we tailored portfolio assessment to extend beyond a mere compilation of student work. The portfolios became diagnostic tools used to assess students' abilities, as well as reflective instruments to strengthen students' metacognitive awareness.

Preparation

In the beginning of the school year, Theresa frequently discusses learning strategies with her second graders so they can evolve as learners who discover and reflect on their own thinking. One method she uses is oral cloze, frequently modeled at the beginning of the day. For example, when students work to predict an unknown word while reading the morning message or a poem, Theresa brainstorms insertion possibilities with the children. She focuses them on what word would fit, make sense, sound like language, and begin with the designated sound. Students choose the most appropriate response, which she then places in the text, and they reread it together. Theresa asks how they were able to choose the appropriate word. As they respond, Theresa notes each strategy they explain.

One student, Leah (all students' names are pseudonyms), summarized this experience when she said, "Oh, I get it! First we see if it makes sense, then we check to see if the sounds are the same, and then when we go back and read it again we see if it sounds like language." Theresa's aim is to make each reader and writer consciously aware of and familiar with the language that is used to describe and practice proficient reading.

Self-awareness of the learning process is also developed during literature reading. Students are taught to identify books that are "too hard, too easy, and just right." We practice together many times, and students orally reflect on their identification of level. This eventually leads to a written reflection of their daily progress in book logs, and they become aware of their own changing abilities. From this experience, Jon was able to internalize and articulate when a "too hard" book became "just right" and when a "just right" book became "too easy." He knew that he was "improving as a reader."

Students practice these techniques for several weeks before we discuss the term *reflection*. With direction, children are encouraged to continually ask questions of their own learning and to seek the answers, in order to become more reflective about, aware of, and in control of their own learning strategies. We encourage students to use appropriate self-evaluating language.

Shortly after the children understand reading and writing workshop, Theresa introduces the concept of portfolios. For example, Theresa reads *Grandma's Scrapbook* by Josephine Nobisso (1990) and *Seven Blind Mice* by Ed Young (1992) and discusses ways in which we change and grow. She then introduces the concept of portfolios and self-reflection, relating the children's work to the examples in the literature just read. Theresa also asks those students who have portfolios from the previous year to bring them in to share. The class brainstorms what they think a portfolio is. A typical list may consist of the following responses:

> Something that shows how you've changed and grown.
>
> Something you put work in that you are proud of.
>
> Something you save forever.
>
> A treasure.
>
> Something that you put all your work in, good stuff and bad stuff.
>
> Something that shows what you are good at and what you need to work on.

Theresa lets the students know that a portfolio is all of these things and more: They also help students to know how to learn and set goals for the future.

Diagnosis

We believe that the purpose of assessment is to gather evidence of student learning in order to plan and guide literacy instruction (Anthony, Johnson, Mickelson, & Preece, 1991; Rhodes & Shanklin, 1993; Tierney, 1998; Tierney et al., 1991). Theresa begins an individual file for each child on the first day of school that eventually includes a reading interview (Rhodes, 1993), a running record based on miscue analysis, work samples, checklists, anecdotal records on her early observations of reading and writing behaviors, and other diagnostic surveys (Anthony et al., 1991; Rhodes, 1993) she deems relevant. These are kept in a notebook or file box, which makes record keeping clear and accessible.

This collection of assessments and observations becomes the diagnostic section for each portfolio. Theresa keeps an accurate, ongoing record of a child's progress, including insightful observations about what the child does and doesn't do during the reading and writing process. This analysis is based on an overview of the entire learning process and results in making recommendations for strategic instruction. The diagnostic section enables Theresa to discuss strengths and needs with students, parents, and other professionals; make appropriate recommendations for instruction; assess growth on a continual basis; and compare student self-reflections to her own diagnosis in order to gain insight into a student's understanding of his or her own learning.

Collections

An open invitation is extended to parents to view the contents of the collection folders at any time. During the first week of school, parents receive a letter to explain the portfolio process, which is reinforced again at open house and at parent conferences. We use large folders in plastic crates for students to collect artifacts they may want to include in their portfolios. The folders are labeled with each child's name and contain individual manila folders for reading, writing, and math. We find that content area work samples can usually be placed in either reading or writing folders. Students have access to these collections at all times.

Periodically, Theresa checks and reviews the contents of the folders. She photocopies any sample of significance to include in the diagnostic section of the portfolio.

Sorting

As the collections grow and thicken, it becomes necessary to sort them periodically. Theresa models the procedure for sorting work from each folder. Students are directed to choose a certain number of pieces (this number can vary depending on the individual capabilities of each student and the number of items included in their folders). These pieces represent learning that students want to select and reflect on for their portfolios. Sometimes Theresa will give specific directions: "Choose two math papers that demonstrate growth," or "You must choose your reading log reflection for your portfolio." She may invite discussion, "Should you put only your best work in? Why or why not?" Theresa also holds conferences with individual children to encourage them to include certain pieces.

For some children, choosing the contents of the portfolio is initially overwhelming, and they need guidance in the sorting process. All sorting is done with another student's input, and the partners discuss with each other why they are choosing to select certain pieces. Theresa quickly reviews the pieces that remain in the folder in case there is something that she feels might be important for inclusion in the portfolio. If she encourages an additional selection, she discusses its merits with the student. There is little attempt to control the student selection process; it is student-centered. Theresa staples together the remaining work samples from the folder for the students to take home to share with their parents.

This periodic sorting leads the students to a final selection process in which they choose the pieces upon which they will reflect and include in their final portfolio. Periodic sorting enables students to become more self-evaluative and creates a less overwhelming and more manageable process for the students and the teacher.

Goal Setting

Portfolios are driven by the goals that the children and the teacher construct together. Theresa guides children in setting realistic and appropriate goals. First she and the children discuss what they think a goal is. In one such dialogue, Amanda responds that a goal "is the point you get in soccer." Theresa leads the class into a discussion of all the things a player had to do in order to get that soccer goal. Jamie responds that a goal "is something that you think is hard, but over time, when you've reached your goal, you don't think it is hard anymore." Ryan thinks that a goal "is something you practice and practice to get better at." Meghan says a goal "is something you practice until you get it and then you get a new goal." Theresa writes this discussion on chart paper to serve as a model for goal-setting language.

Theresa asks the class to brainstorm ideas about possible goals and records them on chart paper as well. After the brainstorming session, a discussion evolves about what specific goals students may have. Theresa asks, "What are the things that you might want to work on or get better at?" She then models the language for appropriate goal setting by paraphrasing student responses and recording them on chart paper. Theresa elaborates on sample goals by asking students to "Tell me how you might specifically work on these goals." She might expand further, "If you were working on your goal, what might I hear or see you doing?" Theresa records several responses from the group and breaks them down into specific, observable behaviors. Some sample goals that second graders set include the following:

> To get better at reading by putting words that fit, make sense, and sound like language.
>
> Improve my writing by reading my drafts out loud and then changing them.
>
> To improve reading by reading at home and at school.
>
> To work on staying on task by staying in my seat and paying attention to the speaker.
>
> Making sure that when I work no one else is in my way.
>
> Get better at spelling by reading more books.

Theresa confers with each child, and with her help, they construct three specific and appropriate learning goals. She writes the goals on index cards, which are taped to the children's desks to promote awareness of their goals as they work. Theresa frequently needs to refocus the children's attention to their goals. Some children are goal oriented to begin with, but others need to be encouraged and prodded to make their goals important. For these learners, Theresa might question, "Let's look at your goals. What is something you said you wanted to work on while you were reading? How am I going to see you do this? Can you show me an example of this before you start reading today?" This enables children to know what the goal is, identify its purpose, and define a process to achieve it.

The establishment of goals stems from Theresa's diagnosis and daily "kidwatching" (Goodman, 1978). Through observation and interaction, she comes to know the children better as learners. Goal setting provides a strong foundation for future, honest self-evaluation and reflection.

Reflection and Construction

When it is time to create the portfolio at the end of the term, one week is set aside to model and begin construction. Reflection is the process of looking back on what one has done and asking what, why, and how learning has taken place. It also implies a self-evaluative segment in which the learner contemplates what will be done next time to improve. This sets the stage for the establishment of new goals in the future.

An examination of interactions with individual students helps clarify the process. Marty compares a copy of his journal entry from the first day of school. He stares at it for a long time. He then takes out his most current journal entry and compares the two. He states, "Wow! My writing has really changed." Theresa questions Marty, "How has your writing changed?" Marty responds, "I put spaces between my words and use punctuation now." Marty proudly places both pieces in his portfolio and compares them in a written assessment by saying, "I included this in my portfolio because it shows how much my writing has changed. I use spaces and punctuation now." One of Marty's new goals is "to continue to improve my writing by always using capital letters and periods." Theresa is pleased with his implementation of punctuation, awareness of capitalization, and his ability to reflect on his own learning.

Each day, through minilessons, Theresa reflects on a specific type of work: reader response, word bank, writing sample, goals, math, audiotaping. Theresa asks for a volunteer to practice a model reflection. The student shares what she or he wishes to reflect on with the class. Through the process of inquiry, Theresa probes the child to elicit a thorough reflection on his or her work sample.

John answers the question from his Book Log Reflection (see Figure), "What are the things you want to do to become a better reader?" He responds, "Practice the strategies." Theresa probes with "What strategies do you mean?" John answers, "Like saying *blank*, looking at sounds, putting in words that make sense." Theresa further queries, "Why do you want to use these strategies?" John responds, "These will help me when I come to a word I don't know." Without Theresa's questioning, it would have been unclear what John meant by "strategies." With further probing "strategies" becomes clearer to John, as well as to Theresa and the other students.

Role modeling helps students hear and experience self-reflective portfolio language. We teach the process of reflection directly. While the class observes, Theresa works with a child at the overhead projector. The child responds to a reflective question; Theresa paraphrases the student's response into appropriate reflective language and scripts the responses on the overhead projector for the class to see. She continues to question the child in order to clarify, extend, and refine the child's thinking. What the child can do with assistance one day, she or he will be able to do independently in the future (Vygotsky, 1962, 1978).

In December, Theresa works at the overhead with Leah. Leah is reflecting on her October goals:

1. Spell words correctly in my journal and storybook.
2. Reading harder books like *Pippi on the Run* (Lindgren, 1971). Remember to use my blanking strategy.
3. Making sure I am listening to the speaker.

Book log reflection

1. What book did you like best? Why?

2. What was the easiest book to read? Why?

3. What was the hardest book? What did you do to help yourself read it?

4. What book do you remember most? Why?

5. What book taught you the most? How?

6. What are the things you want to do to become a better reader?

Theresa begins by questioning Leah. A portion of the transcript of their work together follows.

T: Okay, Leah, how have you been achieving your goals?

L: I've been trying hard.

T: Okay, how have you been trying hard?

L: [No response.]

T: What have you been doing?

L: [Leah is thinking.]

T: What have you been doing when you read?

L: [No response.]

T: Remember how you wanted to read harder books like *Pippi on the Run*?

L: Oh, when I read my books I say *blank*.

T: Good, and how does that help you?

L: It helps me make sure that what I'm reading makes sense.

T: Anything else?

L: And sounds like language.

T: Great.

Theresa and Leah continue working together. Theresa questions Leah and pushes her thinking. Rather than just parroting what she thinks Theresa wants to hear, Leah is able to clarify her thinking and demonstrate in her reflection that she is consciously aware of exactly how and why the blanking strategy is used. The written overhead reflection follows:

> I have been trying hard. When I read my books, I say *blank* and that helps me make sure that what I'm reading makes sense and sounds like language.

Theresa, Leah, and the class then reread the reflective statement together followed by questions, comments, or confusions from the class. Theresa discusses how important it is for the children to think about what they do as they read. Leah takes the overhead transparency to copy the information on her own goal reflection sheet.

Theresa provides reflective questions as guidelines for all students (see Figure as a sample). She instructs the class to select a piece and to discuss why they are selecting this particular item with a partner. The partner is to probe, question, and ask for clarification. The partner's role, as well as the teacher's role, is to scaffold for the learner. The children then write a reflection statement and place it together with the work sample into the three-ring binder that serves as the final portfolio keeper.

Our experience suggests that participation in the process of diagnostic-reflective portfolios positively influences children's development in reading and writing. This is apparent in reviewing student writing progress, as well as by looking at and comparing the reflective statements the children write. These indicate an awareness of their individual growth.

Reflection of Others

Theresa synthesizes all of her diagnostic data and develops a learning profile for each individual child, which she includes in the diagnostic section of the portfolio. She interprets the collected diagnostic data and sets an action plan to support literacy learning growth. This synthesis helps Theresa to construct new goals with the children and to wed assessment and observation to learning and instruction (Johnston, 1992).

Once Theresa reviews the portfolio, she writes a reflective statement that is addressed to the child. After peer review, children write comments to each other on a page inserted in the back of the portfolios.

Sharing

When portfolios go home in December, March, and June, it is the child who conducts the tour of the portfolios with the parent(s). Children make appointments with their parent(s) for a period of uninterrupted time in which they contrast and compare pieces, point out how and why they have improved, and share future goals. Parents write comments to their child in the space provided. To prepare the children Theresa models a good sharing session. The children practice sharing their portfolios with their portfolio partners before sharing it with their parent(s). After the portfolio is shared at home, it is returned to the classroom.

The portfolios are also used throughout the year in parent–teacher conferences, special education meetings, etc. During parent–teacher conferences, Theresa has the contents of the portfolios out for the parents to view and to use as a starting point for informed discussion. She includes student work samples and the teacher diagnostic pieces. Both the teacher and the parents can look at the concrete evidence of process and product, as well as growth over time.

Conclusion

Theresa and the students, working together, construct diagnostic-reflective portfolios three times throughout the school year. Theresa collects diagnostic data throughout the year that informs her teaching. As the children reflect on their goals at the end of each term, they construct new goals and reassess and direct their own progress. The continual refinement of goals enables the children to make informed decisions about their own learning.

From class discussion to setting individual goals, sorting written pieces to constructing the portfolios, students are immersed in learning experiences that naturally demand reflection on their learning. In addition, children are provided with a multitude of modeling experiences and opportunities to practice reflective language.

Practice in goal setting and experience in constructing a reflective portfolio establish the framework for students to think about what they know, how they know, and what they want to know; to set specific goals for learning; and to implement strategies to construct meaning. Diagnostic-reflective portfolios hold great promise in providing a direct link between children's understanding of reading and writing and the strategies they use to construct meaning while reading and writing. Portfolios establish a closer connection between what children understand they should do and what they actually do in constructing meaning in reading and writing.

In order for children to establish this conscious awareness, they must be assisted in developing a reflective stance on their own learning. Reflective language must be modeled, orally rehearsed, and practiced so that students internalize the true nature of reflecting. Diagnostic-reflective portfolios provide a structure to support and encourage children in their self-evaluative endeavors and to help teachers develop knowledge of their students' strengths and needs.

If I were to write this article in another year, I would write something different. Each year we change and grow with our portfolios. We do not offer a formula for portfolios. We offer a journey of discovery in a second-grade classroom. Like Graves (1992), we too believe that you need to "keep a good idea growing" (p. 1). Portfolio possibilities are limitless; we challenge teachers to venture on their own journey of discovery.

References

Anthony, R., Johnson, T.D., Mickelson, N., & Preece, A. (1991). *Evaluating literacy: A perspective for change*. Portsmouth, NH: Heinemann.

Goodman, Y.M. (1978). Kidwatching: An alternative to testing. *Journal of National Elementary School Principals*, *57*(4), 22–27.

Graves, D.H. (1992). Portfolios: Keep a good idea growing. In D. Graves & B. Sunstein (Eds.), *Portfolio portraits* (pp. 1–12). Portsmouth, NH: Heinemann.

Hill, B.C., & Ruptic, C. (1994). *Practical aspects of authentic assessment: Putting the pieces together*. Norwood, MA: Christopher-Gordon.

Johnston, P.H. (1992). *Constructive evaluation of literate activity*. New York: Longman.

Porter, C., & Cleland, J. (1995). *The portfolio as a learning strategy*. Portsmouth, NH: Heinemann.

Rhodes, L.K. (Ed.). (1993). *Literacy assessment: A handbook of instruments*. Portsmouth, NH: Heinemann.

Rhodes, L.K., & Shanklin, N. (1993). *Windows into literacy: Assessing learners K–8*. Portsmouth, NH: Heinemann.

Rief, L. (1991). *Seeking diversity: Language arts with adolescents*. Portsmouth, NH: Heinemann.

Tierney, R.J. (1998). Literacy assessment reform: Shifting beliefs, principled possibilities, and emerging practices. *The Reading Teacher*, *51*, 374–390.

Tierney, R.J., Carter, M., & Desai, L. (Eds.). (1991). *Portfolio assessment in the reading and writing classroom*. Norwood, MA: Christopher-Gordon.

Valencia, S.W., & Place, N. (1994). Portfolios: A process of enhancing teaching and learning. *The Reading Teacher*, *47*, 666–669.

Vygotsky, L.S. (1962). *Thought and language*. Cambridge, MA: MIT Press.

Vygotsky, L.S. (1978). *Mind in society: The development of higher psychological processes*. Cambridge, MA: Harvard University Press.

Children's Books Cited

Lindgren, A. (1971). *Pippi on the run*. New York: Trumpet.

Nobisso, J. (1990). *Grandma's scrapbook*. New York: Green Tiger Press.

Young, E. (1992). *Seven blind mice*. New York: Scholastic.

We Can Charts: Building Blocks for Student-Led Conferences

JoAnn V. Cleland

"It was a disaster," Sue confessed as she came into my office. She explained that my class session on student-led conferences had so inspired her that she had taken the plunge at the very first conference time of her first year of teaching. "I know it worked for you. What did I do wrong?" she asked.

I was not surprised at Sue's taking such a great challenge so soon in her professional career; she had 10 years' experience as a Title I teaching assistant and possessed a solid understanding of principles for good reading instruction. If anyone was ready, it was Sue. And as I listened to her description of her conferences, it became clear that *she* had done nothing wrong. *I* had failed to explain the vital steps she needed to take months in advance to prepare herself, her students, and their parents for student-led conferences. During the next 2 hours, I shared with Sue my own path to understanding and implementing student-led conferences using We Can Charts.

The Path to Student-Led Conferences

During the past 15 years, focus on authentic assessment has resulted in a proliferation of portfolios in classrooms as additions to or replacements for test scores. Extensive use of student-led conferences has come with portfolio assessment. In the past, parent conferences have been teacher-led events during which adults discussed their perceptions of a child's functional level; much of what was communicated was a mystery to the child. Then we began to let children in on the secrets—the criteria we used to grade them. "If we are to give students the responsibility of explaining their progress, it is imperative—and only fair—that they know how we evaluated them before the conference" (Countryman & Schroeder, 1996, p. 67). In the process, we came to recognize that the learner is the key stakeholder who rightfully should take the lead in this dialogue. "The purpose of student-led conferences is to help the students accept the responsibility for reporting school progress to their parents. This process helps the student in learning accountability for work produced [and] improving communication skills" (Little & Allan, 1989, p. 210).

The true power of a portfolio is its capacity not only to showcase a student's best works, but also to profile progress over time. The way a child evolves as a reader is highly idiosyncratic and can best be described by the child. "For an observer to understand the significance of a portfolio, it's necessary for the maker to explain it" (Hebert & Schultz, 1996, p. 70). But if the child is to describe the worth of his or her portfolio during a parent conference, he or she must be prepared for the self-evaluation experience even before placing work in this collection.

Preparation for Student-Led Conferences

Asking children to take responsibility for evaluating and explaining their own learning cannot occur at the end of the grading period. Before the

From *The Reading Teacher*, 52(6), 588-595. © 1999 by the International Reading Association.

Good sources for setting up portfolio systems

Harp, B. (1991). *Assessment and evaluation in whole language programs*. Norwood, MA: Christopher-Gordon.

Hill, B., & Ruptic, C. (1994). *Practical aspects of authentic assessment: Putting the pieces together*. Norwood, MA: Christopher-Gordon.

Rhodes, L., & Shanklin, N. (1993). *Literacy assessments: A handbook of instruments*. Portsmouth, NH: Heinemann.

Tierney, R., & Desai, L. (1991). *Portfolio assessment in the reading-writing classroom*. Norwood, MA: Christopher-Gordon.

start of the school year, the teacher must plan to help students develop the skills necessary for analyzing their work and articulating their progress. "Promoting students' control of reading relies on conscious and systematic instructional decisions that emerge from a carefully conceived framework of reading goals and objectives" (Forsyth & Roller, 1997/1998, p. 346). To this end, Sue and I listed the preparations she would need to make for the upcoming school year:

1. Determine expected learner outcomes.
2. Plan means of setting expectations with students and parents during the first week of school.
3. Plan lessons to elicit students' demonstrations and analyses of the reading skills and strategies (expected learner outcomes) to be listed on the We Can Chart.
4. Set procedures for helping students develop ownership of the We Can Chart and the reading strategies it contains.
5. Plan specific instruction on self-analysis of during-reading strategies.
6. Decide how to give students practice in articulating their self-analyzed progress.
7. Set the schedule and process for students' preparation for leading the conferences.
8. Plan logistics for the actual conference time.

These steps should not be viewed as rigid but rather as possible means of operationalizing principles for marrying effective instruction and assessment. Steps may be modified, omitted, or augmented depending upon individual teaching styles, grade levels, and school cultures. The explanations that follow are suggestions that may serve as guidelines for other teachers trying to implement student-led conferences for the first time.

1. Determine expected learner outcomes. The teacher makes a list of expected proficiencies as a guide for decision making about day-to-day activity in the classroom. These expected learner outcomes for the year may be mandated by the school, district, or state, or the teacher may need to identify the strategies and skills that will drive instruction and assessments. This is the time to identify the types of items that will be collected as evidence of competence on each outcome and to determine the organizational system to be used. It is not possible to present here the range of possible portfolio systems, but perhaps it is important to highlight the need for at least two files per child:

- the teacher folder containing anecdotal notes, observation checklists test records, etc.; and
- the student folder(s) containing a directory of works matched to numbered and dated items in the collection, works in progress, final products with the student's reflections, etc.

A list of several good resources describing organizational systems for portfolios is included in the sidebar.

2. Set expectations during week 1. During the first week of school, a baseline product in each significant category (e.g., a tape of oral reading, a drawing in response to literature, a graphic organizer, a writing sample) is gathered. Through the production of these works, children are introduced to the types of works they will be generating during the year, and the teacher has initial diagnostic measures on each child. Because these items are so critical to showing progress over time, it is probably wise to store them in the teacher's files on the individual children rather than in the students' portfolios.

The teacher guides students to think about their reading through strategy surveys and conversations. Each student completes a goal sheet to state the one thing he or she does best as a reader and the one thing he or she would like to improve. Students may have limited capacity to express their knowledge of reading strategies at this point, so the goal-setting procedure may seem superficial. This is normal and may even intensify the power of the student's analysis of growth after 9 weeks.

Also during the first week the teacher distributes the students' portfolios, shows students how they will be used, helps them make their first entries in their directories, and demonstrates the collection, selection, and reflection procedures they will use across the year (Hill & Ruptic, 1994). At meet-the-teacher night she briefly describes to both children and parents how the portfolio system will serve as the framework for the upcoming student-led conferences. She makes clear the connection between the expected learner outcomes and the products that students will be gathering before the first conference. A summary chart may help parents see the long-range plan (see Figure 1).

3. Elicit student demonstrations and analyses of the reading skills and strategies stated within the expected learner outcomes. Once baseline data are in place, it is time for instruction to begin. Having targeted a specific initial skill or strategy, the teacher creates an experience in which the children will be able to use this reading tool successfully. For instance, if she or he has chosen matching pictures to words, the class may read from a big book, stopping at words not in most students' sight vocabulary but shown in the illustrations. As they "read" these words, the teacher expresses pride. At the end of the book, she or he comes back and asks the children to tell how they figured out these new words. Without a doubt, at least one child will describe the picture strategy. The teacher then writes or paraphrases a child's explanation of this technique to begin the We Can Chart:

> We are readers. We can
>
> • use pictures to help us figure out new words.

As with "What Can You Show Us?" activities, the "heart of the [process] is student demonstration [of what] they know" (Richgels, Poremba, & McGee, 1996, p. 635). The critical element is the teacher's careful orchestration of a lesson that leads the children to successfully use, identify, and articulate an effective reading strategy. Middle-grade students may identify strategies like using prior knowledge to understand characters' motives, becoming familiar with word parts to determine meanings of new vocabulary, or sensing a turn in the main character's behavior to identify story climax. The skilled teacher provides the opportunity for students to put a targeted reading strategy into action, asks for a response, and then helps them discover the strategy used to reach that response by asking questions like "How did you know that?" or "What makes you think so?"

4. Build student ownership of the strategies. As students experience other strategies, the chart grows. Whenever an addition is made, the teacher leads a chart chant or discussion to reinforce past learning while helping children continue to build a repertoire of ways to construct meaning from print. By the time of the first conference, a substantial list is in place—and the students feel they own it, since they have been full participants in producing it.

Here is a chart generated by 7-year-olds during the first 9-week grading period.

Figure 1
Summary chart

	Student	Teacher	Parent/Guardian
Week 1	Generates baseline products for targeted learner outcomes.	Collects and stores baseline products in teacher folder on student.	Reviews expectations for the year.
		Uses baseline information to plan instruction.	
Week 1	Makes initial goal sheet.	Makes copy of goal sheet for teacher folder on student.	Shares relevant information about student.
Ongoing	Gathers products in working folder.	Designs instruction to foster independent, strategic reading.	Asks about ongoing work, but does not expect daily take-homes.
End of grading period	Chooses works for showcase portfolio to show growth since baseline.	Confers with student about progress.	
	Sets new goal.		
	Prepares take-home folder of other finished work.	Schedules parent conferences.	Schedules parent conferences.
End of grading period	Explains progress to parents through contents of showcase portfolio.		Reacts to contents of showcase portfolio.
	Shares new goal.	Assists with setting new goal.	Participates in plans for new goal.
	Gives parents take-home folder.		Reviews take-home folder at home.

We are good readers. We can

- use pictures to help us figure out new words.
- predict what will happen next.
- use letter sounds to help us figure out words.
- make pictures in our heads from the words.
- ask ourselves, "Does this make sense?"
- use words we know to figure out new words.
- think about what we would feel like if we were in the story.
- figure out why characters do what they do.
- watch for punctuation marks.
- use expressive voices when we read out loud.

The list contains strategies one might find in a scope and sequence for reading, but the casual organization and wording show the children's collaborative involvement in constructing the chart. Simultaneously, the socialization during review of good-reader strategies energizes the children's understanding of the reading process.

5. Plan specific instruction on self-analysis. While peer conversations and chanting help children state effective reading strategies, head knowledge is not enough. The ultimate goal is individual internalization; each child must find his or her own way to apply the information on the We Can Charts to the ongoing quest for meaning. In the middle and upper grades, we can explicitly teach students how to self-monitor while they read. Techniques similar to those used for taking anecdotal notes can be shared with children. Perhaps the easiest way is to have students jot in learning logs the strategies they use to "get clicking" again when they have "clunked." Figure 2 shows a small sample of a fifth grader's learning log.

Students gain an empowering sense of control over their own learning when they begin coding their thinking processes during self-correction. But here a word of caution is needed. Just as teachers space their use of running records or anecdotal notes so as not to interrupt the flow of teaching, students should be asked to bring their self-monitoring strategies to the conscious level only periodically. This occasional experience can be intriguing and empowering to students if they view it as a periodic experiment to see how they are doing. The fifth grader whose log is presented in Figure 2 compared it to taking her pulse in health class every 8 or 9 weeks.

On a more regular basis, children can learn to check the performances and products they generate in response to reading. Even young children can hear the difference between robot reading and the sound of storytelling, can feel the difference between a flat performance and an animated delivery, can spot the difference between a random list and a graphic organizer, and can see the difference between a drawing that merely shows a place and one that includes important actions. When students know the "important aspects of the product or performance," quality of learning improves (Khattri, Kane, & Reeve, 1995, p. 81). We point the way for children to become independent learners when "[w]e teach them how to assess the value of their work" (Hebert & Schultz, 1996, p. 70).

6. Give students practice in articulating their self-analyzed progress. During the construction of the We Can Chart, students participate in the creation of criteria for quality

Figure 2
Fifth grader's learning log

What word made me clunk?	What did I do to get clicking again?	Did it work?
advisor	WP (advise)	Yes
gecko	CC (a flip of its long tail) & PC	Yes Got the meaning, but still couldn't pronounce
palace (I read *place*)	CA & CC (king)	Yes
munch (I read *much*)	CA & CC (You can't much food!)	Yes
Sire (I'd been saying *sir*)	CA & CC (king)	Yes

CA = Closer Attention to all letters
PC = Picture Clue
CC = Context Clue
WP = Word Parts

work. They are led not only to apply but also to articulate what they do as good readers. In a study of 9-year-olds' self-monitoring behaviors, those children who were able to articulate how they self-corrected during silent reading were more successful on frustration-level passages than those who self-corrected in an intuitive manner (Cleland, 1988). Clearly, it is important that we provide opportunity for children to bring to the conscious level and verbalize what they do to check their own mental processing of print. "Good readers...monitor their own progress and achievements," and as they specify what helps them succeed, "they develop 'ownership' of their reading that reflects pride in their accomplishment" (Paris et al., 1992, p. 91). In fact, as students prepare for student-led conferences, they seem "eager to explain or demonstrate what they are doing" (Kohn, 1996, p. 55).

7. Set the schedule and process for last-minute student preparations for leading the conference. Approximately a week before conference day, students begin intensive preparation for leading the conversations about their portfolios. First the teacher returns the baseline products. This is usually an "aha!" moment for students. As they look at the We Can Chart, they see specific areas of positive change over 8 weeks' time.

Next students review the entries in their directories to select one piece per category (see step 2) to highlight their progress. All other finished pieces are placed in a take-home folder, and all unfinished work is placed in the under-construction folder or pocket. Each piece selected as a showcase work is paired with its baseline match, and the child prepares a reflection cover page telling why he or she chose this particular work sample as evidence of growth.

Because students have been using the We Can Charts daily to evaluate their efforts, writing the reflections is a relatively easy task. Here is a sample of a second grader's reflection cover for her "best GO" (graphic organizer) that she wrote while referring to the We Can Chart shown in step 4.

> I choze this I Think—Now I Think Chart because it shoze I can predict. I draw befor I read I draw aftr I read and I ges prde cloze sep the end Mrs. I sez thats oka because a good arthr makes a suprize for the end.
>
> [I chose this "I Think—Now I Think Chart" because it shows I can predict. I drew before I read, I drew after I read, and I guessed pretty close except the end. Mrs. I says that's okay, because a good author makes a surprise for the end.]

Each day during readers' workshop time, students pair off to role-play the conference presentation. Partners take turns playing child and parent. For even more practice, children change partners. In this way children have multiple opportunities to prepare to present their portfolios: explaining their work, telling why they chose certain pieces to showcase, showing how they have progressed on their goals, and identifying new areas of concentration for continued growth. Also, children hear several of their peers describe their work and goals. All refer to the class We Can Chart, reinforcing the ongoing learning within the community of readers and anchoring individual mental maps for processing print.

During this time the teacher systematically circulates to talk privately with each child and shares information from her or his own folder on the child's progress. There are to be no surprises at conference time; the child has heard in advance what will be said and is in charge of both sharing and eliciting information.

8. Plan logistics for the actual conference time. By the time parents arrive for the conference, children know just what they will do and say. As parents arrive, they are first given an opportunity to review everything posted in the room and available at the child's desk. The students tell their parents about the We Can Charts and show them their pieces displayed in group projects or on class bulletin boards. They describe the directory as the record of all their work, explain how the baseline efforts have been paired with exemplary pieces to show progress, and give parents the take-home folder of the other finished pieces from their working portfolios. Each child then makes a presentation comparing baseline and showcase works. Next children bring their parents and their work to the teacher. The children ask the teacher to contribute her or his viewpoint and encourage their parents to do the same.

The children close the conference by stating their goals for the next grading period and requesting support from parents and teacher. If the goal seems unrealistic, either too minimal or too advanced, all present converse and reach consensus. A new goal is written, all sign the goal sheet, and the teacher takes responsibility for preparing copies for all parties to hold and act upon until the next conference time. Here is a sample of a past and future goal sheet prepared by a fourth grader.

> I am a good reader.
>
> I have gotten better at describing the events that shape the plot of a story and finding the turning point.
>
> I would like to get to be even better at reading.
>
> I want to learn how to use prefixes, suffixes, and endings to decide what long words mean and how to pronounce them.

Once again, the teacher has structured the experience so the child can be successful and assume the leading role, but stands by to coach as needed.

An Active Learner

The use of We Can Charts as tools to promote independent, strategic readers is embedded in an understanding of the conditions of learning known to give children optimal opportunity for literacy development (Cambourne, 1988). Students are fully engaged throughout. The teacher immerses them in authentic experiences with real texts, during which the teacher enables students to demonstrate reading strategies. They then bring these strategies to the conscious level as they construct the We Can Chart. Repeated reminders that "We Can," through ongoing references to the chart, empower students; they expect future success and assume responsibility for their own learning. They have a means of internalizing reading strategies as they use them on a regular basis, analyze their effectiveness, and make adjustments based on their metacognitive processing. All the while they are not really left on their own; they receive steady support and feedback from the teacher, peers, and parents that are vital to their progress.

A Knowledgeable Teacher

When I introduced the concept of student-led conferences to Sue and her classmates, I posed it as an ultimate goal rather than a first-year teacher's task. Sue's determination to make it work *now* showed a level of readiness attributable to her solid knowledge base about how children process print to make meaning. She had brought to conscious level the variety of reading strategies that interact during proficient reading; she had identified them and knew how to provide prompts that children could eventually emulate to become independent strategy users. She understood the school curriculum and could list the grade-level strategies that she would target to help students build an appropriate We Can Chart. She was a devotee of discovery learning and had developed an instructional style that lent itself to planning guided reading experiences through which she elicited children's generation of items for the We Can Chart. In short, she had three teacher traits necessary for the implementation of a student-centered conference plan: a strong understanding of reading strategies, the ability to organize a pattern for cyclical strategy development, and instructional skills for planning and guiding students' self-discoveries.

Even with these master teacher qualities, Sue admitted that she planned to invite her grade-level colleagues to join her effort. She knew their support would increase her staying power and, she hoped, maximize the benefits to children.

Benefits

Three major benefits evolve from the use of We Can Charts as a component of reading assessment and evaluation. First, We Can Charts provide a dynamic set of guidelines for children to use to measure their progress. Commercial and district check charts have been posted on classroom walls for decades, but the hallmark of the We Can Chart is its origin. "Signs, exhibits, or lists created by students rather than teachers" (Kohn, 1996, p. 55) empower learners as the teacher releases responsibility for learning to children (Pearson & Gallagher, 1983). At a recent parent conference, a first grader showed her parents the reading We Can Chart and said, "We can read and we even made up the reasons why!" The wording may lack precision, but the message was clear: Children thrive on the joys of discovery and ownership.

Second, the gathering of multiple perspectives is currently viewed as a healthy approach, but it is important that the child have the leading voice and be the one at the locus of control. It is the child's learning being reviewed. The child not only holds the most knowledge about his or her own mental processes, but also has the most to gain by setting goals for improvement and for soliciting others' support.

Third, during the student-led conference, parents survey their child's progress over time, and do not measure the child's work against that of other children. We are "interested in...whether each child is growing, not whether he is better than the next child across the district or the country.... [O]ur reference point should be the child's work" (Harmon, 1992, p. 250). By referring to the We Can Charts parents can gauge their child's progress in light of the criteria set by the class. The spirit is not competitive but communal.

When Sue left my office, both of us had metamorphosed. She was committed to beginning the next fall with a yearlong process that would guide her children to be responsible for assessing and reporting their own reading development, and I was determined to change the way I deliver instruction about student-led conferences. We both were ready to "walk" our students through procedures to help them succeed in their respective roles within a process that puts learners in control of interpreting their own growth.

References

Cambourne, B. (1988). *The whole story: Natural learning and the acquisition of literacy in the classroom*. New York: Ashton Scholastic.

Cleland, J. (1988). *An analysis of fourth graders' self-monitoring of comprehension during silent reading*. Unpublished doctoral dissertation, Northern Arizona University, Flagstaff, AZ.

Countryman, L., & Schroeder, M. (1996). When students lead parent-teacher conferences. *Educational Leadership, 53*(7), 64–68.

Forsyth, S., & Roller, C. (1997/1998). Given this, then...what? Helping children become independent readers. *The Reading Teacher, 51*, 346–348.

Harmon, S. (1992). Snow White and the seven warnings. *The Reading Teacher, 46*, 250–253.

Hebert, E., & Schultz, L. (1996). The power of portfolios. *Educational Leadership, 53*(7), 69–70.

Hill, B., & Ruptic, C. (1994). *Practical aspects of authentic assessment: Putting the pieces together*. Norwood, MA: Christopher-Gordon.

Khattri, N., Kane, M., & Reeve, A. (1995). Research report: How performance assessments affect teaching and learning. *Educational Leadership, 53*(3), 80–83

Kohn, A. (1996). What to look for in a classroom. *Educational Leadership, 54*(1), 54–55.

Little, A., & Allan, J. (1989). Student-led parent-teacher conferences. *Elementary School Guidance and Counseling, 23*, 210–218.

Paris, S., Calfee, R., Filby, N., Hiebert, E., Pearson, P.D., Valencia, S., Wolf, K., & Hansen, J. (1992). A framework for authentic literacy assessment. *The Reading Teacher, 46*, 88–98.

Pearson, P.D., & Gallagher, M. (1983). The instruction of reading comprehension. *Educational Psychology, 8*, 317–344.

Richgels, D., Poremba, K., & McGee, L. (1996). Kindergartners talk about print: Phonemic awareness in meaningful contexts. *The Reading Teacher, 49*, 632–642.

Student-Generated Rubrics: Bringing Students Into the Assessment Process

Mary Jo Skillings and Robbin Ferrell

"Perhaps the greatest potential value of classroom assessment is realized when we open the assessment process up and welcome students into that process as full partners" (Stiggins, 1997, p.18). Involving students in the development of performance targets can be an effective instructional tool because students who are given the task of analyzing quality work and its critical components become better performers themselves (Stiggins, 1997).

Performance-based assessments, such as rubrics, are not new to the educational community. Over the past decade many states in the U.S. have mandated fundamental revisions of their assessment practices to include learning tasks that are open ended, aligned more closely to real-life learning situations and the nature of learning, and involve a variety of measures that inform students of their progress in reading performance goals (California Department of Education Elementary Grades Task Force, 1992; Wiggins, 1989). The nature of the assessments teachers use should create a relationship between assessment and instruction that is "more natural, ongoing, and constructive" (Tierney, Readence, & Dishner, 1995, p. 482).

Highly competent teachers use assessment measures to inform their instruction and at times as a means of instruction. Rubrics are frequently the tools used to identify key elements of proficiency, particularly for assessing reading fluency or writing development. These rubrics assist both the teacher and the learner in determining the necessary elements for each level of performance. However, these levels of performance are usually developed by educators rather than by students. The purpose of this article is to highlight a performance assessment process where the teacher and the students work together to generate specific performance standards.

Teacher-Researchers in the Classroom

I (Mary Jo Skillings) met Robbin Ferrell when I worked as a university professor in partnership with a local school district's mentor program. Robbin presented her use of student-generated rubrics to a group of beginning teachers. I asked if I could observe in her classroom and if we could work together to study how the process evolved with her second- and third-grade students. Over a period of two years, we observed, recorded, and questioned the process. Student interviews, classroom observations, and videotaped sessions were conducted as we looked at how Robbin's students learned to assume more control in developing the criteria for their performance on a variety of reading and writing tasks.

Starting Points

Robbin explained what prompted her to begin this process. "Our district began using rubrics for assessing students' writing performance levels for inclusion in writing portfolios. It became apparent to me that when I displayed a set of criteria with examples for establishing performance levels, my students were supported and were more successful in meeting performance goals. They had a clearer picture of what the end results

From *The Reading Teacher*, 53(6), 452–455. © 2000 by the International Reading Association.

of an assignment should be. This was particularly effective with children in my class who were from other language backgrounds. Why not extend this process to other areas? I wanted my students to be more actively engaged, to better understand my expectations for assignments, and to have a better grasp of the concepts. I decided to gradually bring the students into the process of developing their own rubrics." Robbin worked to help her class "solve the mystery of the meaning of success" (Stiggins, 1997, p. 38) in a series of small steps.

Setting the Stage

At the beginning of the school year, Robbin started using teacher-developed rubrics with her students to get them accustomed to this form of assessment. The next step in the process was to bring the students into the actual development of a rubric by first asking questions that connected them to real-life situations that required establishing criteria. She asked her class to develop a rubric of five standards for a "Best Place to Eat," an "Okay Place to Eat," and a "Not So Good Place to Eat." They established a rating of 3 for highest and 1 for lowest choice of a place to eat (see Table 1).

Robbin's students agreed on the essential elements of what they thought would be important if they got to decide on a place to eat. Then they deliberated about the other two levels. Robbin pointed out to them that they needed to look at each point of the "Best Place to Eat" and consider how this point would change for the other two levels. After completing several of these, the process moved from the real-life situations into more structured development of a rubric that involved students' performance on reading and writing tasks. Robbin's students gradually became partners with the teacher in developing assessment tools.

Robbin explained it this way, "The first rubrics I used were extremely structured and were used both to teach and to assess if the students understood the concepts I wanted them to learn. It was important for me to make sure that my students had both the experiences and the information they needed to be successful with an assignment." She provided an environment that included a wide assortment of literature, fiction and nonfiction books, magazines, maps, flyers, and menus. She used many examples of graphic organizers such as Venn diagrams, story maps, and word webs. All of these were accessible and prominently displayed in the classroom. Additionally, she aligned the development of her assessments with the *California Academic Standards for the Language Arts: Reading, Writing, Listening and Speaking Content Standards for Grades K–12* (Commission for the Establishment of Academic Content and Performance Standards, 1998). Robbin planned the exact requirements for the assignment. "I knew what I had taught them and I knew what I wanted them to show me that they had learned. It was a time-consuming process, particularly in the beginning stages, but it was important for es-

Table 1
Best place to eat rubric

3	2	1
• They have special kids' meals with prizes • Food comes fast • Food is good • A special place to play • Noise is okay	• Some kids' meals but no prizes • Food is a little slow • Food is okay • Space to play is small • Not too much noise	• No special kids' meals • Food takes a long time • Food isn't all that good • No special place to play • You have to be quiet

tablishing a foundation for them. I didn't want them going in all directions."

Teacher-Student Collaboration in Structured Rubric Development

The class had been studying the literary elements of character, plot, and setting. The focus of this lesson was on attempting to get students to understand the literary elements of character development using *Cinderella*. The underlying objective was to include the students in assessing their own learning about characterization. First Robbin read a traditional version of *Cinderella*. She explained the lesson with the specific tasks written on a chart that delineated what students were expected to know and to demonstrate for the assignment. Students were to choose a character and write four things the character did in the story. Students were to be able to explain what motivated the characters to act as they did in the story. They needed to include an illustration and an appropriate setting.

Robbin already had in mind what she felt were the important criteria for the development of the rubric. She used three performance levels "because I have found it is easier at this stage to differentiate among the levels." The three-level rubric designing session began with the question "If you were to get the very best grade on the assignment, what would you have to do?" Students responded with the various requirements that were anchored within the assignment chart while Robbin recorded their exact words.

> "You have to pick a character from *Cinderella*."
>
> "You need to have four things that your character did in the story."
>
> "There need to be two reasons we think the character did what he did."
>
> "There needs to be a picture that is right for the story."

Robbin continued the discussion with a variety of probing questions and included the responses for the criteria for "best paper." "I let the students make the decisions on these questions before I include it as part of the criteria," she explained. The questions included these:

> Does there need to be a heading?
>
> Do the sentences need to be complete?
>
> Does all of the information need to be correct?

"For a top paper, you have to remember everything and put it in," explained one student. Students then began to add criteria on their own without the teacher's leading questions, and they expressed knowledge of expectations for the assignment. Additional criteria for classroom assignments were added:

> "You need to have your name and date in the upper right side."
>
> "It has to be neat."
>
> "For showing the ball, you should show the prince in a palace."

Robbin again directed students' attention to the assignment and agreed that they should write why their characters acted the way they did. Finally, the class had developed a standard for a paper to be considered a "best paper." Then she assigned it a grade, or a level of 3. Robbin asked, "Who thinks they can get a number 3 paper?" Every hand went up. Robbin explained that she does not assign a level until criteria are set because students can identify with a good grade rather than a number 3.

After the standard was established for the best grade, the same process was followed for the next category, an "okay" or number 2 paper. Robbin again asked her students to think about what would cause a paper to be a number 2 or an "okay" paper. The students lowered the standards in some cases. They suggested the following:

- There might be only three things the character did in the story.
- The picture might not be colored or have enough details in it.
- It might have only one reason for the character doing what he did.

- The sentences could be complete but it might not be as neat.

Finally, Robbin questioned, "What makes a paper that is not very good, a level 1 paper, a paper that might have to be done over?" The process was repeated with the standards adjusted to a lower level. Students' comments were recorded as they thought about the assignment and the criteria for their work. In addition to meeting the assignment requirements for the lesson, Robbin addressed the additional criteria for headings and neatness, and these were added to the rubric. She also reminded students of where they could get help with the information if they needed it. She discussed looking in their books, looking on the class charts, or reviewing previous assignments. The structured language arts rubric in Table 2 was developed by Robbin and her students.

Robbin led the students through all of the criteria from the very best paper and adjusted it for each of the standards. The assignment was reviewed with the students, and the charts were placed within easy access for reference. As students worked they frequently referred back to the rubrics for cross-checking their papers.

Expanding the Possibilities

Robbin began to move students beyond the constraints of a prescribed set of criteria. She continued to use structured rubrics for instruction and assessing student understandings for many reading and writing tasks, but she also began to expand the rubrics for more open-ended activities. Thus she began to open up the rubrics to a higher level of student ownership. The students were able to choose what they would do and how they would do it. This step was taken later in the year and after many occasions to work with rubrics. She used rubrics as opportunities for her students to negotiate new connections they had made and to be able to use a variety of forms to represent new concepts they had learned. "I wanted them to have choices and to have a broader vision of what they could do to satisfy the requirements of the lesson. I have students who are able to achieve higher levels of performance when they are able to express themselves through more involved expressive modes, such as telling another student who then writes the version down." Robbin used the familiar rubric form but invited students to "think about what other ways you could use to demonstrate, to show what you know."

Table 2
Structured character rubric

3	2	1
• Choose a character • Write four things the character did • Write two reasons for character's actions • Illustrate character in appropriate setting with at least three details • Complete sentences • Proper heading • Neatly done	• Choose a character • Write two to three things the character did • Write one reason for character's actions • Illustrate character in appropriate setting with at least two details • Most sentences are complete • Heading complete • Not as neat	• Choose a character • Write one thing the character did • No reason given for the character's actions • Illustration wrong for setting—few details • Some sentences not complete • Heading incomplete • Paper is messy

The expanded rubric started with a reading lesson from a traditional version of a familiar story, *Goldilocks and the Three Bears*. Robbin led the students through the creation of a story map which included the setting, characters, problem (plot), and solution. On the following day, she read aloud a different version of the story, *Somebody and the Three Blairs* (Tolhurst, 1990). She asked the students to think about, "How can you show your understanding of this new story? How does this story compare with the traditional version?" She and the students generated ideas, which she listed on the board. Most of the ideas represented activities that students had done previously as learning exercises.

- Do a story map for the new story.
- Write a new ending for either story with an illustration.
- Do a Venn diagram comparing the two stories; include illustrations to show comparisons.
- Do a Venn diagram comparing a character from each story, include illustrations to show comparisons.

In addition to the list, Robbin told the students that they could add any other ideas that they might think of later. Next came the development of an open-ended rubric. Through the discussion and questioning process that Robbin had promoted and developed with her students, she and the class designed a rubric. At this point she wanted to be less in control of orchestrating the mode of the outcomes and to have her students move in the direction of making decisions about how to express their knowledge. Students linked the performance levels to the requirements on the board. They began to broaden the field when a student asked, "Could I tell my ending on the tape recorder and then write it down?" Robbin asked the class, "Would that satisfy the requirements?" The class decided that it would, provided that an illustration was included. Again the lesson was aligned to the California Standards in Language Arts. Table 3 is the expanded version of a teacher- and student-generated rubric.

Through the use of this more expanded form of rubric, Robbin found that both her lower achieving students and higher achieving students were able to be successful in showing their knowledge. By having the liberty to demonstrate their knowledge through their different learning styles, Robbin's more capable students were able to take the assignment to an even higher level of performance.

Standards Lead to Thinking

"Learning is a consequence of thinking" (Perkins, 1992, p. 78). Through the use of

Table 3
Expanded rubric

3 Very best level	2 Okay level	1 Not so good level
• Shows clear understanding • Shows creativity • Illustrations colored with details • Correct spelling • Done on time • Neatly done • Proper heading	• Some understanding • A little creativity • A few colors and details • Some spelling errors • Done on time–1 day late • Not neatest work • Proper heading	• Not so clear understanding • Little or no creativity • Little coloring & details • Many spelling errors • More than 1 day late • Sloppy work • May have proper heading

rubrics, Robbin has invited her students to think more deeply about their learning. Robbin has expanded her use of rubrics to include teaching math processes, science, and social studies. The use of rubrics has become an integral part of the set of strategies she uses to assist children in concept attainment and also to assess their learning. Bringing students into the development of the criteria, like bringing them into the development of their personal portfolios, supports them in their abilities to build their own performance standards (Danielson, 1996).

When students complete an assignment or a physical product, teachers have specific criteria or standards for the designation as "best work." Students also need such standards for making the distinction between a best product, an acceptable, or an unacceptable product. When students begin to see this distinction and examples of exemplary work, their own standards tend to increase (Danielson, 1996). Involving students in this process of self-evaluation empowers them in the development of critical thinking skills.

The classroom teacher may use rubrics as a tool for teaching concepts or for assessing what students know about a subject. This process takes time and preparation. It is begun by modeling the thinking that goes into the development of criteria. Then students are brought into the creation of a class rubric. Students also need assisted practice in looking at samples of work at each level to begin to make comparisons and to determine the elements that demonstrate a high-quality, acceptable, or less than acceptable product.

The strength of using rubrics as a learning situation or as an assessment strategy lies in its success in developing metacognitive skills; this ability to think about one's thinking is critical in a world of continuous change. Through metacognition, students can develop those skills that are transferable to new learning situations (Abbott, 1997). Students in Robbin's room have increased confidence in their ability to learn because they are in a classroom where they help develop the standards for work that demonstrates knowledge of the concepts.

Robbin uses the scored rubrics as "a starting point for additional instruction." After assigning scores, she confers with students to have them "discover" why they earned the scores. "Sometimes I show a student who has received a lower score a number 3 paper, and we discuss the gaps and matches between their paper and the higher paper. Sometimes I give them the chance to do the assignment again, and other times we just try to apply the findings to the next assignment."

This process can be modified to meet the needs of children of all abilities, and is especially effective with second-language learners due to the repetition and the variety of ways the concepts are presented. Robbin stressed the importance of the development of the sense of community, which is essential for creating a low-anxiety environment. The repeated practice of working through the setting of criteria and the modeling done by the classroom teacher all contribute to the effectiveness of the process for all learners.

Students' responses to the use of rubrics are the most revealing. "You mean all I have to do to get the best grade is what we wrote?" Students in Robbin's room are using rubrics to assess the quality of their work and reflect on any gaps in their knowledge or missing elements and to search for ways they can improve. Her students frequently raise their hands and ask if they should develop rubrics as a next step. They are actively engaged in finding solutions for working out the tangles of new learning.

References

Abbott, J. (1997). To be intelligent. *Educational Leadership, 54*, 6–10.

California Department of Education Elementary Grades Task Force. (1992). Measures for success. *It's Elementary!*, 65–71.

The Commission for the Establishment of Academic Content and Performance Standards. (1998). *California academic standards for the language arts: Reading, writing, listening and speaking content standards for grades K–12*. Sacramento, CA: Author.

Danielson, C. (1996). Designing rubrics for authentic assessment. *Education Update ASCD Conference Report on Teaching & Learning Assessment, 38*, 1–2.

Perkins, D. (1992). *Smart schools. From training memories to educating minds.* New York: Free Press.

Stiggins, R. (1997). *Student-centered classroom assessment.* Columbus, OH: Merrill.

Tierney, R.J., Readence, J., & Dishner, E. (1995). *Reading strategies and practices.* Needham Heights, MA: Allyn & Bacon.

Tolhurst, M. (1990). *Somebody and the three Blairs.* New York: Orchard.

Wiggins, G. (1989). Teaching to the (authentic) test. *Educational Leadership, 46,* 41–47.

Performance Assessments in Reading and Language Arts

John T. Guthrie, Peggy Van Meter, and Ann Mitchell

Teachers are inventing a wide variety of exciting new ways to integrate reading and writing instruction into the teaching of literature, history, geography, and science. These integrations reflect the view that reading and writing are inextricably linked to knowledge, strategies, and dispositions for learning. Teachers see students as builders and explorers who use resources including texts, peers, and experience to discover meaning and solve self-defined problems. For these teachers, traditional assessments seem incomplete. When instruction is based on trade books, group thinking activities, and projects that may involve the home and community, traditional assessments often fail to capture students' motivational development and higher-order competencies. In this column, we discuss a performance assessment designed to reflect a wide spectrum of literacy processes that appear in an integrated curriculum (Grant, Guthrie, Bennett, Rice, & McGough, 1993).

What Is a Performance Assessment in Reading?

Our performance assessment in reading has three fundamental qualities. First, the assessment is instructional, simulating the teaching environment that we maintain in the classroom. As students participate in the assessment, they interact with texts, draw, write, and use their newfound knowledge to solve problems in ways that parallel the typical instructional unit. Consistent with classroom instruction, we expect students to learn, and we record the new concepts they acquire. The assessment is a small unit of instruction for both the students and teachers.

Second, this performance assessment is realistic. It is a mirror of classroom literacy, reflecting authentic and regularly occurring tasks in reading, writing, and problem solving. In integrated curricula, students may write observations from a field trip into a journal, read journals to each other, discuss trade books on topics observed in the field trip, and develop ways to teach what they have learned to other students. Similar connections across learning activities are part of this performance assessment in reading.

Third, this performance assessment provides a public record of tasks students have accomplished. The task in this assessment includes a text (something to read), a response to the text (a way of writing or expressing understanding), and a quality statement (which describes the student performance). This sequence of tasks brings literacy learning to light, enabling students, teachers, and others to observe students as they interact with instruction.

What Does Student Performance Look Like?

This performance assessment accompanies an integrated curriculum, Concept-Oriented Reading Instruction (CORI; Grant et al., 1993), for the third and fifth grades in two schools. Topics used for the assessments include owls, phases of the moon, trees, tides, ponds, and simple machines. To chart growth, we use two topics, one that is closely tied to the curriculum and a second that

From *The Reading Teacher*, *48*(3), 266–271.

is less related to it. This permits teachers to see content-based gains as well as generalized gains in reading strategies. Our performance assessments are designed to enable students to perform seven distinct but connected tasks: (1) statement of prior knowledge (stating what they know about the topic), (2) searching (finding resources and ideas about the topic), (3) drawing (expressing what they have learned through drawing), (4) writing (communicating their learning through composition), (5) problem solving (addressing a related problem using conceptual knowledge learned during the unit), (6) informational text comprehension (understanding an expository text related to the theme), and (7) narrative text comprehension (understanding and responding to a literary text on the theme of the unit).

These assessments are conducted in classrooms as instructional units lasting 4–6 days. One teacher began the performance assessment on owls and how they adapt to their environment by asking the whole class what they knew about owls. Discussion was brief and did not convey new information to students. The teacher then moved the class into Stage 1 and asked students to write down their prior knowledge by responding to the question: "What are the different parts of an owl and how do these parts help it live?" We will follow two third-grade students, Sandra and William, as they perform each of the tasks.

Stage 1: Statement of prior knowledge. Sandra recorded her prior knowledge as follows (we have not edited this excerpt): "A owl can eat a lot of food. The owl lives like people. The eat corn. He can live like people. The owl will live good like people."

The quality of the student's performance on each stage is judged using a rubric, which distinguishes lower levels of quality from higher levels of quality. Rubrics enable us to chart student growth, to profile a student's strengths and weaknesses, and to discuss the effectiveness of instruction. Here we present the general rubric for each stage, although specific rubrics for each topic are also needed for complete coding. We created five levels for most rubrics and assigned points to each level.

The rubric for statement of prior knowledge was:

1. No conception (student writes nothing at all or the answer does not contain information relevant to the question).
2. Preconception (student may list objects or parts and their functions may be vaguely described; the answer is scientifically incorrect but demonstrates an understanding that there are relationships among objects or events relevant to the concept).
3. Partial conception (student answer is scientifically correct and shows a limited understanding of some of the relationships among a few of the relevant objects or events but the statements are vague).
4. Incomplete conception (student answer is scientifically correct, shows an understanding of relationships among many but not all of the relevant objects or events, and the relationships are clear but incomplete).
5. Full conception (student answer is scientifically correct, shows an understanding of relationships among all important objects or events, and the relationships are depicted in clear and complete form).

Sandra's statement of prior knowledge was a Preconception, which we assigned a level of 2. An example of an Incomplete conception (4) was given by William, whose statement was that: "the eyes help it see at night to catch its prey and he takes his prey with his clawed feet and he swoops to get it with his giant wings."

William's prior knowledge contained an understanding of several parts of the owl and the survival value of these parts.

Stage 2: Search. Next, we gave students a booklet containing 12 selections of text, which simulated the format of a trade book, containing a table of contents, index, glossary, and chapter headings. Each selection was a 1–3 page excerpt from a trade book on the topic of birds. Half of the selections were relevant to the question (What are the different parts of an owl and how do these parts help it live?) and half were not. As the students read through the packets, they maintained a log to record the packet they were reading, why they chose the packet, and what they learned from it. We gave students a form for their logs, divided into sections 1–8, one for each packet they read, as illustrated here. We did not have 12 sections because we did not expect third graders to read all 12 packets.

Sandra's search log looked like Table 1.

To describe the quality of search for information we coded the logs into five levels:

Table 1
Sandra's search log

A Packet letter	B Why did you pick this packet?	C What did you learn from this packet?
1. D	The owl eat a lot of mouse and can get quiet	I learn the owls can get quiet mouse and eat the mouse to
2.	mouse to Because it is a good	and owls do not miss a thing.
3. B	Birds can fly to trees and some Birds can not fly to a trees.	King Birds, the mother a father will have the baby and Be it will Be Birds.
4.	I put this is about Birds mother has the baby	I put this about the father go get the Baby and get and love.
5.		
6. A	Introducing like to end fish and like to eat Sea birds.	it eat a lot to like and eat fish to like.
7.		
8.		

1. No search (no evidence of search or selection of materials).
2. Minimum (students chose at least two relevant packets as well as some irrelevant ones, took good notes from one packet, and gave one clear reason for choosing one of the packets).
3. Moderate (students chose at least three relevant packets and very few irrelevant ones with appropriate reasons for their selections and good notes on two packets).
4. Adequate (students chose at least four relevant packets with few or no irrelevant ones, giving clear reasons for all their selections and clear notes).
5. Proficient (students selected all of the relevant packets with no irrelevant ones and all of their notes were related to the theme. Their reasons for choosing packets were diverse, and their notes showed that they learned during the course of the reading and note taking activity).

Sandra's log of her activities (rated a 2) contained two packets that were related to the theme. She did not, however, know the difference between a reason for choosing a packet and what she learned from the texts that she chose. Sandra's notes from the first packet clearly stated that owls can "get a quiet mouse and eat the mouse." But her notes from the second packet were not highly elaborated beyond the notion that birds have babies. This was a Minimum search (2).

William used a more well-developed search strategy than Sandra. The log of his activities, which is given in Table 2, was rated Adequate (4).

Table 2
William's log of activities

A Packet letter	B Why did you pick this packet?	C What did you learn from this packet?
1. D	I picked it because it tells alot about owls and how they are.	I learned that owls can see in the dark and I learned that they can twist there head all the way around. I also learned that they can twist it.
2. I	I picked it because I shows you how birds get their food.	I learned that birds need their sharp claws to get their food.
3. G	I pick this packet because it tells how birds feed their babies	I learned that birds feed their babies by dropping worms, insects, and bread in their mouth.
4. H	I picked it because it tells (no continuation)	I learned that they need their feet to help them swim.

William chose four packets related to the theme and no irrelevant ones. He showed that he could distinguish the reasons for his choices from what he had learned from the texts. He first learned about how owls see in the dark and turn their heads around. From the next packet he learned that owls use their claws during hunting. From the third text he learned that birds feed babies by dropping food into their mouths, and last he discovered that different birds have different types of feet which are adapted to their environments.

Stage 3: Drawing. After students searched for information, we asked them to make a picture that showed everything they knew about owls. These third graders were asked to make a drawing to teach second graders about owls, without using their notes. We described the quality of student drawings with the same rubric used for describing their statements of prior knowledge: No conception, Preconception, Partial conception, Incomplete conception, and Full conception. Sandra's drawing was a Preconception (2) because she presents some of the parts of the owl, but the functions are not described and the relationships among the parts were vague (see Figure). William's drawing was an Incomplete Conception (4). It is scientifically correct and it shows an understanding of relationships among parts of an owl, but his drawing omitted several parts of the owl that were described in the text. Because this part of the assessment focused on students' understanding, we accepted invented spelling and punctuation.

Stage 4: Writing. We next asked students to write a statement that showed their understanding of the topic using their drawing and what they remembered. As in the Concept-Oriented Reading Instruction, we did not encourage copying or rote learning. Students were expected to construct and reorganize their thoughts continually to express them in writing, without using notes from their search activity. Sandra's written statement of how the parts of an owl help it to live was the following: "The owl can see thing and get the thing and it eat them. Owl like mouse and water and owl can get quite thing. Owl eat a lot to be love and live from food and can fly to and fly to a tree and like tree to and eat thing in tree. I thing owl will like it."

Using the same rubric that we used to describe prior knowledge, we classified Sandra's written understanding as a Partial conception (3). Comparing Sandra's written statement to her prior knowledge, we can see that she gained conceptual knowledge during the assessment. As the notes in her search log indicate, she learned that owls have exceptional eyes for hunting mice.

William's written understanding was an Incomplete conception (4) as follows: "The eyes help it see in the dark. A hooked beak to tear meat in half and a long wing span help it fly swiftly. The claws help catch mice and hang on branches."

Although William understood the owl as a predator more fully than Sandra at the time of the writing task, Sandra learned more new concepts during the assessment than William. William's task performance does not give evidence that he gained conceptual knowledge about owls.

Stage 5: Problem solving. Students then used their knowledge to write a solution to a new problem: "Suppose you saw a type of owl that was blind. But these owls are living a very good life. What things would these owls have to be good at to be able to keep living? What would the body parts of these owls be like? Please explain your answer."

Sandra wrote, "The owl can hear thing but this is not so good. I will like to know what can do when owl are blind. I will not like to be blind. I will like to know how it is some owl have friend and friend like to help people. Maybe the friend will help her or him see thing and hear thing and eat thing. I think owl will not go out in the day and will be wild."

During her search activity, Sandra learned that owls could see even in the dark and capture "quiet things." In the new problem when the owl was deprived of sight, Sandra could not employ the concept of adaptation to generate newly developed senses for the owl, although she understood that such information was called for. She solved the owl's problem by giving the owl a friend.

Students' drawings about owls

Although Sandra was aware that the question called for information about the senses and their adaptations, her solution did not illustrate the concepts of adaptation of body parts to the environment. In contrast, William solved the new problem by writing: "he will have to hear his prey and then catch it, if it was a great horned owl he would have to keep his tufts of feathers up so that he could signal his family, maybe he would have to use his wings to feel around when he is flying, maybe he could smell where his prey is in the woods."

The rubric for problem solving consisted of the following:

1. No solution (no answer given).
2. Presolution (solution is scientifically incorrect or not relevant to the problem; some conceptual knowledge of the topic is evident).
3. Partial solution (some objects are present but the concepts are not applied to solving the problem; solution is scientifically correct, but the answer is vague or incomplete).
4. Incomplete solution (all objects and/or events are present and the concepts are related to solving the problem, but the answer is incomplete or vague).
5. Full solution (all objects and events are present; the concepts are fully applied and the answer is complete).

In solving the new problem, Sandra's notion that the owl could make friends which would help her see things was not realistic (a Presolution 2), although she showed that serious adjustments would have to take place. William's solution contained the generative concept that adaptations of other senses such as hearing and feeling in the wings would increase to help support the owl in hunting. But his statement was an Incomplete solution (4) because there are many other adaptations that might have been included.

Stage 6: Informational text comprehension. During the search stage of the assessment, different students use different text selections and their notes may not reflect their full comprehension of the material. A relatively low level search performance may reflect a low text-selection strategy or low text comprehension ability or both. because text comprehension is fundamental, we gave students two tasks. One was a short informational text containing related illustrations. The accompanying question required students to integrate information from both the text and the illustration. This informational text explained the development of a bird inside an egg.

The rubric to describe the quality of students' responses to informational text was:

1. No answer (no answer; answer relies on prior knowledge not related to the text; or information is incorrect, nonspecific, or verbatim copy).
2. Accurate (response accurately integrates information from two or more parts of the text).
3. Elaborated (response connects an integrated statement with additional information in the text that elaborates, explains, or contextualizes the statement).

Sandra's response was not related to the text, nor was it very coherent (No answer 1): "I now that egg has a red line on the yolk and the egg will have to get water a food to grow and you can see the hen babyes and the baby can float in the egg."

William's response was based on appropriate segments of text, and he added shape and color (Elaborated 3): "inside of an egg is a baby chick and yolk for the baby to eat. The baby looks like a bird. the yolk is light yellow."

Stage 7: Narrative text comprehension. Students read a 350-word excerpt from "Izzard the Lizard," a story in which a girl brings to the classroom a lizard that entertains and distracts the students. Three questions required the students to: (a) reproduce a brief portion of text from memory, (b) give an explanation for an important event, and (c) provide a personal reaction to a character, event, or theme. We include narrative because our integrated curriculum contains literary as well as informational books.

Quality of narrative comprehension was judged with a rubric based on responses to all of the questions. Student responses to the reproductive, explanatory, and open-extension questions were rated as appropriate (accurate and text-based) or elaborated (embellished with details and characterizations). The scoring scheme was: 1—no appropriate responses; 2—one appropriate response; 3—two appropriate responses; 4—three appropriate responses; 5—three appropriate responses and at least two elaborated responses. Although all of the responses cannot be given here, Sandra received an overall score of 1 and William received a 4.

To the question, "Why couldn't Izzard go to school anymore?" Sandra wrote, "I thing the Izzard will be good but it will be log and the teacher will be happy."

William said, "Because the class wasn't waching the teacher. they where waching Izzard."

What Are the Advantages of a Performance Assessment and Who Does It Help?

Developing an assessment challenged us to examine our teaching aims and objectives. We clarified what we wanted students to learn and what evidence we would accept as indicators that they had learned. This process helped us to understand where we were going in our teaching as well as where our students had been in their learning (Gaskins et al., 1994). Many of these instructional benefits are shared with portfolio assessment (Valencia & Place, 1993). This performance assessment can be placed in a student's portfolio, providing a common task that permits teachers to compare students and to chart growth over time.

Students benefit from this assessment because they can use the tasks as a basis for their own self-appraisal. Students can reflect on whether they used their background knowledge in their search and whether they applied their search findings to their writing and problem solving. We believe that administrators and policy makers may benefit from performance assessments, too, because the assessments reflect the shape of the curriculum and teachers' aspirations for authentic learning. By communicating the outcomes of the assessment to administrators as well as to other teachers, we have been able to make public the higher-order accomplishments of our students on a diversity of important and realistic tasks. We believe that a performance assessment that simulates instruction can be a stage where schooling and its appraisal are acted out together.

What Are the Demands on and Responsibilities of Teachers Who Want to Conduct This Performance Assessment?

One teacher can design, administer, and evaluate the results of this performance assessment, but the demands on the teacher's time will be prohibitive. We recommend that a group of teachers with similar curricula and goals at a given grade level, perhaps across several schools, join together to develop a performance assessment. A cluster of teachers within a school or an entire district may design, administer, score, interpret, and report a performance assessment. The assessment presented in this article may be used as a starting point for the development of instructional assessments that are tailored to the curricula, student populations, and cultural contexts of particular schools or districts.

References

Gaskins, I.W., Guthrie, J.T., Satlow, E., Ostertag, J., Six, L., Byrne, J., et al. (1994). Integrating instruction of science, reading, and writing: Goals, teacher development, and assessment. *Journal of Research in Science Teaching, 31*(9), 1039-1056.

Grant, R., Guthrie, J., Bennett, L., Rice, M.E., & McGough, K. (1993). Developing engaged readers through concept-oriented reading instruction. *The Reading Teacher, 47*, 338-340.

Valencia, S.W., & Place, N. (1993). Literacy portfolios for teaching, learning and accountability: The Bellevue literacy assessment project. In S.W. Valencia, E.F. Hiebert, & P.A. Afflerbach (Eds.), *Authentic reading assessment* (pp. 134-167). Newark, DE: International Reading Association.

Formal Assessment Tools

- What are the benefits of using formal, measurement-type assessment tools with students? Do they invite unwanted comparisons? When can comparison be helpful to achievement? When can it be problematic?
- What dimensions of oral language development are relevant to literacy development? How can you assess this development?
- What is phonological awareness? How do you assess it, and what instruction supports students' phonological awareness?
- How does phonics assessment differ from a test of phonemic awareness?
- Why include children's attitudes toward reading in an assessment system?
- How can data on readers' self-perceptions be used to improve instruction?

Each of the five articles in this section presents a formal, or measurement-oriented, assessment protocol to use with individuals or whole groups. Subjected to the rigors of validation and reliability, each assessment instrument can be administered with confidence by teachers to systematically uncover what students know and are able to do and to plan for instruction.

The first instrument, Teacher Rating of Oral Language and Literacy (TROLL), is designed to track several dimensions of language progress for young children. This assessment tool not only effectively taps many language abilities that support literacy achievement but is also realistic for teachers to administer. As David K. Dickinson, Allyssa McCabe, and Kim Sprague report on TROLL, they also reveal how a teacher uses assessment results to change her instructional practice—thus increasing language-learning opportunities for her students with the most language challenges.

Phonological awareness is a dimension of early literacy that is now measured in nearly every early childhood educational setting. Because of its high level of validity and reliability and ease to administer and interpret, the Yopp–Singer Test of Phoneme Segmentation is a respected and widely used test for assessing children's phonemic awareness. According to Hallie Kay Yopp, one of the purposes of pinpointing a child's phonemic awareness is to design active, playful, and meaningful instruction that draws attention to "the sound structure of language."

Direct and systematic phonics instruction is once again prominent in reading education. The Tile Test, developed by Kimberly A. Norman and Robert C. Calfee, is designed to reveal a picture of young learners' understanding of phonics. The Tile Test recording sheet, administration guidelines, and scoring information support test implementation. Explanation of how test results applied to two students reveals how teachers can use test information to support literacy learning.

The Elementary Reading Attitude Survey, now a classic assessment tool, was developed by Michael C. McKenna and Dennis J. Kear. This efficient and reliable public domain instrument enables teachers to estimate the attitude level of students about reading. Garfield, the comic strip character created by Jim Davis, depicts four emotions repeatedly used throughout the survey to represent the choice of attitudes for each survey item. The collected data help teachers make observations such as a discrepancy between a student's reading ability and attitude. McKenna and Kear illustrate ways to think about the results and possibilities for monitoring attitudinal changes.

In the tradition of McKenna and Kear, William A. Henk and Steven A. Melnick developed a normed, valid, reliable, and easy to administer affective reading survey. Their survey, aimed for use with students in grades 4 through 6, focuses on students' self-perceptions, or self-efficacy. Henk and Melnick relate how a fourth-grade teacher used the perception scale to monitor change in students' affect and how she adjusted instruction for individual readers using results from the assessment.

Additional Reading

- Bottomley, D.M., Henk, W.A., & Melnick, S.A. (1997/1998). Assessing children's views about themselves as writers using the Writer Self-Perception Scale. *The Reading Teacher*, *51*(4), 286–296.
- Clay, M.M. (1985). *The early detection of reading difficulties* (3rd ed.). Portsmouth, NH: Heinemann.
- Clay, M.M. (1993). *An observation survey of early literacy achievement*. Portsmouth, NH: Heinemann.
- Gambrell, L.B., Palmer, B.M., Codling, R.M., & Mazzoni, S.A. (1996). Assessing motivation to read. *The Reading Teacher*, *49*(7), 518–533.
- Kear, D.J., Coffman, G.A., McKenna, M.C., & Ambrosio, A.L. (2000). Measuring attitudes towards writing: A new tool for teachers. *The Reading Teacher*, *54*(1), 10–23.

- Kern, D., Andre, D., Schilke, R., Barton, J., & McGuide, M.C. (2003). Less is more: Preparing students for state writing assessments. *The Reading Teacher, 56*(8), 816–826.
- Langdon, T. (2004). DIBELS: A teacher-friendly literacy accountability tool for the primary classroom. *Teaching Exceptional Children, 37*(2), 54–58.
- New Standards for Speaking and Listening Committee. (2001). *New standards for speaking and listening for preschool through third grade*. Philadelphia: National Center on Education and the University of Pennsylvania.
- Schmitt, M.C. (1990). A questionnaire to measure children's awareness of strategic reading processes. *The Reading Teacher, 43*(7), 454–461.

Create a Statement of Reading Assessment Principles and Practices

Previously you listed your required and choice assessment tools and selected one tool to develop into an assessment partnership with students. Review your lists of assessment tools. Do they include any formal assessments, as described in this section? If so, using the information presented on teachers in these articles, identify ways you can strengthen your use of your formal assessments. Or, select one of the formal assessments in this section. Incorporate it into your assessment toolbox. Develop a plan for administration and anticipate how you could use the results. For example, you might administer the "Garfield Survey" to a student or group of students. Analyze the results collectively and individually. How might you use the survey to confer with a student, or a parent? Pull one survey example and practice talking about it with a peer.

Teacher Rating of Oral Language and Literacy (TROLL): Individualizing Early Literacy Instruction With a Standards-Based Rating Tool

David K. Dickinson, Allyssa McCabe, and Kim Sprague

Keisha is a quiet little girl with tawny skin, long black hair, and large brown eyes. Her teacher has observed that she is shy with other children, reluctant to participate in groups, and often the last to join in activities, but the teacher never has had to reprimand Keisha. Only when the teacher sat down to fill out reports on the language development of each of her students did she realize Keisha has a problem.

CJ is an energetic almost 5-year-old African American boy who attends childcare from 7:00 a.m. to 4:00 p.m. five days a week. His teacher observed that "CJ has demonstrated strong use of his oral language skills since entering my program. CJ speaks clearly and is easily understood by adults." The teacher was enrolled in a college course that focused on enriching children's language and literacy skills. She noticed after completing the TROLL assessment of CJ that he did not always choose to attend to stories in large group and appeared most interested in stories when reading one-on-one or in a small group of no more than three other children where he was able to ask questions as a way to clarify the meaning of a story. She suggested to his mother that his older brothers be encouraged to read to him at home. She also noted that his scores on the language and reading subtotals of the TROLL were high—higher than his writing subtotal—and she was knowledgeable about his exact writing skills and limitations.

Reading, Writing, and Oral Language: Roots of Literacy

Early reading and writing abilities are by now well-known dimensions of early literacy. Through their preschool years, children progressively construct understandings of writing (e.g., Bissex, 1980) and reading (e.g., Sulzby & Teale, 1991). Similarly, the contribution of children's phonological awareness has often been explored and is also widely recognized (Bryant, MacLean, & Bradley, 1990; Cronin & Carver, 1998; Speece, Roth, Cooper, & de la Paz, 1999; Stanovich, 1992; Vellutino & Scanlon, 2001; Wagner, Torgesen, Laughon, Simmons, & Rashotte, 1993; Wagner et al., 1997).

However, there are other lesser known oral language skills relevant to literacy that include the development of narrative ability (Dickinson & Tabors, 2001; see McCabe & Rollins, 1991, for review), use of talk while pretending (Dickinson, 2001; see Pelligrini & Galda, 1993, for review), and varied vocabulary usage (Tabors, Beals, & Weizman, 2001). To be able to read and write effectively, children must develop strong oral language skills (Dickinson &

From *The Reading Teacher*, 56(6), 554-564. © 2003 by the International Reading Association.

McCabe, 1991; Dickinson & Tabors, 2001; Snow, 1983; Snow, Burns, & Griffin, 1998). Oral language skills blossom during the preschool years, but they are also very vulnerable and in need of stimulation during this time, as a number of major organizations involved in the education of young children have recognized.

A Call for Developmentally Appropriate Assessment

The International Reading Association (IRA) and the National Association for the Education of Young Children (NAEYC) jointly formulated a position statement regarding early literacy development (1998). The statement acknowledges the difficulty that teachers face, for example, in kindergarten classrooms where a five-year range in children's literacy skills is not uncommon (Riley, 1996). Estimating where each child is in terms of the acquisition of speaking, listening, reading, and writing skills is critical to providing developmentally appropriate instruction to all children in this wide range. The position statement is quite clear that

> throughout these critical years *accurate assessment* of children's knowledge, skills, and dispositions in reading and writing will help teachers better match instruction with how and what children are learning. However, early reading and writing cannot simply be measured as a set of narrowly defined skills on standardized tests. These measures often are not reliable or valid indicators of what children can do in typical practice, nor are they sensitive to language variation, culture, or the experiences of young children. (International Reading Association & National Association for the Education of Young Children, 1998, p. 38; emphasis added)

As if these difficulties were not enough, preschool teachers face time constraints and typically have not been trained to evaluate children's language development as it relates to the acquisition of literacy or their emergent reading and writing skills. In response to this need, we present an accessible means of evaluating each child in a classroom for literacy-related abilities. One way to help teachers track children's development is by periodic reflection on demonstrations of early literacy. Even though teachers may lack prior formal training regarding assessment of language and literacy development, we have found that they can recognize critical aspects of this development. Using the Teacher Rating of Oral Language and Literacy (TROLL) to evaluate children can help teachers assess the effectiveness of an educational program.

New Standards: Speaking and Listening for Preschool Through Third Grade

Because speaking and listening are so critical for literacy development in early childhood, the New Standards project, a program of the National Center on Education and the Economy (Tucker & Codding, 1998), has developed research-based standards for speaking and listening in preschool through third grade (New Standards Speaking and Listening Committee, 2001). These standards complement those already developed for reading and writing. The speaking and listening standards include specific recommendations for teachers regarding beneficial habits of conversation, useful kinds of talk such as narratives and explanations, and language conventions relevant to early childhood. Many programs are concerned with ensuring that their students meet such national standards.

Development of TROLL

To guide teachers' observations of children's individual language and literacy skills and interests, we created an instrument that focuses on key abilities. In constructing this tool, we drew on the same body of theory and research that was the foundation for the speaking and listening standards. Indeed, we contributed to both efforts. TROLL is a tool developed by the first author to provide teachers with a way to track the language and literacy skills and interests of children in their classrooms and is represented in its entirety in Table 1. Although it was developed for

Table 1
Teacher Rating of Oral Language and Literacy (TROLL)

Language use

1. How would you describe this child's willingness to **start a conversation** with adults and peers and continue trying to communicate when he or she is not understood on the first attempt? Select the statement that best describes how hard the child works to be understood by others.

Child almost never begins a conversation with peers or the teacher and never keeps trying if unsuccessful at first.	Child sometimes begins conversation with either peers or the teacher. If initial efforts fail he or she often gives up quickly.	Child begins conversations with both peers and teachers on occasion. If initial efforts fail, he or she will sometimes keep trying.	Child begins conversations with both peers and teachers. If initial efforts fail, he or she will work hard to be understood.
1	2	3	4

2. How well does the child **communicate personal experiences** in a clear and logical way? Assign the score that best describes this child when he or she is attempting to tell an adult about events that happened at home or some other place where you were not present.

Child is very tentative, only offers a few words, requires you to ask questions, has difficulty responding to questions you ask.	Child offers some information, but information needed to really understand the event is missing (e.g., where or when it happened, who was present, the sequence of what happened).	Child offers information and sometimes includes the necessary information to understand the event fully.	Child freely offers information and tells experiences in a way that is nearly always complete, well sequenced, and comprehensible.
1	2	3	4

3. How would you describe this child's pattern of **asking questions** about topics that interest him or her (e.g., why things happen, why people act the way they do)? Assign the score that best describes the child's approach to displaying curiosity by asking adults questions.

To your knowledge, the child has never asked an adult a question reflecting curiosity about why things happen or why people do things.	On a few occasions the child has asked adults some questions. The discussion that resulted was brief and limited in depth.	On several occasions the child has asked interesting questions. On occasion these have lead to an interesting conversation.	Child often asks adults questions reflecting curiosity. These often lead to interesting, extended conversations.
1	2	3	4

(continued)

Table 1 (continued)
Teacher Rating of Oral Language and Literacy (TROLL)

4. How would you describe this child's use of talk while **pretending** in the house area or when playing with blocks? Consider the child's use of talk with peers to start pretending and to carry it out. Assign the score that best applies.

Child rarely or never engages in pretend play or else never talks while pretending.	On occasion the child engages in pretending that includes some talk. Talk is brief, may only be used when starting the play, and is of limited importance to the ongoing play activity.	Child engages in pretending often and conversations are sometimes important to the play. On occasion child engages in some back-and-forth pretend dialogue with another child.	Child often talks in elaborate ways while pretending. Conversations that are carried out "in role" are common and are an important part of the play. Child sometimes steps out of pretend play to give directions to another.
1	2	3	4

5. How would you describe the child's ability to **recognize and produce rhymes**?

Child cannot ever say if two words rhyme and cannot produce a rhyme when given examples (e.g., rat, cat).	Child occasionally produces or identifies rhymes when given help.	Child spontaneously produces rhymes and can sometimes tell when word pairs rhyme.	Child spontaneously rhymes words of more than one syllable and always identifies whether words rhyme.
1	2	3	4

6. How often does child use a **varied vocabulary** or try out new words (e.g., heard in stories or from teacher)?

Never	Rarely	Sometimes	Often
1	2	3	4

7. When child speaks to adults other than you or the teaching assistant, **is he or she understandable**?

Never	Rarely	Sometimes	Often
1	2	3	4

8. How often does child **express curiosity** about how and why things happen?

Never	Rarely	Sometimes	Often
1	2	3	4

Language subtotal __________

(continued)

Table 1 (continued)
Teacher Rating of Oral Language and Literacy (TROLL)

Reading

9. How often does child like to hear books read in the full group?

Never	Rarely	Sometimes	Often
1	2	3	4

10. How often does child attend to stories read in the full group or small groups and react in a way that indicates comprehension?

Never	Rarely	Sometimes	Often
1	2	3	4

11. Is child able to read storybooks on his or her own?

Does not pretend to read books	Pretends to read	Pretends to read and reads some words	Reads the written words
1	2	3	4

12. How often does child remember the story line or characters in books that he or she heard before either at home or in class?

Never	Rarely	Sometimes	Often
1	2	3	4

13. How often does child look at or read books alone or with friends?

Never	Rarely	Sometimes	Often
1	2	3	4

14. Can child recognize letters? (choose one answer)
    - None of the letters of the alphabet 1
    - Some of them (up to 10)..2
    - Most of them (up to 20)..3
    - All of them 4

15. Does child recognize his or her own first name in print?

No	Yes
1	2

16. Does child recognize other names?

No	One or two	A few (up to four or five)	Several (six or more)
1	2	3	4

17. Can child read any other words?

No	One or two	A few (up to four or five)	Several (six or more)
1	2	3	4

(continued)

Table 1 (continued)
Teacher Rating of Oral Language and Literacy (TROLL)

18. Does child have a beginning understanding of the relationship between sounds and letters (e.g., the letter *B* makes a "buh" sound)?

No	One or two	A few (up to four or five)	Several (six or more)
1	2	3	4

19. Can child sound out words that he or she has not read before?

No	Once or twice	One syllable words often	Many words
1	2	3	4

Reading subtotal ________

Writing

20. What does child's writing look like?

Only draws or scribbles	Some letter-like marks	Many conventional letters	Conventional letters and words
1	2	3	4

21. How often does child like to write or pretend to write?

Never	Rarely	Sometimes	Often
1	2	3	4

22. Can child write his or her first name, even if some of the letters are backward?

Never	Rarely	Sometimes	Often
1	2	3	4

23. Does child write other names or real words?

No	One or two	A few (up to four or five)	Several (six or more)
1	2	3	4

24. How often does child write signs or labels?

Never	Rarely	Sometimes	Often
1	2	3	4

25. Does child write stories, songs, poems, or lists?

Never	Rarely	Sometimes	Often
1	2	3	4

Writing subtotal ________ (out of 24 possible)
Oral language subtotal ________ (out of 32 possible)
Reading subtotal ________ (out of 42 possible)
Total TROLL score ________ (out of 98 possible)

research purposes separate from the New Standards initiative, TROLL addresses all the central speaking and listening skills in the New Standards, as well as many of the early reading and writing skills covered by the companion reading and writing standards. Of special interest is the fact that it allows teachers to track children's interests in various language and literacy activities—something that no direct assessment tool can capture.

Using TROLL to Inform Instruction

No formal training is required to use the TROLL instrument; however, it is most effective if teachers know about language and literacy development. In other words, TROLL can make knowledgeable teachers better. This tool is designed for classroom teachers to easily track the language and literacy development of all their students. The TROLL requires only 5 to 10 minutes for each child and need not disrupt classroom activities (it can be completed during naptime).

Teachers can use the information to inform their teaching by identifying (a) children who are displaying evidence of serious delay and who may need formal assessment by audiologists or speech-language pathologists and (b) children who are showing high levels of literacy development and therefore need special additional challenges in this area. Furthermore, by completing TROLL several times over the course of a year, teachers can track the progress of all their students.

Second, teachers could combine results for all the children in their class to determine which areas need more systematic instruction. For example, if all children in a class score relatively low on rhymes, their teacher might want to begin providing numerous opportunities to listen to and produce rhyming chants, songs, and poems.

Teachers should consider using TROLL ratings of children as a basis for discussions with parents. In fact, as we saw in the case of CJ at the outset of this article, teachers are likely to initiate such discussions without anyone urging them to do so. (Recall that the teacher recommended that CJ's mother get his older brothers to read with him one-on-one because that was an effective setting for the child.)

Parents can also serve as a source for ratings using the TROLL. In particular, teachers of bilingual children often have a difficult time rating the language competence of children who speak English as a second language (ESL). Of course, if a teacher can rate a child's competence in a language other than English, it would be of great interest to rate the child's skill in both English and his or her first language. Whenever possible, educators need to involve the parents of ESL students. In fact, maternal reports of preschoolers' literacy (when children were 3 or 4 years old) significantly predicted much of the variation in kindergarten tests, grade 1 teacher assessments, and direct assessments of decoding given near the end of first grade (Dickinson & DeTemple, 1998). Thus, if TROLL were used collaboratively with parents, it could provide a powerful way to organize a multifaceted conversation about a child's full range of language and literacy development.

TROLL Has Been Used Extensively

Over the last several years, TROLL has been used with 973 children in the context of research examining early literacy development. Over 100 teachers have been involved in this process.

One measure of a good test is that all items on the test tap related abilities. We analyzed responses for 534 of these preschool children and found strong indications that TROLL meets standards expected of research tools in this regard. Specifically, Cronbach's alpha estimates of internal consistency ranged from .77 to .92 for separate subscales, indicating strong internal consistency. For the total TROLL scores, alphas exceeded .89 for each age.

Another way of determining the value of a tool is the extent to which a child's performance on that tool compares to performance on other measures. After all, TROLL relies on a teacher's professional judgment or perception of a child's development rather than formal testing of actual development. It is therefore reassuring to find that, for this sample, the ratings teachers provided using TROLL compared favorably to formal assessments by researchers. These measures included the well-established Peabody Picture Vocabulary Test (PPVT-III), which is a measure of receptive vocabulary, as well as measures of emergent literacy and early phonological awareness. Teacher ratings of children's language and literacy development on the TROLL show moderate associations with children's scores on all three of those direct assessments despite the fact that teachers never saw those test results. So in about five minutes, and with no special training on the TROLL, teachers themselves can index what specially trained researchers would spend 25–30 minutes per child assessing.

Of course, the TROLL teacher ratings do not agree completely with the researchers' tests. This difference partly reflects the fact that TROLL assesses other factors that teachers take into consideration as they rate individual children—factors that are not captured in the direct, formal assessments. TROLL captures the kind of information the position statement by IRA and NAEYC recommended be captured in assessment. Formal tests measure how well a child does at only one point in time; children may be tired or sick on the day of the PPVT-III assessment and receive a dismal score for their receptive vocabulary, whereas their teacher knows that on most days they are quick to pick up on the vocabulary of classroom units and articulate when sharing stories of personal experience. The TROLL score is not as vulnerable to fluctuations in a child's performance as are the formal tests.

Furthermore, as noted earlier, the TROLL includes information about the child's engagement in literacy activities and patterns of use of oral language. Formal assessments do not tap such interests and inclinations to use language and print in any way. And yet, a child's initiative in this area could be an important determinant of the child's future success.

Overall, children's scores improve from fall to spring. However, the correlations between TROLL scores and direct assessment measures of literacy are generally less reliable in the spring than in the fall, which is just the opposite of what one would predict. After all, teachers have had far more interaction with children—and should therefore be *more* sensitive to their reading and writing skills—in the spring than in the fall. In fact, however, there is no firm correlation between teacher TROLL scores in the spring and formal assessments of children's emergent literacy conducted at that time, although correlations with vocabulary (PPVT) and phonological awareness (EPAP) remain moderately strong. Unfortunately, this may reflect the fact that teachers do not revisit their assessment of children's literacy skills as much as they should. In the fall, teachers may arrive at judgments about a child's accomplishments that they fail to update. Children's progress in language and literacy may go undetected by their teachers. This finding is sobering.

One danger of any judgment is that it can become a self-fulfilling prophecy (Rosenthal & Jacobsen, 1968). Teachers' opinions of children at the very outset of their education can predict children's success just by virtue of the teacher giving extra attention, motivation, or instruction to those children they expect to become the most accomplished. Conversely, teacher expectations—never revisited—can predict other children's failure by virtue of overlooking children expected to fail.

This lack of revision of judgments about literacy skills and interests points to the value of teachers carrying out periodic informal assessments of children to provide concrete evidence of children's growth. For example, teachers can ask children to write their own or others' names or to identify letters in them.

In general, then, rather than contribute to self-fulfilling prophecies of children's success or failure, we hope that TROLL will predict possible failure to learn to read in order to prevent such failure. That is, we hope that teachers will use this instrument to give struggling children the help they need to succeed so that they never have to experience failure at a later point. Specifically, we (Dickinson, 2001) recommend that teachers make sure that one or more adults read with small groups of children every day and ensure that all children have this experience once a week. Teachers can also set aside time when children tell stories. Finally, teachers need to introduce varied and challenging vocabulary as a routine part of the curriculum.

What TROLL Scores Mean

Table 2 displays what different scores on TROLL indicate about a child's overall developmental level. For example, a score of 66 in the spring indicates that the child is making progress that is average for 4-year-olds in this sample. The sample consisted only of low-income children, so these scores should be regarded as provisional. However, we argue that the well-known academic disadvantages of low-socioeconomic status (SES) preschool children (e.g., Stipek & Ryan, 1997) make this sample important in its own right. If a child from a low-SES family scores at the 10th percentile, for example, this result cannot be dismissed as a result of economic disadvantage; such a child is scoring very poorly relative to his or her economic peers. Scores at the 75th and, especially, the 90th percentile, however, should prompt a teacher to provide opportunities for children to read more advanced

Table 2
What TROLL scores mean

3-year-olds' TROLL scores		4-year-olds' TROLL scores		5-year-olds' TROLL scores		Relative standing on the TROLL	Recommendations/ meaning
Fall *n* = 115	Spring *n* = 55	Fall *n* = 336	Spring *n* = 234	Fall *n* = 83	Spring *n* = 229		
40	44	43	46	51	55	10th percentile	Assessment of child by audiologist, speech-language pathologist. Discuss concerns with parents.
44	49	52	55	59	65	25th percentile	Assessment of child by speech-language pathologist, extra involvement in extended conversations, and other literacy activities.
51	56	61	66	68	76	50th percentile	Child is performing at an average level.
61	62	71	74	75	85	75th percentile	Child is performing above average.
68	69	80	84	85	91	90th percentile	Child should be encouraged to read and write at advanced levels in school and at home.

Note. Our data come from a low-income sample. In national studies children from such homes tend to receive less support for early language and literacy development than children from economically advantaged homes. Children from more advantaged backgrounds would be expected to receive somewhat higher ratings than those reported above (roughly 5–6 points higher on average).

books, engage in writing frequently, and talk at length about challenging and interesting topics.

Program Evaluation Potential: TROLL Measures Appropriate Language and Literacy Instruction

As we mentioned, children's scores on TROLL might well serve as an impetus to plan systematic language and literacy instruction for a class. In fact, such instruction has been implemented by a number of Head Start programs in the Boston, Massachusetts, area, where TROLL detected changes that occurred as a result of program improvement efforts. Head Start teachers and their supervisors volunteered to participate in a professional development program called LEEP (Literacy Environment Enrichment Program). They received academic credit for participating in two intensive three-day blocks separated by three months. TROLL scores for children whose teachers participated in LEEP were significantly higher than for children whose teachers did not. Specifically, children in LEEP classrooms gained more overall from fall to spring on average in comparison to a control group.

Furthermore, the classrooms that supported such advances had improved classroom language and literacy practices. Teachers who participated in LEEP made greater efforts to engage children in conversations and to provide opportunities for children to write and to use books. The change that appeared to reflect the most major shift was the extent to which teachers planned activities with the intention of having children practice literacy-related skills. Enriching the literacy environment had one additional effect that might come as a surprise. Children whose teachers participated in LEEP displayed significantly more growth in social skills than their peers, as assessed by the Social Skills Rating System (Gresham & Elliott, 1990). Children who are busy talking, reading, and writing—activities registered by TROLL—were more likely to be viewed by their teachers as developing stronger skills in collaborating with others.

Case Studies

We conclude by returning to Keisha and CJ. Keisha scored the lowest on the TROLL of anyone in her class of 4-year-olds—a total of 44 points. Her teacher realized that she spent far more time talking to Keisha's high-scoring classmates than she did to Keisha. Children who already were the most advanced talkers were the ones who asked questions, participated in group discussions, and took many opportunities to explain activities to other children or tell stories about themselves. The teacher found that in her classroom, as in the classrooms of other preschool teachers (see Dickinson & Tabors, 2001), the old adage of "the rich get richer" applied to language and literacy development. The teacher also realized that several of the children who misbehaved also received low scores, and she made an effort to involve them in more conversations. Two such boys, in particular, seemed to thrive on this extra attention for desirable behavior and were noticeably better behaved by the end of the year.

In the coming weeks, Keisha's teacher made a concentrated effort to involve her in conversation every day. The teacher also shared her TROLL assessment of Keisha with the child's mother, who acknowledged that she had been struggling with a number of issues and had not had much time to talk with Keisha, let alone read with her. The teacher recommended regular trips to the library and setting aside time at meals just to talk about the day. By the end of the year, Keisha was far more talkative and began to initiate looking at books on her own. She did not have to fail at reading in order to get the help she needed to succeed. Keisha benefited from the kind of early intervention strongly recommended by Snow et al. (1998, pp. 318–319).

CJ's teacher responded to his advanced skills (he scored 71, which placed him above the 90th percentile) by making sure that his brothers read to him frequently and by involving him a couple of times a week in small-group book reading, when she encouraged his conversations and explained a number of terms in books that were unfamiliar to him.

Tracking children's language and literacy development is a critical yet challenging task. The TROLL provides one means for teachers to accomplish this and can provide a starting point for productive conversations with colleagues and parents.

References

Bissex, G.L. (1980). *GNYS at wrk: A child learns to write and read.* Cambridge, MA: Harvard.

Bryant, P., MacLean, M., & Bradley, L. (1990). Rhyme, language, and children's reading. *Applied Psycholinguistics, 11*(3), 237-252.

Clay, M.M. (1979). *Stones—The concepts about print test.* Exeter, NH: Heinemann.

Cronin, V., & Carver, P. (1998). Phonological sensitivity, rapid naming, and beginning reading. *Applied Psycholinguistics, 19*(3), 447-462.

Dickinson, D.K. (2001). Large-group and free-play times: Conversational settings supporting language and literacy development. In D.K. Dickinson & P.O. Tabors (Eds.), *Beginning literacy with language* (pp. 223-256). Baltimore, MD: Brookes.

Dickinson, D.K., & DeTemple, J. (1998). Putting parents in the picture: Maternal reports of preschoolers' literacy as a predictor of early reading. *Early Childhood Research Quarterly, 13*(2), 241-263.

Dickinson, D.K., & McCabe, A. (1991). The acquisition and development of language: A social interactionist account of language and literacy development. In J.F. Kavanagh (Ed.), *The language continuum from infancy to literacy* (pp. 1-40). Parkton, MD: York.

Dickinson, D.K., & Tabors, P.O. (2001). *Beginning literacy with language: Young children learning at home and school.* Baltimore, MD: Brookes.

Gresham, F.M., & Elliott, S.N. (1990). *Social skills rating system: Ages 3-5.* Circle Pines, MN: American Guidance Service.

International Reading Association & National Association for the Education of Young Children. (1998). Learning to read and write: Developmentally appropriate practices for young children. *Young Children, 53*(4), 30-46.

McCabe, A., & Dickinson, D.K. (2001, Summer). Good talk, close listening: Laying solid foundations for literacy. *Children and Families*, pp. 21-22.

McCabe, A., & Rollins, P.R. (1991). *Assessment of preschool narrative skills: Prerequisite for literacy.* Miniseminar presented at the Annual Convention of the American Speech-Language-Hearing Association, Atlanta, GA.

New Standards for Speaking and Listening Committee. (2001). *New standards for speaking and listening for preschool through third grade.* Philadelphia: National Center on Education and the University of Pennsylvania.

Pellegrini, A.D., & Galda, L. (1993). Ten years after: A reexamination of symbolic play and literacy research. *Reading Research Quarterly, 28*, 162-175.

Riley, J. (1996). *The teaching of reading.* London: Paul Chapman.

Rosenthal, R., & Jacobsen, L. (1968). *Pygmalion in the classroom: Teacher expectation and pupils' intellectual development.* New York: Holt, Rinehart and Winston.

Snow, C.E. (1983). Literacy and language: Relationships during the preschool years. *Harvard Educational Review, 53*, 165-189.

Snow, C.E., Burns, M.S., & Griffin, P. (Eds.). (1998). *Preventing reading difficulties in young children.* Washington, DC: National Academy Press.

Speece, D.L., Roth, F.P., Cooper, D.H., & de la Paz, S. (1999). The relevance of oral language skills to early literacy: A multivariate analysis. *Applied Psycholinguistics, 20*(2), 167-190.

Stanovich, K.E. (1992). Speculations on the causes and consequences of individual differences in early reading acquisition. In P.B. Gough, L.C. Ehri, & R. Treiman (Eds.), *Reading acquisition* (pp. 307-342). Hillsdale, NJ: Erlbaum.

Stipek, D.J., & Ryan, R.H. (1997). Economically disadvantaged preschoolers: Ready to learn but further to go. *Developmental Psychology, 33*(4), 711-723.

Sulzby, E., & Teale, W. (1991). Emergent literacy. In R. Barr, M. Kamil, P. Mosenthal, & P.D. Pearson (Eds.), *Handbook of reading research* (Vol. II, pp. 727-758). New York: Longman.

Tabors, P.O., Beals, D.E., & Weizman, Z.O. (2001). "You know what oxygen is?" Learning new words at home. In D.K. Dickinson & P.O. Tabors (Eds.), *Beginning literacy with language: Young children learning at home and school* (pp. 93-110). Baltimore, MD: Brookes.

Tucker, M.S., & Codding, J.B. (1998). *Standards for our schools: How to set them, measure them, and reach them.* San Francisco, CA: Jossey-Bass.

Vellutino, F.R., & Scanlon, D.M. (2001). Emergent literacy skills, early instruction, and individual differences as determinants of difficulties in learning to read: The case for early intervention. In S.

Neuman & D. Dickinson (Eds.), *Handbook of early literacy research* (pp. 295–321). New York: Guilford.

Wagner, R.K., Torgesen, J.K., Laughon, P., Simmons, K., & Rashotte, C.A. (1993). Development of young readers' phonological processing abilities. *Journal of Educational Psychology, 85*, 83–103.

Wagner, R.K., Torgesen, J.K., Rashotte, C.A., Hecht, S.A., Barker, T.A., Burgess, S.R., et al. (1997). Changing relations between phonological processing abilities and word-level reading as children develop from beginning to skilled readers: A 5-year longitudinal study. *Developmental Psychology, 33*, 468–479.

A Test for Assessing Phonemic Awareness in Young Children

Hallie Kay Yopp

Two decades ago few educational researchers and practitioners were familiar with the concept of phonemic awareness. In the last several years, however, phonemic awareness has captured the attention of many individuals in both the research community and elementary classrooms, and this interest is likely to continue for some time. What is this concept that has attracted so much attention? Phonemic awareness, as the term suggests, is the awareness of phonemes, or sounds, in the speech stream. It is the awareness that speech consists of a series of sounds.

Most youngsters enter kindergarten lacking phonemic awareness. Indeed, few are conscious that sentences are made up of individual words, let alone that words can be segmented into phonemes.

By the end of first grade, however, many (but not all) children have gained this awareness and can manipulate phonemes in their speech. For example, they can break spoken words into their constituent sounds, saying "/d/-/i/-/g/" when presented with *dig*; they can remove a sound from a spoken word, saying "rake" when asked to take the /b/ off the beginning of the word *break*; and they can isolate the sound they hear at the beginning, middle, or end of a word. (Parallel lines surrounding a letter [e.g., /z/] are used to represent the sound rather than the name of the letter. For the ease of the reader, typical spellings of sounds will be used within these lines rather than the symbols used in phonetic transcriptions.)

Research has demonstrated that phonemic awareness is a very important ability. There is substantial evidence that phonemic awareness is strongly related to success in reading and spelling acquisition (Ball & Blachman, 1991; Liberman, Shankweiler, Fischer, & Carter, 1974; Perfetti, Beck, Bell, & Hughes, 1987; Share, Jorm, Maclean, & Matthews, 1984; Treiman & Baron, 1983; Yopp, 1992a). In a review of the research, Stanovich (1986) concluded that phonemic awareness is a more potent predictor of reading achievement than nonverbal intelligence, vocabulary, and listening comprehension, and that it often correlates more highly with reading acquisition than tests of general intelligence or reading readiness. He restated this conclusion recently in the pages of *The Reading Teacher*: "Most importantly, [phonemic awareness tasks] are the best predictors of the ease of early reading acquisition—better than anything else that we know of, including IQ" (Stanovich, 1994, p. 284).

A growing number of studies indicate that phonemic awareness is not simply a strong predictor, but that it is a necessary prerequisite for success in learning to read (Bradley & Bryant, 1983, 1985; Tunmer, Herriman, & Nesdale, 1988; see also Stanovich's 1994 discussion). For instance, Juel and Leavell (1988) determined that children who enter first grade lacking phonemic awareness are unable to induce spelling–sound correspondences from print exposure or to benefit from phonics instruction. Likewise, in her comprehensive survey of the research on learning to read, Adams (1990) concluded that children who fail to acquire phonemic awareness "are severely handicapped in their ability to master print" (p. 412).

The importance of phonemic awareness appears to cut across instructional approaches, as

From *The Reading Teacher*, *49*(1), 20–29. © 1995 by the International Reading Association.

evidenced by the work of Griffith, Klesius, and Kromrey (1992), who found that phonemic awareness is a significant variable in both whole language and traditional classrooms. Few now would argue with the claim that this ability is essential for reading progress.

Given the evidence that phonemic awareness is necessary for success in reading development, many researchers are sounding the call for teachers of young children to include experiences in their curriculum that facilitate the development of phonemic awareness (Griffith & Olson, 1992; Juel, 1988; Lundberg, Frost, & Petersen, 1988; Mattingly, 1984). Particular attention needs to be given to those children lacking this ability. How, then, can teachers determine which students have this critical ability?

Any assessment instrument used to identify those students needing more activities that facilitate phonemic awareness must be both reliable and valid. The purpose of this article is to provide teachers with a tool for assessing phonemic awareness, and to offer evidence of its reliability and validity. The Yopp–Singer Test of Phoneme Segmentation is easy to administer, score, and interpret.

The Instrument

The Yopp–Singer Test of Phoneme Segmentation measures a child's ability to separately articulate the sounds of a spoken word in order. For example, given the orally presented word *sat*, the child should respond with three separate sounds: /s/-/a/-/t/. Note that sounds, not letter names, are the appropriate response. Thus, given the four-letter word *fish*, the child should respond with three sounds: /f/-/i/-/sh/ (see the 22-item Test). Words were selected for inclusion on the basis of feature analysis and word familiarity. (For a complete discussion of the word list rationale, see Yopp, 1988.) The test is administered individually and requires about 5 to 10 minutes per child.

Children are given the following directions upon administration of the test:

> Today we're going to play a word game. I'm going to say a word and i want you to break the word apart. You are going to tell me each sound in the word in order. For example, if I say "old," you should say "/o/-/l/-/d/" [The administrator says the sounds, not the letters.] Let's try a few words together.

The practice items are *ride*, *go*, and *man*. The examiner should help the child with each sample item—segmenting the item for the child if necessary and encouraging the child to repeat the segmented sounds. Then the child is given the 22-item test. Feedback is given to the child as he or she progresses through the list. If the child responds correctly, the examiner nods or says, "That's right." If the child gives an incorrect response, he or she is corrected. The examiner provides the appropriate response.

A child's score is the number of items correctly segmented into all constituent phonemes. No partial credit is given. For instance, if a child says "/c/-/at/" instead of "/c/-/a/-/t/," the response may be noted on the blank line following the item but is considered incorrect for purposes of scoring. Correct responses are only those that involve articulation of each phoneme in the target word.

A blend contains two or three phonemes and each of these should be articulated separately. Hence, item 7 on the test, *grew*, has three phonemes: /g/-/r/-/ew/. Digraphs, such as /sh/ in item 5, *she*, and /th/ in item 15, *three*, are single phonemes. Item 5, therefore, has two phonemes and item 15 has three phonemes. If a child responds with letter names instead of sounds, the response is coded as incorrect, and the type of error is noted on the test.

Teachers of young children should expect a wide range of performance on this test. A sample of kindergarteners drawn from the public schools in a west coast city in the United States obtained scores ranging from 0 to 22 correct (0% to 100%) during their second semester. The mean (average) score was 11.78, with a standard deviation of 7.66 (Yopp, 1988, see below). Similar findings from a sample of kindergartners on the east coast of the United States were reported by Spector (1992): the mean score was 11.39 with a standard deviation of 8.18.

Yopp-Singer Test of Phoneme Segmentation

Student's name____________________________________ Date______________

Score (number correct)______________

Directions: Today we're going to play a word game. I'm going to say a word and I want you to break the word apart. You are going to tell me each sound in the word in order. For example, if I say "old," you should say "/o/-/l/-/d/." (*Administrator: Be sure to say the sounds, not the letters, in the word.*) Let's try a few together.

Practice items: (*Assist the child in segmenting these items as necessary.*) ride, go, man

Test items: (*Circle those items that the student correctly segments; incorrect responses may be recorded on the blank line following the item.*)

1. dog ______________________
2. keep ______________________
3. fine ______________________
4. no ______________________
5. she ______________________
6. wave ______________________
7. grew ______________________
8. that ______________________
9. red ______________________
10. me ______________________
11. sat ______________________
12. lay ______________________
13. race ______________________
14. zoo ______________________
15. three ______________________
16. job ______________________
17. in ______________________
18. ice ______________________
19. at ______________________
20. top ______________________
21. by ______________________
22. do ______________________

Students who obtain high scores (segmenting all or nearly all of the items correctly) may be considered phonemically aware. Students who correctly segment some items are displaying emerging phonemic awareness. Students who are able to segment only a few items or none at all lack appropriate levels of phonemic awareness. Without intervention, those students scoring very low on the test are likely to experience difficulty with reading and spelling.

Teachers' notes on the blank lines of the test will be helpful in understanding each child. Some children may partially segment—perhaps dividing words into chunks larger than phonemes. These children are beginning to have an insight into the nature of speech. Others may simply repeat the stimulus item or provide nonsense responses regardless of the amount of feedback and practice given. They have very little insight into the phonemic basis of their speech. Still others may simply offer letter names.

If the letter names are random (e.g., given *red* the child responds "n-b-d-o"), the teacher learns that the child lacks phonemic awareness but knows some letter names. If the letter names are close approximations to the conventional spelling of the words (e.g., given *red* the child responds "r-a-d"), the teacher knows that either the child has memorized the spellings of some words or that he or she is phonemically aware and has mentally segmented the items, then verbally provided the examiner with the letters corresponding to those sounds—an impressive feat! The examiner should repeat the instructions in this case to make sure the child fully understands the task.

Data on the Instrument

A number of years ago I undertook a study to compare tests of phonemic awareness that appeared in the literature and to examine the reliability and validity of each (Yopp, 1988). Nearly 100 second-semester kindergarten youngsters drawn from three public elementary schools in a southern California school district that serves children from a lower middle to an upper middle class population were each administered 10 different phonemic awareness tests over a period of several weeks. Children ranged in age from 64 to 80 months with an average age of 70 months, and were predominantly White, with 1% Black, 2% Asian, and 15% with Spanish surnames. All children were fluent English speakers.

Performance on the phonemic awareness tests was compared, the reliability of each test was calculated, and a factor analysis was conducted to determine validity. One of the tests in the battery, the Yopp–Singer Test of Phoneme Segmentation, had a reliability score (Cronbach's alpha) of .95, indicating that it can be appropriately used in the assessment of individuals. Experts in tests and measurement tell us that instruments should have reliability coefficients above .85 (Hills, 1981) or even .90 (Jensen, 1980) if they are to be used to make decisions about individuals.

Analyses also indicated that the Yopp–Singer Test is a valid measure of phonemic awareness. Construct validity was determined through a factor analysis (for details see Yopp, 1988). Predictive validity was determined by collecting data on the reading achievement of the same students each year beginning in kindergarten and concluding when the students were in sixth grade; spelling achievement data were obtained in grades 2 to 6. Thus, seven years of longitudinal data are available. (See Yopp, 1992a for details on this study.) A test of nonword decoding was administered in kindergarten. In order to determine reading and spelling achievement in grades 1 through 6, records of the students' performance on the Comprehensive Test of Basic Skills (CTBS, 1973), a timed, norm-referenced, objectives based test, were obtained. This standardized test, widely used by school districts as part of their regular testing program, includes word attack, vocabulary, comprehension, and spelling subtests in the reading and spelling achievement battery. These tests are described in Table 1.

Table 2 presents the correlations between performance on the Yopp–Singer Test of Phoneme Segmentation administered in kindergarten and all subtests on the reading and spelling achievement battery throughout the grade levels

Table 1
Descriptions of reading and spelling tests used to determine predictive validity

Nonword Reading Test

The nonword reading test was administered for the purpose of determining each child's ability to use sound-symbol correspondences to decode nonwords. Children were assessed on their ability to sound and blend printed nonwords such as *paz* and *kov*.
Administered in kindergarten.

CTBS Word Attack Subtest

The word attack section requires students to identify letters corresponding to the initial or final single consonant, cluster, or digraph sounds or the medial vowels heard in orally presented words. Recognition of sight words is also measured in this subtest.
Administered during grades 1 through 3.

CTBS Vocabulary Subtest*

The vocabulary section measures children's ability to identify a word associated with an orally presented category or definition, in addition to identifying same-meaning words or unfamiliar words in context.
Administered during grades 1 through 6.

CTBS Reading Comprehension Subtest*

The reading comprehension section is used to measure children's comprehension of both sentences and stories. Children are asked to respond to objective questions after reading each selection.
Administered during grades 1 through 6.

CTBS Spelling Subtest

The spelling section measures children's ability to recognize correctly spelled words.
Administered during grades 2 through 6.

*A "total" reading scores is generated for each child that combines the vocabulary and comprehension subtests.

as well as the kindergarten nonword reading measure. Each of the correlations is significant: performance on the Yopp–Singer Test of Phoneme Segmentation has a moderate to strong relationship with performance on the nonword reading test given in kindergarten and with the subtests of the CTBS—word attack, vocabulary, comprehension, and spelling (and the total score)—through grade 6. Thus, the phonemic awareness test has significant predictive validity.

Because reading and spelling achievement are related to phonemic awareness and to future reading and spelling achievement, these impressive correlations (as high as .78) do not address the question of whether a measure of phonemic awareness truly contributes to the prediction of reading and spelling performance years later, independent of previous reading and spelling achievement. For instance, a significant correlation between phonemic awareness in kindergarten and reading in grade 1 might be obtained because reading performance in kindergarten and grade 1 are highly correlated, and reading performance in kindergarten and phonemic awareness in kindergarten are highly correlated.

Thus, the relationship between phonemic awareness in kindergarten and reading in first grade might simply be a byproduct of these other relationships. We want to know whether a measure of phonemic awareness obtained in

Table 2
Correlation of performance on phonemic awareness task administered in Grade K with performance on reading and spelling subtests, Grades K-6

Grade level	Subtests					
	Nonword	Word Attack	Vocabulary	Comprehension	Total	Spelling
K	.67**					
1		.46**	.66**	.38**	.62**	
2		.62**	.72**	.55**	.67**	.53**
3		.56**	.66**	.62**	.67**	.44**
4			.51**	.62**	.58**	.60**
5			.56**	.57**	.59**	.55**
6			.78**	.66**	.74**	.46**

* $p<.05$ ** $p<.01$

kindergarten contributes to the prediction of future reading and spelling achievement above and beyond the contribution that past reading and spelling achievement makes on future achievement in reading and spelling. Does performance on a measure of phonemic awareness offer us any unique insights into future performance in reading and spelling?

In order to rule out the effect of reading and spelling achievement over the years on subsequent reading and spelling performance, partial time-lag correlations were also conducted. These correlations are "partial" in that they partial out, or eliminate, the effects of one variable (in this case, past reading or spelling performance) on another (in this case, later reading or spelling performance); they are "time-lag" in that they examine the relationship between two variables over time (earlier phonemic awareness performance and later reading or spelling achievement). The partial time-lag correlations are presented in Table 3.

Each correlation coefficient indicates the strength of the relationship between performance on the phonemic awareness test in kindergarten and performance on reading and spelling subtests in grades 1–6 when the previous year's achievement in these areas has been controlled. Thus, the .54 correlation found in Table 3 between phonemic awareness in kindergarten and vocabulary in grade 5 is the strength of the relationship after fourth-grade vocabulary performance has been accounted for.

Table 3 reveals that most of the correlations remain significant, some as high as .51, .54, and .55. Thus, they reveal that scores on the Yopp–Singer Test of Phoneme Segmentation make a unique contribution to predicting students' reading and spelling achievement above and beyond their previous achievement in these areas.

The power of a 5- to 10-minute, 22-item test administered in kindergarten to predict students' performance in reading and spelling achievement years later, even after controlling for previous reading and spelling achievement, is quite surprising. In his review of the research on phonemic awareness, Stanovich (1994) noted the strong relationship between performance on a number of simple, short phonemic awareness tasks and reading acquisition and suggests that the power of such simple tasks to predict reading acquisition is one of the reasons for the tremendous research energy currently devoted to this line of inquiry.

Table 3
Partial time-lag correlation of performance on phonemic awareness task administered in Grade K with performance on reading and spelling subtests, Grades 1-6, controlling for performance on reading and spelling subtests administered the previous year

Grade level	Subtests: Word Attack	Vocabulary	Comprehension	Total	Spelling
1	.33**	.55**	.08	.43**	
2	.51**	.36**	.43**	.32**	
3	.20	.19	.43**	.33**	.11
4		-.05	.38**	.10	.43**
5		.54**	.18	.36*	.26
6		.51**	.45**	.47**	-.05

* $p<.05$ ** $p<.01$

Implications

What do these findings mean for teachers? They mean that we now have a tool—one that is both valid and reliable as well as simple and quick to administer—that can be used to determine a child's phonemic awareness, and we have the knowledge that performance on this measure is significantly related to a child's achievement in reading and spelling for years to come.

What can we do with this information? We can identify children quite early who are likely to experience difficulty in reading and spelling and give them appropriate instructional support. Fortunately, a growing body of evidence indicates that training of phonemic awareness is possible and that it can result in significant gains in subsequent reading and spelling achievement (Ball & Blachman, 1991; Bradley & Bryant, 1983; Cunningham, 1990; Lie, 1991; Lundberg et al., 1988). Thus, a child need not be labeled "phonemically unaware" and therefore inevitably a "poor" reader. Phonemic awareness is an ability that teachers and reading/language arts specialists can develop in many students.

Some researchers have argued that systematic training in phonemic awareness should be part of every youngster's education before the onset of formal reading instruction (Mattingly, 1984; Tunmer et al., 1988). The need for this, of course, depends upon the abilities of the individual children in the classroom. Further, in many classrooms the onset of formal reading will be difficult to identify—there is no onset of "formal" instruction and reading is not differentiated from prereading.

A growing number of teachers hold an emergent literacy perspective, viewing literacy as an evolving process that begins during infancy and they provide a wealth of valuable literacy experiences for children very early on. Certainly these experiences should not be withheld until children become phonemically aware!

However, it is important for teachers and other practitioners to appreciate that children will likely make little sense of the alphabetic principle without phonemic awareness, and so phonemic awareness should be developed as part of the larger literacy program for many children. Fortunately, phonemic awareness activities can be readily incorporated into preschool, kindergarten, and early primary grade classrooms. Recent articles in *The Reading Teacher* (Griffith & Olson, 1992; Yopp, 1992b) have provided suggestions for helping young children focus on the sounds of language through stories, songs, and games. A few suggestions will be highlighted here.

Griffith and Olson (1992) and I (Yopp, 1995) suggest that one simple means to draw children's attention to the sound structure of language is through the use of read-aloud books. Many children's books emphasize speech sounds through rhyme, alliteration, assonance, phoneme substitution, or segmentation and offer play with language as a dominant feature. For instance, P. Cameron's *"I Can't," Said the Ant* (1961) makes use of a simple rhyme scheme, Seuss's *Dr. Seuss's ABC* (1963) uses alliteration as each letter of the alphabet is introduced, and his *There's a Wocket in My Pocket* (1974) incorporates initial phoneme substitution to create a household of humorous nonsense creatures.

I have suggested (Yopp, 1995) that such books can be read and reread, their language can be enjoyed and explored in class discussions, predictions that focus on language can be encouraged, and additional verses or alternate versions of the texts can be created using the language patterns provided. (See Yopp, 1995, for an annotated bibliography of books to develop phonemic awareness.)

A guessing game that I have used successfully both with groups of children and in individualized settings is "What am I thinking of?" (Yopp, 1992b). This game encourages children to blend orally spoken sounds together. The teacher tells the children a category and then speaks in a segmented fashion the sounds of a particular item in that category. For instance, given the category "article of clothing," the teacher might say the following three sounds: "/h/-/a/-/t/." Children's attempts to blend the sounds together to say "hat" are applauded and the game continues. Eventually, children may become the leaders and take turns providing their peers with segmented words for blending.

Categories may be selected to relate to curriculum areas under investigation (e.g., "I'm thinking of one of the types of sea animals we have been learning about—it is a /c/-/r/-/a/-/b/") or as an extension of integrated literacy experiences. When teaching about bears and their habitats, teachers may encourage children to write about bears, listen to stories about bears, view films about bears, create art projects involving bears, and learn poems and songs about bears. After singing the song, "The bear went over the mountain," children may play the guessing game to hypothesize the kinds of things seen by the bear on his outing (*A Treasury of Literature*, 1995)—"he saw a /t/-/r/-/ee/."

Common children's songs can be easily altered to emphasize the sounds of language. For instance, the initial sounds of words can be substituted. Instead of "merrily, merrily, merrily, merrily" in "Row, Row, Row Your Boat," children can suggest other sounds to insert in the initial position—"jerrily, jerrily, jerrily, jerrily" or "terrily, terrily, terrily, terrily." Young children often find such manipulations of sounds amusing and are likely to be heard singing nonsensical lyrics on the playground.

Concrete objects may help children attend to the sounds in speech. Elkonin boxes have been used in Reading Recovery to help low achieving readers focus on the sounds in words (Clay, 1985). A series of connected boxes are drawn across a page. The number of boxes corresponds to the number of sounds in a target word. The word *chick*, for example, is represented by three boxes. As the teacher slowly says the word, he or she models moving an object such as a chip into each box (from left to right) as each sound is articulated. The child eventually takes over the process of articulating the word and moving the objects into place.

Ultimately, the moving of chips into the boxes is replaced by the writing of letters in the boxes. (In the case of *chick* two letters are written in the first box because two letters spell the first sound: *ch*. Likewise, two letters are written in the third and final box: *ck*.) This activity is purposeful in the larger context of literacy acquisition when used to support children as they attempt to record thoughts or communicate in writing. (For a similar activity to facilitate phonemic awareness and support invented spelling, see Cunningham & Cunningham, 1992.)

Note that these activities fit into a meaning-based framework. Phonemic awareness should not be addressed as an abstract isolated skill to be acquired through drill type activities. It can be a natural, functional part of literacy experiences throughout the day.

Use of the Test

The Yopp–Singer Test of Phoneme Segmentation was designed for use with English-speaking kindergartners. It may be used as a general assessment tool in order for teachers to learn more about their students and so develop suitable experiences; or it may be used selectively as teachers observe individual children experiencing difficulty with literacy-related tasks. Certainly, it need not be administered to the child who is already reading. Independent reading implies the existence of phonemic awareness. Further, phonemic awareness is not an end to itself—rather, it is one aspect of literacy development.

First-grade teachers, too, may wish to administer the test to students at the beginning of the school year in order to determine the phonemic awareness needs of the children in the classroom. Reading/language arts specialists or clinicians who work with children experiencing difficulty in literacy acquisition may also wish to assess their students' phonemic awareness as part of a larger diagnostic survey. And, although there are currently no data regarding the use of this particular test with older populations, we know that often older nonreaders lack phonemic awareness.

This instrument may be helpful to teachers of older individuals, including adult emerging readers, as they begin to build a profile of the strengths and needs of the individuals with whom they work. If phonemic awareness is poor, then it is appropriate to include activities that support its development in the larger picture of literacy experiences.

Should students who are limited in English proficiency be given this test? There are no data on using this test with an EL (English learner) population. Further, the issue is problematic since not only is there a potential problem with understanding task directions and familiarity with vocabulary (recall that the items on the test were selected, in part, on the basis of word familiarity), but there is also the possibility that performance on the test could be influenced by the fact that some speech sounds that exist in the English language may not exist in a student's dominant language.

Research does indicate that phonemic awareness is a critical variable in languages that have an alphabetic orthography (i.e., ones that map speech at the level of the phoneme rather than larger units). Therefore, the ideas presented in this article apply to children learning to read in an alphabetic script. The next step for educational researchers, therefore, is to develop reliable, valid assessment tools in other alphabetic languages to help teachers working with populations of children who are reading in languages other than English.

Conclusion

One of many insights that individuals must gain along the path to literacy is phonemic awareness. Research has shown that phonemic awareness is a more potent predictor of success in reading than IQ or measures of vocabulary and listening comprehension, and that if it is lacking, emergent readers are unlikely to gain mastery over print. However, teachers can provide activities that facilitate the acquisition of phonemic awareness. With an assessment device readily available, practitioners can quickly identify those children who may benefit most from phonemic awareness activities and reduce the role that one factor—phonemic awareness—plays in inhibiting their success in reading and spelling.

References

Adams, M.J. (1990). *Beginning to read: Thinking and learning about print*. Cambridge, MA: MIT Press.

Ball, E.W., & Blachman, B.A. (1991). Does phoneme segmentation training in kindergarten make a difference in early word recognition and developmental spelling? *Reading Research Quarterly, 26,* 49–66.

Bradley, L., & Bryant, P. (1983). Categorizing sounds and learning to read: A causal connection. *Nature, 301,* 419–421.

Bradley, L., & Bryant, P. (1985). *Rhyme and reason in reading and spelling.* Ann Arbor, MI: University of Michigan Press.

Cameron, P. (1961). *"I can't," said the ant.* New York: Coward-McCann.

Clay, M.M. (1985). *The early detection of reading difficulties* (3rd ed.). Portsmouth, NH: Heinemann.

Cunningham, A.E. (1990). Explicit versus implicit instruction in phonemic awareness. *Journal of Experimental Child Psychology, 50,* 429–444.

Cunningham, P.E., & Cunningham, J.W. (1992). Making Words: Enhancing the invented spelling-decoding connection. *The Reading Teacher, 46,* 106–115.

Griffith, P.L., Klesius, J.P., & Kromrey, J.D. (1992). The effect of phonemic awareness on the literacy development of first grade children in a traditional or a whole language classroom. *Journal of Research in Childhood Education, 6,* 86–92.

Griffith, P.L., & Olson, M.W. (1992). Phonemic awareness helps beginning readers break the code. *The Reading Teacher, 45,* 516–523.

Hills, J.R. (1981). *Measurement and evaluation in the classroom* (2nd ed.). Columbus, OH: Charles E. Merrill.

Jensen, A.R. (1980). *Bias in mental testing.* New York: Free Press.

Juel, C. (1988). Learning to read and write: A longitudinal study of 54 children from first through fourth grades. *Journal of Educational Psychology, 80,* 437–447.

Juel, C., & Leavell, J.A. (1988). Retention and nonretention of at-risk readers in first grade and their subsequent reading achievement. *Journal of Learning Disabilities, 21,* 571–580.

Liberman, I.Y., Shankweiler, D., Fischer, F.W., & Carter, B. (1974). Explicit syllable and phoneme segmentation in the young child. *Journal of Experimental Child Psychology, 18,* 201–212.

Lie, A. (1991). Effects of a training program for stimulating skills in word analysis in first-grade children. *Reading Research Quarterly, 23,* 263–284.

Lundberg, I., Frost, J., & Petersen, O. (1988). Effects of an extensive program for stimulating phonological awareness in preschool children. *Reading Research Quarterly, 23,* 263–285.

Mattingly, I.G. (1984). Reading, linguistic awareness, and language acquisition. In J. Downing & R. Valtin (Eds.), *Language awareness and learning to read* (pp. 9–25). New York: Springer-Verlag.

Perfetti, C., Beck, I., Bell, L., & Hughes, C. (1987). Phonemic knowledge and learning to read are reciprocal: A longitudinal study of first grade children. *Merrill-Palmer Quarterly, 33,* 283–319.

Seuss, Dr. (1963). *Dr. Seuss's ABC.* New York: Random House.

Seuss, Dr. (1974). *There's a wocket in my pocket.* New York: Random House.

Share, D., Jorm, A., Maclean, R., & Matthews, R. (1984). Sources of individual differences in reading acquisition. *Journal of Educational Psychology, 76,* 1309–1324.

Spector, J.E. (1992). Predicting progress in beginning reading: Dynamic assessment of phonemic awareness. *Journal of Educational Psychology, 84,* 353–363.

Stanovich, K.E. (1986). Matthew effects in reading: Some consequences of individual differences in the acquisition of literacy. *Reading Research Quarterly, 21,* 360–407.

Stanovich, K.E. (1994). Romance and reason. *The Reading Teacher, 47,* 280–291.

A treasury of literature. (1995). Orlando, FL: Harcourt Brace.

Treiman, R., & Baron, J. (1983). Phonemic-analysis training helps children benefit from spelling-sound rules. *Memory and Cognition, 11,* 382–389.

Tunmer, W., Herriman, M., & Nesdale, A. (1988). Metalinguistic abilities and beginning reading. *Reading Research Quarterly, 23,* 134–158.

Yopp, H.K. (1988). The validity and reliability of phonemic awareness tests. *Reading Research Quarterly, 23,* 159–177.

Yopp, H.K. (1992a). *A longitudinal study of the relationships between phonemic awareness and reading and spelling achievement.* Paper presented at the annual meeting of the American Educational Research Association, San Francisco, CA.

Yopp, H.K. (1992b). Developing phonemic awareness in young children. *The Reading Teacher, 45,* 696–703.

Yopp, H.K. (1995). Read-aloud books for developing phonemic awareness: An annotated bibliography. *The Reading Teacher, 48,* 538–542.

Tile Test: A Hands-On Approach for Assessing Phonics in the Early Grades

Kimberly A. Norman and Robert C. Calfee

The goal of early reading instruction is to help students move as quickly as possible toward independent comprehension of a broad range of texts. Phonics instruction is one gateway toward this goal by providing students with the skills to decode unfamiliar words encountered in new and challenging passages. All children should possess independent reading skills like the young reader who imagines fish being pulled by an invisible thread while reading *Swimmy* (Lionni, 1973). The challenge for growth in comprehension, sometimes referred to as the "fourth-grade slump" (Hirsch, 2003), is to promote in students a willingness—indeed, an enthusiasm—to move beyond known words and safe passages. The foundation for such progress lies in the acquisition of skills, strategies, and confidence in taking risks with print.

Increased attention to "proven practice," particularly in the area of phonics, has led to a call for increases in the amount of time devoted to phonics instruction in the primary grades (National Institute of Child Health and Human Development, 2000). The past three decades of cognitive research have revealed that *understanding* is critical to apply knowledge and strategies in new settings (Bransford, Brown, & Cocking, 2000). However, instruction in phonemic awareness and phonics typically relies on opportunities for practice rather than experiences that promote understanding. How do we help children develop strategic knowledge about the orthographic system and apply that knowledge? How can we assess strategic knowledge of the sort that will enable students in the later grades to independently access text?

In this article, we present an approach for thinking about assessment in a strategic manner. Imagine an ideal setting where you can sit with individual students and engage in a conversation designed to reveal a picture of what they know and can do. The Tile Test is designed to do just that; in a reasonable amount of time, you can examine students' understanding of the English orthographic system. It provides a hands-on interactive experience with letters and sounds for teachers who want to delve more deeply into students' underlying thinking. The test has four distinctive features. First is *efficiency*; much can be learned in a minimum amount of time (5–15 minutes) because you assess the fundamental concepts. The second feature is *flexibility*; the test is composed of individual modules of reading components so you can present the relevant sections to your students. Because it serves as a "shell," teachers can create new versions of the test that focus on the concepts they select. Third, the Tile Test offers rich *clinical opportunities*. Carefully constructed assessment activities allow you to see and hear what students know and how they know it. Finally, it provides the feedback needed to guide instruction.

Understanding Is Essential

We noted earlier that many programs do not emphasize understanding or strategic learning. Consequently, students are presented with isolated objectives that take time to learn and have limited transfer. Some might question whether there is more to phonics than a basic skill, and

From *The Reading Teacher*, 58(1), 42-52. © 2004 by the International Reading Association.

we have argued that understanding is essential to promote rapid and transferable learning. Over the past decade we have examined ways to teach phonics for understanding and have developed tools that reveal students' knowledge and strategies for approaching words (Calfee, Norman, Trainin, & Wilson, 2001). Word Work (Calfee, 1998), a decoding-spelling framework, is an approach to teaching phonics that fosters students' exploration of the system and scaffolds students as they explain their thinking. The Word Work strategy builds on the historical and morphophonemic structure of English orthography (Venezky, 1999). Students in the primary grades need to rapidly master words from the Anglo-Saxon layer of English; Word Work focuses on the most productive letter–sound correspondences from this layer, with a particular emphasis on the central importance of vowels as the "glue" that connects consonants (Venezky).

Students begin with phonemic awareness by turning their attention to how they articulate or produce sounds in their mouths. *Articulatory phonemic awareness* draws upon principles from the motor theory of speech perception (Liberman & Mattingly, 1985) to guide students to examine the features of consonant production (manner, place, and voicing). As first graders attend to their speech, they explain that "the air comes out really fast—it explodes" when producing the popping sounds (plosives) *p*, *t*, and *k*. For the hissing sounds (fricatives), students' explorations of *f* and *s* lead to comments that "the air is coming out kind of slow" and "soft on your hand."

Once familiar with a small collection of consonants, students begin to use vowels (glue letters) to build words. The word *pat* is built by "putting your lips together and popping, gluing in the /a:::/ sound, and then tapping your tongue to the roof of your mouth." As students explain how they build words in this fashion, they use the *metaphonic principle*, learning to decode and spell by understanding the system rather than through rote memorization. Therefore, the teacher continually asks students to explain. For example, *dime* is pronounced that way because the final *e* tells the *i* to say its name. Notice that the system integrates decoding and spelling in a single process. Students' reflective talk supports conceptual understanding of English orthography because the talk mirrors their understanding—students become aware of what they know. This, in turn, facilitates the application of their knowledge and strategies to reading and writing across the curriculum (Vygotsky, 1978). (For a discussion of the research findings that support the promotion of metacognitive discussions in primary-grade classrooms, see Calfee & Norman, 2003; Trainin, Calfee, Norman, & Wilson, 2002.)

Determining Understanding

How can you as a teacher, whatever phonics program you are using, determine your students' understanding? First, you have to actively engage the students in working with the code so they can reveal what they know. Second, you need to study how students think about letter–sound correspondences and apply this knowledge. Both can be accomplished by having students work with letter tiles to construct words. Hands-on manipulation of letters reveals their ability to identify and represent phonemes, what they know about the role of vowels in words, and their application of decoding and spelling strategies. Third, you need to scaffold students' talk in order to understand what they know. For instance, how do students approach an unfamiliar word when decoding or spelling? Because metacognitive awareness is important for children to apply their knowledge in different contexts, answers to these questions are important to teachers. The Tile Test is built on these learning principles (Bransford et al., 2000).

In the next section, we present a comprehensive description of the tool, followed by directions for administering it with young children. In later sections we discuss how to analyze and interpret the results, use the information to plan instruction, and adapt the tool to fit your classroom context and curriculum.

Description of the Tile Test

The Tile Test is an individually administered diagnostic assessment designed to quickly evaluate early readers' and writers' understanding of letters, sounds, words, and sentences. A complete description and assessment materials are available online at www.education.ucr.edu/read_plus. The skills tested include several of those generally accepted as necessary for successful beginning reading and spelling: phoneme awareness, letter and sound correspondences, decoding and spelling of words, sight-word reading, and the application of decoding and spelling in sentences. Additional activities have students respond to metalinguistic questions to assess the level of problem-solving strategies known and applied when using English orthography.

The Tile Test is intended for use with students in midkindergarten through first grade, although it may be used with students of any age or language background who are learning the building blocks of English orthography. An expanded version of the Tile Test assesses orthographic concepts extending through second grade and is described later. The entire test can be administered in one session of about 10–15 minutes. It is efficient because it quickly assesses fundamental concepts rather than testing everything. We have intentionally chosen consonants that are highly productive and vowels that are very distinctive. Complicating factors, such as *r* and *l* and vowel digraphs, are not included. For present purposes, we do not examine consonant blends or digraphs. We focus on the very core essentials that allow children to demonstrate that they understand the basic principles of English orthography.

Areas of knowledge tested in the first segment of the Tile Test include identification of letters' names and sounds, decoding and spelling of monosyllabic words (consonant–vowel–consonant units), and sight-word reading.

Letters and Sounds

The first section of the Tile Test focuses on the most basic decoding and spelling information—letter–sound correspondence. Using eight letters —two vowels (a, i) and six consonants (p, m, n, s, d, t), teachers can quickly gauge students' general knowledge of letter names and sounds when given visual and auditory stimuli. Letter inversions (p, d) and confusions (m, n) can also be noted in student responses.

Words

Decoding. This section of the test begins with reading simple consonant–vowel–consonant (CVC) words, built with lowercase letter tiles. The progression of the first three words of the series focuses on changes from the previous word of either the initial or final consonant (pat→ sat→ sam) to quickly assess students' processing and functional use of single letter–sound correspondences. The next five words require manipulation of more than one consonant or the vowel.

Spelling. The next section consists of building the progression of words with initial or final consonant variations followed by vowel variations. These tasks gauge students' ability to employ phonemic awareness of individual and blended sounds when spelling, as well as assess their knowledge of applying the vowel system in words. The students use individual, lowercase letter tiles for word building, eliminating the possible confounding that handwriting may introduce.

Metalinguistic questions. During both the decoding and spelling sections, questions are asked to further clarify students' thinking and problem solving when working with words. To assess their knowledge of underlying principles the students are asked to explain *why* they gave their answers. For example, a student replied that she knew how to spell the word *sip* that way because she could "feel her tongue behind her lips" at the beginning of the word. Her response reveals an awareness of not only the sound of the letter but also how the letter is produced or feels—an effective skill when approaching unfamiliar words. By embedding the metalinguistic questions in the decoding and spelling activities, even the youngest students are capable of reflecting on and explaining their thinking processes.

Sight words. This section assesses students' automaticity in reading 17 phonetically regular (e.g., cat, run) and irregular (e.g., the, me) words. Each word is presented on individual word tiles. Words used to begin sentences in the next segment of the test are presented with their initial letter capitalized, and if the word is also found within the sentence, it is presented a second time in lowercase format. Because the word *the* is used twice in one sentence, two word tiles are required.

Sentences

Areas of knowledge tested in the second segment of the Tile Test include the reading and building of sentences. Each sentence is constructed from the sight-word tiles used previously. In the first section, students are asked to read sentences ranging from three to seven words. The test administrator constructs each sentence. Because words such as *sit*, *sat*, *cat*, and *can* are included, some weaknesses in students' word reading strategies can be identified. In the final section of the test, students are asked to build sentences read to them by the test administrator. Students are asked to read the sentences after building, which allows for self-correction. In addition to word recognition, this activity demonstrates students' ability to hold sentences of varying lengths in working memory.

Validity and Reliability of the Tile Test

The Tile Test's validity was tested by examining the relationship of performance on the Tile Test with measures of early reading commonly used in schools. The data show that there is a high degree of agreement (concurrent validity) between the Tile Test and the Developmental Reading Assessment (Celebration Press, 1997), a measure of reading fluency and accuracy ($r = .74$, $p < .001$), suggesting both instruments measure similar constructs. In addition, we found moderate to strong relationships with performance on the Scholastic (1997) Phonemic Awareness Test ($r = .60$, $p < .001$), spelling performance in writing samples ($r = .65$, $p < .001$), and writing assessed with a holistic rubric ($r = .70$, $p < .001$). These data provide further evidence of the relationship between performance on the Tile Test and tasks used to measure students' ability to decode and spell in reading and writing tasks.

The Tile Test has been shown to be a reliable measure of basic decoding and spelling skills. Reliability addresses the trustworthiness of all facets of the test. Cronbach's (1951) alpha, a statistic used to measure the internal consistency of an instrument, was calculated at kindergarten and first grade. These coefficients were .93 for the kindergarten sample and .98 for first grade, indicating that it can be appropriately used in the assessment of individuals. Another index of consistency, test–retest reliability, produced a coefficient alpha of .87–.97.

Administering the Tile Test

This section describes the preparation of assessment materials and provides general guidelines for assessing students. As noted previously, the materials are available online or can be easily created (see the recording sheet in Figure 1 for required materials). (Tip: The Century Gothic font presents *a* and *g* in a format familiar to young students.)

Preparing for the Assessment

Materials. Our usual practice is to use lowercase letter tiles with a horizontal line across the bottom to support students' directionality (see Figure 2). The vowels are distinguished from the consonants by the thickness of the directional line—thick line for vowels, thin line for consonants. Our website includes separate sets of vowels and consonants allowing the vowels to be printed on a colored background, thus offering another distinguishing feature.

Environment. Select a work area large enough to allow the student to easily manipulate the letter tiles in front of him or her. The test administrator should also be able to reach the tiles

Figure 1
Tile Test recording sheet

Student ______________________________ Date ______________

Letters and sounds: Display letter tiles m, a, p, i, s, t, d, n.

"Here are some letters. I'll say the name of a letter and ask you to point to the letter. Point to the card that has the letter *m*." (Record. Continue procedure with each letter.)

"Now, I'll point to a tile and you'll tell me two things about the letter. First, the *name* of the letter and, second, the *sound* that it makes." (Record.)

	Identification	Name	Sound		Identification	Name	Sound
m				s			
a				t			
p				d			
i				n			

Words: Add letter tiles f, b.

Decoding. "Now let's put some letters together to make words. I'll go first and make a word, then I'll ask you to read it for me." (Manipulate only necessary letters. Stop after *sat* and ask the first metalinguistic question.)

pat ______________
sat* ______________
sam ______________
fan ______________
fin ______________
pit ______________
tab ______________
mid ______________

*Metalinguistic question: "How did you know to say *sat* (or other pronunciation) that way?" ______________

Metalinguistic question: Rebuild the word that the student had the most difficulty with but decoded correctly.
"How did you know to say ______________ that way? ______________

Spelling. "Now, I'll say a word, and you'll build it for me." (As you dictate, clearly articulate by "stretching and exaggerating." Example: tan = /ta:::n:::/. Stop after *tad* and ask the first metalinguistic question.)

tan ______________
tad* ______________
mad ______________
sap ______________
sip ______________
tin ______________
pad ______________
fit ______________

*Metalinguistic question: "How did you know to build (spell) *tad* that way?" ______________

Metalinguistic question: Rebuild the word that the student had the most difficulty with but built correctly.
"How did you know to build ______________ that way? ______________

Sight-word reading. Lay out the collection of word cards. "I'll show you some words, and you read each one." (Record.)

I		me		the		a	
is		at		look		dog	
cat		big		map		can	
sat		fat		sit		on	
run							

(continued)

Figure 1 (continued)

Sentences:
Reading. "I'll make a sentence with some words, and you'll read the sentence for me."

I can run. ______________________________

Look at me. ______________________________

I sat on the cat. ______________________________

The map is big. ______________________________

I can look at the dog. ______________________________

Sit the dog on the fat cat. ______________________________

Building. "Now I'll say a sentence, and you'll build it for me." (Ask the student to read the sentence after building it. Record the sentence built and the student's read of it.)

I can sit. ______________________________

The dog is fat. ______________________________

Look at the map.______________________________

A dog can look at me.______________________________

The big cat sat on the dog. ______________________________

General observations: ______________________________

____

____

____

____

comfortably in order to manipulate the tiles at several points during the assessment.

Assessing Students

The first few minutes of the session can be used to build rapport, share the purpose of the session, and help the student to relax. Most find the Tile Test to be an enjoyable experience. We encourage you to approach the situation with an attitude of curiosity; the conversations that ensue from active construction of words and sentences should be fueled by your genuine interest in the student's knowledge and strategies. Because finding the student's best performance is the goal of the Tile Test, allow for conversation and use the probing questions provided.

Letters and Sounds

Begin by laying out the eight individual letter tiles and tell the student that you will say the name of a letter and that he or she should point to that letter. If the student responds correctly, place a check or plus under the "identification" heading on the recording sheet. If incorrect, record the student's response. Continue this process with each letter. The order is not important; you may choose to begin with a letter that you are confident the student will know in order to build early success. Then, explain that you will point to a letter tile and ask the student to respond by saying the name of the letter and the sound that it makes. Check the correct responses and write in the incorrect responses. Restate directions as

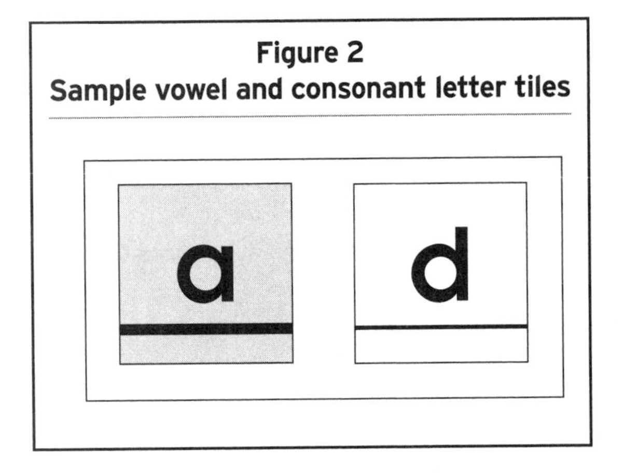

Figure 2
Sample vowel and consonant letter tiles

appropriate. For example, if the student says the name of a letter only, say, "What sound does that letter make?"

Words

Decoding. Add the second collection of letter tiles to the eight used in the previous section. Check that both you and the student can easily reach the tiles and that there is enough space directly in front of the student to build words. To begin, explain that you will put some letters together to make words and that you will ask the student to read them for you.

Build the first word, *pat*, and ask the student to read it to you. Correct responses are marked with a check or plus. For incorrect responses, record the student's exact pronunciation and behaviors, including self-corrections (recorded as SC). You may use the phonetic transcription or your own system. Segmented words read without blending sounds will be marked with slashes between sounds (e.g., /t/ /a/ /p/).

As you build the second word, *sat*, manipulate only the necessary letter tiles. In this case, exchange only the initial consonant, leaving the *-at* in place. After the student decodes *sat* (identified by an asterisk on the recording sheet), ask the first metalinguistic question to tap into the student's understanding of his or her decoding strategy: "How did you know to say *sat* that way?" Record student responses. Use probes as necessary to tap into the full response of the student. For example, if the student provides a limited response or a shrug or says, "I don't know," ask, "What were you thinking or looking at?" "How did you know how to say *sat* instead of *mat*?" (Note: If the student pronounces sat differently [e.g., *sam*], use the student's pronunciation when asking the metalinguistic question "How did you know to say *sam* that way?")

Continue through the word list exchanging the minimum number of letters required to progress from one word to the next. At the end of the word decoding section, ask the second metalinguistic question. First, rebuild the word that the student had the most difficulty with but sounded out correctly. Then say, "This word was kind of hard. You were right when you said (word) for this word. How did you know to say it that way?" If the student is reluctant to answer, provide and document probing questions. If the student reads all words with equal ease, select one that required manipulation of the vowel (e.g., *sit*). Because valuable information can also be gained from students' incorrect attempts, if none of the words are read correctly, select one that is of interest to you.

Spelling. In this activity, the student becomes the word builder—a role that most are eager to assume. Tell the student that you will say a word and that he or she will use the letter tiles to spell the word. When dictating the words, articulate clearly by stretching and exaggerating so the student can attend to each sound (e.g., /ta:::p/, /s:::a:::t/) but do not break the word into individual sounds (/t/ /a/ /p/). Plosives (t, p, k) cannot be stretched, but they can be exaggerated; other consonants, including fricatives (s, v, f) and nasals (m, n), can be stretched by continuing the airflow.

Say the first word, *tan*, and ask the student to build it for you. Once built, ask the student to read the word or "check it." Record the word exactly as the student builds it, noting any self-corrections made along the way. Move to the next word, *tad*, by stating, "If this word says *tan* (previously built word) what would you have to do to make it say *tad*?" Encourage the student to listen to the entire word before building. After the child builds tad, ask the first metalinguistic question (denoted by an asterisk in Figure 1): "How did you know to build *tad* that way?" If necessary, draw from and document the use of the following probes: "What were you thinking when I said the word?" "How did you know to add the *d* instead of a *p*?" "I noticed your mouth moving. How did that help you?"

If the student gives an incorrect response on a particular item, record the response (including behavior and language) and then go to the next word. Do not correct the student in the sense of making the change. For example, if the student spelled *tan* as *fat*, you would not say, "That's not *tan*, that's *fat*." Rather, you would say, "You built the word *fat*. What would you have to do to spell the word *tad*?" When recording students' responses, also note their building strategies (e.g., manipulates all tiles or the minimum required).

At the end of the spelling section, ask the second metalinguistic question. Rebuild the word that the student had the most difficulty with but spelled correctly. Say, "You were right when you built (word) that way. How did you know to spell it that way?" If few words are spelled correctly, you may want to ask the metalinguistic question of an incorrect attempt.

Sight words. Set the letter tiles aside to begin the sight-word reading section. Lay out the collection of word tiles in front of the student and ask him or her to read the words. If the student looks over the words and does not respond, point to a word that you anticipate he or she would know (e.g., I, the, a, cat) in order to build success. Ask, "What is this word?" Once the student has gained momentum, support by saying, "Find other words you know and read them to me." You can support a situation that may be overwhelming for a young reader.

Sentences

Use the sight words from the previous activity to read and build sentences. To begin, build the first sentence and ask the student to read the sentence to you. Record the student's response, including self-corrections and decoding strategies. Continue this process with each of the sentences or until the student is unable to attempt working with the words. Then, move to the building section and have the student become the sentence builder. Say the sentence and ask the student to make it for you. We recommend that the student read the sentence after building to allow for self-correction and to provide additional assessment information. As you continue this process, dictate each sentence slowly and encourage the student to listen to the entire sentence before building. You may choose to read each sentence twice, but in order to assess short-term memory, do not dictate one word at a time.

Decision Rules and Scoring

The purpose of the Tile Test is to assess student performance and feed that information into instruction. Therefore, it is not intended that the administrator instruct students on the concepts of the tool. Students are not provided specific feedback, whether correct or incorrect. General responses should be positive: "You're doing a great job, let's move to the next activity." The two criteria used to decide when to stop are accuracy and speed. If the students' responses are incorrect, even if they are moving through the activities quickly, you probably do not want to continue. In addition, if they struggle with an activity and take a long time then you probably should not continue the specific activity. If students have difficulty in one section (e.g., decoding words), stop the assessment in that section and move to the next section. There are two reasons for attempting each section of the test. First, knowledge in one area may not be indicative of knowledge in another; for example, a student may build words more easily than decode words. Second, the Tile Test was designed around a particular curriculum, and students may have been through a different set of curriculum experiences.

The total score and subsection scores make it possible to monitor growth over time. The total

Table 1
Scoring totals

Test section	Total points
Letters and sounds	
Letter identification	8
Letter name	8
Letter sound	8
Words	
Decoding	8
Spelling	8
Metalinguistic awareness	6
Sight-word reading	17
Sentences	
Reading	6
Building	5

Table 2
Tile Test: Metalinguistic rubric

0 No response. "I don't know."
1 "I know it." "My mom taught me." "I'm smart."
2 Recognition of letters (e.g., "I looked at the letters").
3 Recognition of sounds (e.g., "I sound it out," "I listen to the sounds").
4 Partial linking sounds to letters (e.g., "It starts with a *p* /p/, then /l/") or partial analogy (e.g., "Pat is like cat").
5 Explains the spelling of *each* sound or full analogy (e.g., "Pat is like cat, but it starts with a /p/").
6 Explains how sounds are articulated. "It starts with /p/ my lips are together and the air pops out, my tongue is resting in the middle of my mouth...."

possible points for each subsection are located in Table 1. When scoring, award credit for self-corrections. No partial credit is given.

The metalinguistic questions are scored against the rubric in Table 2. Consider the student's responses to the two decoding and two spelling items when making decisions. To score the sentence reading and building sections, assign 1 point for each complete sentence read (or built) correctly.

Instructional Decisions

The results of the Tile Test can be used to help teachers identify the level of understanding students have about letters, sounds, words, and sentences, as well as the strategies they employ and their awareness of strategy use. Students' responses provide valuable qualitative information that immediately informs instruction. For example, Anthony (all student names are pseudonyms), a kindergarten student, could identify the eight letters in the Tile Test when asked to point to each and provided the name and sound of the six consonants presented in isolation (no vowels). However, when asked to use the letters at the word level, he was unable to link the sounds to the letters when decoding (see Table 3) and had minimal representation of consonants when spelling. When spelling, Anthony identified individual sounds in speech and represented them with letters.

Irvin also identified each of the eight letters in the Tile Test and correctly provided the names and sounds of the consonants and the vowel *a* (short pronunciation) in isolation. He responded that the name of the letter *i* is *e* and is pronounced as /e/ (long pronunciation). When decoding (see Table 3), he identified initial and final consonant sounds but was unable to blend the sounds to form a word. Although he knew the sound for *a* when presented in isolation, he did not identify the vowel in the context of words. When building words with the vowel *a*, Irvin represented each sound with a letter tile. When responding to the metalinguistic question of how he knew to spell *sip* that way (as *sp*), he referenced the vowel stating, "It's not an *a*."

Both these students would benefit from instruction that includes opportunities to manipulate letter tiles to build and decode words. Because Anthony demonstrated letter–sound correspondence for a collection of consonants, he is ready to study vowels and their function in words: The vowel a glues the consonants together to create a word. Prompts to "stretch and exaggerate" when articulating words will help Anthony attend to each and every sound and will help Irvin blend rather than separate sounds. Many children, in our experience, when taught to separate phonemes to decode a word (e.g., /c/-/a/-/t/), must then be taught to blend. Therefore, we never ask a child to break a word into its individual phonemes, so they do not have to be taught to blend the phonemes. Finally, prompts to explain their thinking while working with words will facilitate their application of letter–sound knowledge during phonics instruction and when reading and writing throughout the day.

Table 3
Students' word decoding and spelling

	Anthony	Irvin
Decoding		
pat	p-a-t	/p/ /t/
sat	[no attempt]	/s/ /t/
sam		/s/ /f/
fan		/f/ /h/
sit		/s/ /n/
Spelling		
tan	n t	tan
map		/ma/, map
sip		/sa/, sp
fin		/p/ /a/, fn
sap		/s/ /ap/ /a:::p/, sap

Use of the Tile Test

The Tile Test can be used to collect information before, during, and after instruction to check students' prior knowledge and progress and to plan for future instruction. We suggest that the teacher begin by administering it to a few students.

After you have gained some familiarity with the test, you will find that you can adapt the test for your own needs. One adaptation that takes advantage of the distinct segments that assess different orthographic concepts is to use portions of the test to follow up instruction with all of your students or six to eight focal students. Consider reading ability, language background, gender, and other important factors in your context when selecting students so you gain information regarding the full range of your class.

A second adaptation is to use the Tile Test with small groups of four to six students. You should have a reasonable degree of comfort with the test in order to scaffold students' metaphonic responses. Because there is not always time to assess each student individually, the group administration is well worth the effort. Sample "group assessments" are available on our website.

The third option is to adapt the test to a whole-class administration once students understand the format of the test, have worked with tiles, and have become accustomed to questions that prompt them to talk about the strategies they use when decoding and spelling words. Each student (or pair) has a collection of tiles. As you give a task (e.g., to build the synthetic word *wembick*), walk around and ask students to explain their problem-solving strategies (use the metalinguistic questions and probes presented earlier). Careful note-taking of your observations can guide your instructional planning.

The Tile Test also serves as a shell for incorporating a broad range of orthographic patterns so that you can adapt the test to your curriculum content. After the initial administration, assess different collections of letters and select words to decode and spell that are based on orthographic concepts being studied. For example, when instruction focuses on students' ability to work with the entire collection of short vowels, make the appropriate substitutions in the decoding and spelling segment. Item selection should be made in a principled way. For example, be careful about items like *r*, *l*, and *w*, which influence the vowel pronunciation (include intentionally when appropriate). An expanded version of the Tile Test is available on our website to provide

Figure 3
Decoding real and synthetic word activity from the expanded version of the Tile Test

pat __________	vute __________
sat __________	flass __________
sam __________	lodded __________
hin __________	wembick ________

guidance in creating your own versions and to provide a tool for assessing more complex orthographic concepts (appropriate for use with students through second grade). This version includes the use of individual real and synthetic words (see Figure 3). The synthetic word series assesses knowledge of the basic consonant–vowel–consonant building blocks in monosyllabic and polysyllabic words and includes consonant blends and the long vowel marking system. Synthetic words are included in both the decoding and spelling activities to place the emphasis on sound–symbol relationships. This rationale is supported by research (Felton & Wood, 1992) showing that synthetic word reading is correlated with reading success more highly than verbal IQ. Additional activities have students respond to metalinguistic questions to assess the problem-solving strategies known and applied. Finally, phoneme awareness is tapped by questions about the articulation of consonant sounds in real and synthetic words.

The Tile Test Is Effective and Flexible

The Tile Test provides teachers with an efficient and effective tool for assessing young students' understanding of the English orthographic system. Their problem-solving strategies and awareness of strategy use when decoding and spelling new or unfamiliar words surface through the metaphonic discussions. The flexibility of the tool provides teachers with multiple ways to adapt it for classroom use. Its structure and the ability to match items to the curriculum help teachers think about what is important to know and how to assess the different constructs of literacy. Careful analysis of the students' responses to the activities and metalinguistic questions, coupled with observations of student behaviors in various classroom literacy contexts, can help teachers identify student knowledge before instruction, monitor the impact of instruction, and guide future instruction.

Support for this article was provided by the Spencer Foundation.

References

Bransford, J.D., Brown, A.L., & Cocking, R.R. (Eds.). (2000). *How people learn: Brain, mind, experience, and school.* Washington, DC: National Academy Press.

Calfee, R.C. (1998). Phonics and phonemes: Learning to decode and spell in a literature-based program. In J.L. Metsala & L.C. Ehri (Eds.), *Word recognition in beginning literacy* (pp. 315–340). Mahwah, NJ: Erlbaum.

Calfee, R.C., & Norman, K.A. (2003, April). *Decoding and spelling instruction: Which factors matter most?* Paper presented at the annual meeting of the American Educational Research Association, Chicago, IL.

Calfee, R.C., Norman, K.A., Trainin, G., & Wilson, K.M. (2001). Conducting a design experiment for improving early literacy: What we learned in school last year. In C.M. Roller (Ed.), *Learning to teach reading: Setting the research agenda* (pp. 166–179). Newark, DE: International Reading Association.

Celebration Press. (1997). *Developmental reading assessment.* Glenview, IL: Addison-Wesley.

Cronbach, L.J. (1951). Coefficient alpha and the internal structure of tests. *Psychometrika, 16,* 297–334.

Felton, R.H., & Wood, F.B. (1992). A reading level match study of nonword reading skills in poor readers with varying IQ. *Journal of Learning Disabilities, 25,* 318–326.

Hirsch, E.D. (2003). Reading comprehension requires knowledge—of words and the world: Scientific insights into the fourth-grade slump and the nation's stagnant comprehension scores. *American Educator, 27*(1), 10–48.

Liberman, A.M., & Mattingly, I.G. (1985). The motor theory of speech perception revised. *Cognition, 21*, 1–36.

Lionni, L. (1973). *Swimmy*. New York: Pantheon.

National Institute of Child Health and Human Development. (2000). *Report of the National Reading Panel. Teaching children to read: An evidence-based assessment of the scientific research literature on reading and its implications for reading instruction* (NIH Publication No. 00-4769). Washington, DC: U.S. Government Printing Office.

Scholastic. (1997). *Literacy place: Kindergarten test of phonemic awareness*. Jefferson City, MO: Author.

Trainin, G., Calfee, R.C., Norman, K.A., & Wilson, K. (2002, April). *Supporting metacognitive development: The impact of teacher practice*. Paper presented at the Annual Convention of the International Reading Association, San Francisco, CA.

Venezky, R.L. (1999). *The American way of spelling: The structure and origins of American English orthography*. New York: Guilford.

Vygotsky, L.S. (1978). *Mind in society: The development of higher psychological processes* (M. Cole, V. John-Steiner, S. Scribner, & E. Souberman, Eds. & Trans.). Cambridge, MA: Harvard University Press. (Original work published 1934)

Measuring Attitude Toward Reading: A New Tool for Teachers

Michael C. McKenna and Dennis J. Kear

In 1762, the philosopher Rousseau speculated that any method of teaching reading would suffice given adequate motivation on the part of the learner. While present-day educators might resist such a sweeping pronouncement, the importance of attitude is nevertheless widely recognized. The Commission on Reading in its summary of research (Anderson, Hiebert, Scott, & Wilkinson, 1985) concluded that "becoming a skilled reader requires...learning that written material can be interesting" (p. 18). Smith (1988) observed that "the emotional response to reading...is the primary reason most readers read, and probably the primary reason most nonreaders do not read" (p. 177). Wixson and Lipson (1992) acknowledge that "the student's attitude toward reading is a central factor affecting reading performance." These conclusions are based on a long history of research in which attitude and achievement have been consistently linked (e.g., Purves & Beach, 1972; Walberg & Tsai, 1985).

The recent emphasis on enhanced reading proficiency has often ignored the important role played by children's attitudes in the process of becoming literate. Athey (1985) suggested that one reason for this tendency is that the affective aspects of reading tend to be ill-defined and to involve "shadowy variables" (p. 527) difficult to conceptualize, measure, and address instructionally.

The focus of recent research and development in assessment has been comprehension rather than attitude. Some progress has been made in the development of individually administered, qualitative instruments, but quantitative group surveys, which form a natural complement to qualitative approaches, are often poorly documented in terms of desirable psychometric attributes, such as normative frames of reference and evidence of reliability and validity. Our purpose was to produce a public-domain instrument that would remedy these shortcomings and enable teachers to estimate attitude levels efficiently and reliably. This article presents that instrument along with a discussion of its development and suggestions for its use.

Development of the Scale

Several important criteria were established to guide the development of the instrument. The authors agreed that the survey must (a) have a large-scale normative frame of reference; (b) comprise a set of items selected on the basis of desirable psychometric properties; (c) have empirically documented reliability and validity; (d) be applicable to all elementary students, grades 1 through 6; (e) possess a meaningful, attention-getting, student-friendly response format; (f) be suitable for brief group administration; and (g) comprise separate subscales for recreational and academic reading. We knew of no instrument that possessed all of these characteristics.

A pictorial format was elected because of its natural appeal for children and because of its comprehensibility by the very young. An informal survey of more than 30 elementary teachers indicated that the comic strip character Garfield was more apt to be recognized by children in grades 1 through 6 than any other. Jim Davis, who is the creator of Garfield, and United Features, his publisher, agreed to supply four black-line, camera-ready poses of Garfield,

From *The Reading Teacher*, 43(9), 626-639. © 1990 by the International Reading Association.

ranging from very happy to very upset, and to permit the resulting instrument to be copied and used by educators. (See the Elementary Reading Attitude Survey and scoring sheet prior to the Appendix at the end of this article.)

An even number of scale points avoids a neutral, central category which respondents often select in order to avoid committing themselves even when clear opinions exist (Nunnally, 1967). The use of four points was based on a substantial body of research suggesting that young children typically can discriminate among no more than five discrete bits of information simultaneously (e.g., Case & Khanna, 1981; Chi, 1978; Chi & Klahr, 1975; Nitko, 1983).

Several earlier surveys were used as models in the creation of an item pool from which the final set of items would be constructed (e.g., Estes, 1971; Heathington, 1979; Right to Read, 1976; Robinson & Good, 1987). A total of 39 items were developed, each related to one of two aspects of attitude: (a) attitude toward recreational reading (24 items) or (b) attitude toward academic reading (15 items). To establish a consistent, appropriate expectation on the part of the students, each item was worded with a uniform beginning: "How do you feel...."

This prototype instrument was then administered to 499 elementary students in a middle-sized midwestern U.S. school district. For each of the two item sets (recreational and academic), final sets of 10 items each were selected on the basis of inter-item correlation coefficients. The revised instrument was then administered at midyear to a national sample of over 18,000 children in grades 1-6. Estimates of reliability, as well as evidence of validity, were based on this national sample. A complete description of the technical aspects of the survey appears in the Appendix.

Administering and Scoring the Survey

The Elementary Reading Attitude Survey (ERAS) can be given to an entire class in a matter of minutes, but, as with any normed instrument, it is important that the administration reflect as closely as possible the procedure used with the norming group. The administration procedures are presented in the "Directions for Use" information that accompanies the instrument itself. This process involves first familiarizing students with the instrument and with the purposes for giving it. The teacher next reads the items aloud twice as the students mark their responses.

Each item is then assigned 1, 2, 3, or 4 points, a "4" indicating the happiest (leftmost) Garfield. The scoring sheet that follows the instrument can be used to organize this process and record recreational, academic, and total scores, along with the percentile rank of each. The results are then ready for use.

Using the Survey

Collecting data about students is an empty exercise unless the information is used to plan instruction. Scores on the ERAS can be helpful in this process, but it is important to understand what they can and cannot do as well as how they relate to other sources of information.

Strengths and limitations. This survey provides quantitative estimates of two important aspects of children's attitudes toward reading. Like global measures of achievement, however, they can do little in themselves to identify the causes of poor attitude or to suggest instructional techniques likely to improve it. On the other hand, the instrument can be used to (a) make possible initial conjecture about the attitudes of specific students, (b) provide a convenient group profile of a class (or a larger unit), or (c) serve as a means of monitoring the attitudinal impact of instructional programs.

A classroom plan. A teacher might begin by administering the ERAS during the first few weeks of the school year. Class averages for recreational and academic reading attitude will enable the teacher to characterize the class generally on these two dimensions. Scores for individual students may suggest the need to further explore the nature, strength, and origins of their values and beliefs.

This goal could be pursued through the use of individually conducted strategies such as structured interviews, open-ended sentence instruments, or interest inventories. Reed (1979) suggested using nonreactive measures as well, such as recorded teacher observations following reading instruction and reading-related activities. The combination of these techniques provides a variety of useful information that can be collected in portfolio fashion for individual students.

Survey results can be very useful in deciding what sorts of additional information to pursue. Four general response patterns are especially notable, and we will depict each of them with hypothetical students who are, in fact, composites of many with whom we have worked.

Two profiles involve sizable differences (5 points or more) between recreational and academic scores. Jimmy, a third grader, has a recreational score of 29 and an academic score of 21. The difference suggests a stronger attitude toward reading for fun than for academic purposes. To an extent, this pattern is typical of third graders (compare the means in Table 2 in the Appendix), but not to the degree exhibited in Jimmy's case. Had both scores been higher, Jimmy's teacher might have been justified in disregarding the difference, but a score of 21 is low both in the criterial sense (it is close to the slightly frowning Garfield) and in a normative one (18th percentile rank). Examining the last 10 items of the survey one by one might prove helpful in forming hypotheses about which aspects are troublesome. These can then be tested by carefully observing Jimmy during reading instruction.

For Katy, a fifth grader, assume that the two scores are reversed. By virtue of her stronger attitude toward academic reading, Katy is somewhat atypical. Her academic score of 29 is quite strong in both a criterial sense (it is near the slightly smiling Garfield) and a normative sense (71st percentile rank). Her score of 21 in recreational reading attitude is cause for concern (13th percentile rank), but the strong academic score suggests that her disdain is not total and may be traceable to causes subject to intervention. Because items 1–10 are somewhat global in nature, it is unlikely that scrutinizing her responses will be very helpful. A nonthreatening chat about reading habits may be much more productive in helping her teacher identify Katy's areas of interest and even suggest a book or two. Katy may not have been exposed to a variety of interesting trade books.

Two other profiles involve differences between attitude and ability. These are very real possibilities that require careful attention (Roettger, 1980). Consider Patrick, a second grader whose academic attitude score is 28 and who has been placed in a low-ability group by his teacher. Patrick's relatively positive score (near the smiling Garfield) may encourage his teacher, for it is apt to be higher than others in his reading group. However, more than half of his second-grade peers across the country have stronger attitudes toward reading in school. Data from this study document a widening attitudinal gap between low- and high-ability children as they move through school. Patrick's teacher should be concerned about the likely effects of another frustrating year on his attitude toward instruction. Teaching methods and instructional materials should be scrutinized.

Ironically, the same conclusion might be reached for Deborah, a sixth-grade student of extraordinary ability. Her academic attitude score, however, is only 17, which is quite negative, whether one looks to its position among the pictures or notes that it represents a percentile rank of 11. If Deborah's recreational score were substantially higher, her teacher would be correct in wondering whether the instruction she is receiving is adequately engaging. As with Jimmy, an inspection of her responses to items 11–20 could be helpful, followed by a nonintrusive reading interview and tactful observation. On the other hand, suppose that Deborah's recreational score were also 17. This would place her total score (34) at the 5th percentile rank and suggest a strong disinclination to read despite the ability to do so. This would warrant action on the part of an insightful teacher who is willing to make instructional and leisure reading attractive.

Examples of this nature illustrate how the Elementary Reading Attitude Survey can enter into the process of instructional planning, especially near the beginning of a school year. As the year draws to a close, the survey can again be given, this time to monitor any attitudinal changes of the class as a whole. By comparing class averages from the beginning and end of the year, a teacher can gauge the movement of a class relative both to its own earlier position and to a national midyear average. Estimating yearlong changes for individual students is a less reliable process and should only be attempted with regard to the standard error of measurement for a given subscale and grade level (see Table 2 in the Appendix). We recommend using twice the standard error to construct an adequate confidence interval. In other words, the pre/post difference would, in general, need to be 5 points or more on either the academic or recreational subscale before *any* real change could be assumed. On the total score, the pre/post change would need to be 7 or 8 points.

Conclusion

The instrument presented here builds on the strengths of its predecessors and, it is hoped, remedies some of their psychometric shortcomings. Its placement into the public domain by means of this article provides teachers with a tool that can be used with relative confidence to estimate the attitude levels of their students and initiate informal assessment efforts into the role attitude plays in students' development as readers.

The authors wish to express their sincere thanks to Jim Davis for his Garfield illustrations and for his concern for children's literacy abilities.

References

Anderson, R.C., Hiebert, E.H., Scott, J.A., & Wilkinson, I.A.G. (1985). *Becoming a nation of readers: The report of the Commission on Reading.* Washington, DC: National Institute of Education.

Athey, I.J. (1985). Reading research in the affective domain. In H. Singer & R.B. Ruddell (Eds.), *Theoretical models and processes of reading* (3rd ed., pp. 527-557). Newark, DE: International Reading Association.

Case, R., & Khanna, F. (1981). The missing links: Stages in children's progression from sensorimotor to logical thought. In K.W. Fischer (Ed.), *Cognitive development* (New directions for child development, No. 12). San Francisco: Jossey-Bass.

Chi, M.T. (1978). Knowledge structures and memory development. In R.S. Siegler (Ed.), *Children's thinking: What develops?* Hillsdale, NJ: Erlbaum.

Chi, M.T., & Klahr, D. (1975). Span and rate of apprehension in children and adults. *Journal of Experimental Psychology, 19*, 434-439.

Cronbach, L.J. (1951). Coefficient alpha and the internal structure of tests. *Psychometrika, 16*, 297-334.

Estes, T.H. (1971). A scale to measure attitudes toward reading. *Journal of Reading, 15*, 135-138.

Heathington, B.S. (1979). What to do about reading motivation in the middle school. *Journal of Reading, 22*, 709-713.

Nitko, A.J. (1983). *Educational tests and measurement: An introduction.* New York: Harcourt Brace Jovanovich.

Nunnally, J.C. (1967). *Psychometric theory.* New York: McGraw-Hill.

Purves, A.C., & Beach, R. (1972). *Literature and the reader: Research in response to literature, reading interests, and the teaching of literature.* Urbana, IL: National Council of Teachers of English.

Reed, K. (1979). Assessing affective responses to reading: A multi-measurement model. *Reading World, 19*, 149-156.

Right to Read Office. (1976). *Reading interest/attitude scale.* Washington, DC: United States Office of Education.

Robinson, R., & Good, T.L. (1987). *Becoming an effective reading teacher.* New York: Harper & Row.

Roettger, D. (1980). Elementary students' attitudes toward reading. *The Reading Teacher, 33*, 451-453.

Rousseau, J-J. (1762/1979). *Emile, or on education* (A. Bloom, Trans.). New York: Basic Books.

Smith, F. (1988). *Understanding reading: A psycholinguistic analysis of reading and learning to read* (4th ed.). Hillsdale, NJ: Erlbaum.

Statistical abstract of the United States. (1989). Washington, DC: Bureau of Census, Department of Commerce.

Walberg, H.J., & Tsai, S. (1985). Correlates of reading achievement and attitude: A national assessment study. *Journal of Educational Research, 78*, 159-167.

Wixson, K.K., & Lipson, M.Y. (1992). *Reading diagnosis and remediation.* Glenview, IL: Scott, Foresman.

Elementary Reading Attitude Survey

School_____________________ Grade__________ Name_________________________________

1. How do you feel when you read a book on a rainy Saturday?

2. How do you feel when you read a book in school during free time?

3. How do you feel about reading for fun at home?

4. How do you feel about getting a book for a present?

2

5. How do you feel about spending free time reading?

6. How do you feel about starting a new book?

7. How do you feel about reading during summer vacation?

8. How do you feel about reading instead of playing?

3

9. How do you feel about going to a bookstore?

10. How do you feel about reading different kinds of books?

11. How do you feel when the teacher asks you questions about what you read?

12. How do you feel about doing reading workbook pages and worksheets?

4

13. How do you feel about reading in school?

14. How do you feel about reading your school books?

15. How do you feel about learning from a book?

16. How do you feel when it's time for reading class?

5

17. How do you feel about the stories you read in reading class?

18. How do you feel when you read out loud in class?

19. How do you feel about using a dictionary?

20. How do you feel about taking a reading test?

Elementary Reading Attitude Survey scoring sheet

Student name ______________________________

Teacher ______________________________

Grade ______________ Administration date ______________

Scoring guide	
4 points	Happiest Garfield
3 points	Slightly smiling Garfield
2 points	Mildly upset Garfield
1 point	Very upset Garfield

Recreational reading	Academic reading
1. ______	11. ______
2. ______	12. ______
3. ______	13. ______
4. ______	14. ______
5. ______	15. ______
6. ______	16. ______
7. ______	17. ______
8. ______	18. ______
9. ______	19. ______
10. ______	20. ______
Raw score: ______	Raw score: ______

Full scale raw score (Recreational + Academic): ______________

Percentile ranks		
	Recreational	
	Academic	
	Full scale	

Elementary Reading Attitude Survey Directions for Use

The Elementary Reading Attitude Survey provides a quick indication of student attitudes toward reading. It consists of 20 items and can be administered to an entire classroom in about 10 minutes. Each item presents a brief, simply worded statement about reading, followed by four pictures of Garfield. Each pose is designed to depict a different emotional state, ranging from very positive to very negative.

Administration

Begin by telling students that you wish to find out how they feel about reading. Emphasize that this is *not* a test and that there are no "right" answers. Encourage sincerity.

Distribute the survey forms and, if you wish to monitor the attitudes of specific students, ask them to write their names in the space at the top. Hold up a copy of the survey so that the students can see the first page. Point to the picture of Garfield at the far left of the first item. Ask the students to look at this same picture on their own survey form. Discuss with them the mood Garfield seems to be in (very happy). Then move to the next picture and again discuss Garfield's mood (this time, a *little* happy). In the same way, move to the third and fourth pictures and talk about Garfield's moods—a little upset and very upset. It is helpful to point out the position of Garfield's *mouth*, especially in the middle two figures.

Explain that together you will read some statements about reading and that the students should think about how they feel about each statement. They should then circle the picture of Garfield that is closest to their own feelings. (Emphasize that the students should respond according to their own feelings, not as Garfield might respond!) Read each item aloud slowly and distinctly; then read it a second time while students are thinking. Be sure to read the item number and to remind students of page numbers when new pages are reached.

Scoring

To score the survey, count four points for each leftmost (happiest) Garfield circled, three for each slightly smiling Garfield, two for each mildly upset Garfield, and one point for each very upset (rightmost) Garfield. Three scores for each student can be obtained: the total for the first 10 items, the total for the second 10, and a composite total. The first half of the survey relates to attitude toward recreational reading; the second half relates to attitude toward academic aspects of reading.

Interpretation

You can interpret scores in two ways. One is to note informally where the score falls in regard to the four nodes of the scale. A total score of 50, for example, would fall about mid-way on the scale, between the slightly happy and slightly upset figures, therefore indicating a relatively indifferent overall attitude toward reading. The other approach is more formal. It involves converting the raw scores into percentile ranks by means of Table 1. Be sure to use the norms for the right grade level and to note the column headings (Rec = recreational reading, Aca = academic reading, Tot = total score). If you wish to determine the average percentile rank for your class, average the raw scores first; then use the table to locate the percentile rank corresponding to the raw score mean. Percentile ranks cannot be averaged directly.

Appendix
Technical Aspects of the Elementary Reading Attitude Survey

The norming project

To create norms for the interpretation of scores, a large-scale study was conducted in late January 1989, at which time the survey was administered to 18,138 students in Grades 1-6. A number of steps were taken to achieve a sample that was sufficiently stratified (i.e., reflective of the American population) to allow confident generalizations. Children were drawn from 95 school districts in 38 U.S. states. The number of girls exceeded by only 5 the number of boys. Ethnic distribution of the sample was also close to that of the U.S. population (Statistical abstract of the United States, 1989). The proportion of blacks (9.5%) was within 3% of the national proportion, while the proportion of Hispanics (6.2%) was within 2%.

Percentile ranks at each grade for both subscales and the full scale are presented in Table 1. These data can be used to compare individual students' scores with the national sample and they can be interpreted like achievement-test percentile ranks.

Table 1
Mid-year percentile ranks by grade and scale

Raw	Grade 1			Grade 2			Grade 3			Grade 4			Grade 5			Grade 6		
Scr	Rec	Aca	Tot	Rec	Aca	Tot	Rec	Aca	Tot	Rec	Aca	Tot	Rec	Aca	Tot	Rec	Aca	Tot
80			99			99			99			99			99			99
79			95			96			98			99			99			99
78			93			95			97			98			99			99
77			92			94			97			98			99			99
76			90			93			96			97			98			99
75			88			92			95			96			98			99
74			86			90			94			95			97			99
73			84			88			92			94			97			98
72			82			86			91			93			96			98
71			80			84			89			91			95			97
70			78			82			86			89			94			96
69			75			79			84			88			92			95
68			72			77			81			86			91			93
67			69			74			79			83			89			92
66			66			71			76			80			87			90
65			62			69			73			78			84			88
64			59			66			70			75			82			86
63			55			63			67			72			79			84
62			52			60			64			69			76			82
61			49			57			61			66			73			79
60			46			54			58			62			70			76
59			43			51			55			59			67			73
58			40			47			51			56			64			69
57			37			45			48			53			61			66
56			34			41			44			48			57			62
55			31			38			41			45			53			58
54			28			35			38			41			50			55

(continued)

Table 1
Mid-year percentile ranks by grade and scale (continued)

Raw Scr	Grade 1			Grade 2			Grade 3			Grade 4			Grade 5			Grade 6		
	Rec	Aca	Tot	Rec	Aca	Tot	Rec	Aca	Tot	Rec	Aca	Tot	Rec	Aca	Tot	Rec	Aca	Tot
53			25			32			34			38			46			52
52			22			29			31			35			42			48
51			20			26			28			32			39			44
50			18			23			25			28			36			40
49			15			20			23			26			33			37
48			13			18			20			23			29			33
47			12			15			17			20			26			30
46			10			13			15			18			23			27
45			8			11			13			16			20			25
44			7			9			11			13			17			22
43			6			8			9			12			15			20
42			5			7			8			10			13			17
41			5			6			7			9			12			15
40	99	99	4	99	99	5	99	99	6	99	99	7	99	99	10	99	99	13
39	92	91	3	94	94	4	96	97	6	97	98	6	98	99	9	99	99	12
38	89	88	3	92	92	3	94	95	4	95	97	5	96	98	8	97	99	10
37	86	85	2	88	89	2	90	93	3	92	95	4	94	98	7	95	99	8
36	81	79	2	84	85	2	87	91	2	88	93	3	91	96	6	92	98	7
35	77	75	1	79	81	1	81	88	2	84	90	3	87	95	4	88	97	6
34	72	69	1	74	78	1	75	83	2	78	87	2	82	93	4	83	95	5
33	65	63	1	68	73	1	69	79	1	72	83	2	77	90	3	79	93	4
32	58	58	1	62	67	1	63	74	1	66	79	1	71	86	3	74	91	3
31	52	53	1	56	62	1	57	69	0	60	75	1	65	82	2	69	87	2
30	44	49	1	50	57	0	51	63	0	54	70	1	59	77	1	63	82	2
29	38	44	0	44	51	0	45	58	0	47	64	1	53	71	1	58	78	1
28	32	39	0	37	46	0	38	52	0	41	58	1	48	66	1	51	73	1
27	26	34	0	31	41	0	33	47	0	35	52	1	42	60	1	46	67	1
26	21	30	0	25	37	0	26	41	0	29	46	0	36	54	0	39	60	1
25	17	25	0	20	32	0	21	36	0	23	40	0	30	49	0	34	54	0
24	12	21	0	15	27	0	17	31	0	19	35	0	25	42	0	29	49	0
23	9	18	0	11	23	0	13	26	0	14	29	0	20	37	0	24	42	0
22	7	14	0	8	18	0	9	22	0	11	25	0	16	31	0	19	36	0
21	5	11	0	6	15	0	6	18	0	9	20	0	13	26	0	15	30	0
20	4	9	0	4	11	0	5	14	0	6	16	0	10	21	0	12	24	0
19	2	7		2	8		3	11		5	13		7	17		10	20	
18	2	5		2	6		2	8		3	9		6	13		5	18	
17	1	4		1	5		1	5		2	7		4	9		6	11	
16	1	3		1	3		1	4		2	5		3	6		4	8	
15	0	2		0	2		0	3		1	3		2	4		3	6	
14	0	2		0	1		0	1		1	2		1	2		1	3	
13	0	1		0	1		0	1		0	1		1	2		1	2	
12	0	1		0	0		0	0		0	1		0	1		0	1	
11	0	0		0	0		0	0		0	0		0	0		0	0	
10	0	0		0	0		0	0		0	0		0	0		0	0	

Reliability

Cronbach's alpha, a statistic developed primarily to measure the internal consistency of attitude scales (Cronbach, 1951), was calculated at each grade level for both subscales and for the composite score. These coefficients ranged from .74 to .89 and are presented in Table 2.

It is interesting that with only two exceptions, coefficients were .80 or higher. These were for the recreational subscale at Grades 1 and 2. It is possible that the stability of young children's attitudes toward leisure reading grows with their decoding ability and familiarity with reading as a pastime.

Table 2
Descriptive statistics and internal consistency measures

		Recreational Subscale				Academic Subscale				Full Scale (Total)			
Grade	N	M	SD	S_eM	Alpha[a]	M	SD	S_eM	Alpha	M	SD	S_eM	Alpha
1	2,518	31.0	5.7	2.9	.74	30.1	6.8	3.0	.81	61.0	11.4	4.1	.87
2	2,974	30.3	5.7	2.7	.78	28.8	6.7	2.9	.81	59.1	11.4	3.9	.88
3	3,151	30.0	5.6	2.5	.80	27.8	6.4	2.8	.81	57.8	10.9	3.8	.88
4	3,679	29.5	5.8	2.4	.83	26.9	6.3	2.6	.83	56.5	11.0	3.6	.89
5	3,374	28.5	6.1	2.3	.86	25.6	6.0	2.5	.82	54.1	10.8	3.6	.89
6	2,442	27.9	6.2	2.2	.87	24.7	5.8	2.5	.81	52.5	10.6	3.5	.89
All	18,138	29.5	5.9	2.5	.82	27.3	6.6	2.7	.83	56.8	11.3	3.7	.89

[a] Cronbach's alpha (Cronbach, 1951).

Validity

Evidence of construct validity was gathered by several means. For the recreational subscale, students in the national norming group were asked (a) whether a public library was available to them and (b) whether they currently had a library card. Those to whom libraries were available were separated into two groups (those with and without cards) and their recreational scores were compared. Cardholders had significantly higher ($p < .001$) recreational scores ($M = 30.0$) than noncardholders ($M = 28.9$), evidence of the subscale's validity in that scores varied predictably with an outside criterion.

A second test compared students who presently had books checked out from their school library versus students who did not. The comparison was limited to children whose teachers reported not requiring them to check out books. The means of the two groups varied significantly ($p < .001$), and children with books checked out scored higher ($M = 29.2$) than those who had no books checked out ($M = 27.3$).

A further test of the recreational subscale compared students who reported watching an average of less than 1 hour of television per night with students who reported watching more than 2 hours per night. The recreational mean for the low televiewing group (31.5) significantly exceeded ($p < .001$) the mean of the heavy televiewing group (28.6). Thus, the amount of television watched varied inversely with children's attitudes toward recreational reading.

The validity of the academic subscale was tested by examining the relationship of scores to reading ability. Teachers categorized norm-group children as having low, average, or high overall reading ability. Mean subscale scores of the high-ability readers ($M = 27.7$) significantly exceeded the mean of low-ability readers ($M = 27.0$, $p < .001$), evidence that scores were reflective of how the students truly felt about reading for academic purposes.

The relationship between the subscales was also investigated. It was hypothesized that children's attitudes toward recreational and academic reading would be moderately but not highly correlated.

Facility with reading is likely to affect these two areas similarly, resulting in similar attitude scores. Nevertheless, it is easy to imagine children prone to read for pleasure but disenchanted with assigned reading and children academically engaged but without interest in reading outside of school. The intersubscale correlation coefficient was .64, which meant that just 41% of the variance in one set of scores could be accounted for by the other. It is reasonable to suggest that the two subscales, while related, also reflect dissimilar factors—a desired outcome.

To tell more precisely whether the traits measured by the survey corresponded to the two subscales, factor analyses were conducted. Both used the unweighted least squares method of extraction and a varimax rotation. The first analysis permitted factors to be identified liberally (using a limit equal to the smallest eigenvalue greater than 1). Three factors were identified. Of the 10 items comprising the academic subscale, 9 loaded predominantly on a single factor while the 10th (item 13) loaded nearly equally on all three factors. A second factor was dominated by 7 items of the recreational subscale, while 3 of the recreational items (6, 9, and 10) loaded principally on a third factor. These items did, however, load more heavily on the second (recreational) factor than on the first (academic). A second analysis constrained the identification of factors to two. This time, with one exception, all items loaded cleanly on factors associated with the two subscales. The exception was item 13, which could have been interpreted as a recreational item and thus apparently involved a slight ambiguity. Taken together, the factor analyses produced evidence extremely supportive of the claim that the survey's two subscales reflect discrete aspects of reading attitude.

The Reader Self-Perception Scale (RSPS): A New Tool for Measuring How Children Feel About Themselves as Readers

William A. Henk and Steven A. Melnick

Recently, reading educators and researchers have shown renewed interest in how affective factors influence children's academic achievement and behavior (Alvermann & Guthrie, 1993). As a result, our longheld intuitions about the powerful impact that attitudes, values, beliefs, desires, and motivations exert on literacy learning have begun to receive the focused attention they deserve.

Because of research in the affective domain, we now know with greater certainty that children who have made positive associations with reading tend to read more often, for longer periods of time, and with greater intensity. This deeper engagement translates into superior reading achievement (Anderson, Fielding, & Wilson, 1988; Foertsch, 1992). At the same time, we know that when children feel negatively about reading, their achievement tends to suffer. These children will either avoid reading altogether or read with little real involvement. Perhaps this is why, in a recent national poll, teachers ranked motivating students and creating an interest in reading as their first priority (O'Flavahan et al., 1992).

The movement toward greater consideration of affective influences on reading achievement is long overdue but somewhat understandable (Athey, 1985; Mathewson, 1985). Educators and researchers have recognized for some time the importance of knowing as much as possible about the many affective elements that shape readers' engagement (Morrow & Weinstein, 1986). Unfortunately, because affect tends to be difficult to measure, the tools necessary to make truly valid appraisals have not been available (Henk, 1993). Consequently, teachers have been hindered in adjusting classroom learning climates to foster maximum literacy growth.

To help teachers better address the role of affect in reading, we describe an important psychological construct, *reader self-efficacy*, and introduce a new scale to measure this aspect of literacy. The new scale can be administered to groups of students for the purposes of instruction, assessment, and research, and it provides data on affect that make individual reading evaluations more complete.

Reader Attitudes and Self-Perceptions

Fortunately, educators have made some important strides in measuring affective elements in recent years. For instance, McKenna and Kear (1990) have developed the Elementary Reading Attitude Survey (ERAS), a public domain instrument that measures elementary students' attitudes toward both school-based and recreational forms of reading. The ERAS has been used

From *The Reading Teacher*, 48(6), 470-482. © 1995 by the International Reading Association.

extensively by primary and intermediate level teachers to determine the overall attitude levels of classes, and it has also provided insights into the reading habits and achievement levels of individual children. Besides its inviting response format that makes use of the comic strip character Garfield the cat, a major advantage of the ERAS has been its extensive norming. Unlike many affective scales, the ERAS exhibits solid validity and reliability characteristics, two critical attributes given the potential importance of attitudinal indicators.

Following in this tradition of instrument development, we created the Reader Self-Perception Scale (RSPS) to measure how intermediate-level children feel about themselves as readers (Henk & Melnick, 1992). The RSPS was developed in response to calls in the professional literature for instruments that measure the way readers appraise themselves (Winograd & Paris, 1988; Wixson, Peters, Weber, & Roeber, 1987). Valencia (1990) refers to this notion of reader self-evaluation as "perception of self as reader," a concept important in both statewide and individual portfolio assessment contexts.

Like the Elementary Reading Attitude Survey, the RSPS has been validated systematically and measures a dimension of affect that almost certainly influences attitudes toward reading. At the same time, the construct tapped by the Reader Self-Perception Scale is different enough from reading attitude to warrant special consideration. The two instruments also differ in terms of grade level appropriateness. While the ERAS can be used in the primary grades through grade 6, the RSPS purposely focuses on intermediate-level readers. This targeting stems from developmental research that has consistently indicated that prior to fourth grade, children do not estimate their academic performance accurately, nor attribute its causes properly (Blumenfeld, Pintrich, Meece, & Wessels, 1982; Nicholls, 1978; Stipek, 1981). By contrast, children in the intermediate grades are less likely to attribute their achievement to luck or effort and more likely to attribute performance to ability (Nicholls, 1979; Ruble, Boggiano, Feldman, & Loebl, 1980).

Self-Efficacy and Reading

The Reader Self-Perception Scale is based on Bandura's (1977, 1982) theory of perceived self-efficacy. Bandura defines self-efficacy as a person's judgments of her or his ability to perform an activity, and the effect this perception has on the ongoing and future conduct of the activity. In short, self-perceptions are likely to either motivate or inhibit learning (Schunk, 1982, 1983a, 1983b; Zimmerman & Ringle, 1981). Self-efficacy judgments are thought to affect achievement by influencing an individual's choice of activities, task avoidance, effort expenditure, and goal persistence (Bandura & Schunk, 1981; Schunk, 1984).

In reading, self-perceptions can impact upon an individual's overall orientation toward the process itself. Children who believe they are good readers probably enjoy a rich history of reader engagement and exhibit a strong likelihood of continued positive interactions with text. By contrast, children who perceive themselves as poor readers probably have not experienced much in the way of reading success. They almost surely will not look toward reading as a source of gratification. In this sense, it is not hard to imagine direct links between readers' self-perceptions and their subsequent reading behavior, habits, and attitudes. That is, how an individual feels about herself or himself as a reader could clearly influence whether reading would be sought or avoided, the amount of effort that would occur during reading, and how persistently comprehension would be pursued (Henk & Melnick, 1992).

The basic self-efficacy model (Bandura, 1977, 1982; Schunk, 1984) predicts that individuals take four basic factors into account when estimating their capabilities as a reader: Performance (a very broad category that includes past success, amount of effort necessary, the need for assistance, patterns of progress, task difficulty, task persistence, and belief in the effectiveness of instruction), Observational Comparison, Social Feedback, and Physiological States.

Overall, our previous research into the sources of information that children in the intermediate grades use to make reader self-perception judgments (Henk & Melnick, 1992, 1993) supports this four-factor model. However, as we indicate in the later section on Validation, we found it necessary to redefine the Performance category more narrowly. Consequently, our first source is Progress (PR). We define this scale as how one's perception of present reading performance compares with past performance. The second source, Observational Comparison (OC), deals with how a child perceives her or his reading performance to compare with the performance of classmates. The third source, Social Feedback (SF), includes direct or indirect input about reading from teachers, classmates, and people in the child's family. Finally, the Physiological States (PS) source refers to internal feelings that the child experiences during reading. The entire Reader Self-Perception Scale is reproduced in Appendix A with items coded by scale to illustrate various item types.

It is important to understand that the four sources of information used in making reader self-perception judgments do not operate in isolation from one another (Marshall & Weinstein, 1984). A very natural overlap exists between the categories. For instance, personal perceptions of progress (PR) will be based, in part, not only upon children's observations of how their performance compares with classmates' performance (OC), but also upon the kinds of positive social feedback (SF) they receive, and their internal comfort while reading (PS). In fact, the scales relate so much to one another that interactions among them are inescapable.

These interactions confirm the idea that literacy learning is both complex and socially situated (Alvermann & Guthrie, 1993). In making reader self-perceptions, individual children may value one or more sources over the others. Much of this valuing process will be related to the social context in which the literacy learning occurs. Of course, observational comparison and social feedback are, by their very nature, socially situated. Even aspects of the physiological states category possess social dimensions, especially in the case of internal feelings experienced during oral reading (Filby & Barnett, 1982). Viewed in this social perspective, the classroom, the home, and anywhere else that reading occurs represent contexts for learning about oneself as a reader.

Why the RSPS?

Somewhat surprisingly, there have been very few attempts to develop instruments for measuring reader self-perceptions. The few scales that do exist definitely have their merits, but all possess some notable limitations (Boersma, Chapman, & MacGuire, 1979; Cohen, McDonell, & Osborn, 1989; Mitman & Lash, 1988). For instance, some scales measure self-perceptions of general achievement or language arts proficiency, but do not focus on reading achievement specifically. Others have very few items, and these items tend to measure reader self-efficacy indirectly at best. Often, major elements of reading such as word recognition, word analysis, fluency, and comprehension are not represented in the item pool as they are in the Reader Self-Perception Scale.

Another major problem with many of the scales is that they have not undergone adequate norming. Some are based on small samples, and others have not considered possible scales. A further major concern is that none of the existing reader self-perception instruments appear to be grounded in learning theory. By contrast, the RSPS takes its lead from a well-regarded learning-theory framework and is steeped in a solid tradition of supportive research in the affective domain (Athey, 1985; Mathewson, 1985).

Although previous quantitative scales have fallen short of the mark, several useful structured interview formats are available for qualitative assessment of individual readers' self-perceptions (See Blumenfeld, Pintrich, Meece, & Wessels, 1982; Borko & Eisenhart, 1986; Canney & Winograd, 1979; Filby & Barnett, 1982; Gordon, 1990; Nicholls, 1979; Stipek & Weisz, 1981). Individual data collections can be extremely informative, but they tend to be time consuming and therefore of somewhat less practical value. To date, only the group-administered Reader Self-Perception Scale accounts adequately for concerns related to focus, norming, theoretical grounding, and practicality. Beyond these advantages, the RSPS offers a wide range of assessment, instructional, and research applications that are outlined in later sections.

Description of the Instrument

The Reader Self-Perception Scale consists of 1 general item and 32 subsequent items that represent the four scales (Progress, Observational Comparison, Social Feedback, and Physiological States). The general item was used simply to prompt the children to think about their reading ability. The remaining items deal with overall reading ability as well as aspects of word recognition, word analysis, fluency, and comprehension. Wording of the items was kept simple so that reading ability itself would not confound the assessment. In addition, all items were stated positively to foster straightforward decision making.

Brief written directions to the children appear directly on the instrument. The possible responses and their respective abbreviations are also included. The introductory material also contains a sample item and an accompanying explanation. Before duplicating the instrument for student use, the codes to the left of the items should be covered or removed.

In taking the RSPS, children are asked to read each item and to rate how much they agree or disagree with the statement. They make their ratings using a 5-point Likert system (1 = Strongly Disagree, 2 = Disagree, 3 = Undecided, 4 = Agree, and 5 = Strongly Agree). Because the number of items varies according to the scale (PR = 9; OC = 6; SF = 9; PS = 8), the maximum possible scores will differ for each scale (PR = 45; OC = 30; SF = 45; PS = 40).

Administration and Scoring

The RSPS takes approximately 15 to 20 minutes to complete. The teacher is asked to explain the purpose of the assessment to the children and to work through the example so that all children understand what they are to do. Children are encouraged to ask questions about any aspect of the instrument they don't understand. The teacher should emphasize that the children should be as honest as possible and that there are no right answers. Specific directions to the teacher are provided in Appendix B.

Scoring of the RSPS is accomplished by summing the raw scores for each of the four scales. The scoring sheet in Appendix C has been provided to help compute scores for the Progress, Observational Comparison, Social Feedback, and Physiological States scales. To calculate the scores, the child's completed RSPS is placed alongside a scoring sheet. With the exception of item 1, the scorer transfers the child's responses to each item on the RSPS to the answer sheet using the numerical scoring key (e.g.,

Table 1
Number of items and internal consistency reliabilities for each scale

Scale	Number of items	Alpha reliabilities
Progress	9	.84
Observational Comparison	6	.82
Social Feedback	9	.81
Physiological States	8	.84

Note. The RSPS consists of 33 items with 32 items representing the four scales shown here plus 1 general item ("I think I am a good reader").
n = 1,525.

SA = 5; SD = 1). After all responses are recorded, the scorer simply adds the number in each column to get a raw score for each scale.

The child's scores can then be compared with the norming data in Table 2. Any score for a scale that is slightly below, equal to, or slightly greater than the mean indicates that the child's self-perceptions are in the normal range. On the other hand, scores that are a good deal lower than the scale's mean would be a cause for concern. When the difference exceeds the size of the standard deviation, the child's scores are in the low range. Rough low range cut-off points for the scales would be: Progress (34), Observational Comparison (16), Social Feedback (27), and Physiological States (25). By the same token, scores that exceed the mean by an amount equal to or greater than the standard deviation would indicate high reader self-perceptions (i.e., PR = 44+; OC = 26+; SF = 38+; PS = 37+).

Assessment and Instructional Uses

Information obtained from the Reader Self-Perception Scale can be used for both whole group and individual assessments and interventions. Teachers can gain a sense of how the general classroom climate affects children's self-efficacy judgments in reading. These conclusions can be drawn by examining group performance on the total scale and on the four individual scales. For example, after results of the RSPS are available for interpretation, teachers might feel the need to (a) devise more meaningful and considerate ways to communicate reading progress to their students, (b) modify their current classroom oral reading practices, (c) revise their grouping techniques, (d) pay closer attention to the reading materials they assign, (e) become more sensitive to indirect signals they send to children regarding their reading performance, (f) counsel the class and the parents about constructive feedback, or (g) strive to make the children more physically and mentally comfortable during the act of reading.

Data from the RSPS can also be useful for monitoring individual children. For instance, scores for the total scale and for the four subscales might be maintained in portfolios to demonstrate changes in self-perceptions over time. A child's results from the beginning of the school year could be compared with those obtained at the midpoint or at the end of the year. Likewise, RSPS results for a child could be compared from year to year. Regardless of timeline, individual instructional adjustments could flow naturally from the findings.

Table 2
Descriptive statistics by scale and grade level

		Progress			Observational Comparison			Social Feedback			Physiological States		
Grade level	*n*	Mean	SD	SE	Mean	SD	SE	Mean	SD	SE	Mean	SD	SE
4	506	39.6	4.8	.21	20.7	4.7	.21	33.2	5.3	.24	31.8	5.9	.26
5	571	39.5	5.2	.22	21.0	4.8	.20	32.7	5.4	.22	31.0	6.4	.27
6	402	39.0	5.1	.25	21.3	4.6	.23	32.0	5.5	.27	30.5	6.2	.31
Total	1,479	39.4	5.0	.13	20.9	4.7	.12	32.7	5.4	.14	31.2	6.2	.16

Note. Total possible raw scores are Progress (45), Observational Comparison (30), Social Feedback (45), and Physiological States (40).

Besides a portfolio application, the scale could help teachers to detect and assist children whose self-perceptions are somewhat below the norm. Depending upon their individual profiles, these children might require one or more of the following instructional adjustments: (a) more frequent and concrete illustrations of their progress; (b) opportunities to read in situations where their performance compares favorably with the performance of peers; (c) increased positive reinforcement from the teacher, parents, and classmates; and (d) modeling of the enjoyment, appreciation, relaxation, and gratification that can be gained from reading. For example, low scores on the physiological states scale could signal that the teacher needs to be especially enthusiastic with a particular child, to strive to make her or his reading engagements consistently pleasurable, and to provide the child with a rich array of engaging literature.

Many of these adjustments can be accomplished by carefully estimating and orchestrating the interest, familiarity, and readability of texts. Self-perceptions can also be enhanced when teachers prepare children well for all reading assignments and group them wisely and flexibly. Children with low reader self-perceptions will function best in classrooms where patience is the rule and individual differences are not only tolerated but respected and valued. Additional encouragement and assistance can go a long way in building positive reader self-perceptions.

The Reader Self-Perception Scale can also be used to help identify children who are at risk due to a severe lack of confidence in their reading ability. These children need to be assessed more thoroughly and treated more intensively. When a child's RSPS profile departs markedly from the norm, the teacher can follow up with a personalized, structured interview like those cited previously. Insights gained from the scale itself and from the interview can be applied in counseling the child. In extreme cases, however, the results may be indicative of a deep-rooted or broader self-esteem problem that demands the expertise of a counselor or school psychologist.

One Teacher's Use

Near the beginning of the school year, Ms. Hogan decided to administer the RSPS to her entire class of fourth graders. Since the children came to her from a building that houses only primary students, she knew very little about them. Ms. Hogan recognized that the children would do a great deal more "reading to learn" in fourth grade, and so she wanted to learn how they felt about themselves as readers because this would influence their response to literacy instruction. Ms. Hogan planned to make adjustments that would benefit the whole class as well as individual children. She also planned to administer the RSPS again at the end of the year to determine if her instruction produced affective growth.

After the children's papers had been scored, she looked closely at the scores and was pleased to note that most of the students felt very good about their reading ability. As a group, the children's mean scores on the Progress, Observational Comparison, and Physiological States scales were quite high (42, 23, and 34, respectively), but the mean score for Social Feedback was only 24. Because this score was well below the average range, Ms. Hogan became concerned. In response, she planned to provide the children with reading materials that would allow her to make frequent use of praise. In addition, she decided to monitor her body language closely to make sure that she sent her students positive messages about their reading performance. She would also work hard to create a more supportive climate for literacy by encouraging the children to praise one another and by advising parents how to offer constructive feedback at home.

One of the children, Patti, scored extremely well on all four scales. It was clear that she had a solid appreciation of her own reading ability. On the other hand, the RSPS profile of another student, Bob, showed average scores for Progress, slightly below average for Physiological States, and well below average for Observational Comparison and Social Feedback. Ms. Hogan wondered if Bob felt fine about his silent reading but lacked confidence when reading aloud. She thought that he might have noticed his oral reading didn't compare well with the other children's, and she wondered if the signals he had received in the past from teachers, classmates, and parents had confirmed his doubts. Ms. Hogan believed that his nearly average score on the Physiological States scale might be the result of Bob's feelings about his silent and oral reading offsetting one another. She decided to monitor the situation carefully during the year, to speak with Bob's previous teachers, and to check his permanent record to see if his oral reading had lagged consistently behind his silent reading.

Ms. Hogan was most concerned about Norm. All of his RSPS scores were very low, and his previous achievement test scores indicated a serious reading problem. Norm was new to the district, and Ms. Hogan suspected that the children in her class might read much better than those at his old school. At first, his progress had been slow because the reading materials were much too difficult for him. Also, from listening to the other children read, he learned very quickly that his reading ability didn't compare well. Other children were impatient when Norm read aloud, and she noticed his discomfort with almost any reading task. Because his reading ability was so limited, Ms. Hogan realized that his low reader self-image had probably been shaped over a long time, but she knew that his recent difficulties had made matters worse. She intended to interview Norm individually to gain insights into his reader self-perceptions; to share her results and concerns with the guidance counselor, school psychologist, and principal; and to make as many appropriate instructional adjustments as possible.

A Final Word

Due to its uniqueness and timeliness, the Reader Self-Perception Scale might be immediately useful in a wide array of literacy contexts. The norming of the instrument has been quite extensive, and the scale provides meaningful data for teachers, administrators, parents, and perhaps the students themselves. For the time being, the scale should only be used in fourth through sixth grades, although with additional norming it might prove to be functional at higher grade levels. We would also caution against using the RSPS below fourth grade, even if the items are read aloud to the students. The instrument has not been tested at lower levels and, as we noted previously, research suggests that children in earlier grades tend not to appraise their reading ability accurately, nor attribute the causes of their achievement properly.

Users of the RSPS and the various stakeholders will ultimately need to decide how the instrument ought to be applied and interpreted. The scale yields a general indication of a child's self-perceptions of reading ability. This indicator should not be confused with more specific self-evaluations of reading skills and strategies that students might make as part of regular classroom instruction. Neither does the scale address self-appraisals of specific word analysis techniques or comprehension abilities such as prediction, imagery, self-regulated learning, retelling proficiency, or critical reflection. Whether the scale's major function is for assessment and instruction or for research, our hope is that with additional norming, the instrument will become a routine reading-related assessment on a par with well-known cognitive and affective measures.

The development of the RSPS was supported in part by the Office of Research and Graduate Studies at Penn State University-Harrisburg.

References

Alvermann, D.E., & Guthrie, J.T. (1993). Themes and directions of the National Reading Research Center. *Perspectives in Reading Research, 1*, 1-11.

Anderson, R.C., Fielding, L.G., & Wilson, P.T. (1988). Growth in reading and how children spend their time outside of school. *Reading Research Quarterly, 23*, 285-303.

Athey, I. (1985). Reading research in the affective domain. In H. Singer & R.B. Ruddell (Eds.), *Theoretical models and processes of reading* (3rd ed., pp. 527-557). Newark, DE: International Reading Association.

Bandura, A. (1977). Self-efficacy: Toward a unifying theory of behavioral change. *Psychological Review, 84*, 191–215.

Bandura, A. (1982). Self-efficacy mechanism and human agency. *American Psychologist, 37*, 122–147.

Bandura, A., & Schunk, D.H. (1981). Cultivating competence, self-efficacy, and intrinsic interest through proximal self-motivation. *Journal of Personality and Social Psychology, 41*, 586–598.

Blumenfeld, P.C., Pintrich, P.R., Meece, J., & Wessels, K. (1982). The formation and role of self-perceptions of ability in elementary classrooms. *The Elementary School Journal, 82*, 401–420.

Boersma, F.J., Chapman, J.W., & MacGuire, T.O. (1979). The student perception of ability scale: An instrument for measuring academic self-concept in elementary school children. *Educational and Psychological Measurement, 39*, 135–141.

Borko, H., & Eisenhart, M. (1986). Students' conceptions of reading and their reading experiences in school. *The Elementary School Journal, 86*, 589–611.

Canney, G., & Winograd, P. (1979). *Schemata for reading and reading comprehension performance* (Tech. Rep. No. 120). Urbana, IL: University of Illinois, Center for the Study of Reading. (ERIC Document Reproduction Service No. ED 169 520)

Cohen, S.G., McDonell, G., & Osborn, B. (1989). Self-perceptions of "at risk" and high achieving readers: Beyond Reading Recovery achievement data. In S. McCormick & J. Zutell (Eds.), *Cognitive and social perspectives for literacy research and instruction* (pp. 117–122). Chicago: National Reading Conference.

Filby, N.N., & Barnett, B.G. (1982). Student perceptions of "better readers" in elementary classrooms. *The Elementary School Journal, 5*, 435–449.

Foertsch, M.A. (1992). *Reading in and out of school: Factors influencing the literacy achievement of American students in grades 4, 8, and 12 in 1988 and 1990* (Vol. 2). Washington, DC: National Center for Education Statistics.

Gable, R.K. (1986). *Instrument development in the affective domain*. Boston: Kluwer-Nijhoff.

Gordon, C. (1990). Changes in readers' and writers' metacognitive knowledge: Some observations. *Reading Research and Instruction, 30*, 1–14.

Henk, W.A. (1993). New directions in reading assessment. *Reading and Writing Quarterly, 9*, 103–120.

Henk, W.A., & Melnick, S.A. (1992). The initial development of a scale to measure "perception of self as reader." In C.K. Kinzer & D.J. Leu (Eds.), *Literacy research, theory, and practice: Views from many perspectives* (41st yearbook of the National Reading Conference; pp. 111–117). Chicago: National Reading Conference.

Henk, W.A., & Melnick, S.A. (1993, December). *Quantitative and qualitative validation of the Reader Self-Perception Scale*. Paper presented at the annual meeting of the National Reading Conference, Charleston, SC.

Marshall, H.H., & Weinstein, R.S. (1984). Classroom factors affecting students' self-evaluation: An interactional model. *Review of Educational Research, 54*, 301–325.

Mathewson, G.C. (1985). Toward a comprehensive model of affect in the reading process. In H. Singer & R.B. Ruddell (Eds.), *Theoretical models and processes of reading* (3rd ed., pp. 841–856). Newark, DE: International Reading Association.

McKenna, M.C., & Kear, D.J. (1990). Measuring attitude toward reading: A new tool for teachers. *The Reading Teacher, 43*, 626–639.

Mitman, A.L., & Lash, A.A. (1988). Students' perceptions of their academic standing and classroom behavior. *The Elementary School Journal, 89*, 55–68.

Morrow, L.M., & Weinstein, C.S. (1986). Encouraging voluntary reading: The impact of a literature program on children's use of library centers. *Reading Research Quarterly, 21*, 330–346.

Nicholls, J.G. (1978). The development of the concepts of effort and ability, perception of academic attainment, and the understanding that difficult tasks require more ability. *Child Development, 49*, 800–814.

Nicholls, J.G. (1979). Development of perception of own attainment and causal attribution for success and failure in reading. *Journal of Educational Psychology, 71*, 94–99.

O'Flahavan, J., Gambrell, L.B., Guthrie, J., Stahl, S., Baumann, J.F., & Alvermann, D.A. (August/September, 1992). Poll results guide activities of research center. *Reading Today*, pp. 10, 12.

Ruble, D.N., Boggiano, A.K., Feldman, N.S., & Loebl, J.H. (1980). Developmental analysis of the role of social comparison in self-evaluation. *Developmental Psychology, 12*, 191–197.

Schunk, D.H. (1982). Effects of effort attributional feedback on children's perceived self-efficacy and achievement. *Journal of Educational Psychology, 74*, 548–556.

Schunk, D.H. (1983a). Ability versus effort attributional feedback: Differential effects on self-efficacy and achievement. *Journal of Educational Psychology, 75*, 848–856.

Schunk, D.H. (1983b). Developing children's self-efficacy and skills: The roles of social comparative information and goal setting. *Contemporary Educational Psychology, 8*, 76–86.

Schunk, D.H. (1984). Self-efficacy perspective on achievement behavior. *Educational Psychologist, 19*, 48–58.

Stipek, D. (1981). Children's perceptions of their own and their classmates' ability. *Journal of Educational Psychology, 73*, 404–410.

Stipek, D., & Weisz, J. (1981). Perceived personal control and academic achievement. *Review of Educational Research, 51*, 101–137.

Valencia, S.W. (1990). A portfolio approach to classroom reading assessment: The whys, whats and hows. *The Reading Teacher, 43*, 338–340.

Winograd, P., & Paris, S.G. (1988). *Improving reading assessment. Writings in reading and language arts*. Lexington, MA: D.C. Heath.

Wixson, K., Peters, C., Weber, E., & Roeber, E. (1987). New directions in statewide reading assessment. *The Reading Teacher, 40*, 749-754.

Zimmerman, B.J., & Ringle, J. (1981). Effects of model persistence and statements of confidence on children's self-efficacy and problem solving. *Journal of Educational Psychology, 73*, 485–493.

Appendix A
The Reader Self-Perception Scale

Listed below are statements about reading. Please read each statement carefully. Then circle the letters that show how much you agree or disagree with the statement. Use the following:

SA = Strongly Agree
A = Agree
U = Undecided
D = Disagree
SD = Strongly Disagree

Example: **I think pizza with pepperoni is the best.**	SA	A	U	D	SD

If you are *really positive* that pepperoni pizza is best, circle SA (Strongly Agree).
If you *think* that is good but maybe not great, circle A (Agree).
If you *can't decide* whether or not it is best, circle U (undecided).
If you *think* that pepperoni pizza is not all that good, circle D (Disagree).
If you are *really positive* that pepperoni pizza is not very good, circle SD (Strongly Disagree).

	1.	I think I am a good reader.	SA	A	U	D	SD
[SF]	2.	I can tell that my teacher likes to listen to me read.	SA	A	U	D	SD
[SF]	3.	My teacher thinks that my reading is fine.	SA	A	U	D	SD
[OC]	4.	I read faster than other kids.	SA	A	U	D	SD
[PS]	5.	I like to read aloud.	SA	A	U	D	SD
[OC]	6.	When I read, I can figure out words better than other kids.	SA	A	U	D	SD
[SF]	7.	My classmates like to listen to me read.	SA	A	U	D	SD
[PS]	8.	I feel good inside when I read.	SA	A	U	D	SD
[SF]	9.	My classmates think that I read pretty well.	SA	A	U	D	SD
[PR]	10.	When I read, I don't have to try as hard as I used to.	SA	A	U	D	SD
[OC]	11.	I seem to know more words than other kids when I read.	SA	A	U	D	SD
[SF]	12.	People in my family think I am a good reader.	SA	A	U	D	SD
[PR]	13.	I am getting better at reading.	SA	A	U	D	SD
[OC]	14.	I understand what I read as well as other kids do.	SA	A	U	D	SD
[PR]	15.	When I read, I need less help than I used to.	SA	A	U	D	SD
[PS]	16.	Reading makes me feel happy inside.	SA	A	U	D	SD
[SF]	17.	My teacher thinks I am a good reader.	SA	A	U	D	SD
[PR]	18.	Reading is easier for me than it used to be.	SA	A	U	D	SD
[PR]	19.	I read faster than I could before.	SA	A	U	D	SD
[OC]	20.	I read better than other kids in my class.	SA	A	U	D	SD
[PS]	21.	I feel calm when I read.	SA	A	U	D	SD

(continued)

Appendix A (continued)
The Reader Self-Perception Scale

[OC]	22.	I read more than other kids.	SA	A	U	D	SD
[PR]	23.	I understand what I read better than I could before.	SA	A	U	D	SD
[PR]	24.	I can figure out words better than I could before.	SA	A	U	D	SD
[PS]	25.	I feel comfortable when I read.	SA	A	U	D	SD
[PS]	26.	I think reading is relaxing.	SA	A	U	D	SD
[PR]	27.	I read better now than I could before.	SA	A	U	D	SD
[PR]	28.	When I read, I recognize more words than I used to.	SA	A	U	D	SD
[PS]	29.	Reading makes me feel good.	SA	A	U	D	SD
[SF]	30.	Other kids think I'm a good reader.	SA	A	U	D	SD
[SF]	31.	People in my family think I read pretty well.	SA	A	U	D	SD
[PS]	32.	I enjoy reading.	SA	A	U	D	SD
[SF]	33.	People in my family like to listen to me read.	SA	A	U	D	SD

Appendix B
The Reader Self-Perception Scale
Directions for administration, scoring, and interpretation

The Reader Self-Perception Scale (RSPS) is intended to provide an assessment of how children feel about themselves as readers. The scale consists of 33 items that assess self-perceptions along four dimensions of self-efficacy (Progress, Observational Comparison, Social Feedback, and Physiological States). Children are asked to indicate how strongly they agree or disagree with each statement on a 5-point scale (5 = Strongly Agree, 1 = Strongly Disagree). The information gained from this scale can be used to devise ways to enhance children's self-esteem in reading and, ideally, to increase their motivation to read. The following directions explain specifically what you are to do.

Administration

For the results to be of any use, the children must: (a) understand exactly what they are to do, (b) have sufficient time to complete all items, and (c) respond honestly and thoughtfully. Briefly explain to the children that they are being asked to complete a questionnaire about reading. Emphasize that this is not a *test* and that there are no *right* answers. Tell them that they should be as honest as possible because their responses will be confidential. Ask the children to fill in their names, grade levels, and classrooms as appropriate. Read the directions aloud and work through the example with the students as a group. Discuss the response options and make sure that all children understand the rating scale before moving on. It is important that children know that they may raise their hands to ask questions about any words or ideas they do not understand.

The children should then read each item and circle their response for the item. They should work at their own pace. Remind the children that they should be sure to respond to all items. When all items are completed, the children should stop, put their pencils down, and wait for further instructions. Care should be taken that children who work more slowly are not disturbed by children who have already finished.

Scoring

To score the RSPS, enter the following point values for each response on the RSPS scoring sheet (Strongly Agree = 5, Agree = 4, Undecided = 3, Disagree = 2, Strongly Disagree = 1) for each item number under the appropriate scale. Sum each column to obtain a raw score for each of the four specific scales.

Interpretation

Each scale is interpreted in relation to its total possible score. For example, because the RSPS uses a 5-point scale and the Progress scale consists of 9 items, the highest total score for Progress is 45 (9 x 5 = 45). Therefore, a score that would fall approximately in the middle of the range (22–23) would indicate a child's somewhat indifferent perception of her or himself as a reader with respect to Progress. Note that each scale has a different possible total raw score (Progress = 45, Observational Comparison = 30, Social Feedback = 45, and Physiological States = 40) and should be interpreted accordingly.

As a further aid to interpretation, Table 2 presents the descriptive statistics by grade level for each scale. The raw score of a group or individual can be compared to that of the pilot study group at each grade level.

Appendix C
The Reader Self-Perception Scale scoring sheet

Student name ______________________________

Teacher ______________________________

Grade ______________________________ Date ______________________________

Scoring key: 5 = Strongly Agree (SA)
4 = Agree (A)
3 = Undecided (U)
2 = Disagree (D)
1 = Strongly Disagree (SD)

Scales

General Perception	Progress	Observational Comparison	Social Feedback	Physiological States
1. ____	10. ____	4. ____	2. ____	5. ____
	13. ____	6. ____	3. ____	8. ____
	15. ____	11. ____	7. ____	16. ____
	18. ____	14. ____	9. ____	21. ____
	19. ____	20. ____	12. ____	25. ____
	23. ____	22. ____	17. ____	26. ____
	24. ____		30. ____	29. ____
	27. ____		31. ____	32. ____
	28. ____		33. ____	
Raw score	____ of 45	____ of 30	____ of 45	____ of 40
Score interpretation				
High	44+	26+	38+	37+
Average	39	21	33	31
Low	34	16	27	25

Appendix D
Validation

A pool of initial items was developed that reflected each of Bandura's (1977) four factors (Performance, Observational Comparison, Social Feedback, and Physiological States). Thirty graduate students in reading were presented the pool of items in random order as well as the conceptual definitions for each of the four factor categories. The graduate students were asked to place each item in the category it seemed to fit best. Based upon feedback received in this judgmental process, modifications were made to the item pool.

The instrument was then administered to 625 students in grades 4, 5, and 6 in two different school districts. Preliminary alpha reliabilities for each scale measured in the mid 70s range. Although alpha reliabilities in this range are quite acceptable for an affective measure (Gable, 1986), the analysis identified some items that did not seem to fit well with the rest of the scale. In addition, an exploratory factor analysis indicated clear scales for Observational Comparison, Social Feedback and Physiological States, but not for the Performance scale. Since the items were not clustering as a single construct, the operational definition of the scale was reexamined. A panel of eight experts (consisting of both university faculty and graduate students enrolled in reading and affective instrument development courses) examined the data more closely and made recommendations. The panel concluded that it was more meaningful to use perceptions of personal progress as the one concrete way readers might be able to make ability judgments apart from the other scales. It was also felt that the progress construct subsumed the majority of the dimensions of the original Performance scale. Thus, the original scale was operationally redefined, and only those items that reflected personal progress were retained. For this reason, the scale was renamed Progress.

After the revisions indicated by the first pilot had been made, an additional 1,479 fourth-, fifth- and sixth-grade children in several urban, suburban and rural school districts were asked to respond. Further reliability analyses indicated scale alphas ranging from .81 to .84 with all items contributing to the overall scale reliability. Table 1 displays the internal consistency reliabilities for each scale by grade level. A factor analysis indicated the existence of each of the expected categories and, as hoped, moderate yet significant relationships were indicated between RSPS scores (total and individual scale) and both the Elementary Reading Attitude Survey (McKenna & Kear, 1990) and a variety of standardized reading achievement measures (Henk & Melnick, 1992, 1993).

Moreover, as Table 2 indicates, the mean scores and standard deviations for each scale were extremely similar across grades, and the corresponding standard errors were desirably low. Children reported the highest relative reader self-perceptions on the Progress scale (39.4 of the maximum possible 45) followed by Physiological States (31.2 of 40), Social Feedback (32.7 of 45), and Observational Comparison (20.9 of 30). Overall, these scores indicate that children tended to think of themselves as capable readers.

Appendix: Culminating Activity and Self-Assessment Rubric

Culminating Activity: Reflecting on What I Have Learned

Using the plan you have been working on in all seven sections of this book, write a reflection on what you have learned about assessment.

1. In your reflection, consider the relationship between your assessment principles and practices. Are they unified? Do they support each other? Explain.

2. Also reflect on which articles were most influential on your plan, and why. What professional knowledge or assessment practices have helped you develop assessment that will best support your readers? What knowledge or practices have changed your views or articulated your stance on assessment?

3. As you look into the future, what goals do you have for assessment? What plans do you have for meeting these goals?

Self-Assessment Rubric

Assess your own growth. Use the following items to help you determine the level of your learning and of your performance on the statement of reading assessment principles and practices.

1. Assessment of my level of acquired understanding of my own principles of assessment:
   - ☐ Emergent understanding—I feel as if I have learned from the readings and exercises and am just beginning to understand the issues surrounding assessment. I can articulate and defend a few of my principles and am just beginning to see the relationships between my principles, student achievement, and my choice of assessment practices.
   - ☐ Expanding understanding—I have acquired a set of assessment principles and feel equipped to explain and justify them. My principles enable the achievement of all students and place me, the teacher, at the heart of "making the difference." I can articulate how my principles and selected assessment practices are unified and support student achievement in reading.
   - ☐ Mature understanding—I have made many connections between my assessment principles and classroom practices and can fully articulate, even analyze, how these support or work against each other and students. I feel capable of using my principles as a rubric for making decisions about which assessment practices best serve my students and as a tool for communication and change.
2. Assessment of my increased knowledge of assessment practices:
   - ☐ Emergent knowledge—Many of the assessment practices that I read about interest me, and I feel capable of selecting a few of them for implementation with students. If asked, I could explain which practices are compatible with my principles.
   - ☐ Expanding knowledge—There are numerous assessment practices in the articles that were familiar to me and/or which I already use. I feel equipped to implement new practices and others in more powerful ways. The readings filled gaps in my knowledge, and I have newly acquired confidence to implement practices that before were confusing or too risky. I recognize how I can use my principles to choose and justify my practices.
   - ☐ Mature knowledge—The readings validated my current approaches to reading assessment. I feel empowered to continue my approaches and am excited to refine my practices using ideas from the teachers in the articles. I recognize a rich relationship between my assessment principles and practices and feel they are highly compatible and support the needs of my diverse students.
3. Assessment of the quality of my statement of reading assessment principles and practices:
   - ☐ Acceptable quality—I will refer to this statement because it reveals important pieces of what I believe about assessment and identifies practices that are essential to sound reading assessment.
   - ☐ High quality—This statement represents my new and more elaborated views on reading assessment. The statement is important to me because it represents my best thinking about children and how to promote their reading achievement. I value the statement because preparing it has caused me to think deeply and articulate my views and knowledge with new levels of confidence.
   - ☐ Leadership quality—This statement represents my principles and practices at a level where I feel motivated to share my ideas with other professionals. Learning about assessment never ends, but I see that I can work collaboratively with my colleagues to reform our practices to further the goal of helping students become lifelong readers.

Subject Index

Note: Page numbers followed by *f* and *t* indicate figures and tables, respectively.

I

J-K

L

M

N

O

P

Q

R

S

T

U-V

W

Y-Z